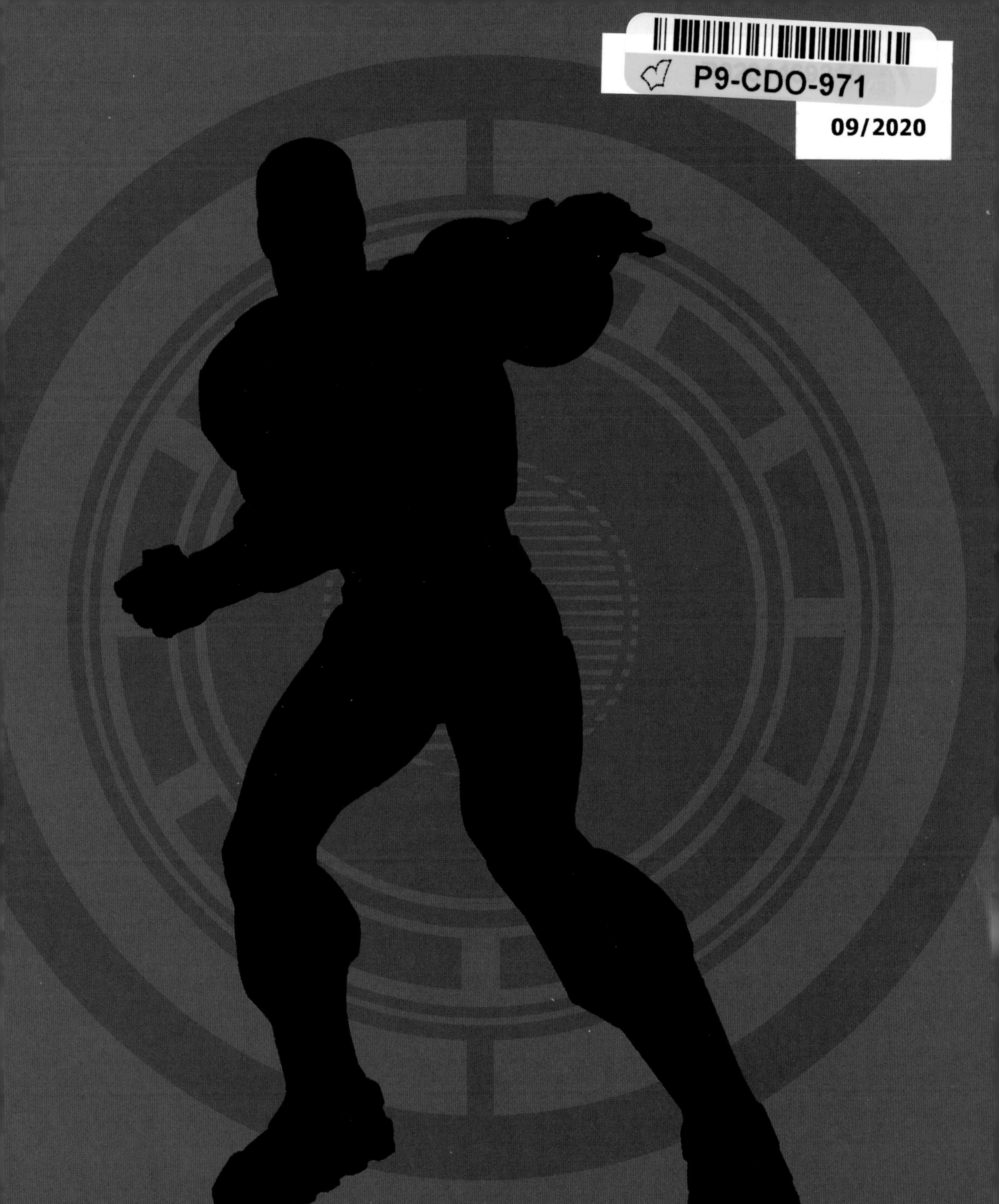

IRON MAN

TH END

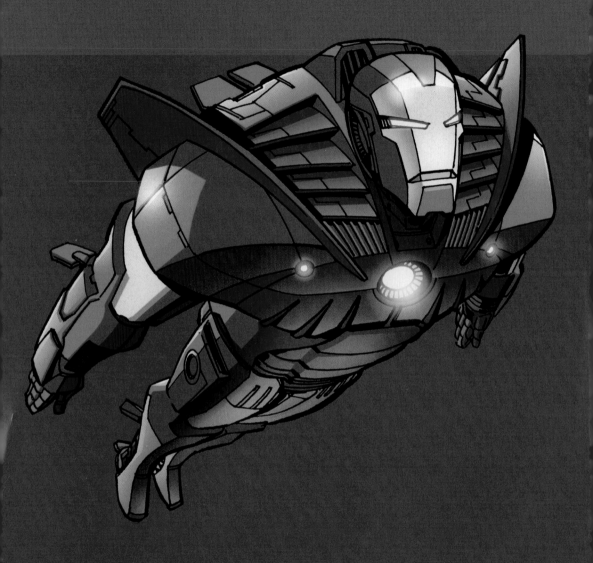

COLLECTION EDITOR
JENNIFER GRÜNWALD

ASSISTANT MANAGING EDITOR
MAIA LOY

ASSISTANT EDITOR
CAITLIN O'CONNELL

EDITOR, SPECIAL PROJECTS
MARK D. BEAZLEY

VP PRODUCTION & SPECIAL PROJECTS
JEFF YOUNGQUIST

BOOK DESIGNERS
ADAM DEL RE WITH **SALENA MAHINA**

SVP PRINT, SALES & MARKETING
DAVID GABRIEL

EDITOR IN CHIEF
C.B. CEBULSKI

IRON MAN: THE END. Contains material originally published in magazine form as IRON MAN: THE END (2008), IRON MAN: REQUIEM (2009), and IRON MAN (1968) #116 and #244. Second edition. First printing 2019. ISBN 978-1-302-92461-4. Published by MARVEL WORLDWIDE, INC., a subsidiary of MARVEL ENTERTAINMENT, LLC. OFFICE OF PUBLICATION: 1290 Avenue of the Americas, New York, NY 10104. © 2019 MARVEL No similarity between any of the names, characters, persons, and/or institutions in this magazine with those of any living or dead person or institution is intended, and any such similarity which may exist is purely coincidental. **Printed in the U.S.A.** KEVIN FEIGE, Chief Creative Officer; DAN BUCKLEY, President, Marvel Entertainment; JOHN NEE, Publisher; JOE QUESADA, EVP & Creative Director; TOM BREVOORT, SVP of Publishing; DAVID BOGART, Associate Publisher & SVP of Talent Affairs; Publishing & Partnership; DAVID GABRIEL, VP of Print & Digital Publishing; JEFF YOUNGQUIST, VP of Production & Special Projects; DAN CARR, Executive Director of Publishing Technology; ALEX MORALES, Director of Publishing Operations; DAN EDINGTON, Managing Editor; SUSAN CRESPI, Production Manager; STAN LEE, Chairman Emeritus. For information regarding advertising in Marvel Comics or on Marvel.com, please contact Vit DeBellis, Custom Solutions & Integrated Advertising Manager, at vdebellis@marvel.com. For Marvel subscription inquiries, please call 888-511-5480. Manufactured between 12/6/2019

THE END

IRON MAN: THE END

WRITER **DAVID MICHELINIE**
PENCILER **BERNARD CHANG**
INKER/CO-PLOTTER **BOB LAYTON**
COLORIST **MIKE CAVALLARO**
LETTERER **ARTMONKEYS STUDIOS**
COVER ART **BOB LAYTON** & **MOOSE BAUMANN**

IRON MAN: REQUIEM

FRAMING SEQUENCE
WRITER **MATT FRACTION**
ARTIST **KANO**
LETTERER **VC's JOE CARAMAGNA**

TALES OF SUSPENSE #39
WRITERS **STAN LEE** & **LARRY LIEBER**
ARTIST **DON HECK**
COLORIST **TOM CHU**

IRON MAN #144
WRITER **DAVID MICHELINIE**
PENCILER **JOE BROZOWSKI**
INKER/CO-PLOTTER **BOB LAYTON**
COLORIST **TOM CHU**
LETTERER **JOHN COSTANZA**

COVER ART **SEAN CHEN**, **SANDU FLOREA** & **FRANK D'ARMATA**
EDITOR **JOHN DENNING**

IRON MAN #116
WRITER **DAVID MICHELINIE**
PENCILER **JOHN ROMITA JR.**
INKER/CO-PLOTTER **BOB LAYTON**
COLORIST **GEORGE ROUSSOS**
LETTERER **ANNETTE KAWECKI**
COVER ART **JOHN ROMITA JR.** & **BOB LAYTON**

IRON MAN #244
WRITER **DAVID MICHELINIE**
ARTIST/CO-PLOTTER **BOB LAYTON**
COLORIST **PAUL BECTON**
LETTERER **JANICE CHIANG**
COVER ART **BOB LAYTON**

IRON MAN CREATED BY **STAN LEE**, **LARRY LIEBER**, **DON HECK** & **JACK KIRBY**

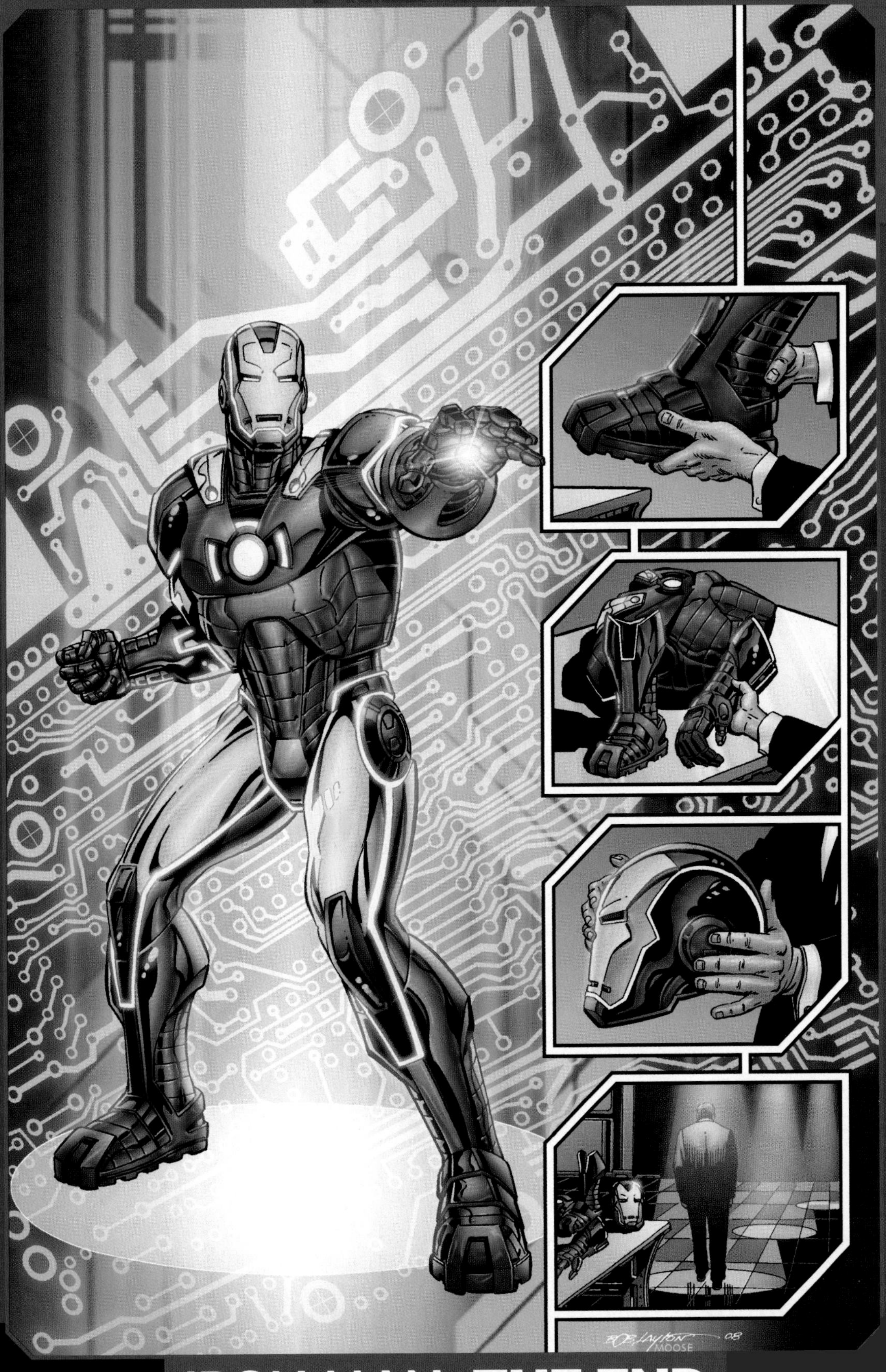
BOB LAYTON 08
MOOSE

IRON MAN: THE END

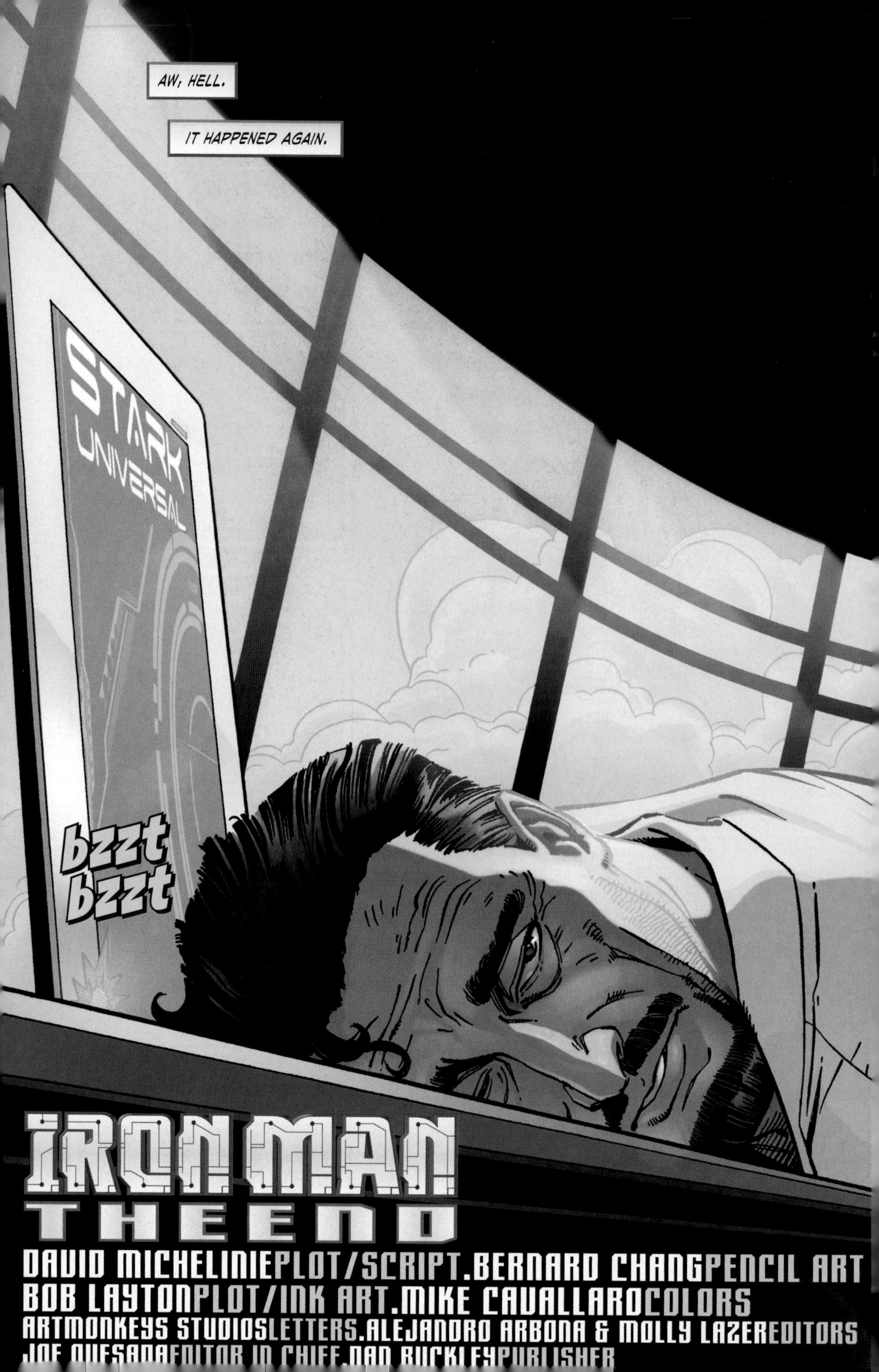

AW, HELL.
IT HAPPENED AGAIN.
STARK UNIVERSAL
bzzt bzzt
IRON MAN
THE END
DAVID MICHELINIE PLOT/SCRIPT. BERNARD CHANG PENCIL ART
BOB LAYTON PLOT/INK ART. MIKE CAVALLARO COLORS
ARTMONKEYS STUDIOS LETTERS. ALEJANDRO ARBONA & MOLLY LAZER EDITORS
JOE QUESADA EDITOR IN CHIEF. DAN BUCKLEY PUBLISHER

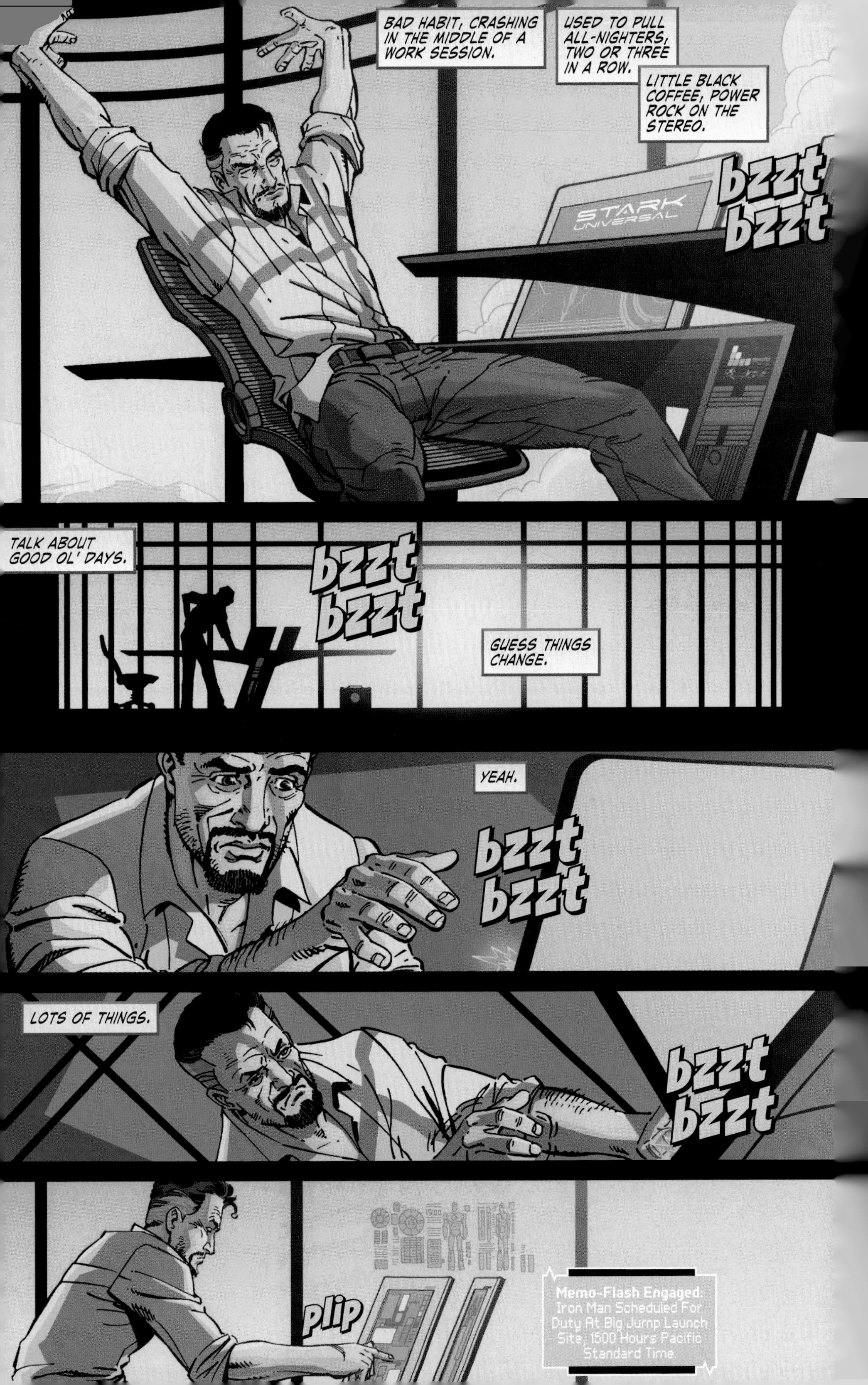

BAD HABIT, CRASHING IN THE MIDDLE OF A WORK SESSION.
USED TO PULL ALL-NIGHTERS, TWO OR THREE IN A ROW.
LITTLE BLACK COFFEE, POWER ROCK ON THE STEREO.
STARK UNIVERSAL
bzzt bzzt
TALK ABOUT GOOD OL' DAYS.
bzzt bzzt
GUESS THINGS CHANGE.
YEAH.
bzzt bzzt
LOTS OF THINGS.
bzzt bzzt
plip
Memo-Flash Engaged:
Iron Man Scheduled For Duty At Big Jump Launch Site, 1500 Hours Pacific Standard Time.

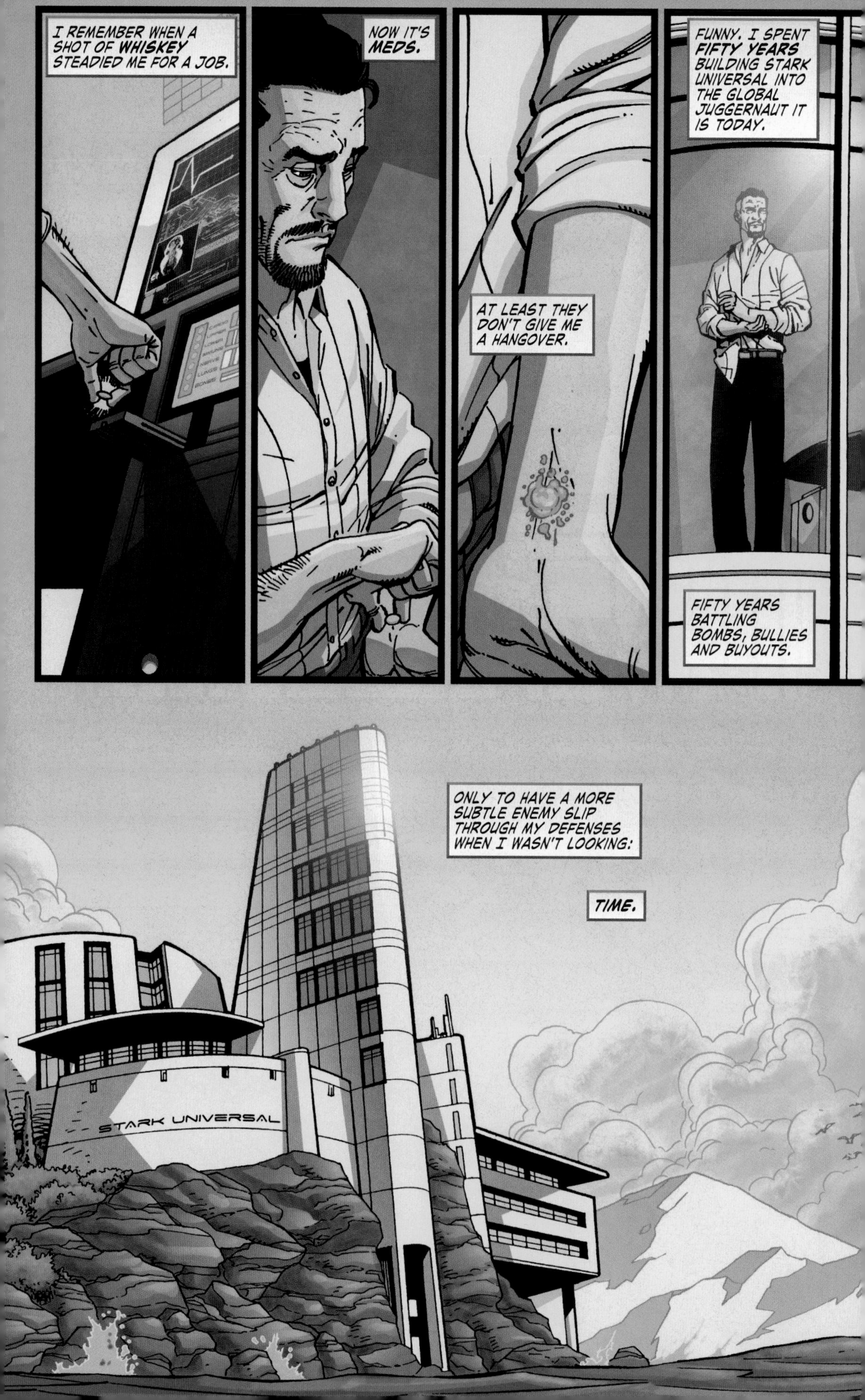
I REMEMBER WHEN A SHOT OF WHISKEY STEADIED ME FOR A JOB.
NOW IT'S MEDS.
AT LEAST THEY DON'T GIVE ME A HANGOVER.
FUNNY. I SPENT FIFTY YEARS BUILDING STARK UNIVERSAL INTO THE GLOBAL JUGGERNAUT IT IS TODAY.
FIFTY YEARS BATTLING BOMBS, BULLIES AND BUYOUTS.
ONLY TO HAVE A MORE SUBTLE ENEMY SLIP THROUGH MY DEFENSES WHEN I WASN'T LOOKING:
TIME.
STARK UNIVERSAL

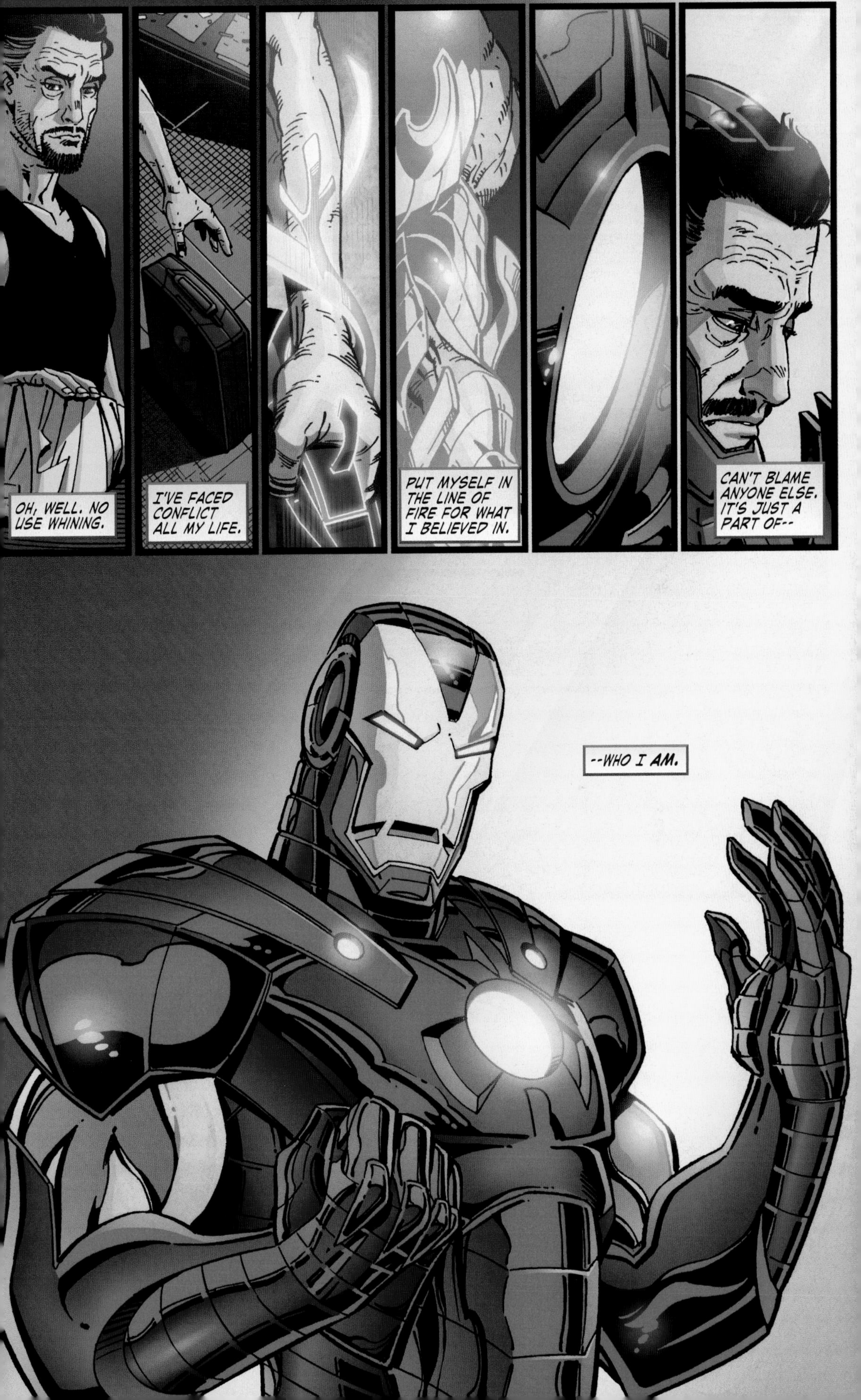
OH, WELL. NO USE WHINING.
I'VE FACED CONFLICT ALL MY LIFE.
PUT MYSELF IN THE LINE OF FIRE FOR WHAT I BELIEVED IN.
CAN'T BLAME ANYONE ELSE. IT'S JUST A PART OF--
--WHO I AM.

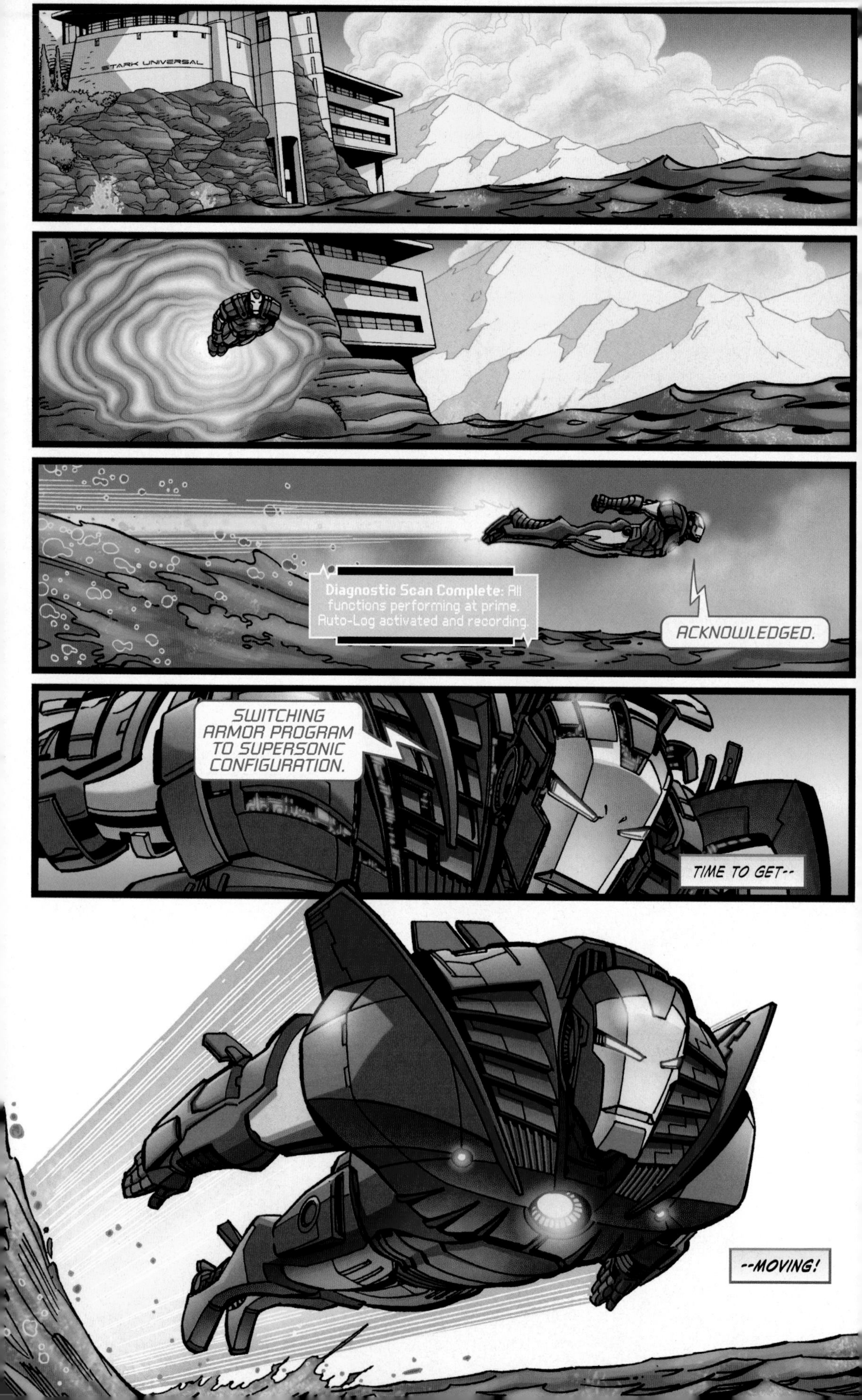
STARK UNIVERSAL
Diagnostic Scan Complete: All functions performing at prime. Auto-Log activated and recording.
ACKNOWLEDGED.
SWITCHING ARMOR PROGRAM TO SUPERSONIC CONFIGURATION.
TIME TO GET--
--MOVING!

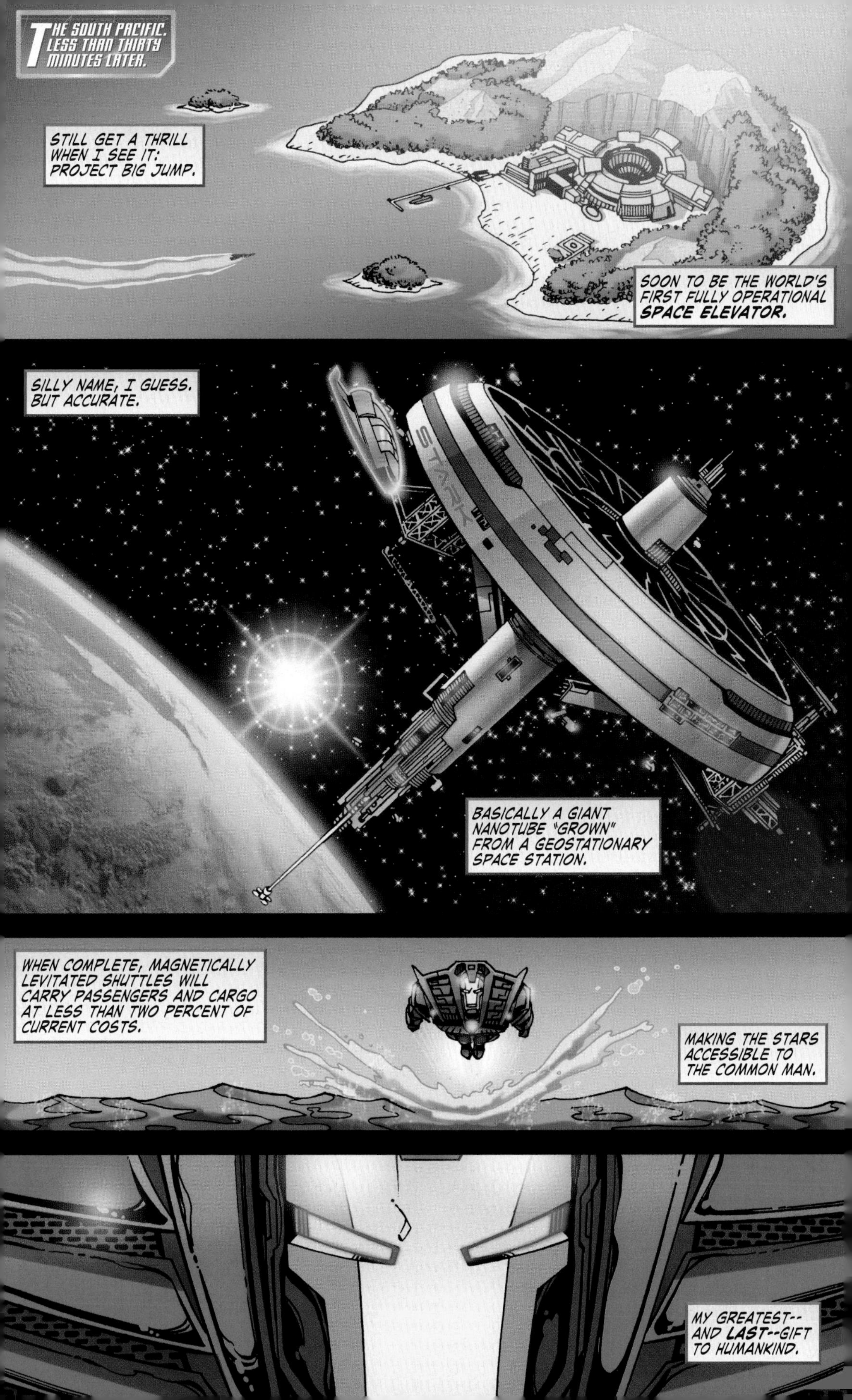

THE SOUTH PACIFIC. LESS THAN THIRTY MINUTES LATER.
STILL GET A THRILL WHEN I SEE IT: PROJECT BIG JUMP.
SOON TO BE THE WORLD'S FIRST FULLY OPERATIONAL SPACE ELEVATOR.
SILLY NAME, I GUESS. BUT ACCURATE.
STARK
BASICALLY A GIANT NANOTUBE "GROWN" FROM A GEOSTATIONARY SPACE STATION.
WHEN COMPLETE, MAGNETICALLY LEVITATED SHUTTLES WILL CARRY PASSENGERS AND CARGO AT LESS THAN TWO PERCENT OF CURRENT COSTS.
MAKING THE STARS ACCESSIBLE TO THE COMMON MAN.
MY GREATEST-- AND LAST--GIFT TO HUMANKIND.

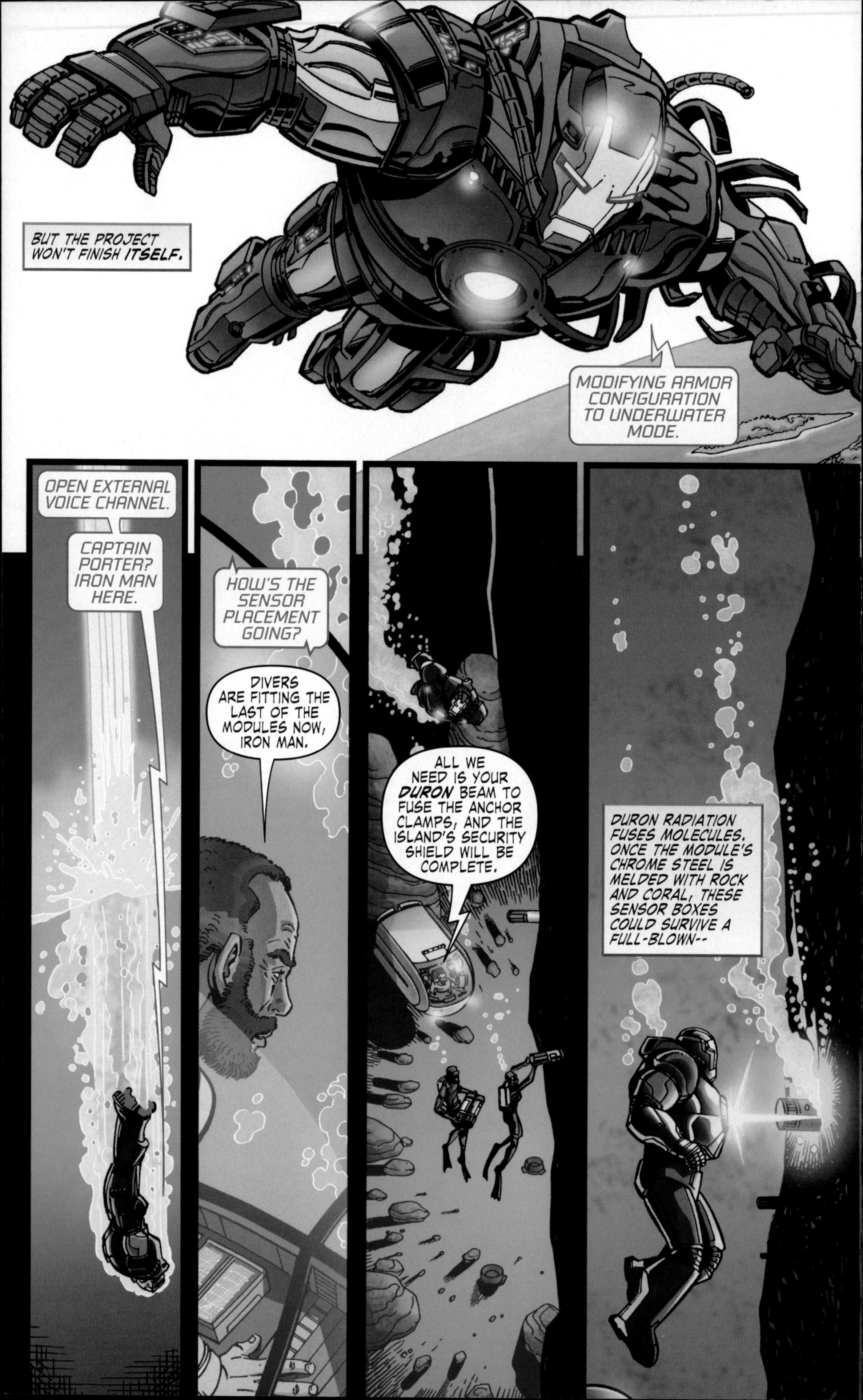
BUT THE PROJECT WON'T FINISH ITSELF.
MODIFYING ARMOR CONFIGURATION TO UNDERWATER MODE.
OPEN EXTERNAL VOICE CHANNEL.
CAPTAIN PORTER? IRON MAN HERE.
HOW'S THE SENSOR PLACEMENT GOING?
DIVERS ARE FITTING THE LAST OF THE MODULES NOW, IRON MAN.
ALL WE NEED IS YOUR DURON BEAM TO FUSE THE ANCHOR CLAMPS, AND THE ISLAND'S SECURITY SHIELD WILL BE COMPLETE.
DURON RADIATION FUSES MOLECULES. ONCE THE MODULE'S CHROME STEEL IS MELDED WITH ROCK AND CORAL, THESE SENSOR BOXES COULD SURVIVE A FULL-BLOWN--

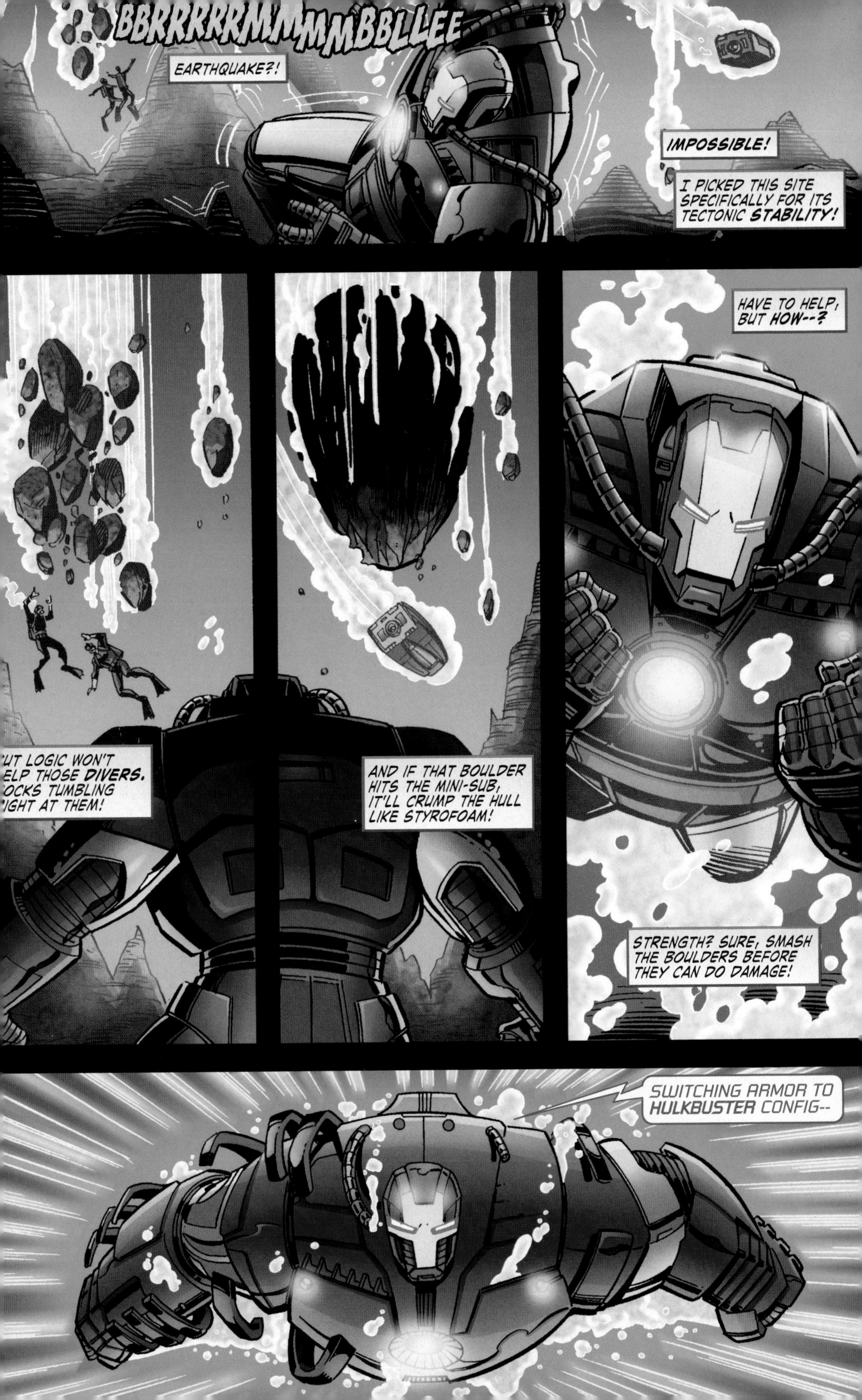
BBRRRRRRMMMMMBBLLEE
EARTHQUAKE?!
IMPOSSIBLE!
I PICKED THIS SITE SPECIFICALLY FOR ITS TECTONIC STABILITY!
UT LOGIC WON'T ELP THOSE DIVERS. OCKS TUMBLING IGHT AT THEM!
AND IF THAT BOULDER HITS THE MINI-SUB, IT'LL CRUMP THE HULL LIKE STYROFOAM!
HAVE TO HELP, BUT HOW--?
STRENGTH? SURE, SMASH THE BOULDERS BEFORE THEY CAN DO DAMAGE!
SWITCHING ARMOR TO HULKBUSTER CONFIG--

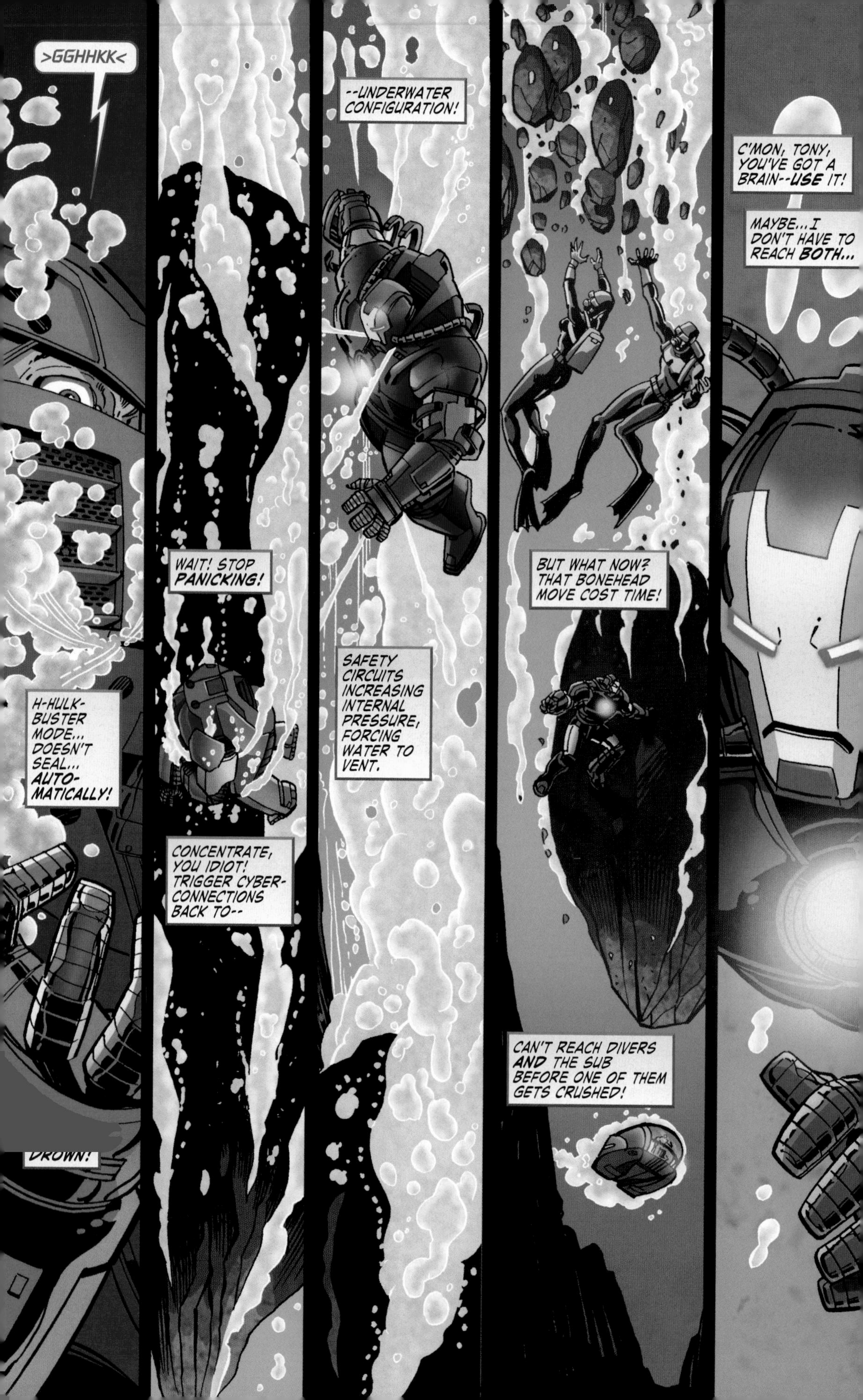

>GGHHKK<
H-HULK-BUSTER MODE... DOESN'T SEAL... AUTO-MATICALLY!
DROWN!
WAIT! STOP PANICKING!
CONCENTRATE, YOU IDIOT! TRIGGER CYBER-CONNECTIONS BACK TO--
--UNDERWATER CONFIGURATION!
SAFETY CIRCUITS INCREASING INTERNAL PRESSURE, FORCING WATER TO VENT.
BUT WHAT NOW? THAT BONEHEAD MOVE COST TIME!
CAN'T REACH DIVERS AND THE SUB BEFORE ONE OF THEM GETS CRUSHED!
C'MON, TONY, YOU'VE GOT A BRAIN--USE IT!
MAYBE...I DON'T HAVE TO REACH BOTH...

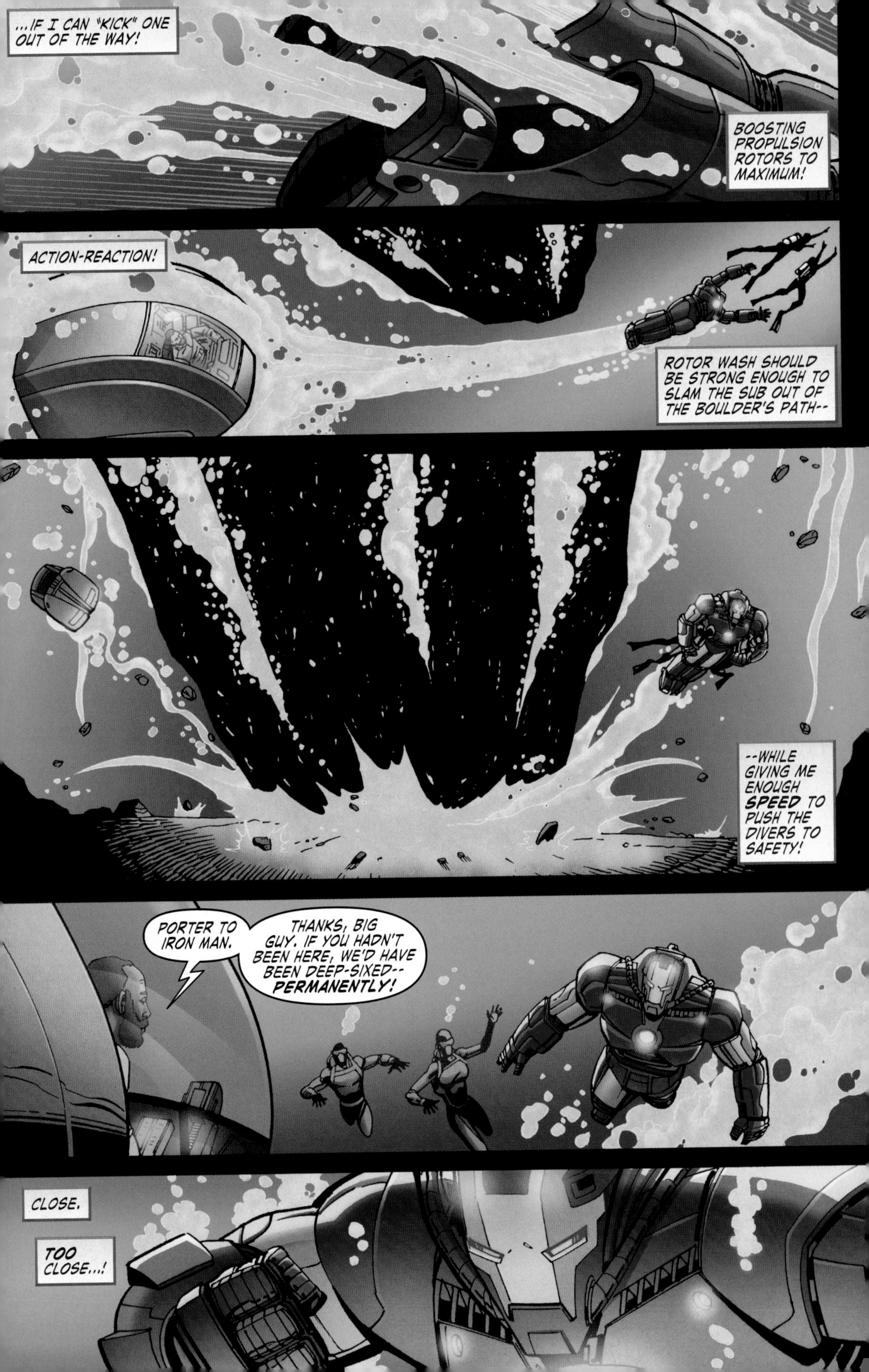
...IF I CAN "KICK" ONE OUT OF THE WAY!
BOOSTING PROPULSION ROTORS TO MAXIMUM!
ACTION-REACTION!
ROTOR WASH SHOULD BE STRONG ENOUGH TO SLAM THE SUB OUT OF THE BOULDER'S PATH--
--WHILE GIVING ME ENOUGH SPEED TO PUSH THE DIVERS TO SAFETY!
PORTER TO IRON MAN.
THANKS, BIG GUY. IF YOU HADN'T BEEN HERE, WE'D HAVE BEEN DEEP-SIXED-- PERMANENTLY!
CLOSE.
TOO CLOSE...!

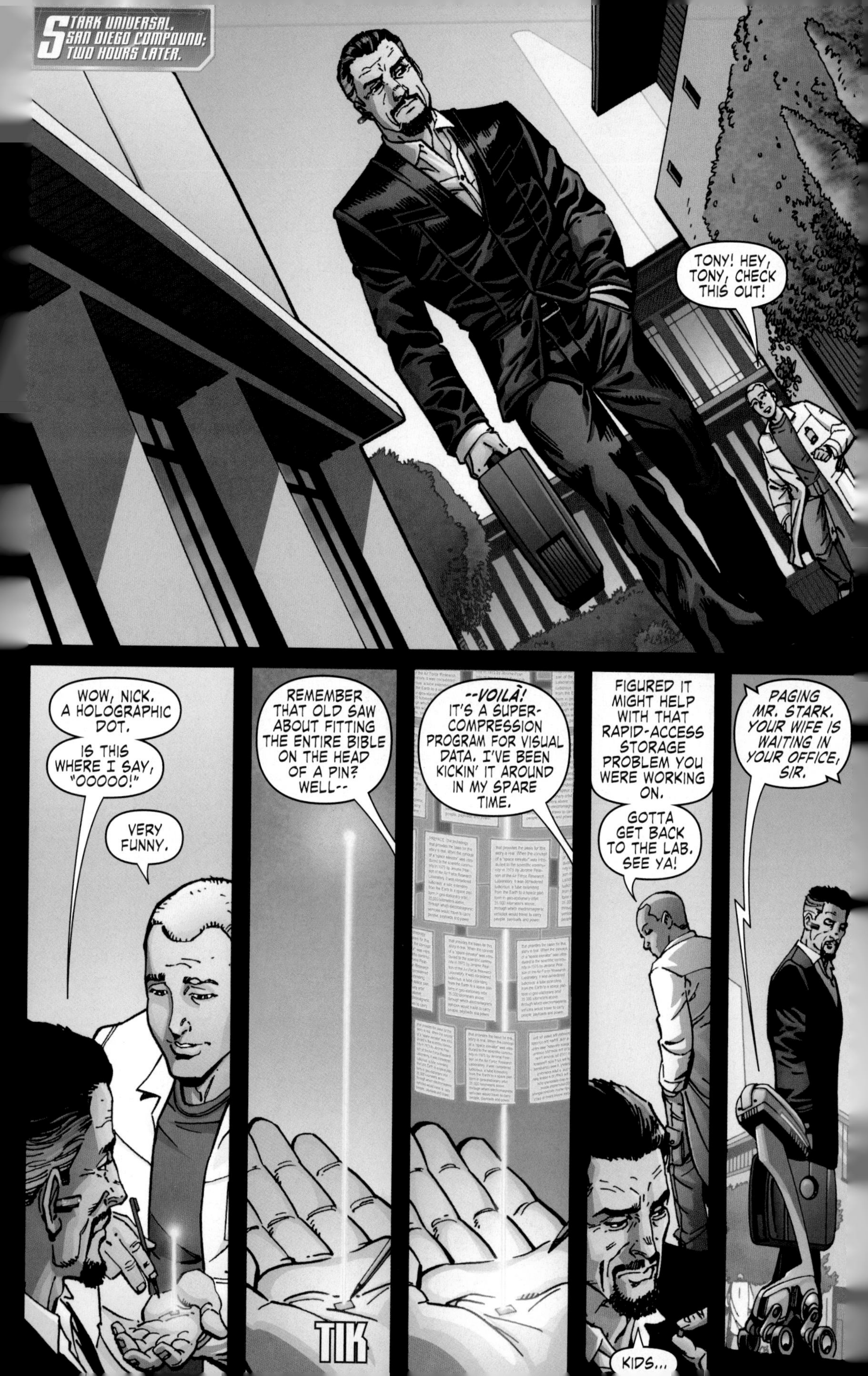
STARK UNIVERSAL, SAN DIEGO COMPOUND: TWO HOURS LATER.
TONY! HEY, TONY, CHECK THIS OUT!
WOW, NICK. A HOLOGRAPHIC DOT.
IS THIS WHERE I SAY, "OOOOO!"
VERY FUNNY.
REMEMBER THAT OLD SAW ABOUT FITTING THE ENTIRE BIBLE ON THE HEAD OF A PIN? WELL--
TIK
--VOILÀ! IT'S A SUPER-COMPRESSION PROGRAM FOR VISUAL DATA. I'VE BEEN KICKIN' IT AROUND IN MY SPARE TIME.
FIGURED IT MIGHT HELP WITH THAT RAPID-ACCESS STORAGE PROBLEM YOU WERE WORKING ON.
GOTTA GET BACK TO THE LAB. SEE YA!
KIDS...
PAGING MR. STARK. YOUR WIFE IS WAITING IN YOUR OFFICE, SIR.

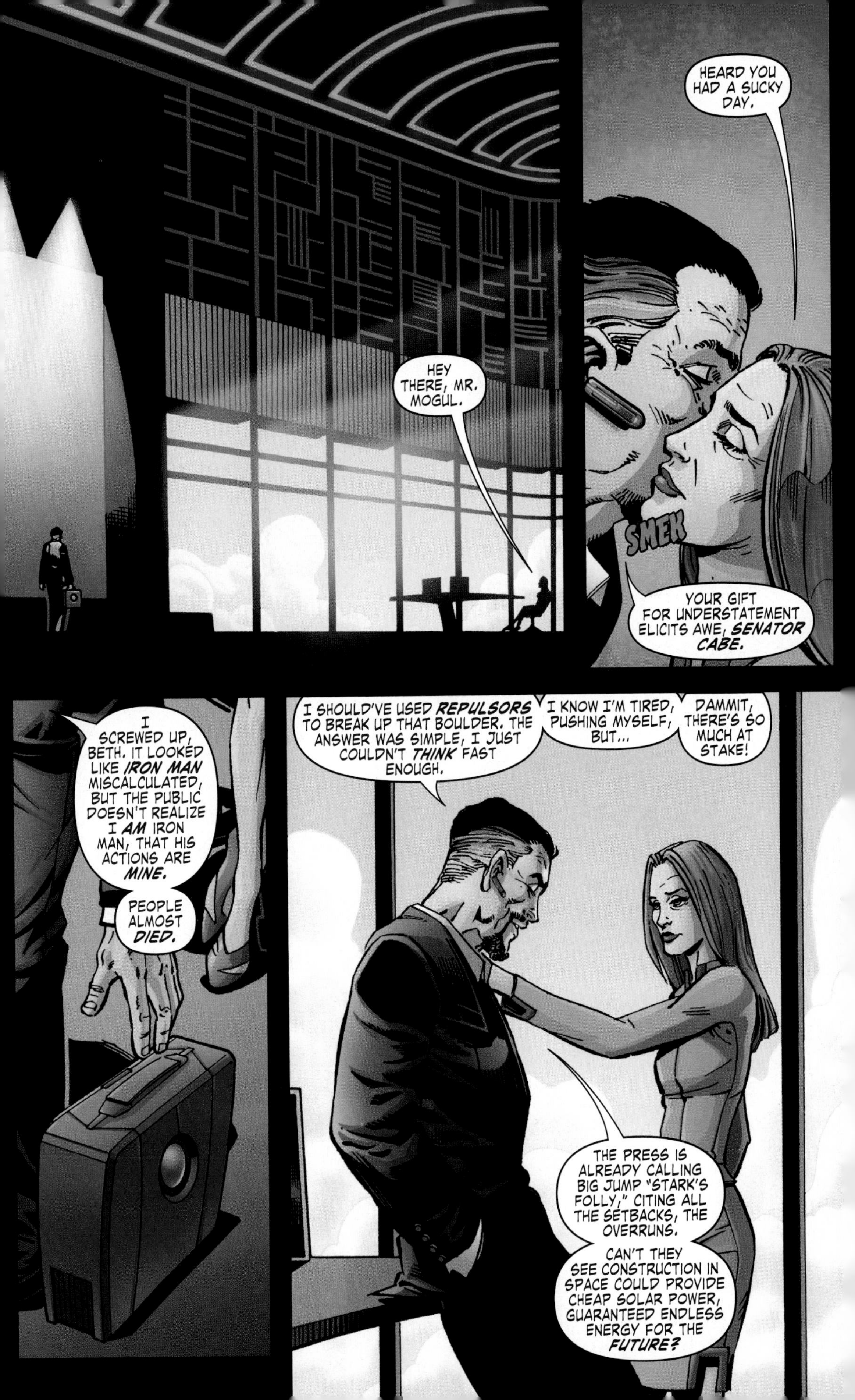
HEY THERE, MR. MOGUL.
HEARD YOU HAD A SUCKY DAY.
SMEK
YOUR GIFT FOR UNDERSTATEMENT ELICITS AWE, SENATOR CABE.
I SCREWED UP, BETH. IT LOOKED LIKE IRON MAN MISCALCULATED, BUT THE PUBLIC DOESN'T REALIZE I AM IRON MAN, THAT HIS ACTIONS ARE MINE.
PEOPLE ALMOST DIED.
I SHOULD'VE USED REPULSORS TO BREAK UP THAT BOULDER. THE ANSWER WAS SIMPLE, I JUST COULDN'T THINK FAST ENOUGH.
I KNOW I'M TIRED, PUSHING MYSELF, BUT...
DAMMIT, THERE'S SO MUCH AT STAKE!
THE PRESS IS ALREADY CALLING BIG JUMP "STARK'S FOLLY," CITING ALL THE SETBACKS, THE OVERRUNS.
CAN'T THEY SEE CONSTRUCTION IN SPACE COULD PROVIDE CHEAP SOLAR POWER, GUARANTEED ENDLESS ENERGY FOR THE FUTURE?

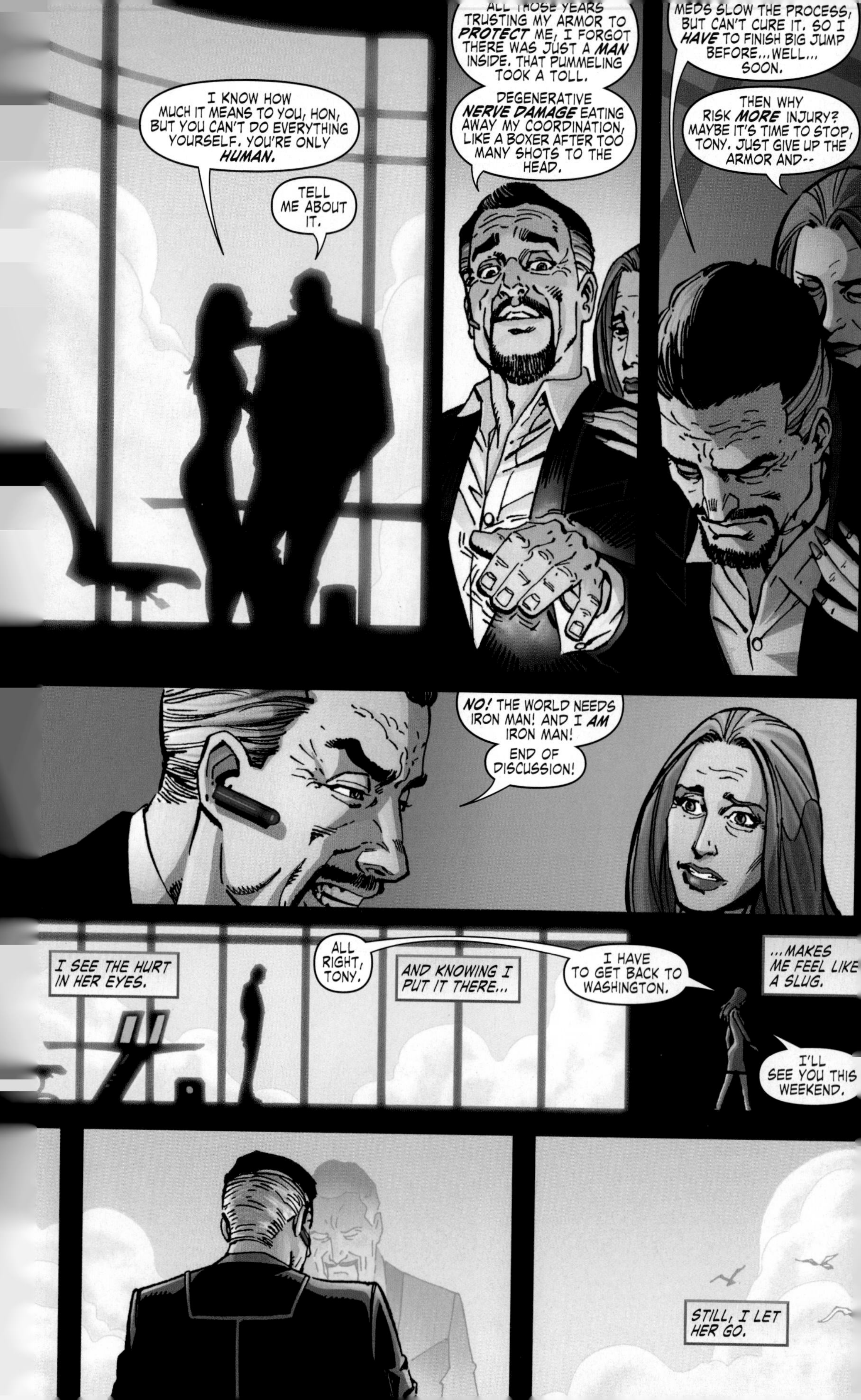
I KNOW HOW MUCH IT MEANS TO YOU, HON, BUT YOU CAN'T DO EVERYTHING YOURSELF. YOU'RE ONLY *HUMAN.*
TELL ME ABOUT IT.
ALL THOSE YEARS TRUSTING MY ARMOR TO *PROTECT* ME, I FORGOT THERE WAS JUST A *MAN* INSIDE. THAT PUMMELING TOOK A TOLL.
DEGENERATIVE *NERVE DAMAGE* EATING AWAY MY COORDINATION, LIKE A BOXER AFTER TOO MANY SHOTS TO THE HEAD.
MEDS SLOW THE PROCESS, BUT CAN'T CURE IT. SO I *HAVE* TO FINISH BIG JUMP BEFORE...WELL... SOON.
THEN WHY RISK *MORE* INJURY? MAYBE IT'S TIME TO STOP, TONY. JUST GIVE UP THE ARMOR AND--
NO! THE WORLD NEEDS IRON MAN! AND I *AM* IRON MAN!
END OF DISCUSSION!
I SEE THE HURT IN HER EYES.
ALL RIGHT, TONY.
AND KNOWING I PUT IT THERE...
I HAVE TO GET BACK TO WASHINGTON.
...MAKES ME FEEL LIKE A SLUG.
I'LL SEE YOU THIS WEEKEND.
STILL, I LET HER GO.

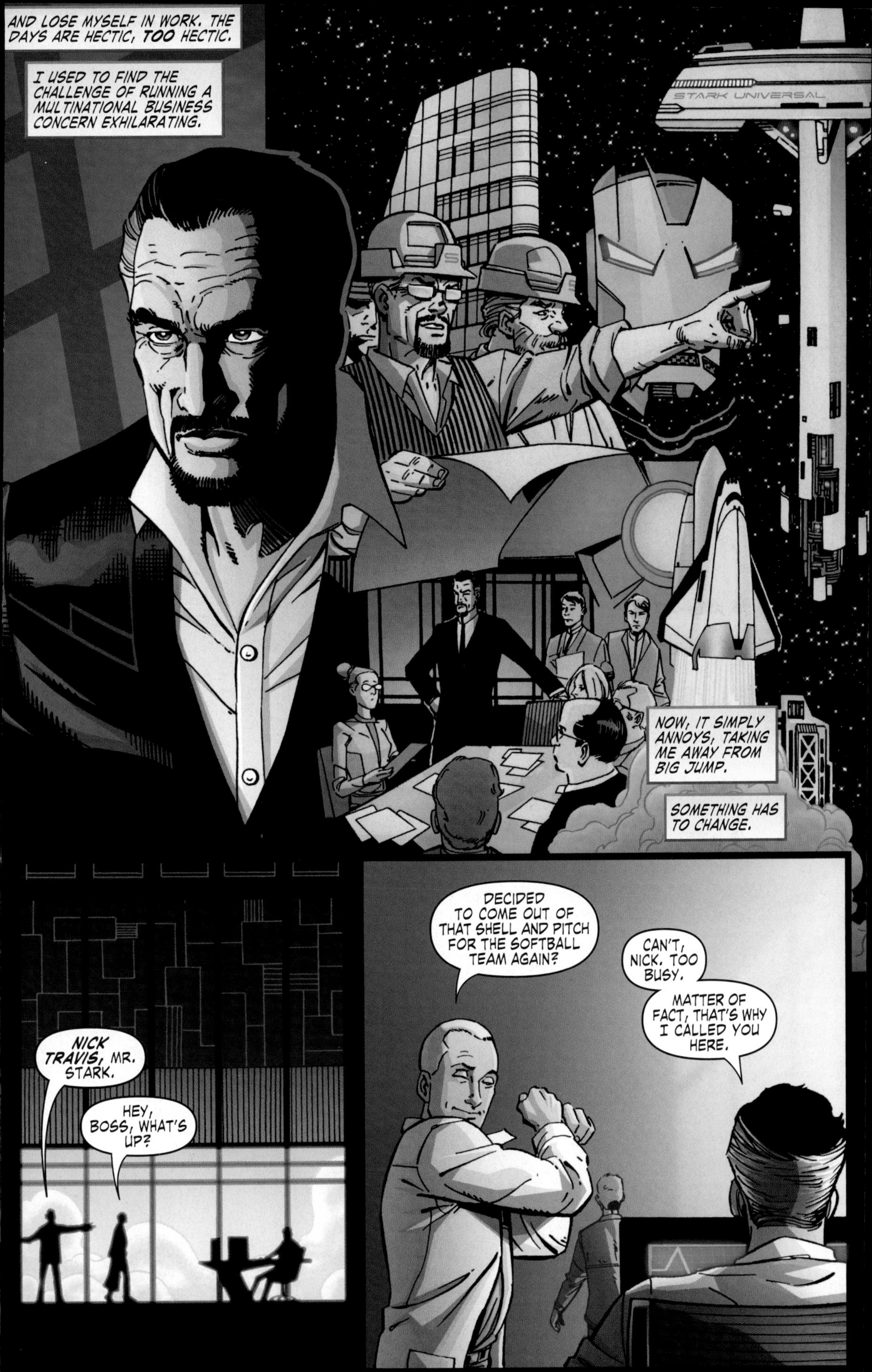
AND LOSE MYSELF IN WORK. THE DAYS ARE HECTIC, TOO HECTIC.
I USED TO FIND THE CHALLENGE OF RUNNING A MULTINATIONAL BUSINESS CONCERN EXHILARATING.
STARK UNIVERSAL
NOW, IT SIMPLY ANNOYS, TAKING ME AWAY FROM BIG JUMP.
SOMETHING HAS TO CHANGE.
NICK TRAVIS, MR. STARK.
HEY, BOSS, WHAT'S UP?
DECIDED TO COME OUT OF THAT SHELL AND PITCH FOR THE SOFTBALL TEAM AGAIN?
CAN'T, NICK. TOO BUSY.
MATTER OF FACT, THAT'S WHY I CALLED YOU HERE.

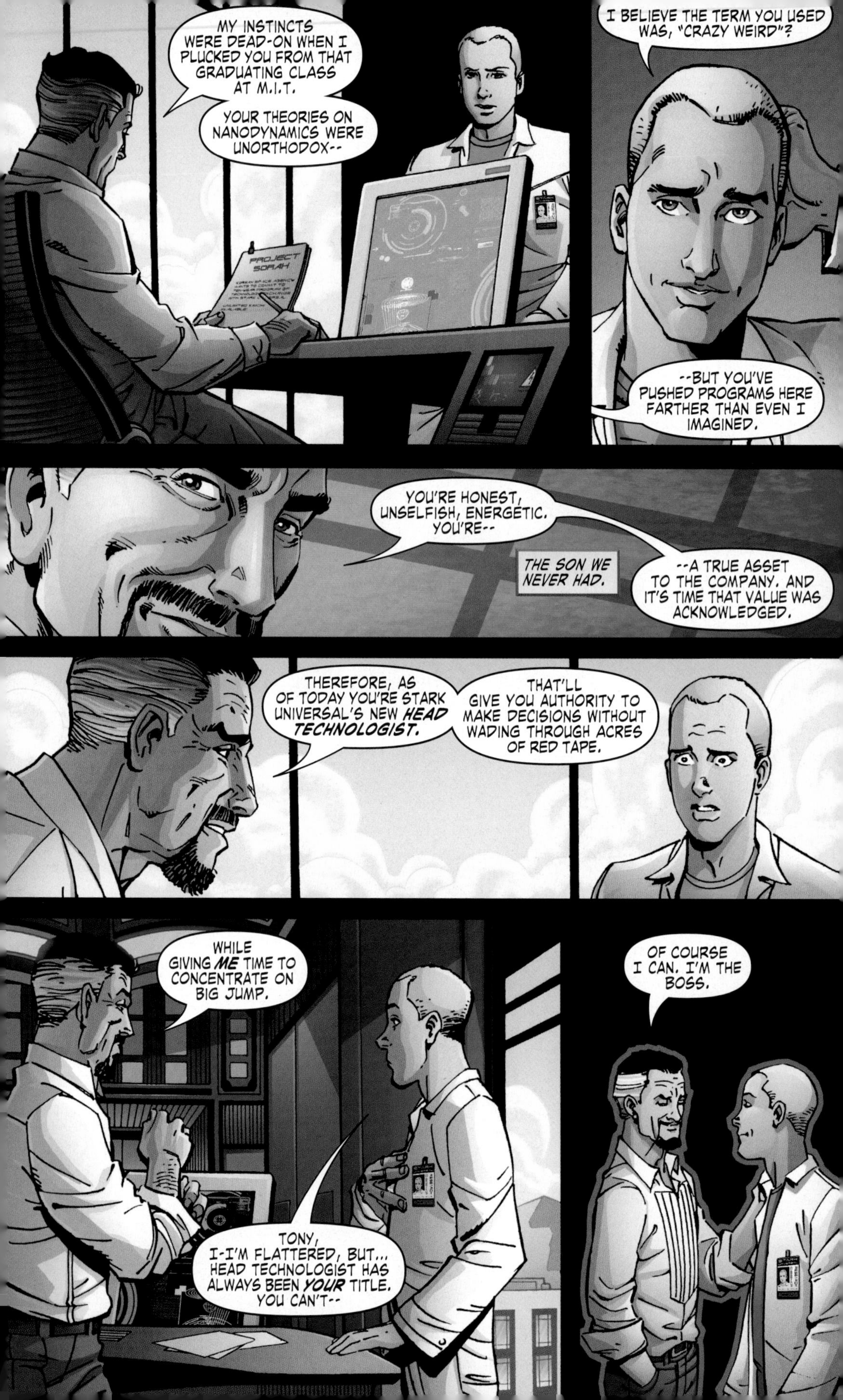

MY INSTINCTS WERE DEAD-ON WHEN I PLUCKED YOU FROM THAT GRADUATING CLASS AT M.I.T.
YOUR THEORIES ON NANODYNAMICS WERE UNORTHODOX--
PROJECT SORAH
I BELIEVE THE TERM YOU USED WAS, "CRAZY WEIRD"?
--BUT YOU'VE PUSHED PROGRAMS HERE FARTHER THAN EVEN I IMAGINED.
YOU'RE HONEST, UNSELFISH, ENERGETIC. YOU'RE--
THE SON WE NEVER HAD.
--A TRUE ASSET TO THE COMPANY. AND IT'S TIME THAT VALUE WAS ACKNOWLEDGED.
THEREFORE, AS OF TODAY YOU'RE STARK UNIVERSAL'S NEW HEAD TECHNOLOGIST.
THAT'LL GIVE YOU AUTHORITY TO MAKE DECISIONS WITHOUT WADING THROUGH ACRES OF RED TAPE.
WHILE GIVING ME TIME TO CONCENTRATE ON BIG JUMP.
TONY, I-I'M FLATTERED, BUT... HEAD TECHNOLOGIST HAS ALWAYS BEEN YOUR TITLE. YOU CAN'T--
OF COURSE I CAN. I'M THE BOSS.

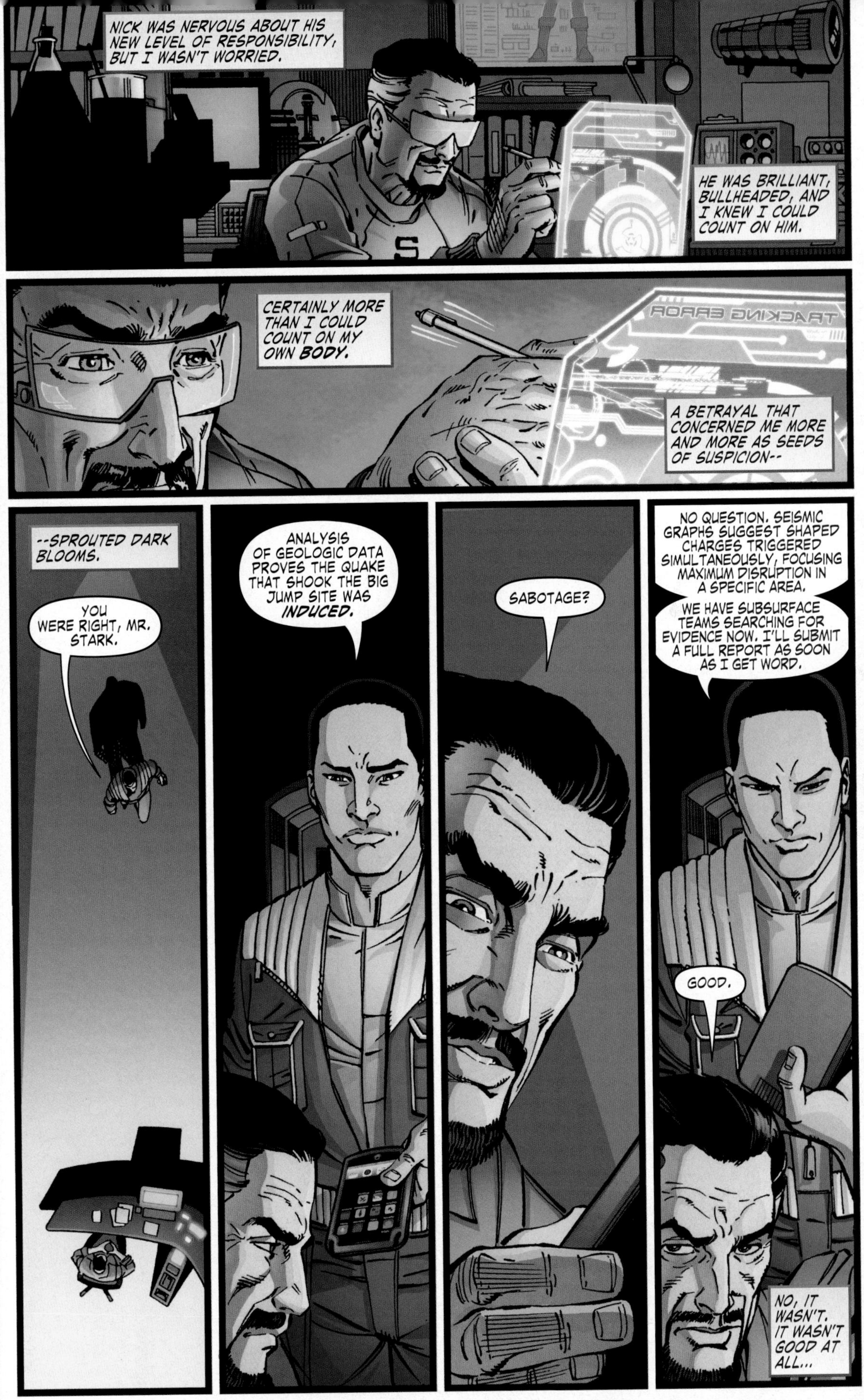
NICK WAS NERVOUS ABOUT HIS NEW LEVEL OF RESPONSIBILITY, BUT I WASN'T WORRIED.
HE WAS BRILLIANT, BULLHEADED, AND I KNEW I COULD COUNT ON HIM.
CERTAINLY MORE THAN I COULD COUNT ON MY OWN BODY.
TRACKING ERROR
A BETRAYAL THAT CONCERNED ME MORE AND MORE AS SEEDS OF SUSPICION--
--SPROUTED DARK BLOOMS.
YOU WERE RIGHT, MR. STARK.
ANALYSIS OF GEOLOGIC DATA PROVES THE QUAKE THAT SHOOK THE BIG JUMP SITE WAS INDUCED.
SABOTAGE?
NO QUESTION. SEISMIC GRAPHS SUGGEST SHAPED CHARGES TRIGGERED SIMULTANEOUSLY, FOCUSING MAXIMUM DISRUPTION IN A SPECIFIC AREA.
WE HAVE SUBSURFACE TEAMS SEARCHING FOR EVIDENCE NOW. I'LL SUBMIT A FULL REPORT AS SOON AS I GET WORD.
GOOD.
NO, IT WASN'T. IT WASN'T GOOD AT ALL...

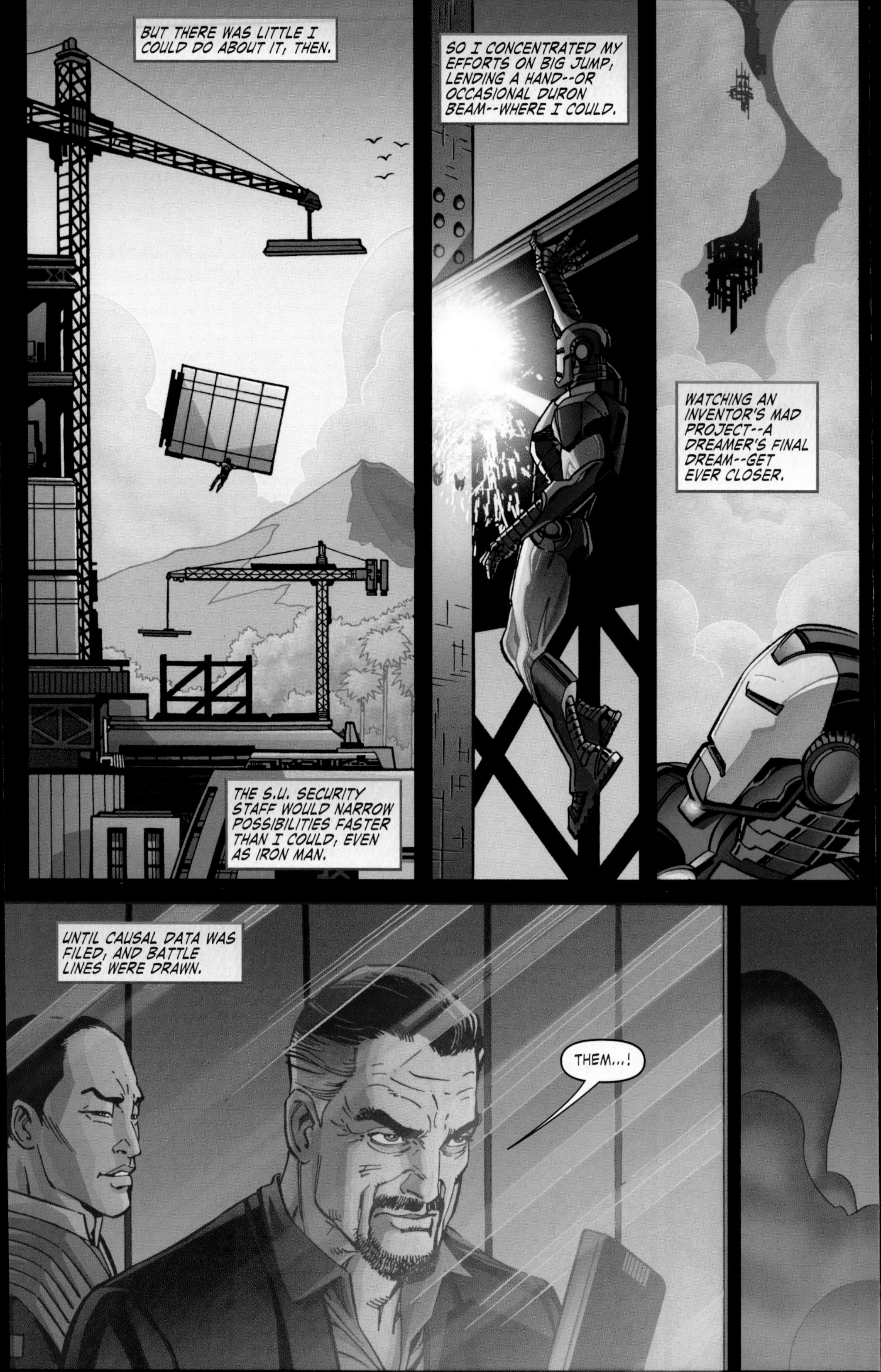
BUT THERE WAS LITTLE I COULD DO ABOUT IT, THEN.
THE S.U. SECURITY STAFF WOULD NARROW POSSIBILITIES FASTER THAN I COULD, EVEN AS IRON MAN.
SO I CONCENTRATED MY EFFORTS ON BIG JUMP, LENDING A HAND--OR OCCASIONAL DURON BEAM--WHERE I COULD.
WATCHING AN INVENTOR'S MAD PROJECT--A DREAMER'S FINAL DREAM--GET EVER CLOSER.
UNTIL CAUSAL DATA WAS FILED, AND BATTLE LINES WERE DRAWN.
THEM...!

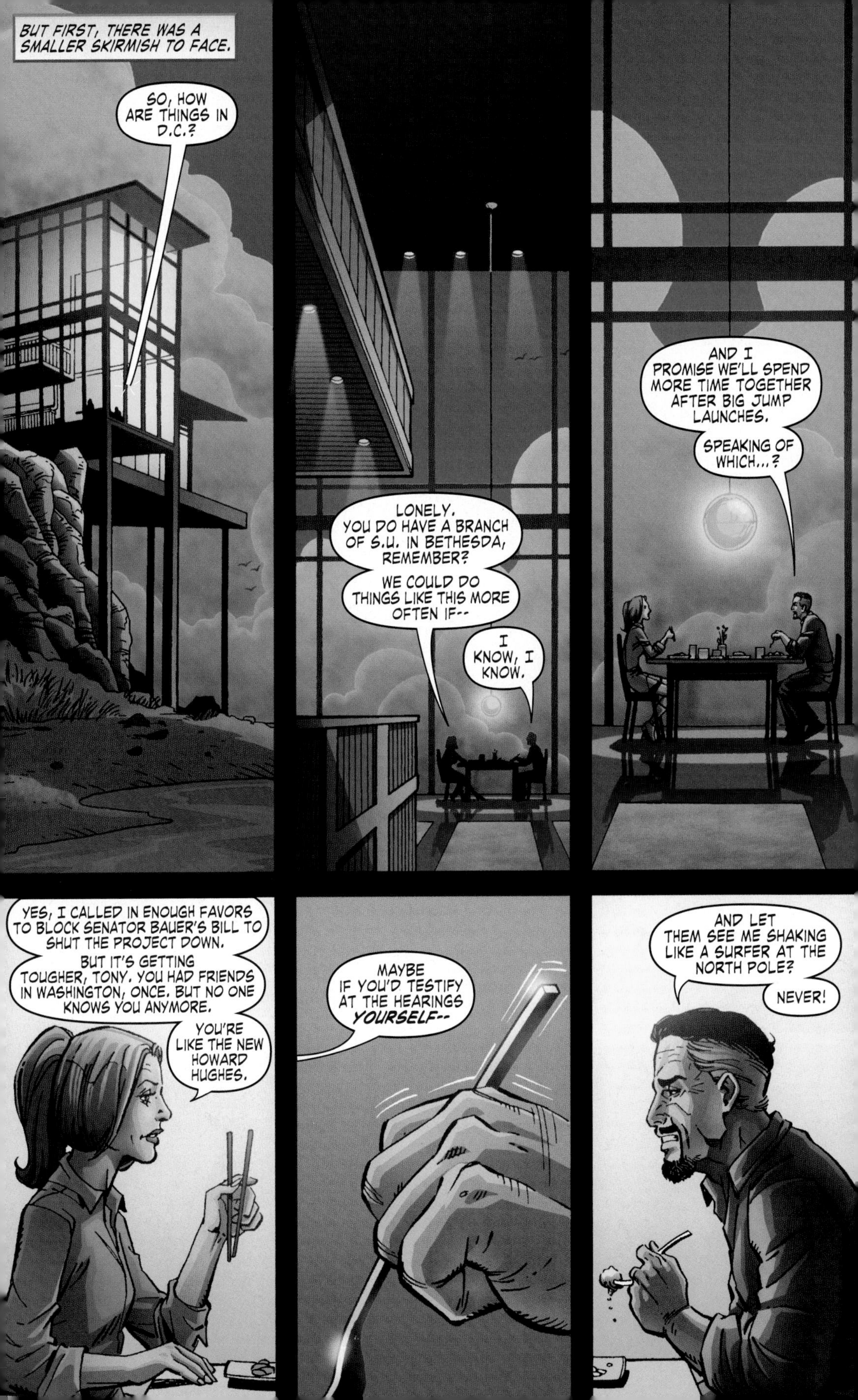
BUT FIRST, THERE WAS A SMALLER SKIRMISH TO FACE.
SO, HOW ARE THINGS IN D.C.?
LONELY. YOU DO HAVE A BRANCH OF S.U. IN BETHESDA, REMEMBER?
WE COULD DO THINGS LIKE THIS MORE OFTEN IF--
I KNOW, I KNOW.
AND I PROMISE WE'LL SPEND MORE TIME TOGETHER AFTER BIG JUMP LAUNCHES.
SPEAKING OF WHICH...?
YES, I CALLED IN ENOUGH FAVORS TO BLOCK SENATOR BAUER'S BILL TO SHUT THE PROJECT DOWN.
BUT IT'S GETTING TOUGHER, TONY. YOU HAD FRIENDS IN WASHINGTON, ONCE. BUT NO ONE KNOWS YOU ANYMORE.
YOU'RE LIKE THE NEW HOWARD HUGHES.
MAYBE IF YOU'D TESTIFY AT THE HEARINGS *YOURSELF--*
AND LET THEM SEE ME SHAKING LIKE A SURFER AT THE NORTH POLE?
NEVER!

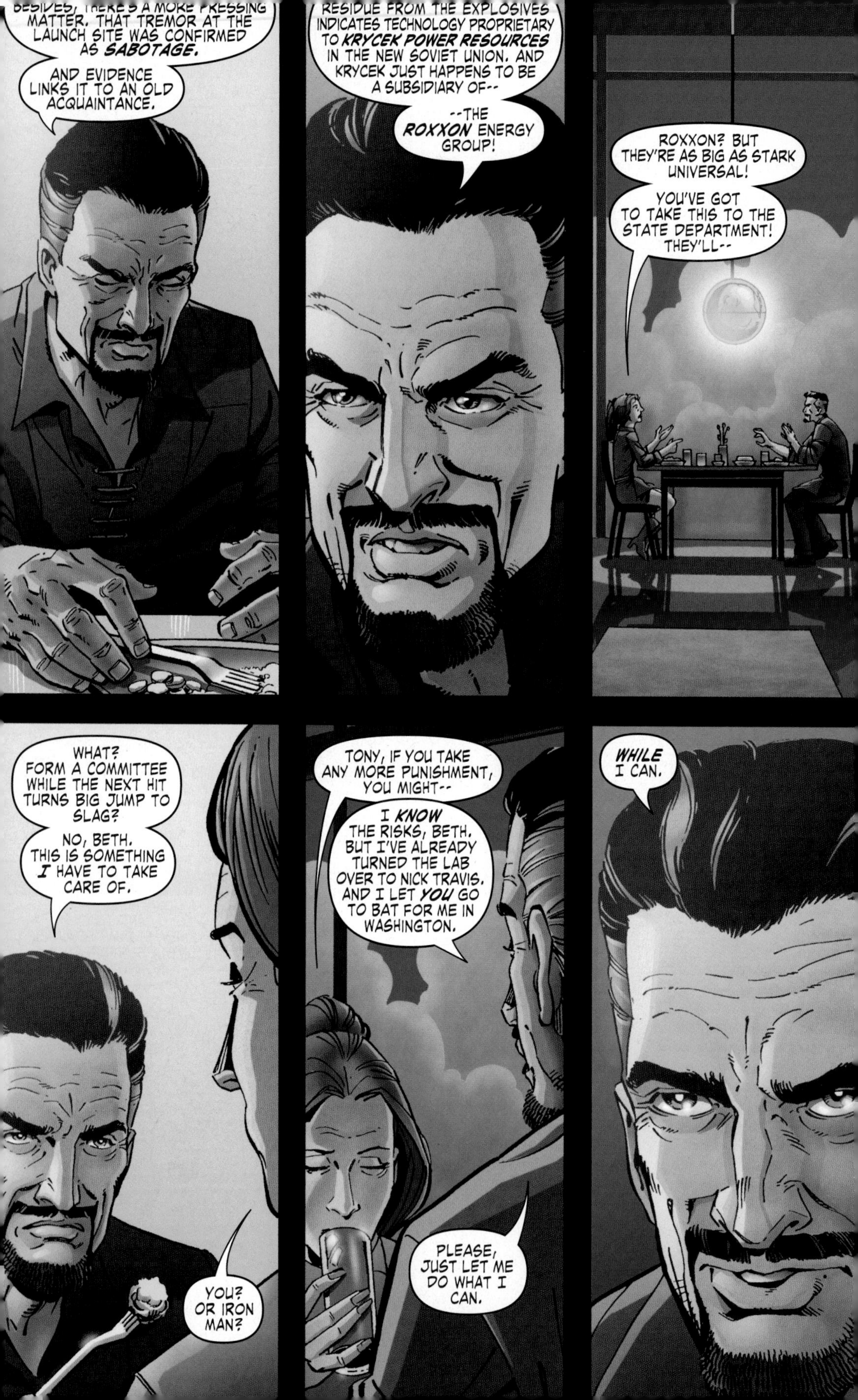

BESIDES, THERE'S A MORE PRESSING MATTER. THAT TREMOR AT THE LAUNCH SITE WAS CONFIRMED AS *SABOTAGE.*
AND EVIDENCE LINKS IT TO AN OLD ACQUAINTANCE.
RESIDUE FROM THE EXPLOSIVES INDICATES TECHNOLOGY PROPRIETARY TO *KRYCEK POWER RESOURCES* IN THE NEW SOVIET UNION. AND KRYCEK JUST HAPPENS TO BE A SUBSIDIARY OF--
--THE *ROXXON* ENERGY GROUP!
ROXXON? BUT THEY'RE AS BIG AS STARK UNIVERSAL!
YOU'VE GOT TO TAKE THIS TO THE STATE DEPARTMENT! THEY'LL--
WHAT? FORM A COMMITTEE WHILE THE NEXT HIT TURNS BIG JUMP TO SLAG?
NO, BETH. THIS IS SOMETHING *I* HAVE TO TAKE CARE OF.
YOU? OR IRON MAN?
TONY, IF YOU TAKE ANY MORE PUNISHMENT, YOU MIGHT--
I *KNOW* THE RISKS, BETH. BUT I'VE ALREADY TURNED THE LAB OVER TO NICK TRAVIS. AND I LET *YOU* GO TO BAT FOR ME IN WASHINGTON.
PLEASE, JUST LET ME DO WHAT I CAN.
WHILE I CAN.

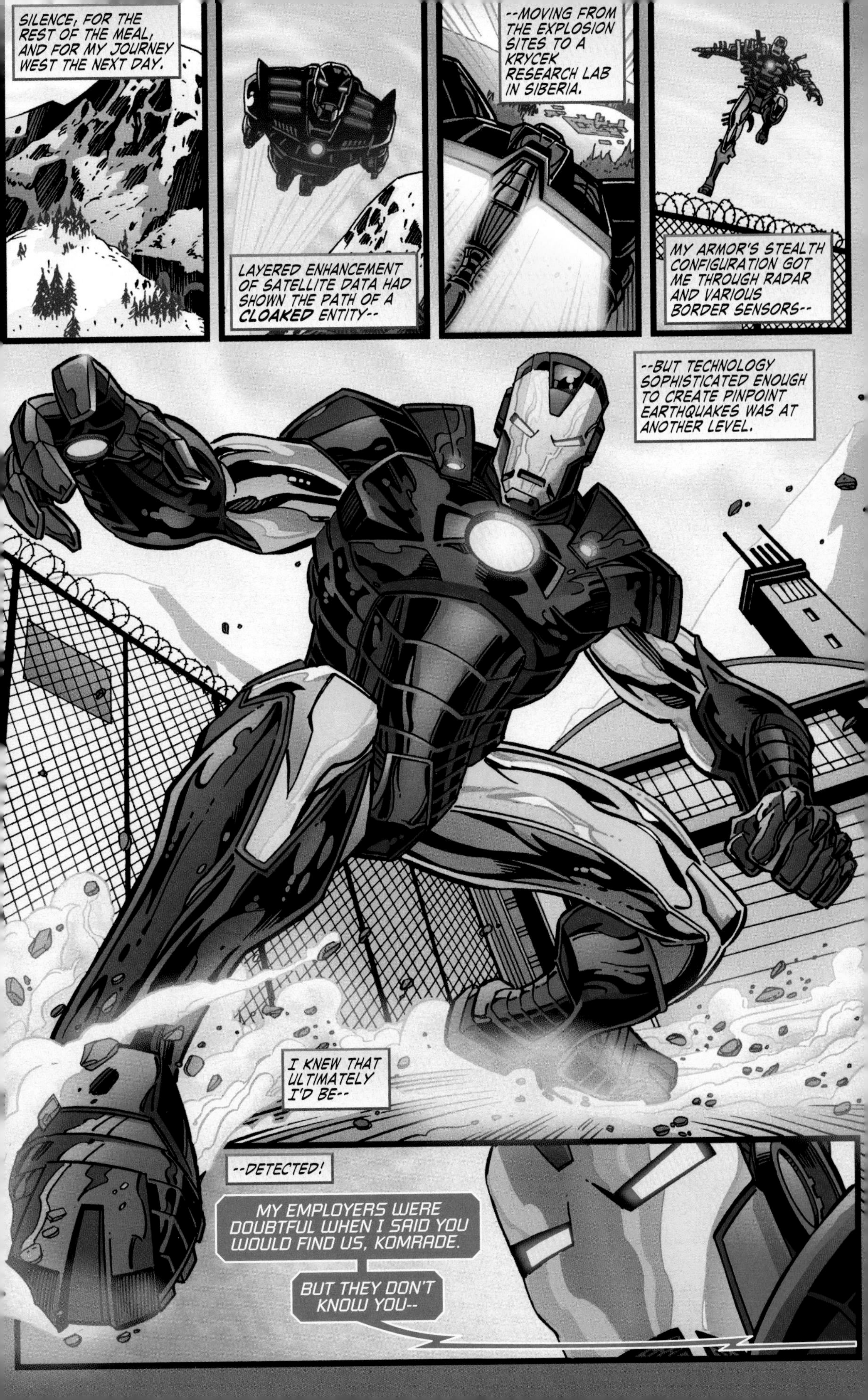
SILENCE, FOR THE REST OF THE MEAL, AND FOR MY JOURNEY WEST THE NEXT DAY.
LAYERED ENHANCEMENT OF SATELLITE DATA HAD SHOWN THE PATH OF A CLOAKED ENTITY--
--MOVING FROM THE EXPLOSION SITES TO A KRYCEK RESEARCH LAB IN SIBERIA.
MY ARMOR'S STEALTH CONFIGURATION GOT ME THROUGH RADAR AND VARIOUS BORDER SENSORS--
--BUT TECHNOLOGY SOPHISTICATED ENOUGH TO CREATE PINPOINT EARTHQUAKES WAS AT ANOTHER LEVEL.
I KNEW THAT ULTIMATELY I'D BE--
--DETECTED!
MY EMPLOYERS WERE DOUBTFUL WHEN I SAID YOU WOULD FIND US, KOMRADE.
BUT THEY DON'T KNOW YOU--

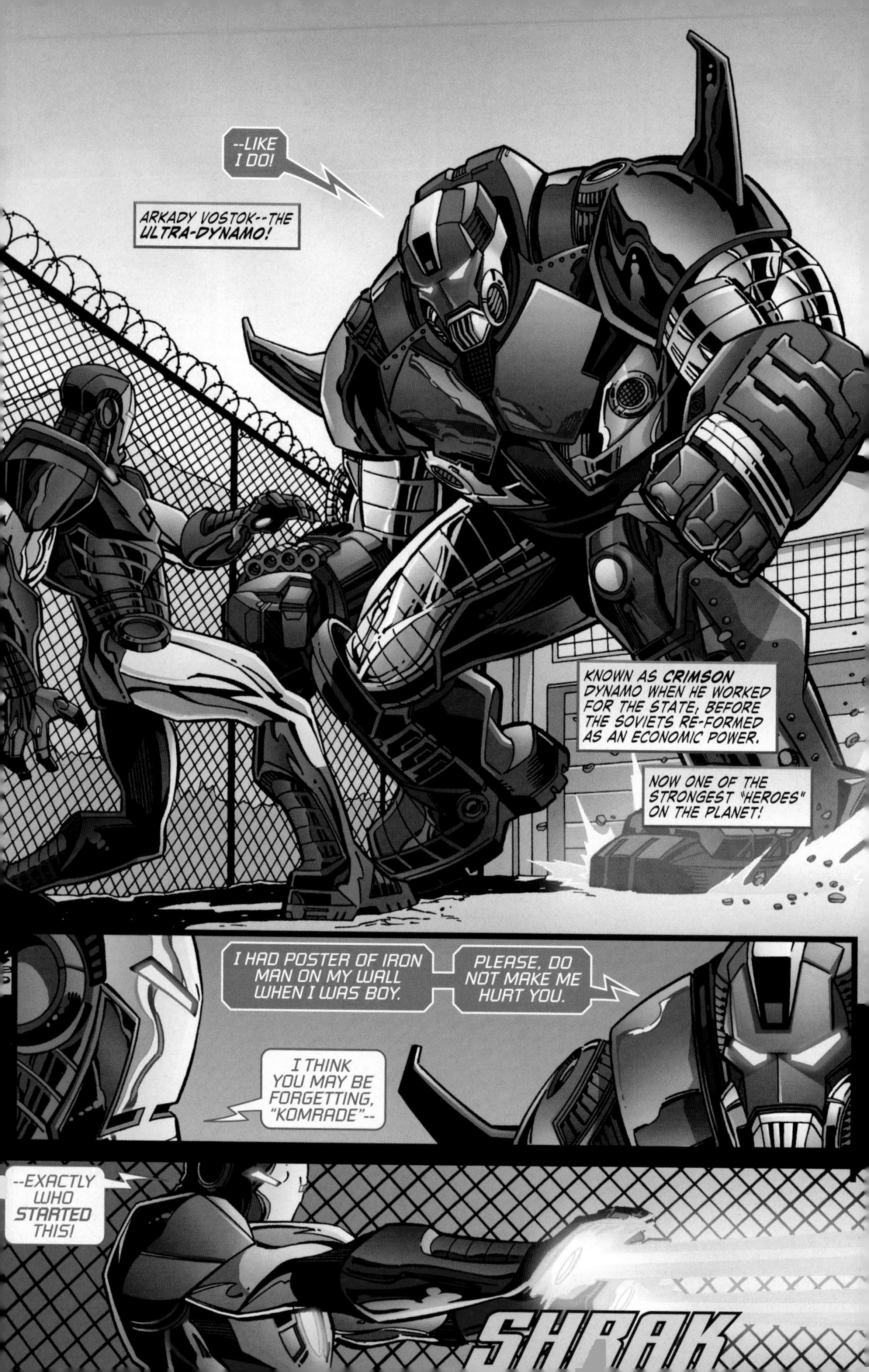
--LIKE I DO!
ARKADY VOSTOK--THE ULTRA-DYNAMO!
KNOWN AS CRIMSON DYNAMO WHEN HE WORKED FOR THE STATE, BEFORE THE SOVIETS RE-FORMED AS AN ECONOMIC POWER.
NOW ONE OF THE STRONGEST "HEROES" ON THE PLANET!
I HAD POSTER OF IRON MAN ON MY WALL WHEN I WAS BOY.
PLEASE, DO NOT MAKE ME HURT YOU.
I THINK YOU MAY BE FORGETTING, "KOMRADE"--
--EXACTLY WHO STARTED THIS!
SHRAK

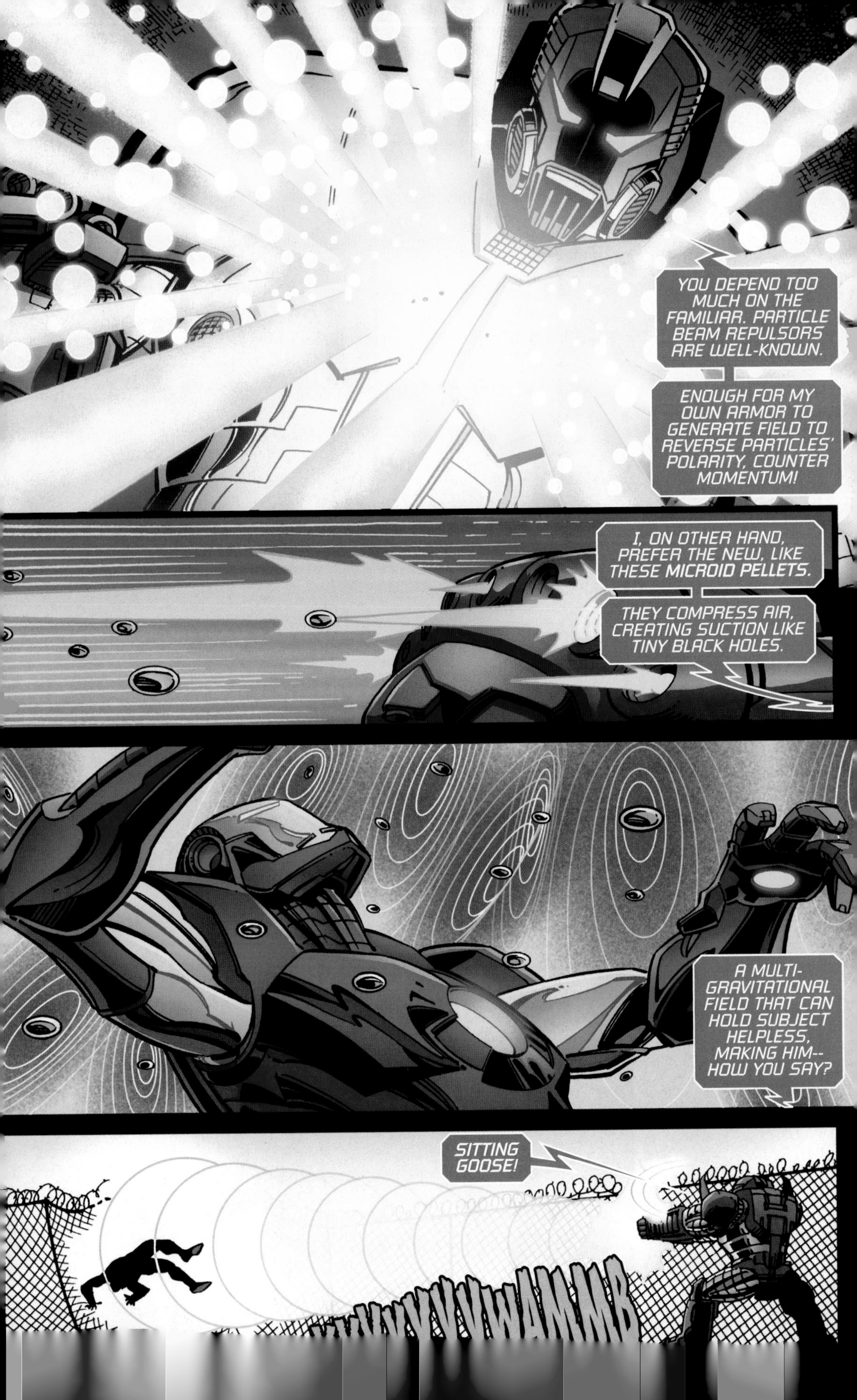
YOU DEPEND TOO MUCH ON THE FAMILIAR. PARTICLE BEAM REPULSORS ARE WELL-KNOWN.
ENOUGH FOR MY OWN ARMOR TO GENERATE FIELD TO REVERSE PARTICLES' POLARITY, COUNTER MOMENTUM!
I, ON OTHER HAND, PREFER THE NEW, LIKE THESE MICROID PELLETS.
THEY COMPRESS AIR, CREATING SUCTION LIKE TINY BLACK HOLES.
A MULTI-GRAVITATIONAL FIELD THAT CAN HOLD SUBJECT HELPLESS, MAKING HIM-- HOW YOU SAY?
SITTING GOOSE!
VVVVVVWAMMB

SHOULD HAVE WAITED UNTIL MY NEXT-GEN ARMOR WAS READY!

IF HE KNOWS SO MUCH, HOW CAN I--

BASICS! YEAH, FALL BACK ON--

--BRUTE STRENGTH!

THROWING STONES? HOW PREHISTORIC.

YOU DISAPPOINT ME, KOMRADE.

VERY WELL. I END THIS QUICKLY.

PIGGYBACK LASERS CARRY ELECTRICAL CHARGE AS SUB-PROGRAM.

LASERS SHOULD DISRUPT MATERIAL OF YOUR ARMOR JUST ENOUGH--

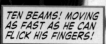

TEN BEAMS! MOVING AS FAST AS HE CAN FLICK HIS FINGERS!

TOO MANY! T-TOO FAST! I CAN'T--!

--TO LET ELECTRIC SHOCK THROUGH.

KZZAP

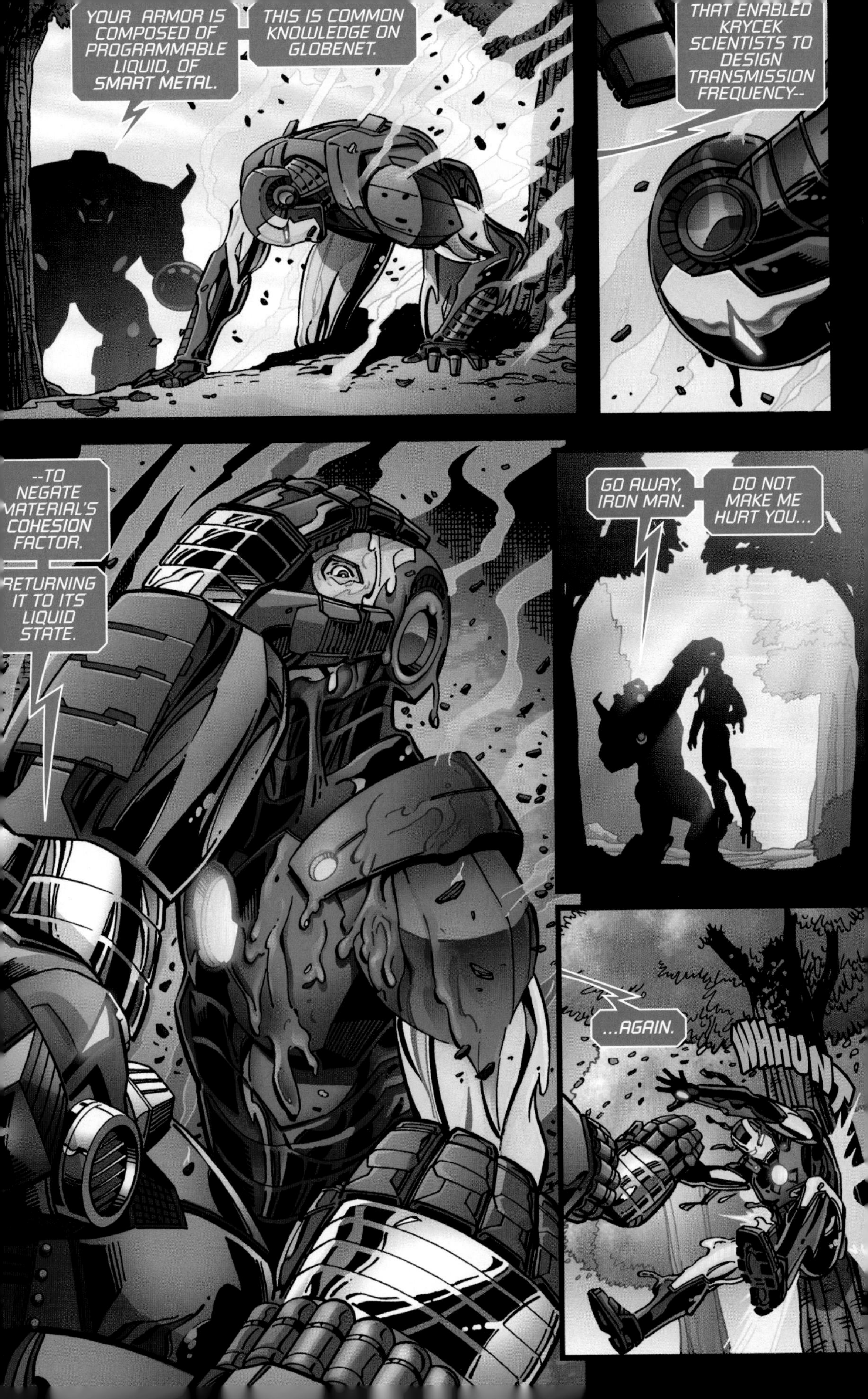
YOUR ARMOR IS COMPOSED OF PROGRAMMABLE LIQUID, OF SMART METAL.
THIS IS COMMON KNOWLEDGE ON GLOBENET.
THAT ENABLED KRYCEK SCIENTISTS TO DESIGN TRANSMISSION FREQUENCY--
--TO NEGATE MATERIAL'S COHESION FACTOR.
RETURNING IT TO ITS LIQUID STATE.
GO AWAY, IRON MAN.
DO NOT MAKE ME HURT YOU...
...AGAIN.
WHHOUN

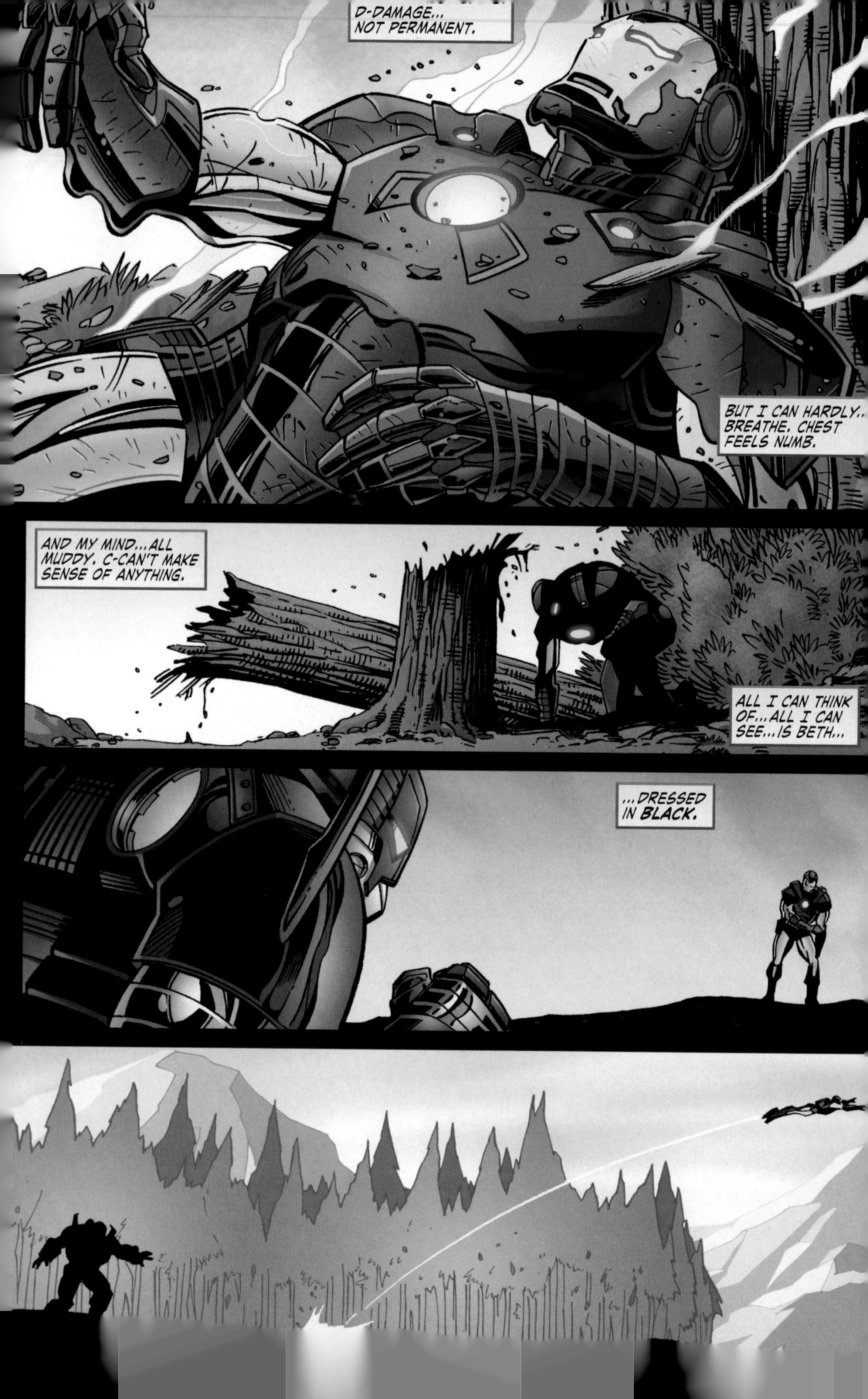
D-DAMAGE... NOT PERMANENT.
BUT I CAN HARDLY... BREATHE. CHEST FEELS NUMB.
AND MY MIND...ALL MUDDY. C-CAN'T MAKE SENSE OF ANYTHING.
ALL I CAN THINK OF...ALL I CAN SEE...IS BETH...
...DRESSED IN BLACK.

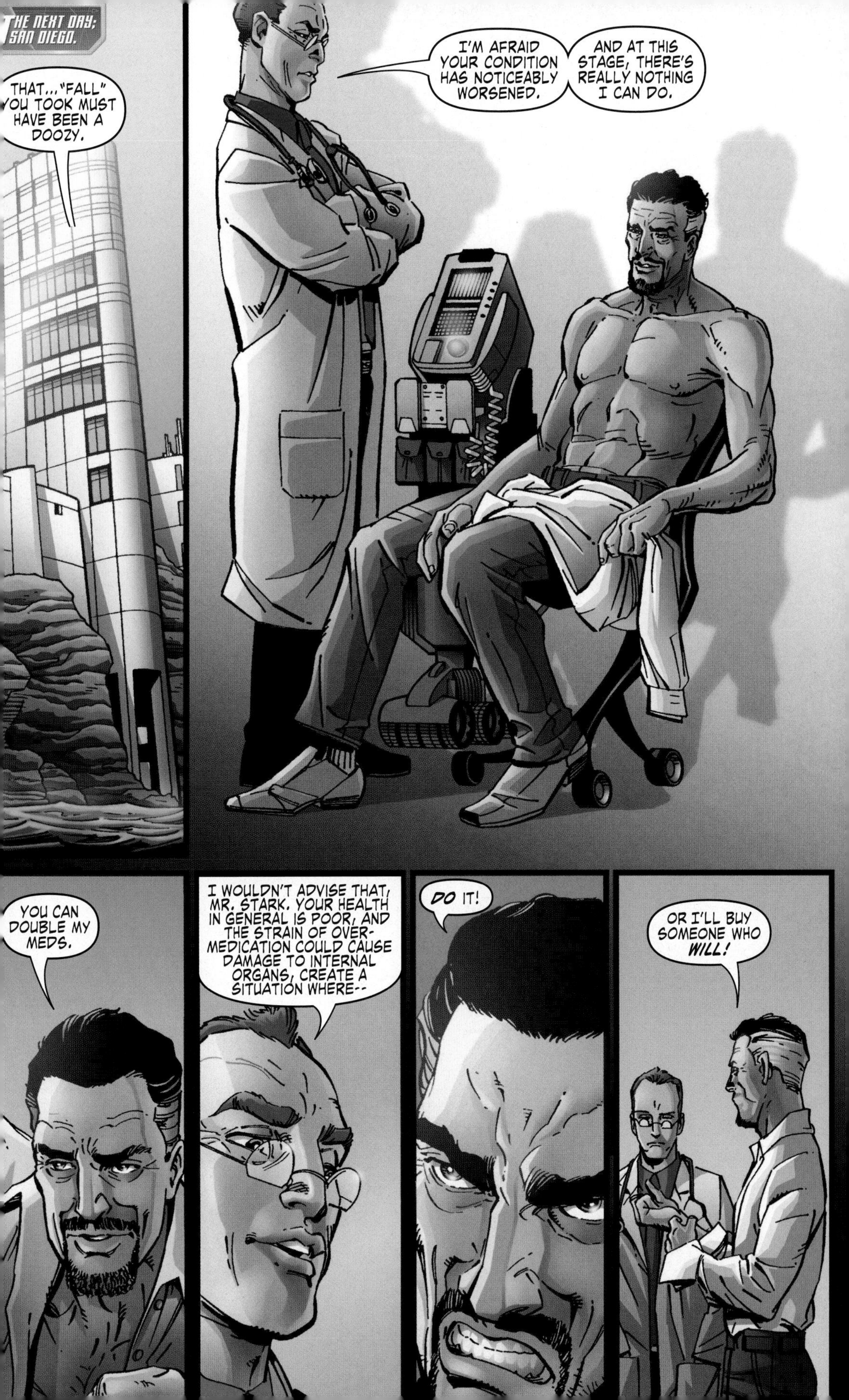
THE NEXT DAY; SAN DIEGO.
THAT..."FALL" YOU TOOK MUST HAVE BEEN A DOOZY.
I'M AFRAID YOUR CONDITION HAS NOTICEABLY WORSENED.
AND AT THIS STAGE, THERE'S REALLY NOTHING I CAN DO.
YOU CAN DOUBLE MY MEDS.
I WOULDN'T ADVISE THAT, MR. STARK. YOUR HEALTH IN GENERAL IS POOR, AND THE STRAIN OF OVER-MEDICATION COULD CAUSE DAMAGE TO INTERNAL ORGANS, CREATE A SITUATION WHERE--
DO IT!
OR I'LL BUY SOMEONE WHO WILL!

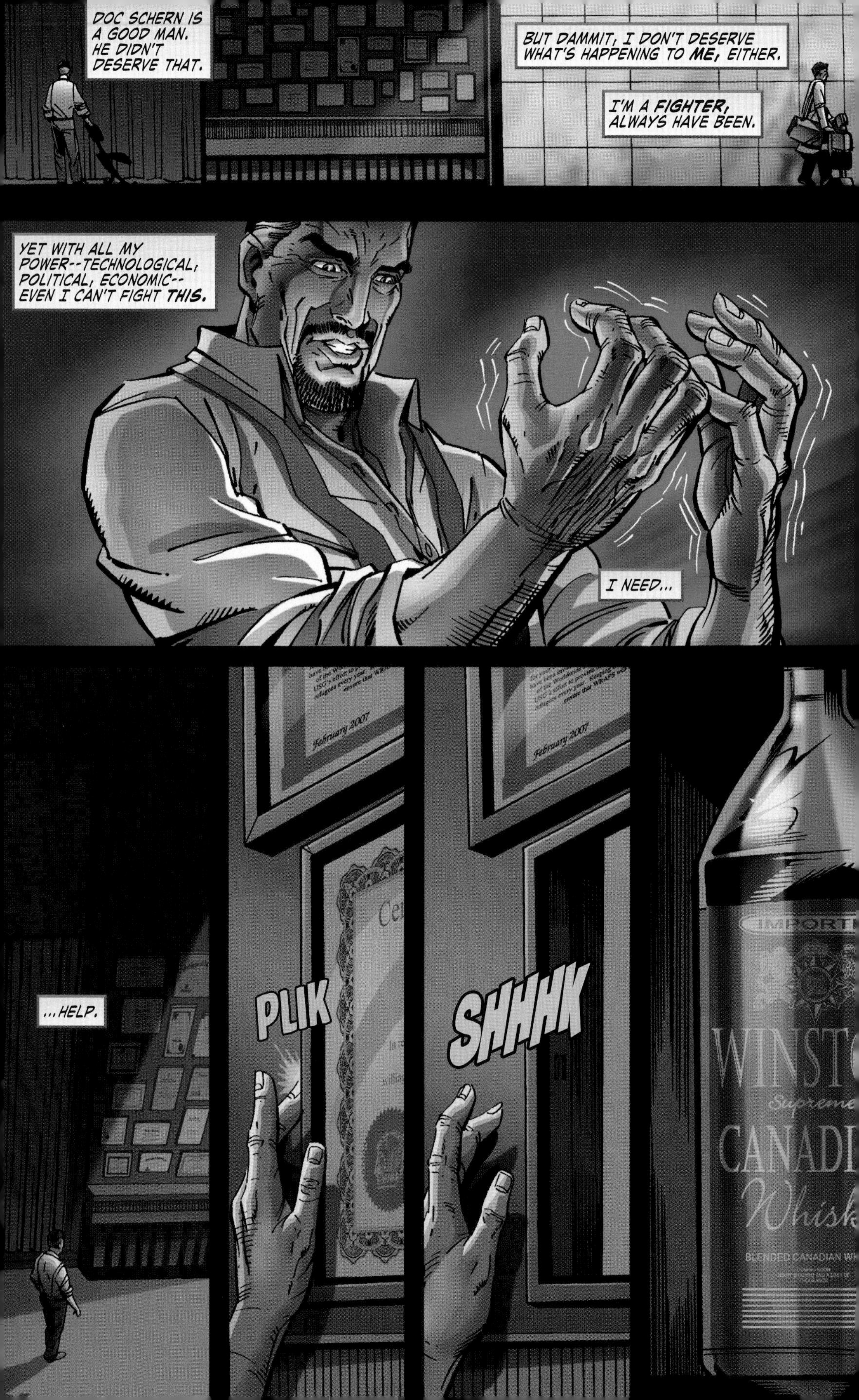
DOC SCHERN IS A GOOD MAN. HE DIDN'T DESERVE THAT.
BUT DAMMIT, I DON'T DESERVE WHAT'S HAPPENING TO ME, EITHER.
I'M A FIGHTER, ALWAYS HAVE BEEN.
YET WITH ALL MY POWER--TECHNOLOGICAL, POLITICAL, ECONOMIC--EVEN I CAN'T FIGHT THIS.
I NEED...
...HELP.
February 2007
PLIK
February 2007
SHHHK
IMPORT
WINSTO
Supreme
CANADI
Whisk
BLENDED CANADIAN WH

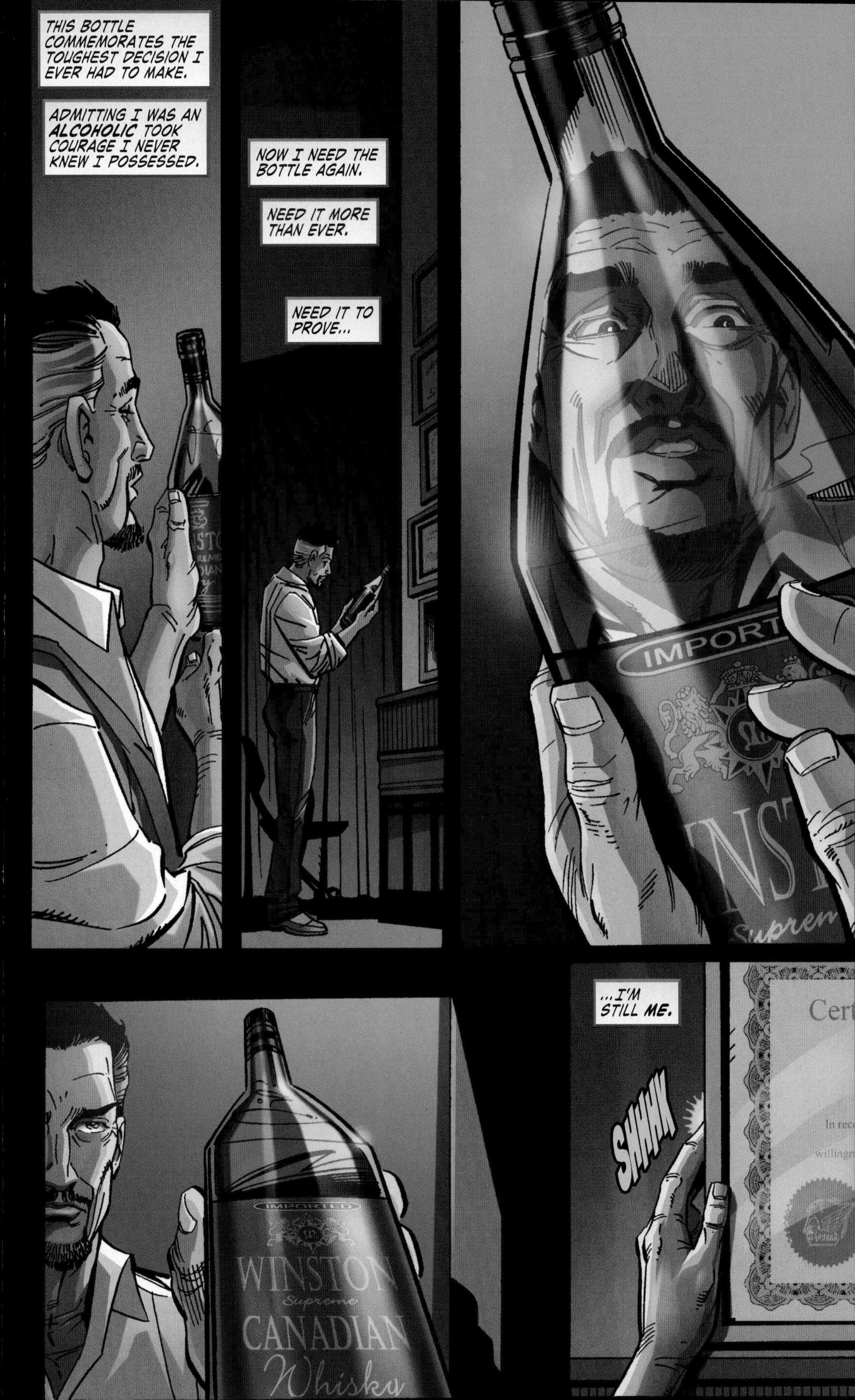
THIS BOTTLE COMMEMORATES THE TOUGHEST DECISION I EVER HAD TO MAKE.
ADMITTING I WAS AN ALCOHOLIC TOOK COURAGE I NEVER KNEW I POSSESSED.
NOW I NEED THE BOTTLE AGAIN.
NEED IT MORE THAN EVER.
NEED IT TO PROVE...
IMPORTED
WINSTON
Supreme
CANADIAN
Whisky
...I'M STILL ME.
SHHHK

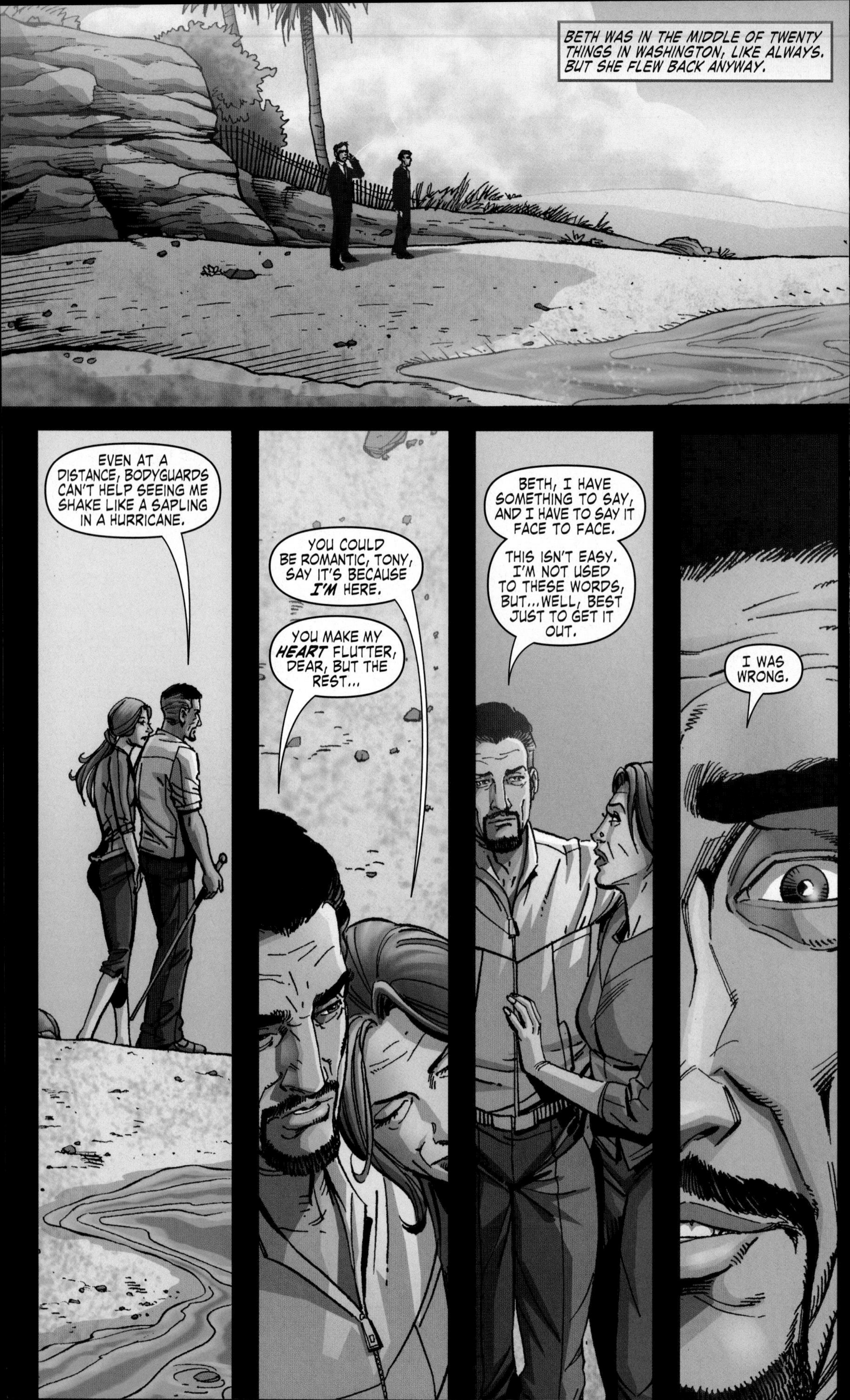
BETH WAS IN THE MIDDLE OF TWENTY THINGS IN WASHINGTON, LIKE ALWAYS. BUT SHE FLEW BACK ANYWAY.
EVEN AT A DISTANCE, BODYGUARDS CAN'T HELP SEEING ME SHAKE LIKE A SAPLING IN A HURRICANE.
YOU COULD BE ROMANTIC, TONY, SAY IT'S BECAUSE *I'M* HERE.
YOU MAKE MY *HEART* FLUTTER, DEAR, BUT THE REST...
BETH, I HAVE SOMETHING TO SAY, AND I HAVE TO SAY IT FACE TO FACE.
THIS ISN'T EASY. I'M NOT USED TO THESE WORDS, BUT...WELL, BEST JUST TO GET IT OUT.
I WAS WRONG.

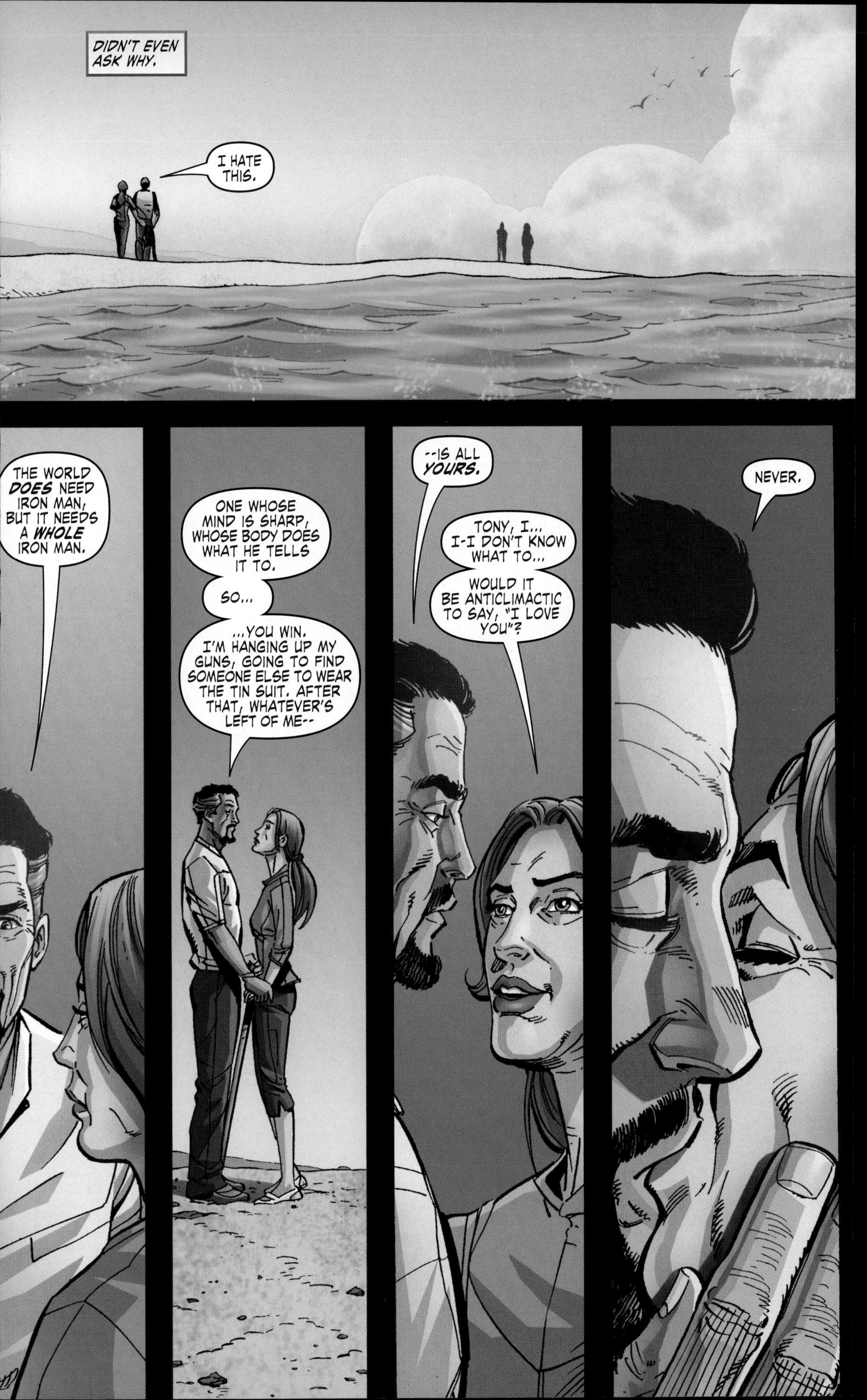

DIDN'T EVEN ASK WHY.
I HATE THIS.
THE WORLD DOES NEED IRON MAN, BUT IT NEEDS A WHOLE IRON MAN.
ONE WHOSE MIND IS SHARP, WHOSE BODY DOES WHAT HE TELLS IT TO.
SO...
...YOU WIN. I'M HANGING UP MY GUNS, GOING TO FIND SOMEONE ELSE TO WEAR THE TIN SUIT. AFTER THAT, WHATEVER'S LEFT OF ME--
--IS ALL YOURS.
TONY, I... I-I DON'T KNOW WHAT TO...
WOULD IT BE ANTICLIMACTIC TO SAY, "I LOVE YOU"?
NEVER.

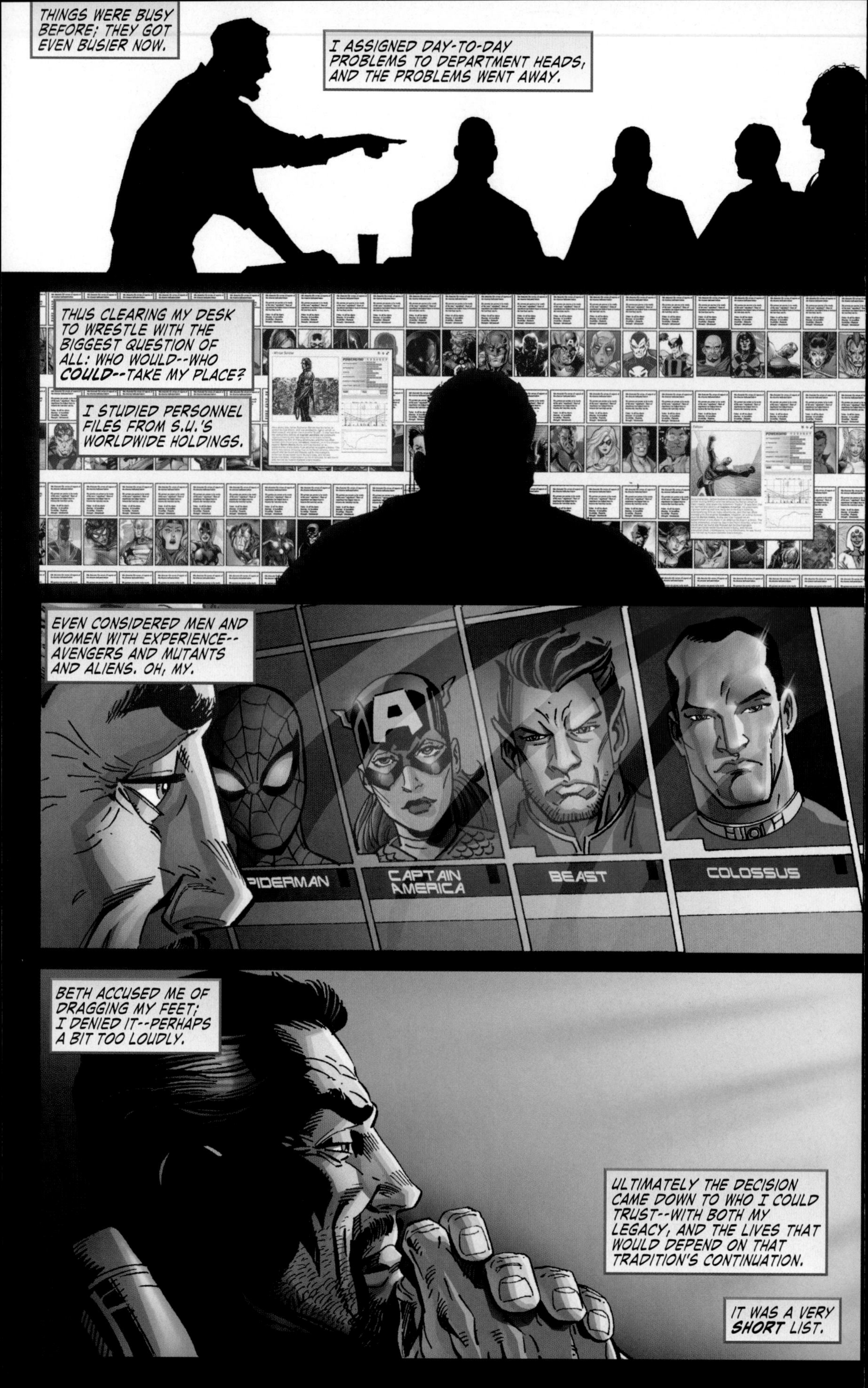
THINGS WERE BUSY BEFORE; THEY GOT EVEN BUSIER NOW.
I ASSIGNED DAY-TO-DAY PROBLEMS TO DEPARTMENT HEADS, AND THE PROBLEMS WENT AWAY.
THUS CLEARING MY DESK TO WRESTLE WITH THE BIGGEST QUESTION OF ALL: WHO WOULD--WHO **COULD**--TAKE MY PLACE?
I STUDIED PERSONNEL FILES FROM S.U.'S WORLDWIDE HOLDINGS.
EVEN CONSIDERED MEN AND WOMEN WITH EXPERIENCE--AVENGERS AND MUTANTS AND ALIENS. OH, MY.
PIDERMAN
CAPTAIN AMERICA
BEAST
COLOSSUS
BETH ACCUSED ME OF DRAGGING MY FEET; I DENIED IT--PERHAPS A BIT TOO LOUDLY.
ULTIMATELY THE DECISION CAME DOWN TO WHO I COULD TRUST--WITH BOTH MY LEGACY, AND THE LIVES THAT WOULD DEPEND ON THAT TRADITION'S CONTINUATION.
IT WAS A VERY **SHORT** LIST.

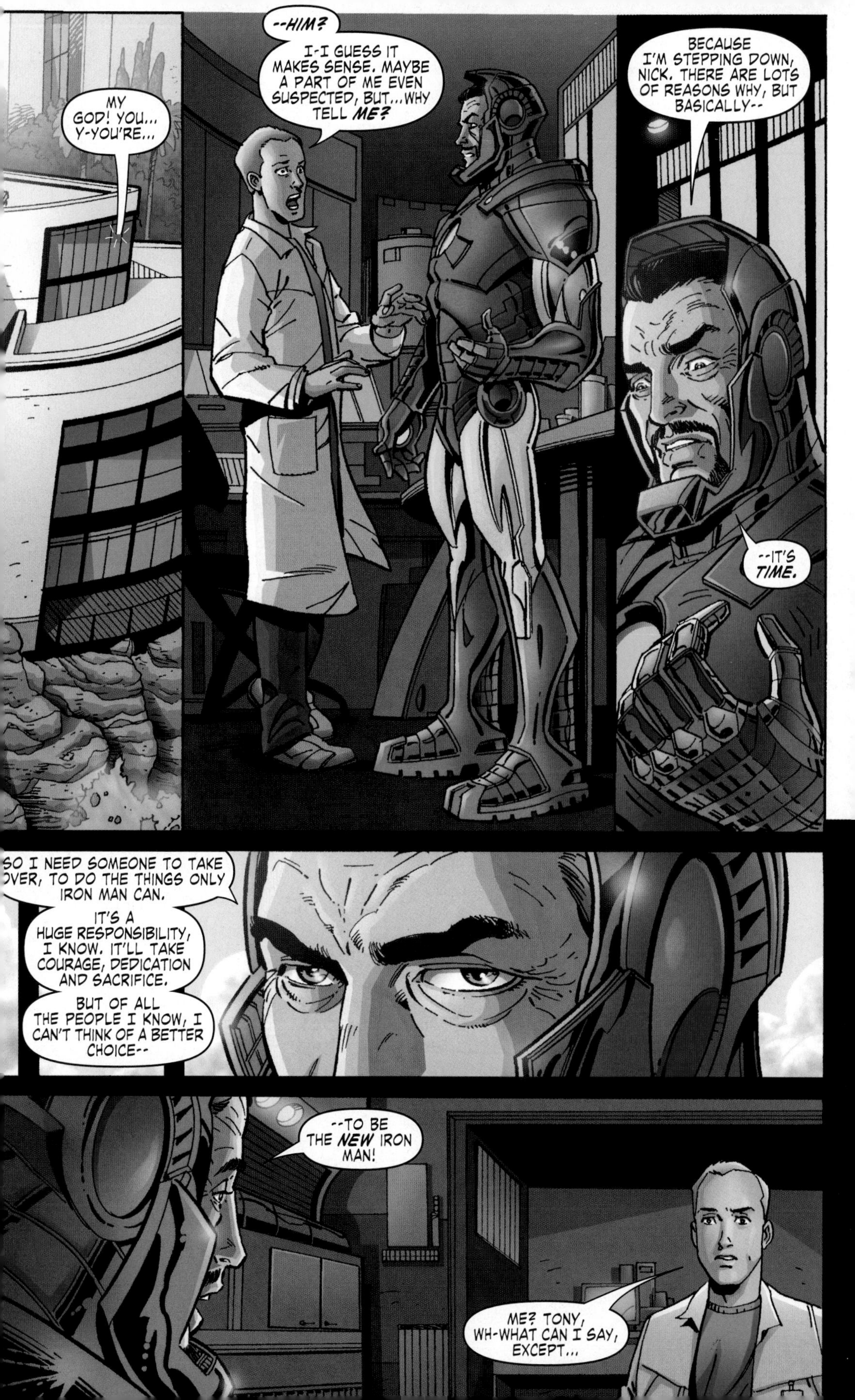
MY GOD! YOU... Y-YOU'RE...
--HIM?
I-I GUESS IT MAKES SENSE. MAYBE A PART OF ME EVEN SUSPECTED, BUT...WHY TELL ME?
BECAUSE I'M STEPPING DOWN, NICK. THERE ARE LOTS OF REASONS WHY, BUT BASICALLY--
--IT'S TIME.
SO I NEED SOMEONE TO TAKE OVER, TO DO THE THINGS ONLY IRON MAN CAN.
IT'S A HUGE RESPONSIBILITY, I KNOW. IT'LL TAKE COURAGE, DEDICATION AND SACRIFICE.
BUT OF ALL THE PEOPLE I KNOW, I CAN'T THINK OF A BETTER CHOICE--
--TO BE THE NEW IRON MAN!
ME? TONY, WH-WHAT CAN I SAY, EXCEPT...

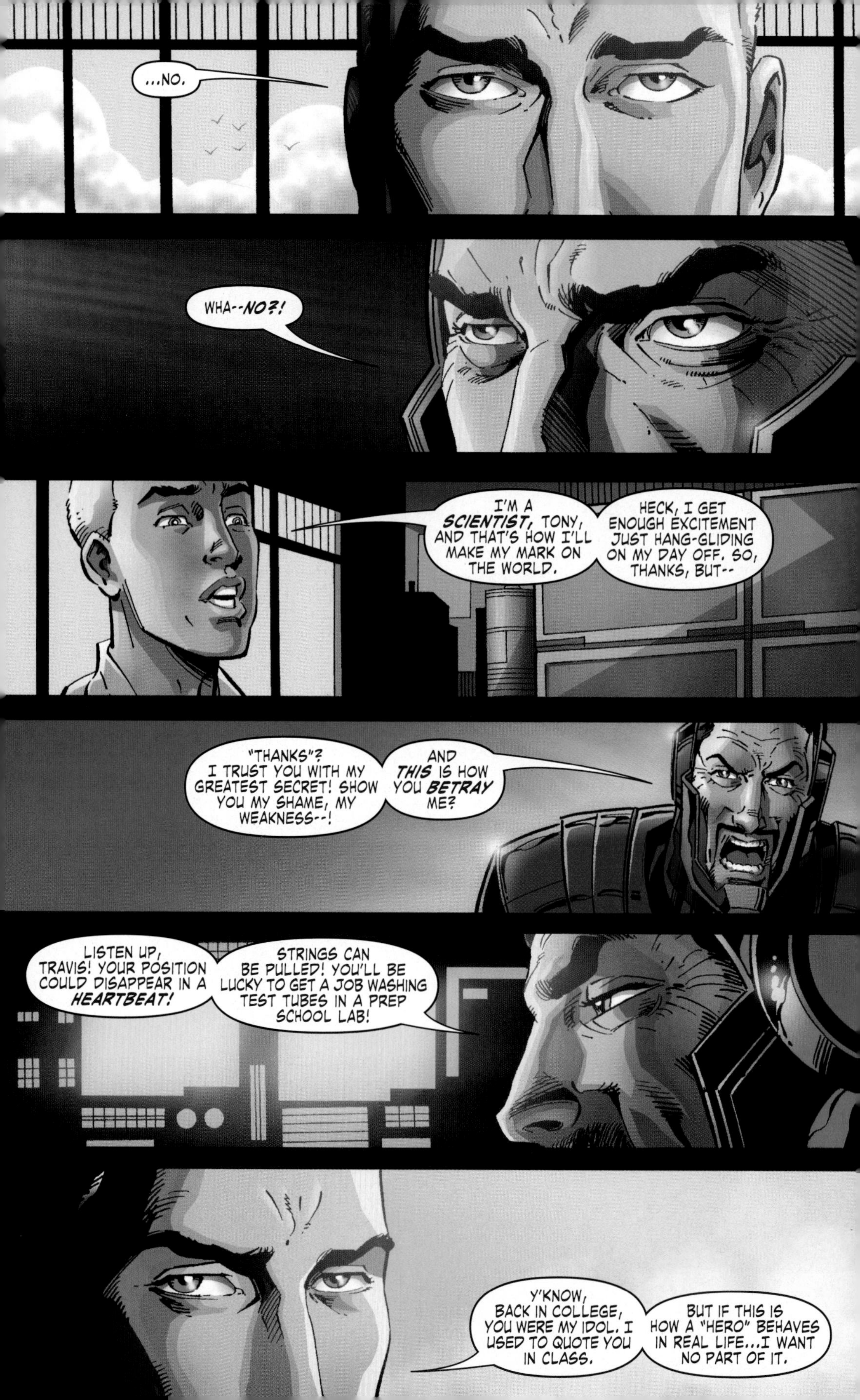
...NO.
WHA--NO?!
I'M A SCIENTIST, TONY, AND THAT'S HOW I'LL MAKE MY MARK ON THE WORLD.
HECK, I GET ENOUGH EXCITEMENT JUST HANG-GLIDING ON MY DAY OFF. SO, THANKS, BUT--
"THANKS"? I TRUST YOU WITH MY GREATEST SECRET! SHOW YOU MY SHAME, MY WEAKNESS--!
AND THIS IS HOW YOU BETRAY ME?
LISTEN UP, TRAVIS! YOUR POSITION COULD DISAPPEAR IN A HEARTBEAT!
STRINGS CAN BE PULLED! YOU'LL BE LUCKY TO GET A JOB WASHING TEST TUBES IN A PREP SCHOOL LAB!
Y'KNOW, BACK IN COLLEGE, YOU WERE MY IDOL. I USED TO QUOTE YOU IN CLASS.
BUT IF THIS IS HOW A "HERO" BEHAVES IN REAL LIFE...I WANT NO PART OF IT.

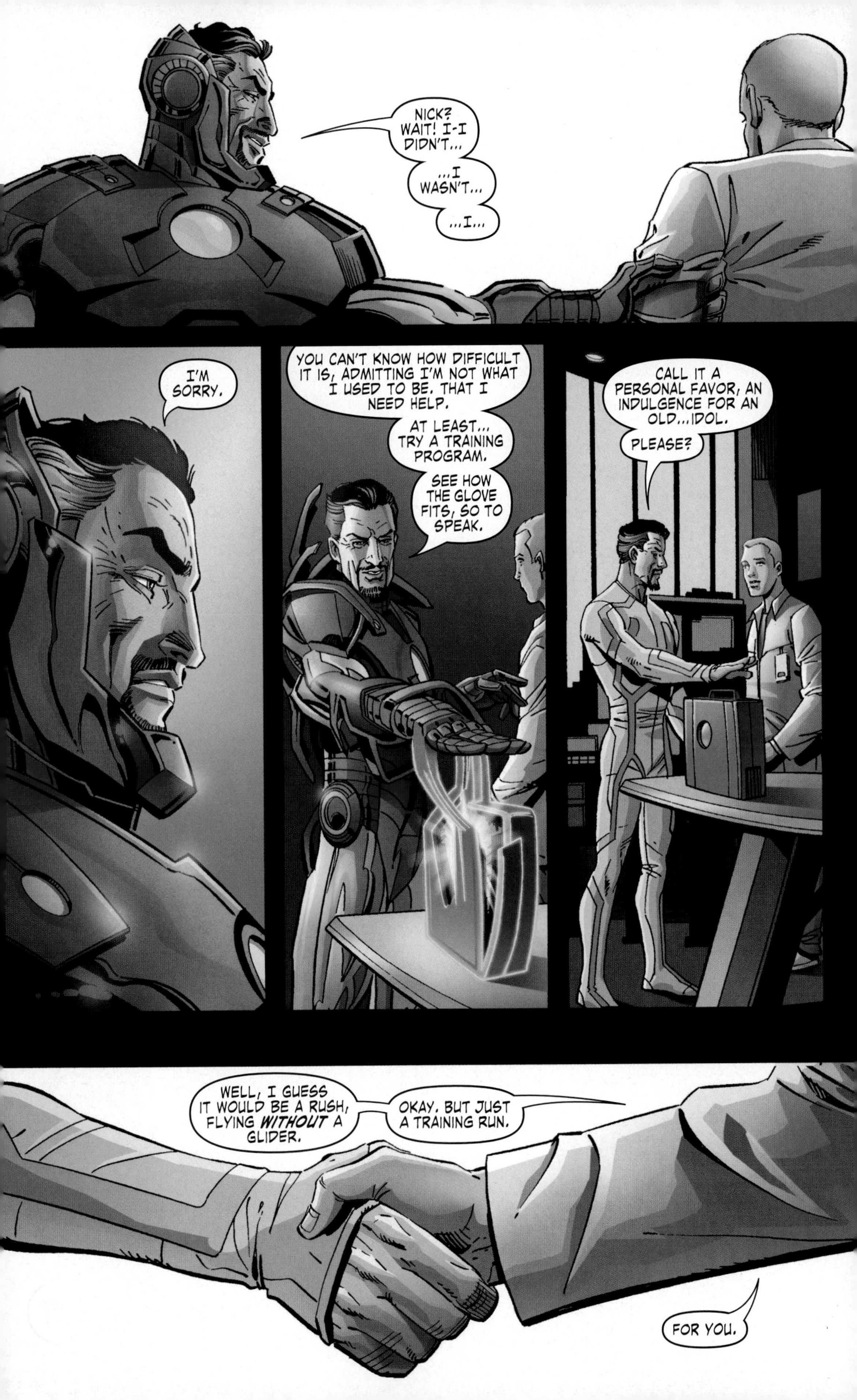
NICK? WAIT! I-I DIDN'T...
...I WASN'T...
...I...
I'M SORRY.
YOU CAN'T KNOW HOW DIFFICULT IT IS, ADMITTING I'M NOT WHAT I USED TO BE. THAT I NEED HELP.
AT LEAST... TRY A TRAINING PROGRAM.
SEE HOW THE GLOVE FITS, SO TO SPEAK.
CALL IT A PERSONAL FAVOR, AN INDULGENCE FOR AN OLD...IDOL.
PLEASE?
WELL, I GUESS IT WOULD BE A RUSH, FLYING *WITHOUT* A GLIDER.
OKAY. BUT JUST A TRAINING RUN.
FOR YOU.

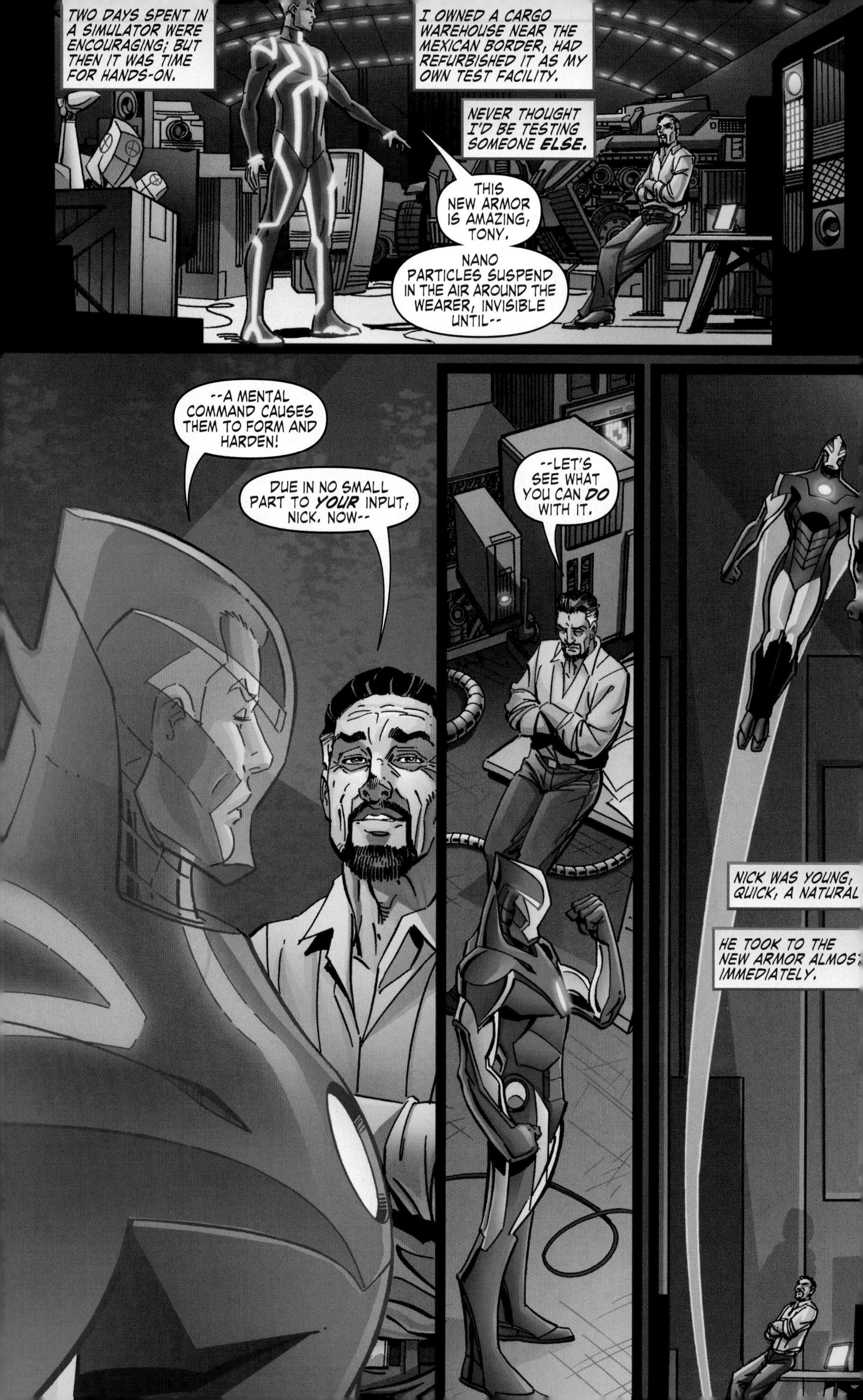
TWO DAYS SPENT IN A SIMULATOR WERE ENCOURAGING; BUT THEN IT WAS TIME FOR HANDS-ON.
I OWNED A CARGO WAREHOUSE NEAR THE MEXICAN BORDER, HAD REFURBISHED IT AS MY OWN TEST FACILITY.
NEVER THOUGHT I'D BE TESTING SOMEONE ELSE.
THIS NEW ARMOR IS AMAZING, TONY.
NANO PARTICLES SUSPEND IN THE AIR AROUND THE WEARER, INVISIBLE UNTIL--
--A MENTAL COMMAND CAUSES THEM TO FORM AND HARDEN!
DUE IN NO SMALL PART TO YOUR INPUT, NICK. NOW--
--LET'S SEE WHAT YOU CAN DO WITH IT.
NICK WAS YOUNG, QUICK, A NATURAL
HE TOOK TO THE NEW ARMOR ALMOST IMMEDIATELY.

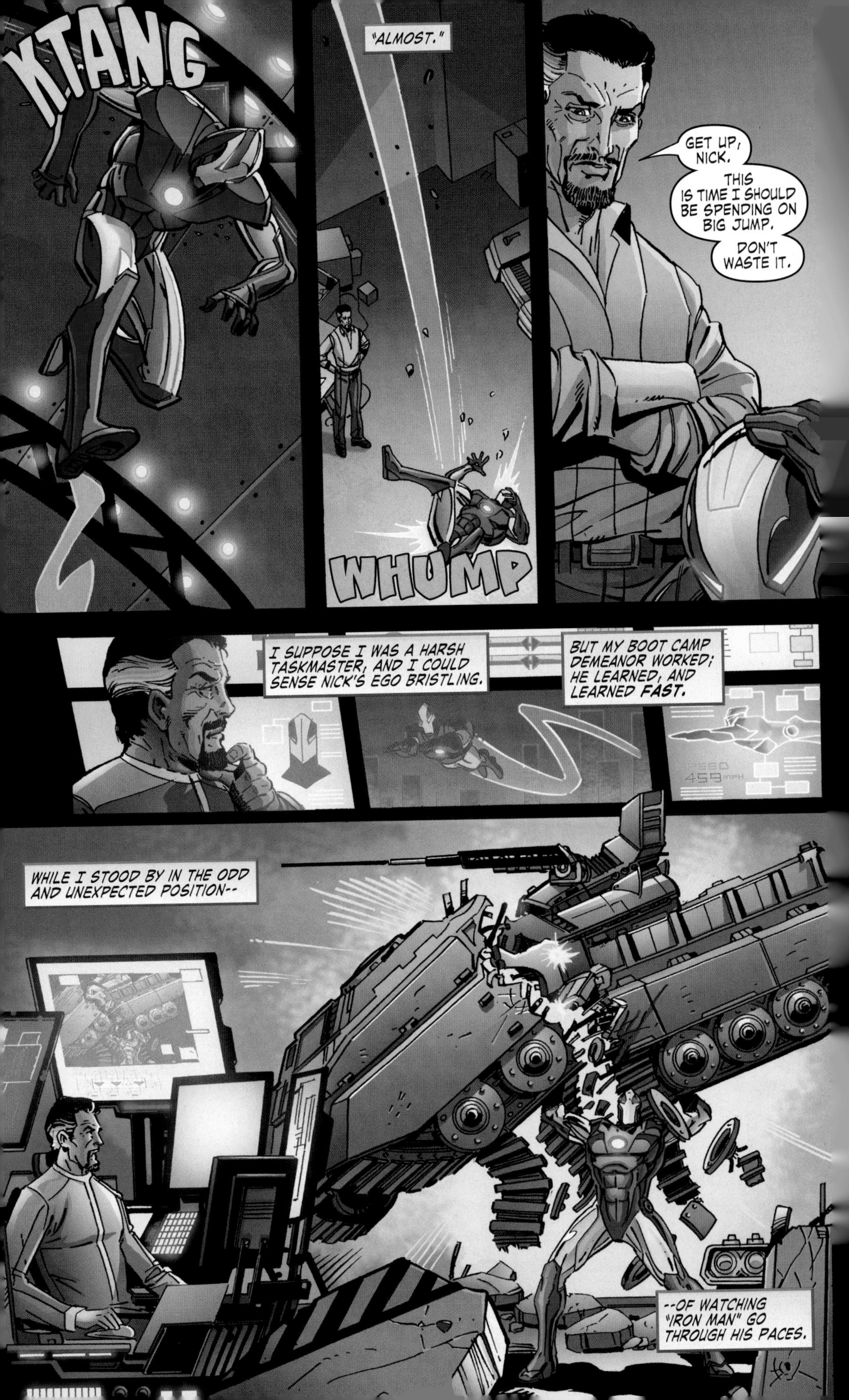
KTANG
"ALMOST."
WHUMP
GET UP, NICK.
THIS IS TIME I SHOULD BE SPENDING ON BIG JUMP.
DON'T WASTE IT.
I SUPPOSE I WAS A HARSH TASKMASTER, AND I COULD SENSE NICK'S EGO BRISTLING.
BUT MY BOOT CAMP DEMEANOR WORKED; HE LEARNED, AND LEARNED FAST.
SPEED 459 MPH
WHILE I STOOD BY IN THE ODD AND UNEXPECTED POSITION--
--OF WATCHING "IRON MAN" GO THROUGH HIS PACES.

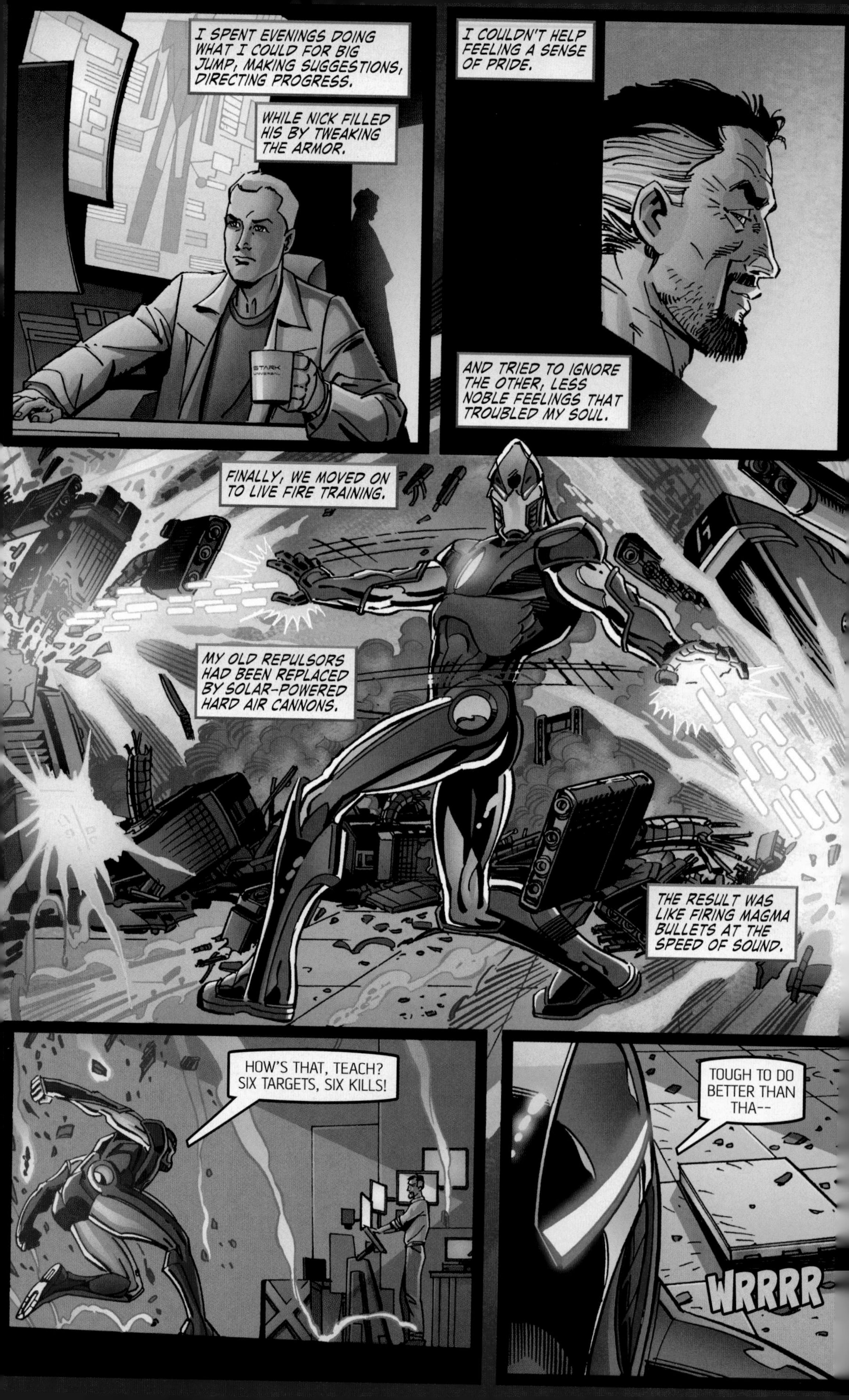
I SPENT EVENINGS DOING WHAT I COULD FOR BIG JUMP, MAKING SUGGESTIONS, DIRECTING PROGRESS.
WHILE NICK FILLED HIS BY TWEAKING THE ARMOR.
STARK
I COULDN'T HELP FEELING A SENSE OF PRIDE.
AND TRIED TO IGNORE THE OTHER, LESS NOBLE FEELINGS THAT TROUBLED MY SOUL.
FINALLY, WE MOVED ON TO LIVE FIRE TRAINING.
MY OLD REPULSORS HAD BEEN REPLACED BY SOLAR-POWERED HARD AIR CANNONS.
THE RESULT WAS LIKE FIRING MAGMA BULLETS AT THE SPEED OF SOUND.
HOW'S THAT, TEACH? SIX TARGETS, SIX KILLS!
TOUGH TO DO BETTER THAN THA--
WRRRR

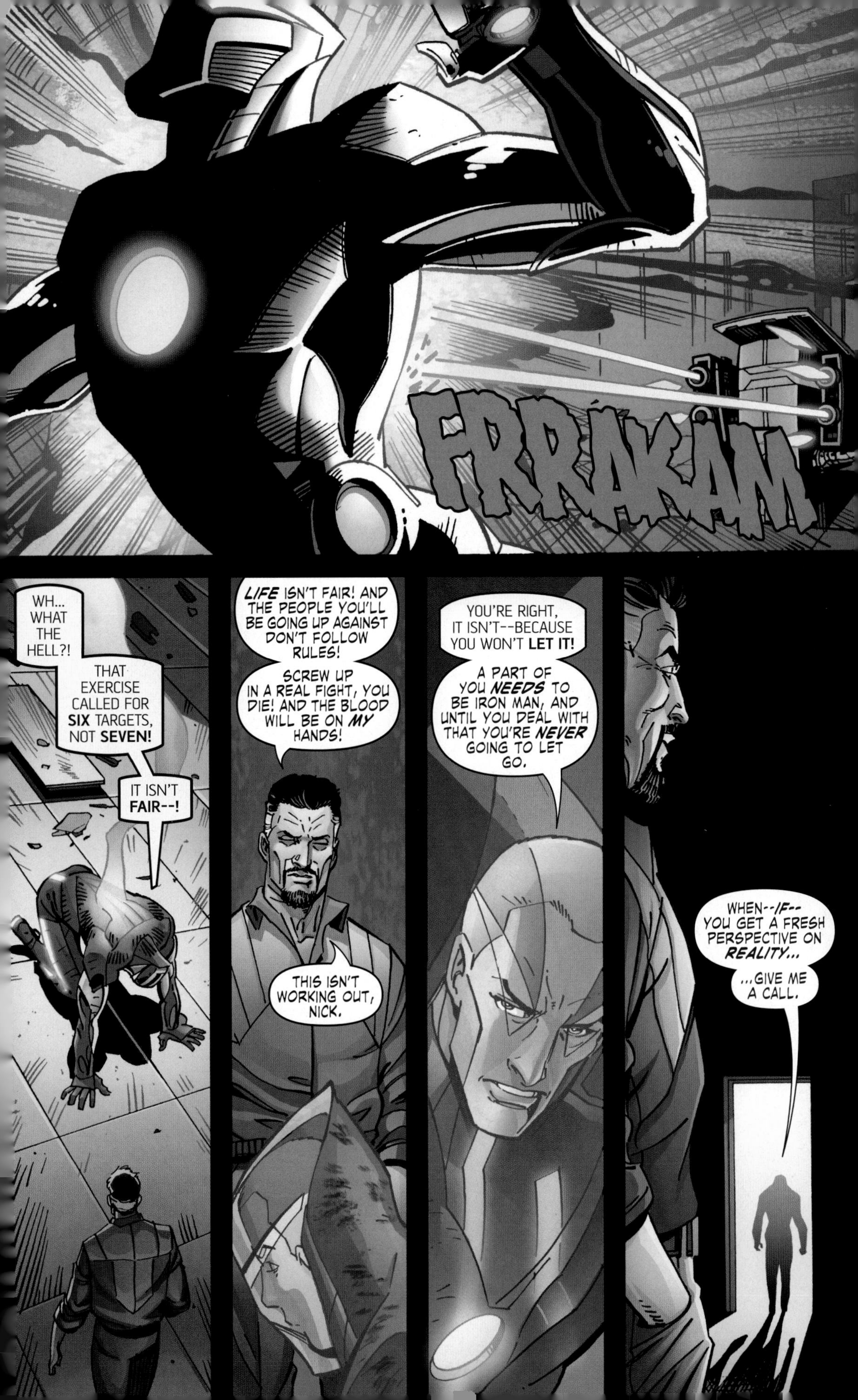
FRRAKAM
WH... WHAT THE HELL?!
THAT EXERCISE CALLED FOR SIX TARGETS, NOT SEVEN!
IT ISN'T FAIR--!
LIFE ISN'T FAIR! AND THE PEOPLE YOU'LL BE GOING UP AGAINST DON'T FOLLOW RULES!
SCREW UP IN A REAL FIGHT, YOU DIE! AND THE BLOOD WILL BE ON MY HANDS!
THIS ISN'T WORKING OUT, NICK.
YOU'RE RIGHT, IT ISN'T--BECAUSE YOU WON'T LET IT!
A PART OF YOU NEEDS TO BE IRON MAN, AND UNTIL YOU DEAL WITH THAT YOU'RE NEVER GOING TO LET GO.
WHEN--IF--YOU GET A FRESH PERSPECTIVE ON REALITY...
...GIVE ME A CALL.

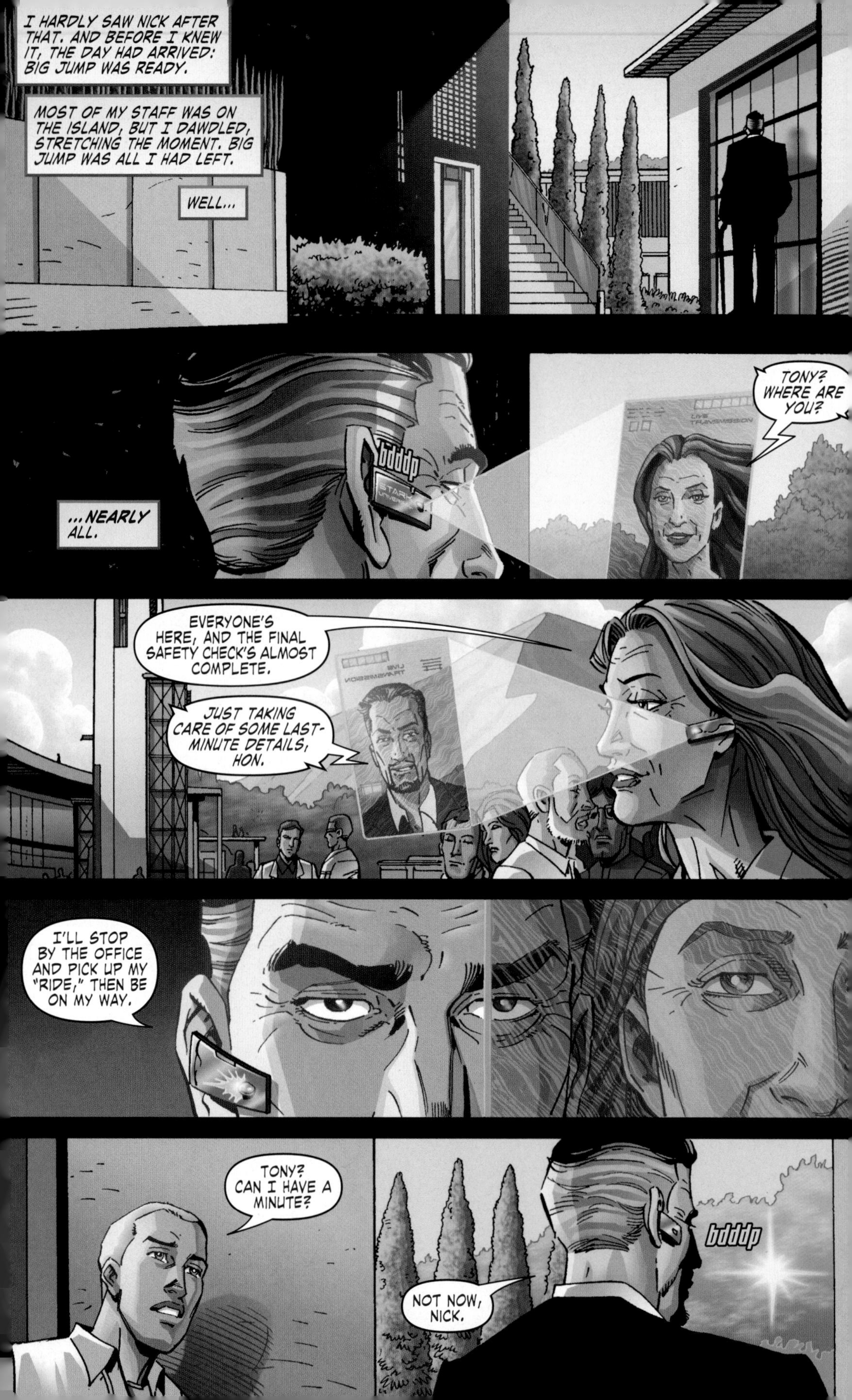
I HARDLY SAW NICK AFTER THAT. AND BEFORE I KNEW IT, THE DAY HAD ARRIVED: BIG JUMP WAS READY.
MOST OF MY STAFF WAS ON THE ISLAND, BUT I DAWDLED, STRETCHING THE MOMENT. BIG JUMP WAS ALL I HAD LEFT.
WELL...
bdddp
...NEARLY ALL.
TONY? WHERE ARE YOU?
EVERYONE'S HERE, AND THE FINAL SAFETY CHECK'S ALMOST COMPLETE.
JUST TAKING CARE OF SOME LAST-MINUTE DETAILS, HON.
I'LL STOP BY THE OFFICE AND PICK UP MY "RIDE," THEN BE ON MY WAY.
TONY? CAN I HAVE A MINUTE?
bdddp
NOT NOW, NICK.

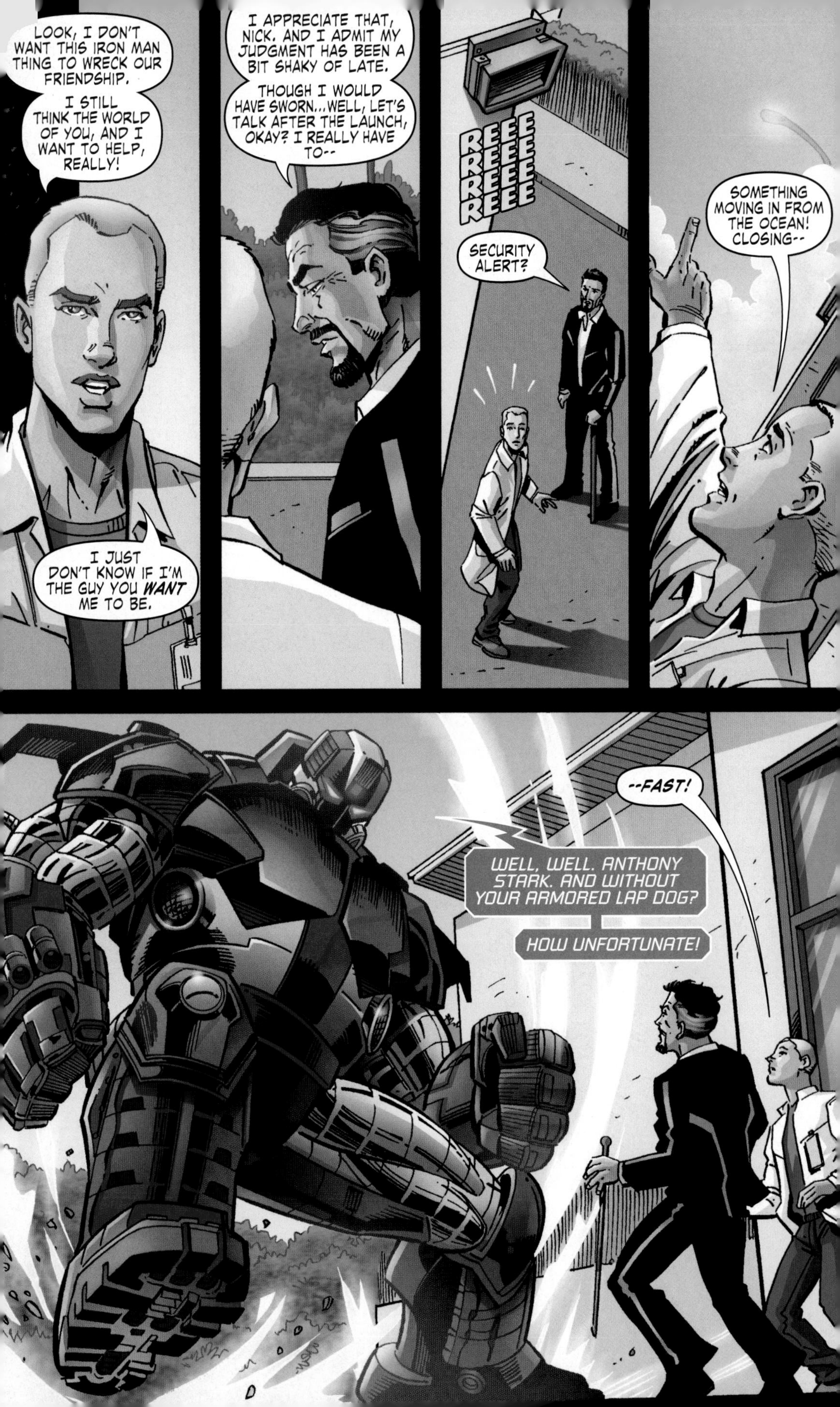

LOOK, I DON'T WANT THIS IRON MAN THING TO WRECK OUR FRIENDSHIP.
I STILL THINK THE WORLD OF YOU, AND I WANT TO HELP, REALLY!
I JUST DON'T KNOW IF I'M THE GUY YOU *WANT* ME TO BE.
I APPRECIATE THAT, NICK. AND I ADMIT MY JUDGMENT HAS BEEN A BIT SHAKY OF LATE.
THOUGH I WOULD HAVE SWORN...WELL, LET'S TALK AFTER THE LAUNCH, OKAY? I REALLY HAVE TO--
REEE REEE REEE REEE
SECURITY ALERT?
SOMETHING MOVING IN FROM THE OCEAN! CLOSING--
--FAST!
WELL, WELL. ANTHONY STARK. AND WITHOUT YOUR ARMORED LAP DOG?
HOW UNFORTUNATE!

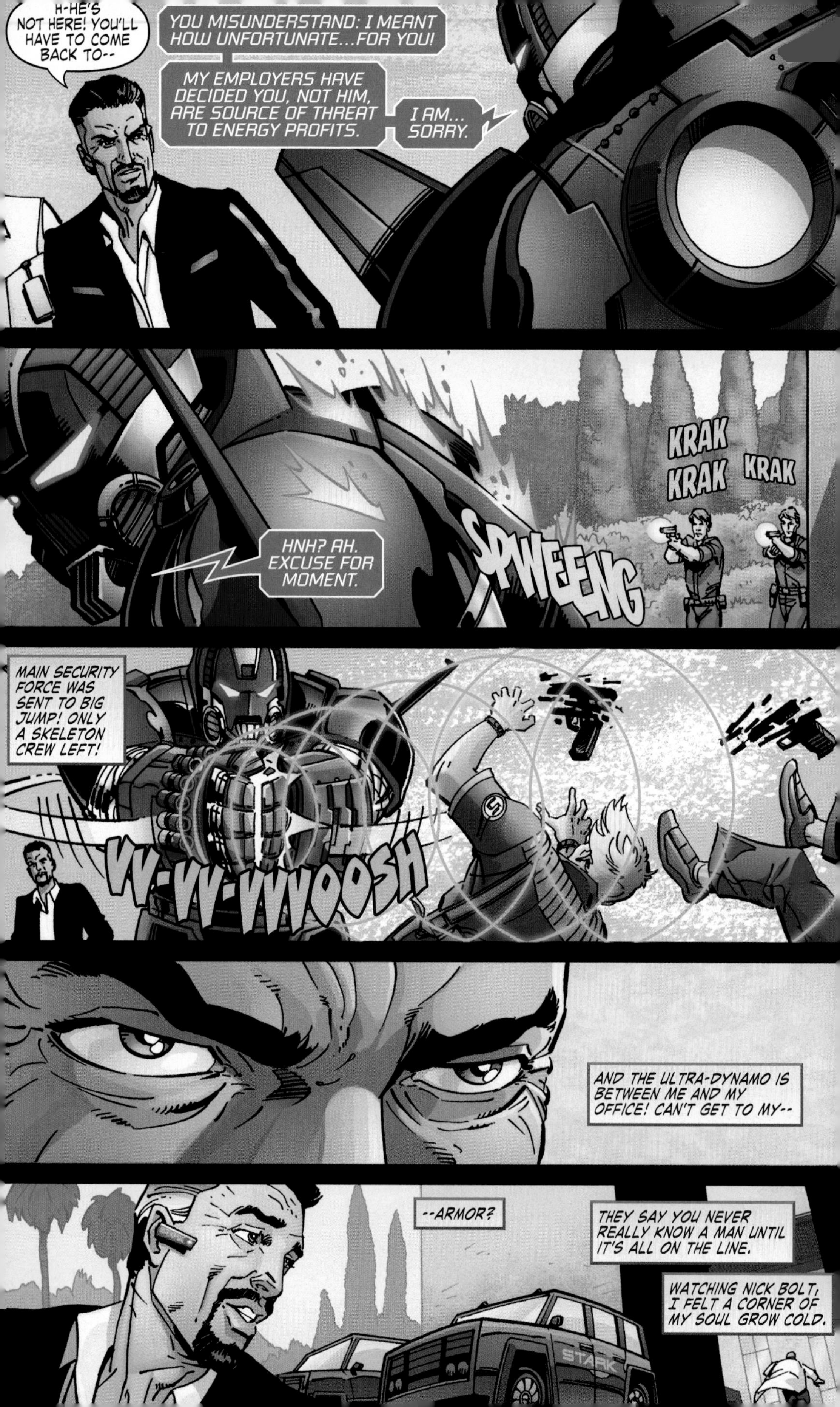

H-HE'S NOT HERE! YOU'LL HAVE TO COME BACK TO--
YOU MISUNDERSTAND: I MEANT HOW UNFORTUNATE...FOR YOU!
MY EMPLOYERS HAVE DECIDED YOU, NOT HIM, ARE SOURCE OF THREAT TO ENERGY PROFITS.
I AM... SORRY.
KRAK KRAK KRAK
HNH? AH. EXCUSE FOR MOMENT.
SPWEEENG
MAIN SECURITY FORCE WAS SENT TO BIG JUMP! ONLY A SKELETON CREW LEFT!
VV-VV-VVVOOSH
AND THE ULTRA-DYNAMO IS BETWEEN ME AND MY OFFICE! CAN'T GET TO MY--
--ARMOR?
THEY SAY YOU NEVER REALLY KNOW A MAN UNTIL IT'S ALL ON THE LINE.
WATCHING NICK BOLT, I FELT A CORNER OF MY SOUL GROW COLD.
STARK

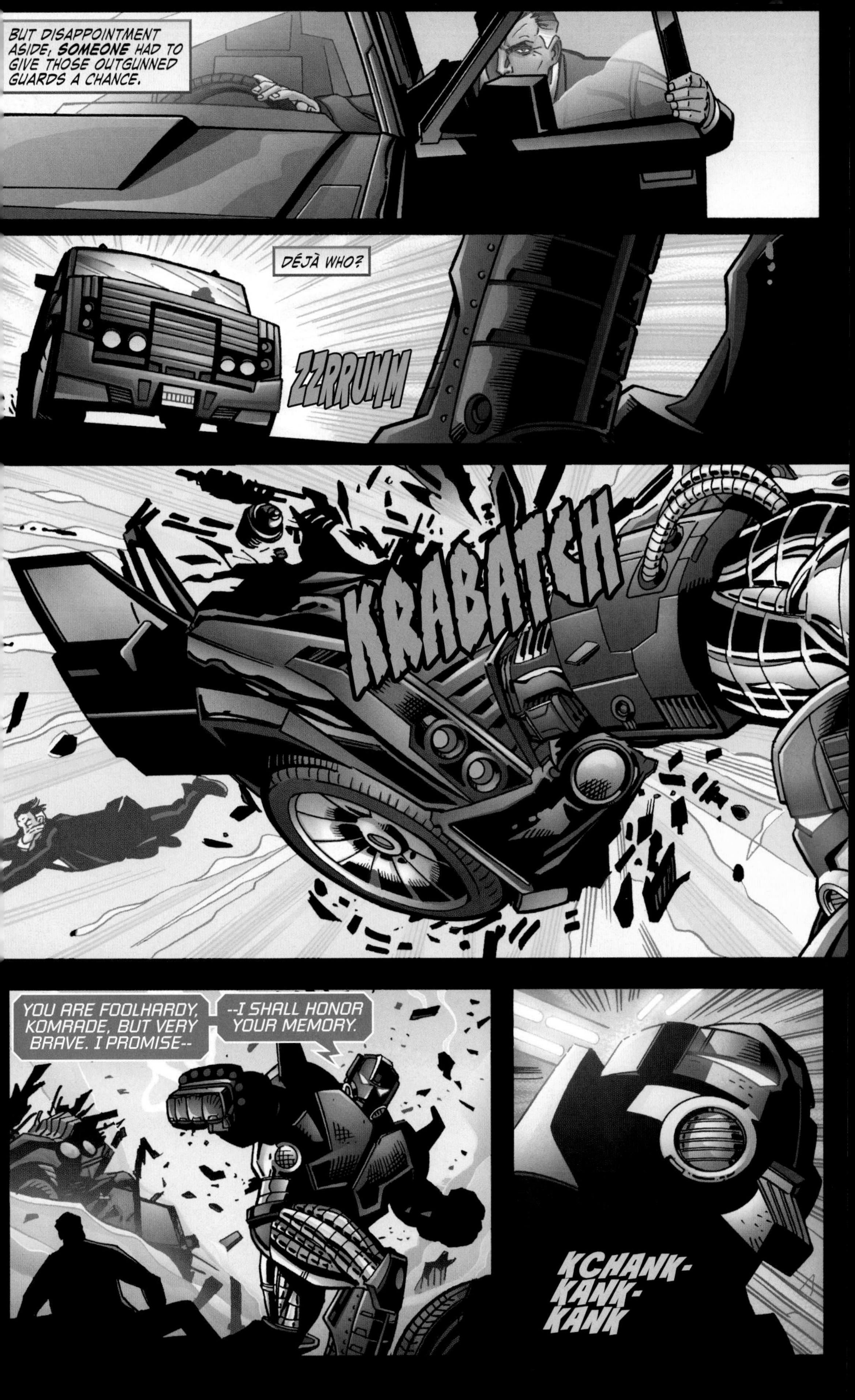
BUT DISAPPOINTMENT ASIDE, SOMEONE HAD TO GIVE THOSE OUTGUNNED GUARDS A CHANCE.
DÉJÀ WHO?
ZZRRUMM
KRABATCH
YOU ARE FOOLHARDY, KOMRADE, BUT VERY BRAVE. I PROMISE--
--I SHALL HONOR YOUR MEMORY.
KCHANK-KANK-KANK

BACK OFF, RED!
THIS LAP DOG'S GOT BITE!
NEW CLOTHES? NOT A PROBLEM.
V-V-VVVAM
I KNOCK YOU IN DIRT, JUST LIKE I DID-- EH?
>WHNGF<
KCHUNG
QUICK.
BUT NOT QUICK ENOUGH...!
LOOK OUT! THOSE MICROID PELLETS--!

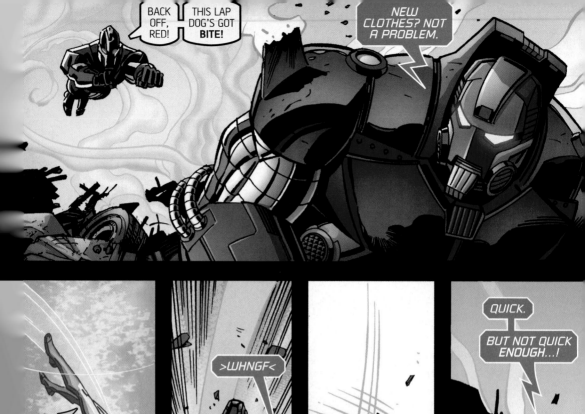

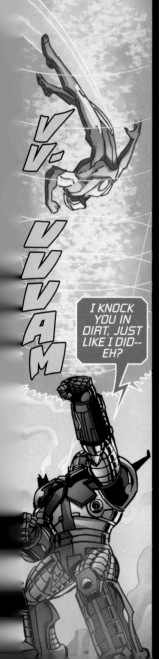

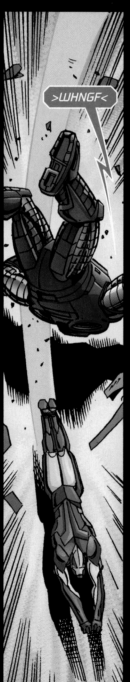

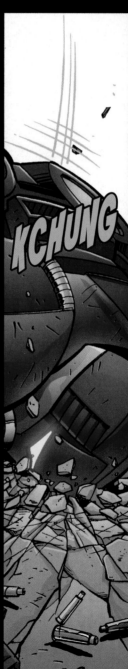

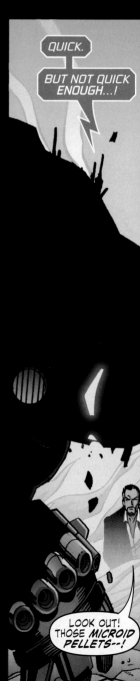

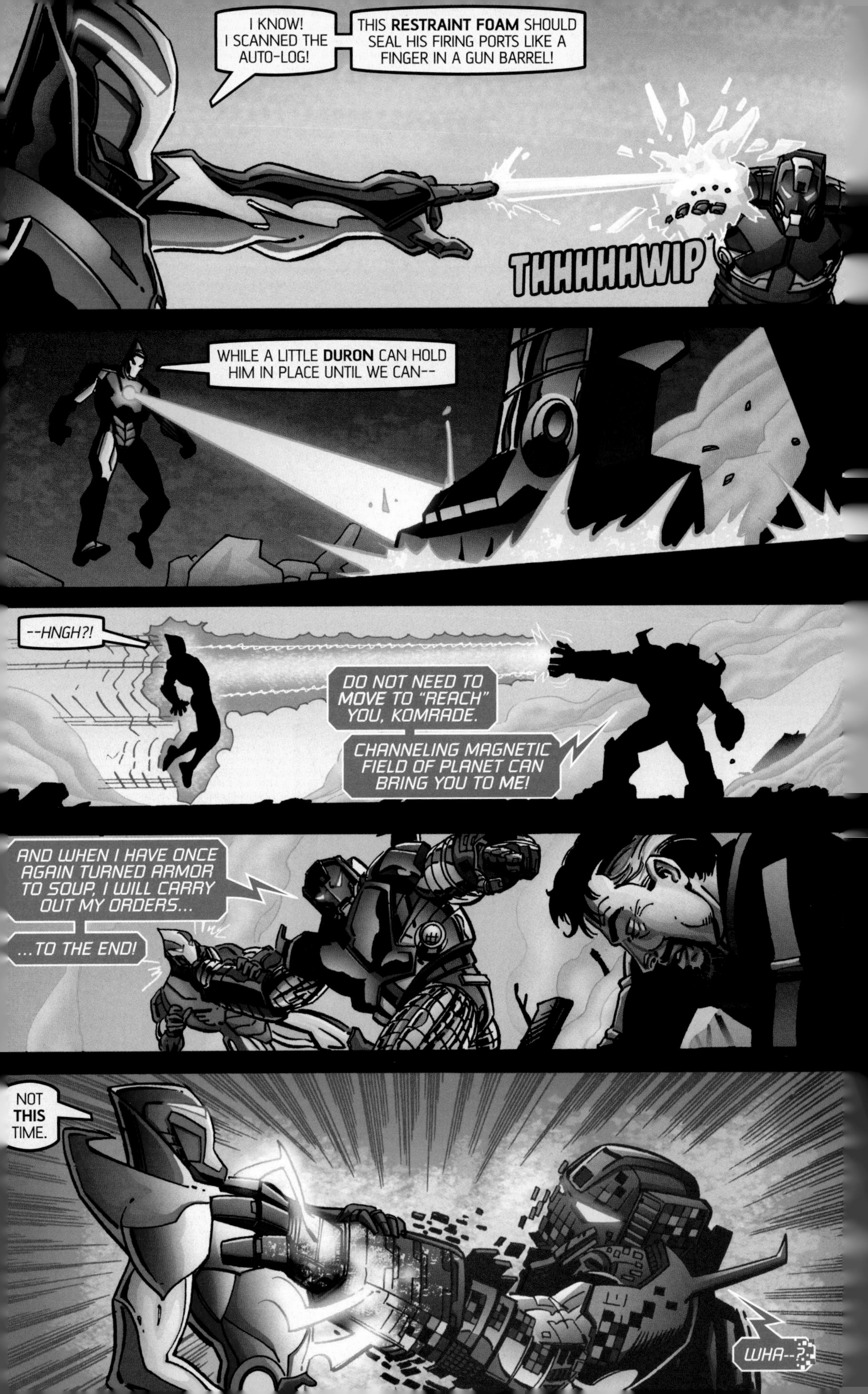
I KNOW! I SCANNED THE AUTO-LOG!
THIS **RESTRAINT FOAM** SHOULD SEAL HIS FIRING PORTS LIKE A FINGER IN A GUN BARREL!
THHHHHWIP
WHILE A LITTLE **DURON** CAN HOLD HIM IN PLACE UNTIL WE CAN--
--HNGH?!
DO NOT NEED TO MOVE TO "REACH" YOU, KOMRADE.
CHANNELING MAGNETIC FIELD OF PLANET CAN BRING YOU TO ME!
AND WHEN I HAVE ONCE AGAIN TURNED ARMOR TO SOUP, I WILL CARRY OUT MY ORDERS...
...TO THE END!
NOT **THIS** TIME.
WHA--?

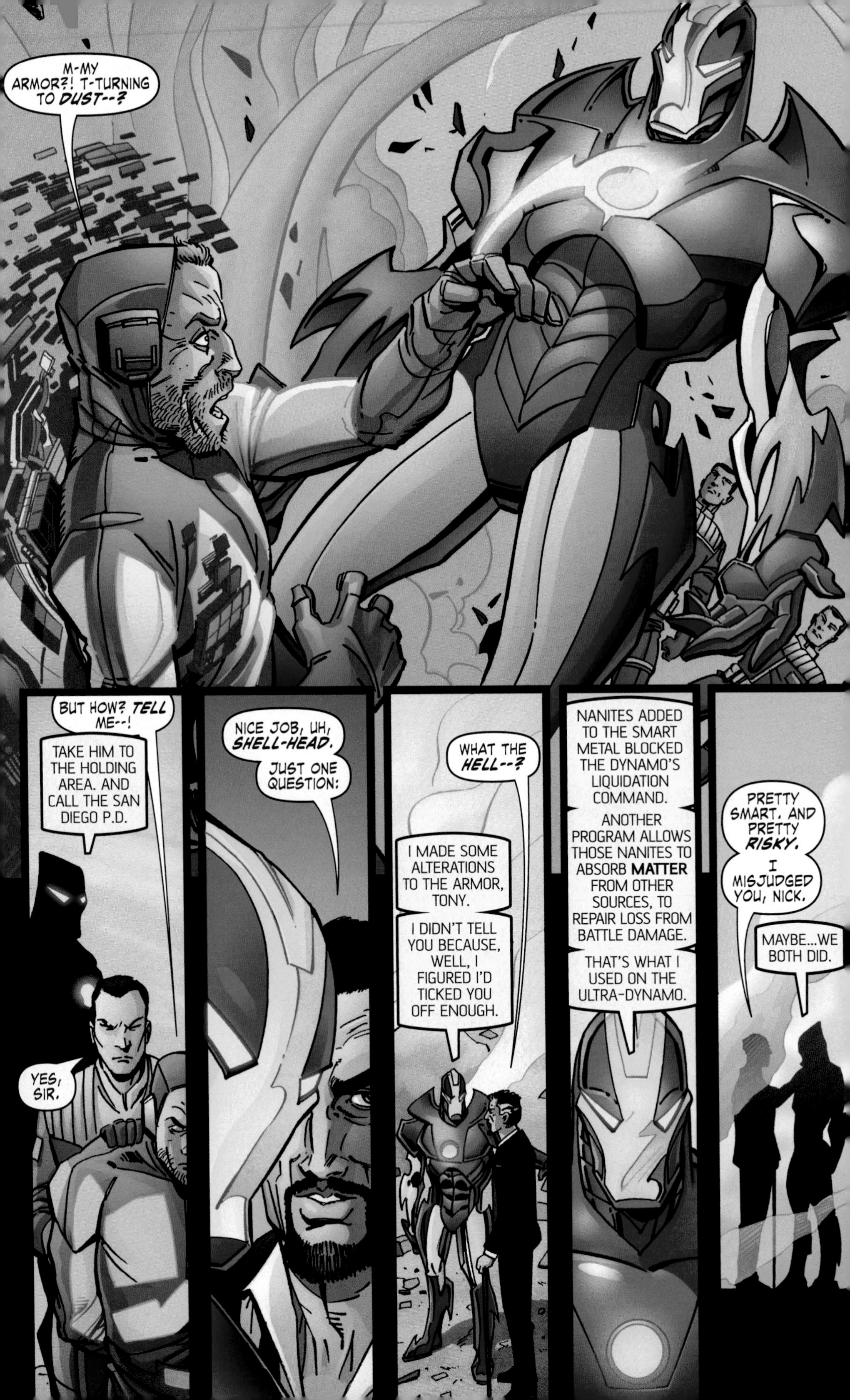

M-MY ARMOR?! T-TURNING TO DUST--?
BUT HOW? TELL ME--!
TAKE HIM TO THE HOLDING AREA. AND CALL THE SAN DIEGO P.D.
YES, SIR.
NICE JOB, UH, SHELL-HEAD.
JUST ONE QUESTION:
WHAT THE HELL--?
I MADE SOME ALTERATIONS TO THE ARMOR, TONY.
I DIDN'T TELL YOU BECAUSE, WELL, I FIGURED I'D TICKED YOU OFF ENOUGH.
NANITES ADDED TO THE SMART METAL BLOCKED THE DYNAMO'S LIQUIDATION COMMAND.
ANOTHER PROGRAM ALLOWS THOSE NANITES TO ABSORB MATTER FROM OTHER SOURCES, TO REPAIR LOSS FROM BATTLE DAMAGE.
THAT'S WHAT I USED ON THE ULTRA-DYNAMO.
PRETTY SMART. AND PRETTY RISKY.
I MISJUDGED YOU, NICK.
MAYBE...WE BOTH DID.

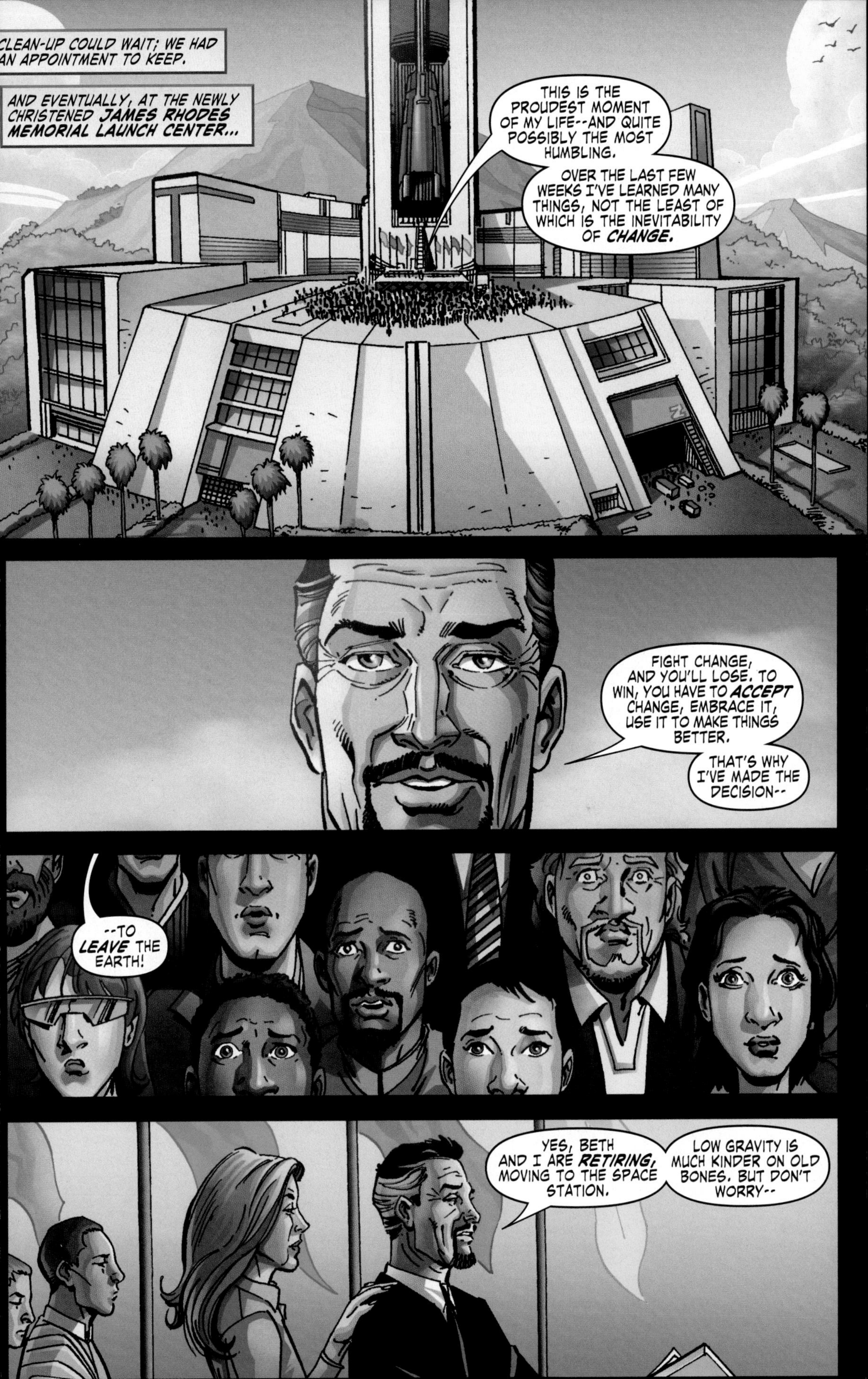
CLEAN-UP COULD WAIT; WE HAD AN APPOINTMENT TO KEEP.
AND EVENTUALLY, AT THE NEWLY CHRISTENED JAMES RHODES MEMORIAL LAUNCH CENTER...
THIS IS THE PROUDEST MOMENT OF MY LIFE--AND QUITE POSSIBLY THE MOST HUMBLING.
OVER THE LAST FEW WEEKS I'VE LEARNED MANY THINGS, NOT THE LEAST OF WHICH IS THE INEVITABILITY OF CHANGE.
FIGHT CHANGE, AND YOU'LL LOSE. TO WIN, YOU HAVE TO ACCEPT CHANGE, EMBRACE IT, USE IT TO MAKE THINGS BETTER.
THAT'S WHY I'VE MADE THE DECISION--
--TO LEAVE THE EARTH!
YES, BETH AND I ARE RETIRING, MOVING TO THE SPACE STATION.
LOW GRAVITY IS MUCH KINDER ON OLD BONES. BUT DON'T WORRY--

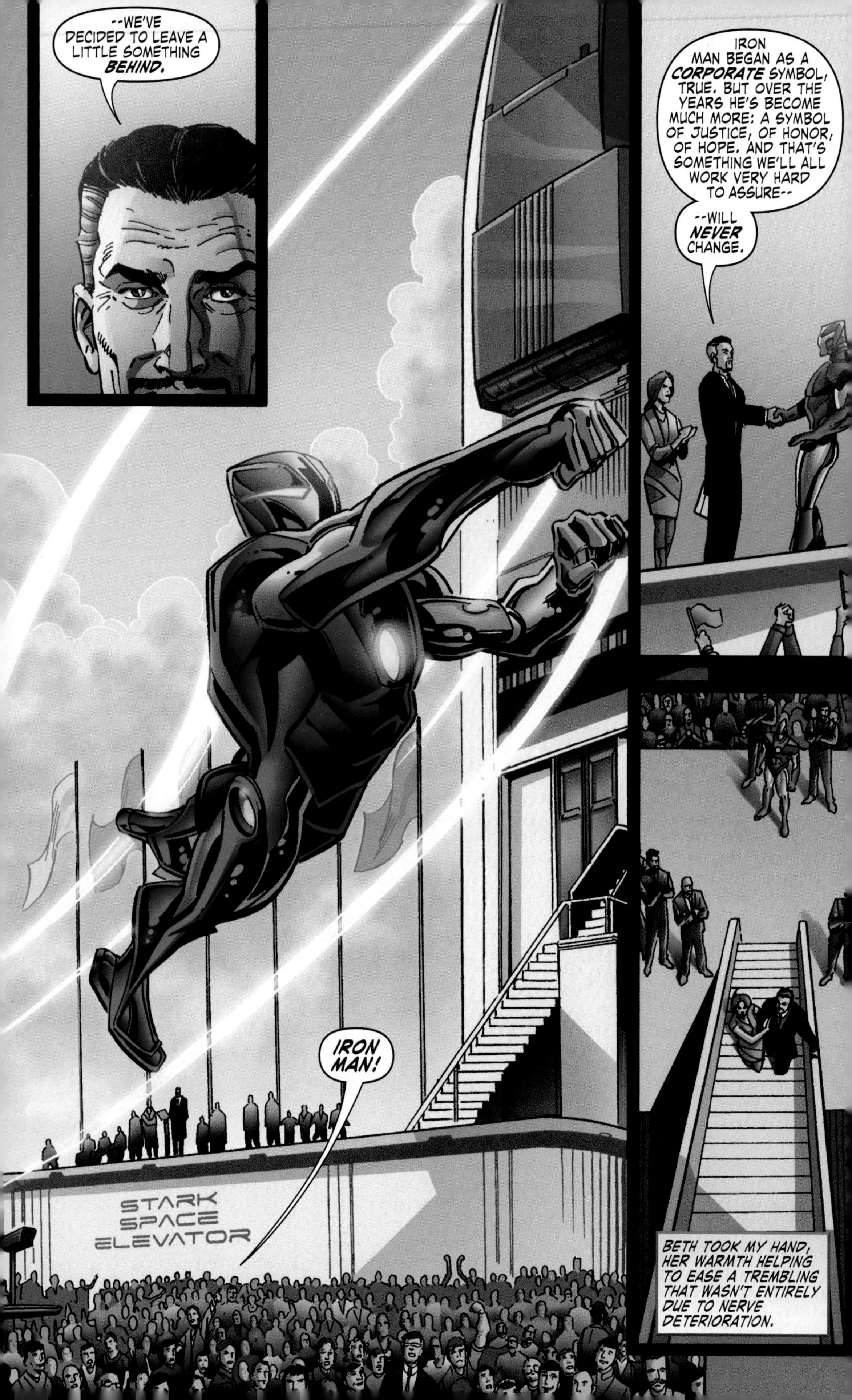
--WE'VE DECIDED TO LEAVE A LITTLE SOMETHING ***BEHIND.***
IRON MAN BEGAN AS A ***CORPORATE*** SYMBOL, TRUE. BUT OVER THE YEARS HE'S BECOME MUCH MORE: A SYMBOL OF JUSTICE, OF HONOR, OF HOPE. AND THAT'S SOMETHING WE'LL ALL WORK VERY HARD TO ASSURE--
--WILL ***NEVER*** CHANGE.
STARK SPACE ELEVATOR
IRON MAN!
BETH TOOK MY HAND, HER WARMTH HELPING TO EASE A TREMBLING THAT WASN'T ENTIRELY DUE TO NERVE DETERIORATION.

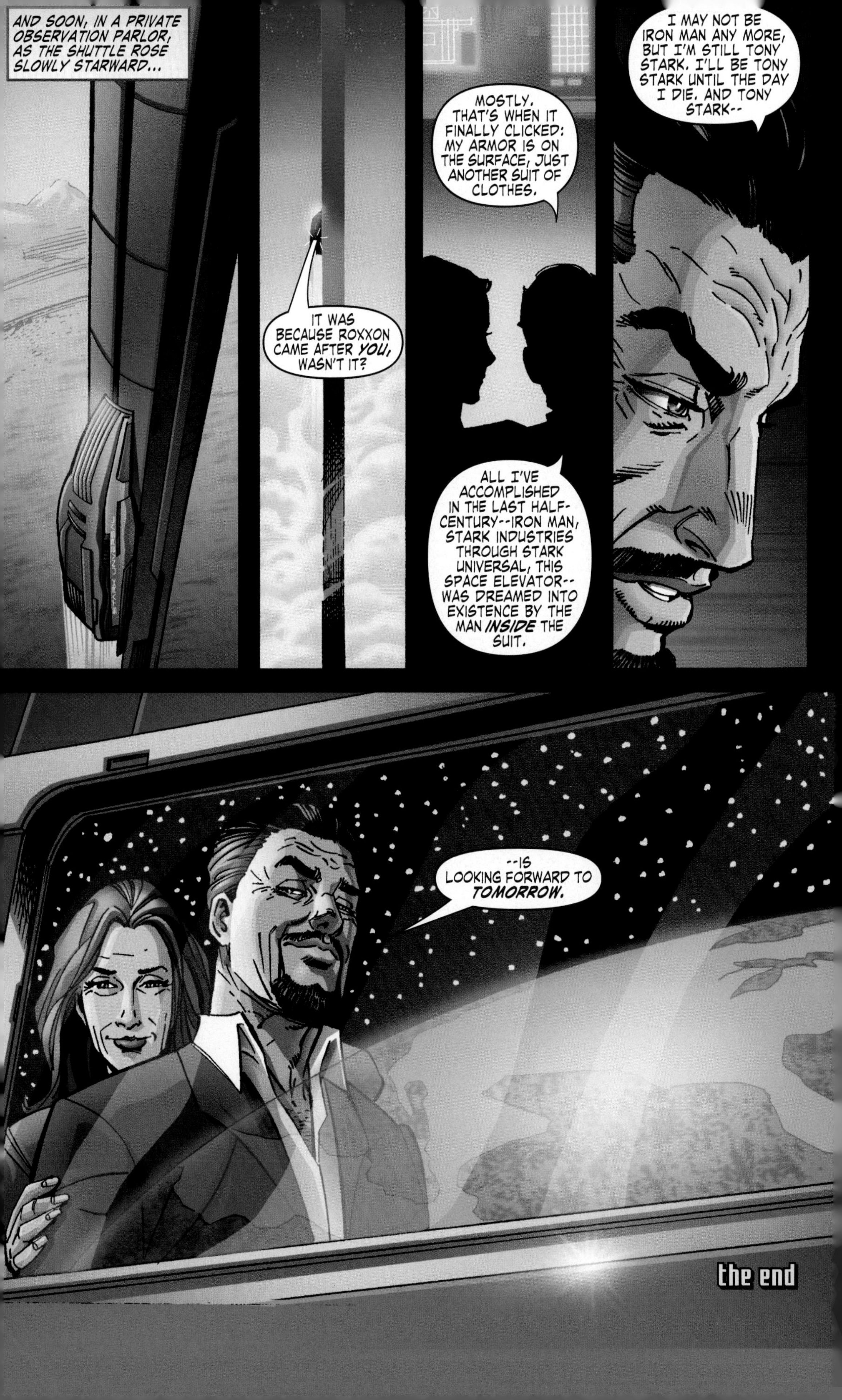
AND SOON, IN A PRIVATE OBSERVATION PARLOR, AS THE SHUTTLE ROSE SLOWLY STARWARD...
STARK UNIVERSAL
IT WAS BECAUSE ROXXON CAME AFTER YOU, WASN'T IT?
MOSTLY. THAT'S WHEN IT FINALLY CLICKED: MY ARMOR IS ON THE SURFACE, JUST ANOTHER SUIT OF CLOTHES.
ALL I'VE ACCOMPLISHED IN THE LAST HALF-CENTURY--IRON MAN, STARK INDUSTRIES THROUGH STARK UNIVERSAL, THIS SPACE ELEVATOR--WAS DREAMED INTO EXISTENCE BY THE MAN INSIDE THE SUIT.
I MAY NOT BE IRON MAN ANY MORE, BUT I'M STILL TONY STARK. I'LL BE TONY STARK UNTIL THE DAY I DIE. AND TONY STARK--
--IS LOOKING FORWARD TO TOMORROW.
the end

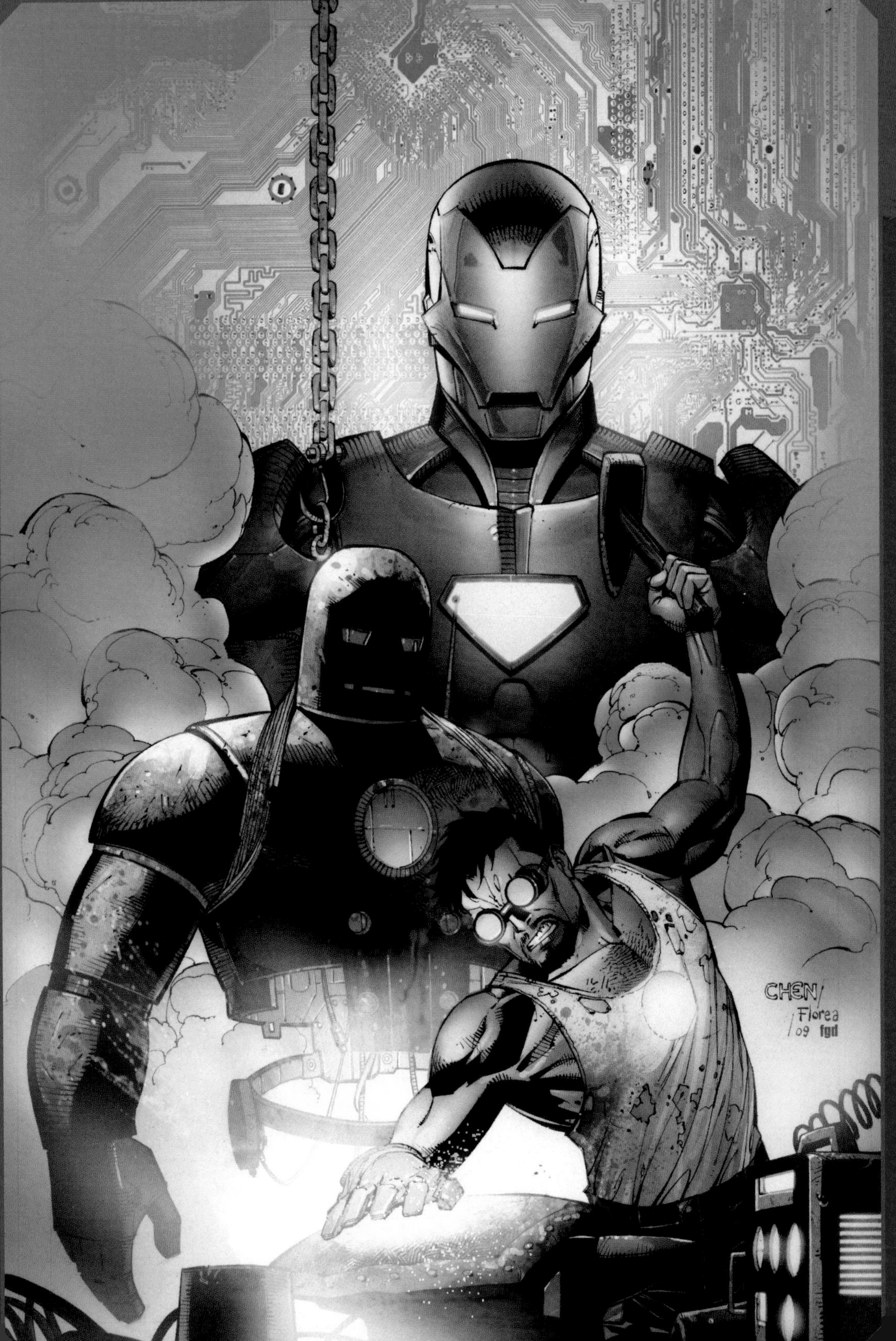
CHEN/
Florea
/09 fgd

IRON MAN: REQUIEM

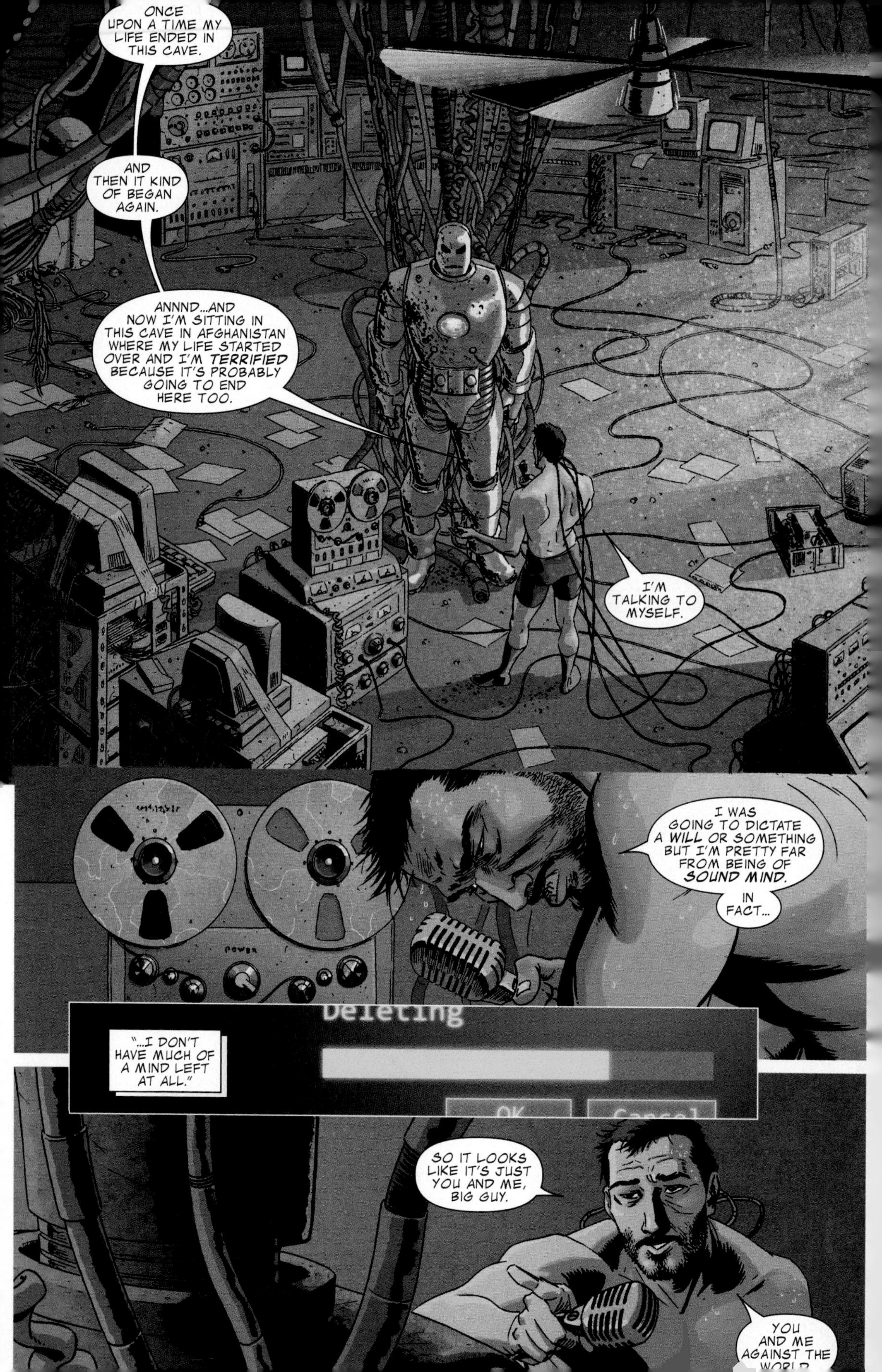

ONCE UPON A TIME MY LIFE ENDED IN THIS CAVE.
AND THEN IT KIND OF BEGAN AGAIN.
ANNND...AND NOW I'M SITTING IN THIS CAVE IN AFGHANISTAN WHERE MY LIFE STARTED OVER AND I'M TERRIFIED BECAUSE IT'S PROBABLY GOING TO END HERE TOO.
I'M TALKING TO MYSELF.
I WAS GOING TO DICTATE A WILL OR SOMETHING BUT I'M PRETTY FAR FROM BEING OF SOUND MIND.
IN FACT...
POWER
Deleting
"...I DON'T HAVE MUCH OF A MIND LEFT AT ALL."
OK
Cancel
SO IT LOOKS LIKE IT'S JUST YOU AND ME, BIG GUY.
YOU AND ME AGAINST THE WORLD

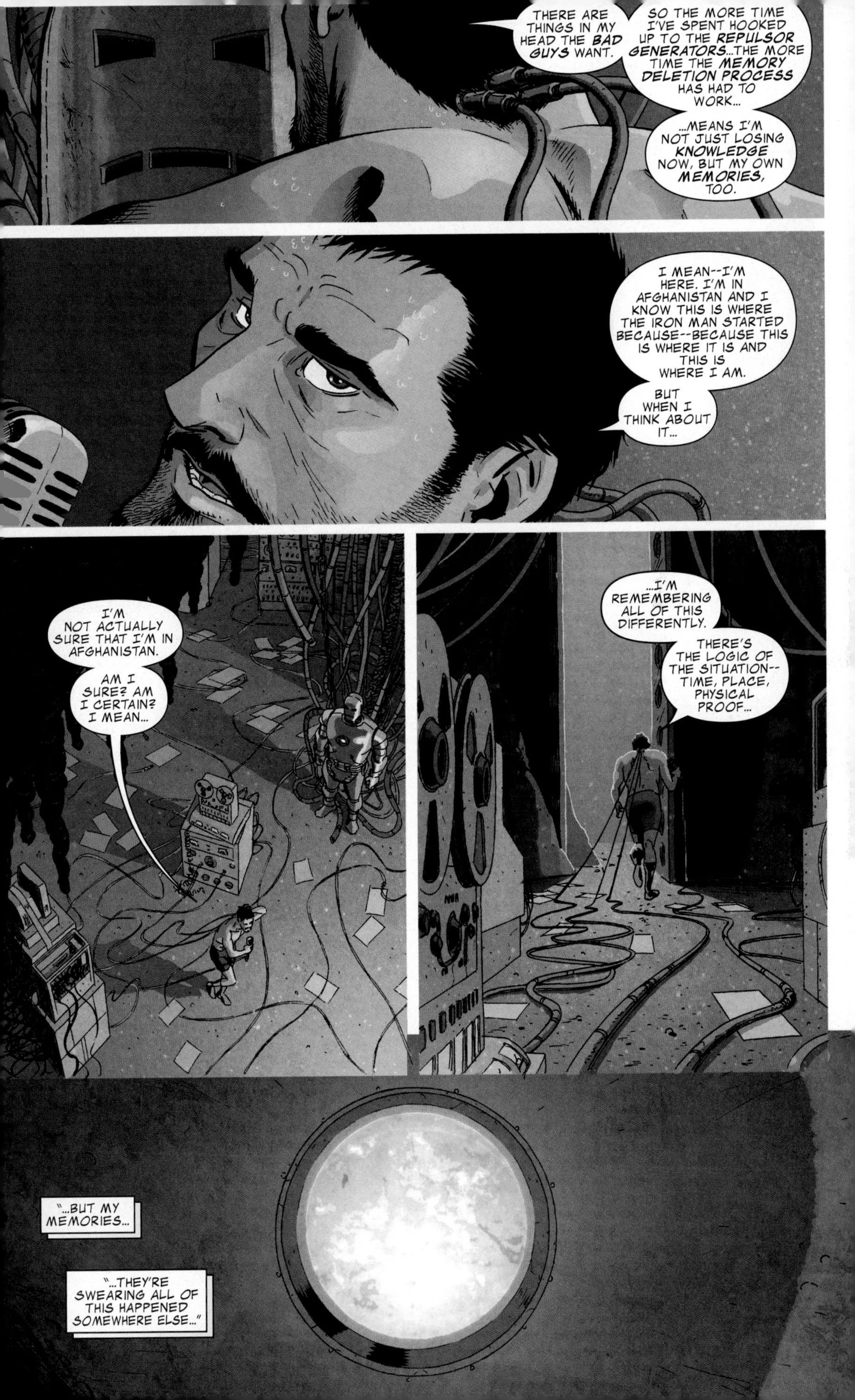
THERE ARE THINGS IN MY HEAD THE BAD GUYS WANT.
SO THE MORE TIME I'VE SPENT HOOKED UP TO THE REPULSOR GENERATORS...THE MORE TIME THE MEMORY DELETION PROCESS HAS HAD TO WORK...
...MEANS I'M NOT JUST LOSING KNOWLEDGE NOW, BUT MY OWN MEMORIES, TOO.
I MEAN--I'M HERE. I'M IN AFGHANISTAN AND I KNOW THIS IS WHERE THE IRON MAN STARTED BECAUSE--BECAUSE THIS IS WHERE IT IS AND THIS IS WHERE I AM.
BUT WHEN I THINK ABOUT IT...
I'M NOT ACTUALLY SURE THAT I'M IN AFGHANISTAN.
AM I SURE? AM I CERTAIN? I MEAN...
...I'M REMEMBERING ALL OF THIS DIFFERENTLY.
THERE'S THE LOGIC OF THE SITUATION--TIME, PLACE, PHYSICAL PROOF...
"...BUT MY MEMORIES...
"...THEY'RE SWEARING ALL OF THIS HAPPENED SOMEWHERE ELSE..."

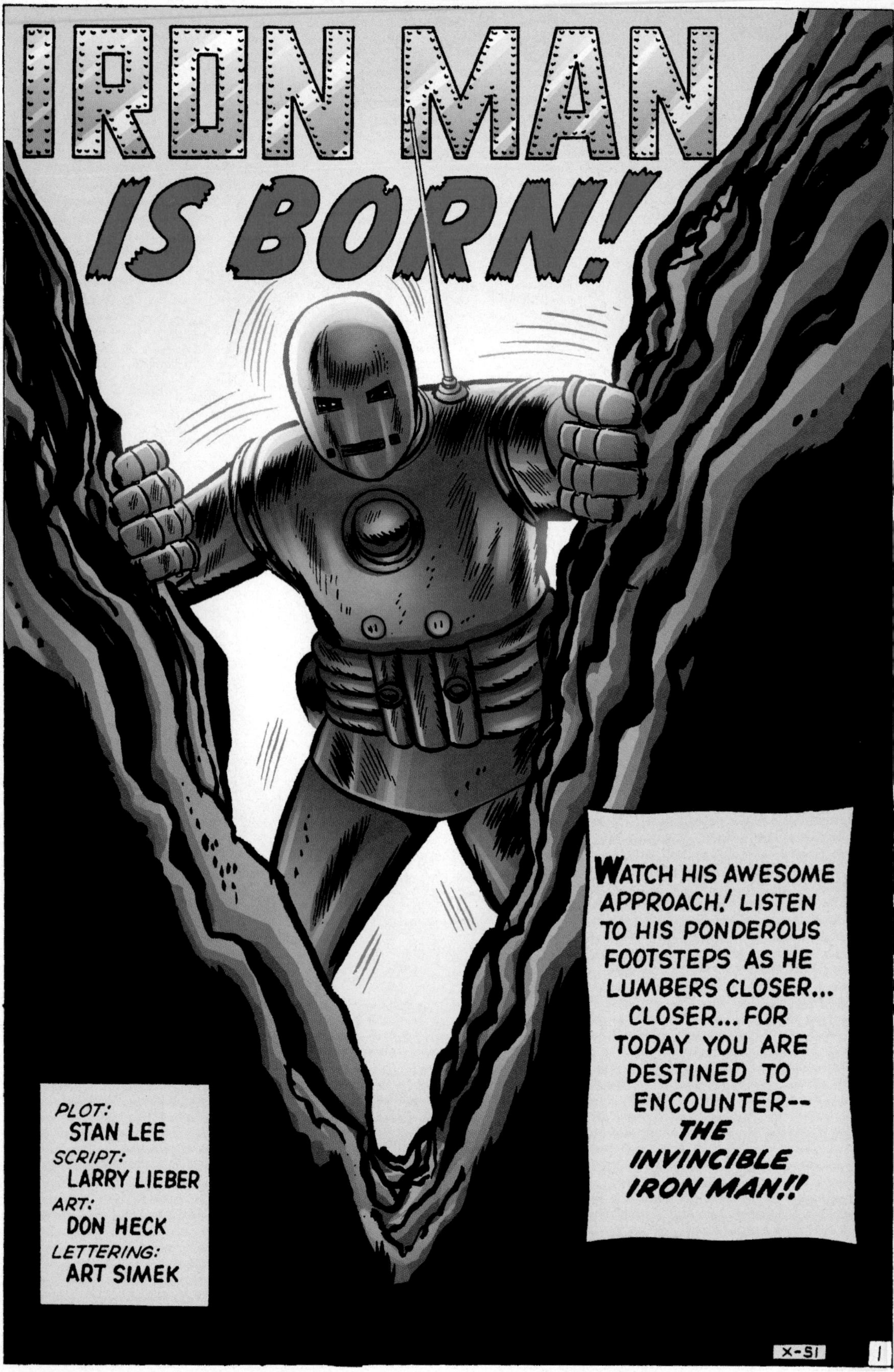
IRON MAN IS BORN!
WATCH HIS AWESOME APPROACH! LISTEN TO HIS PONDEROUS FOOTSTEPS AS HE LUMBERS CLOSER... CLOSER... FOR TODAY YOU ARE DESTINED TO ENCOUNTER-- THE INVINCIBLE IRON MAN!!
PLOT: STAN LEE
SCRIPT: LARRY LIEBER
ART: DON HECK
LETTERING: ART SIMEK
X-51
1

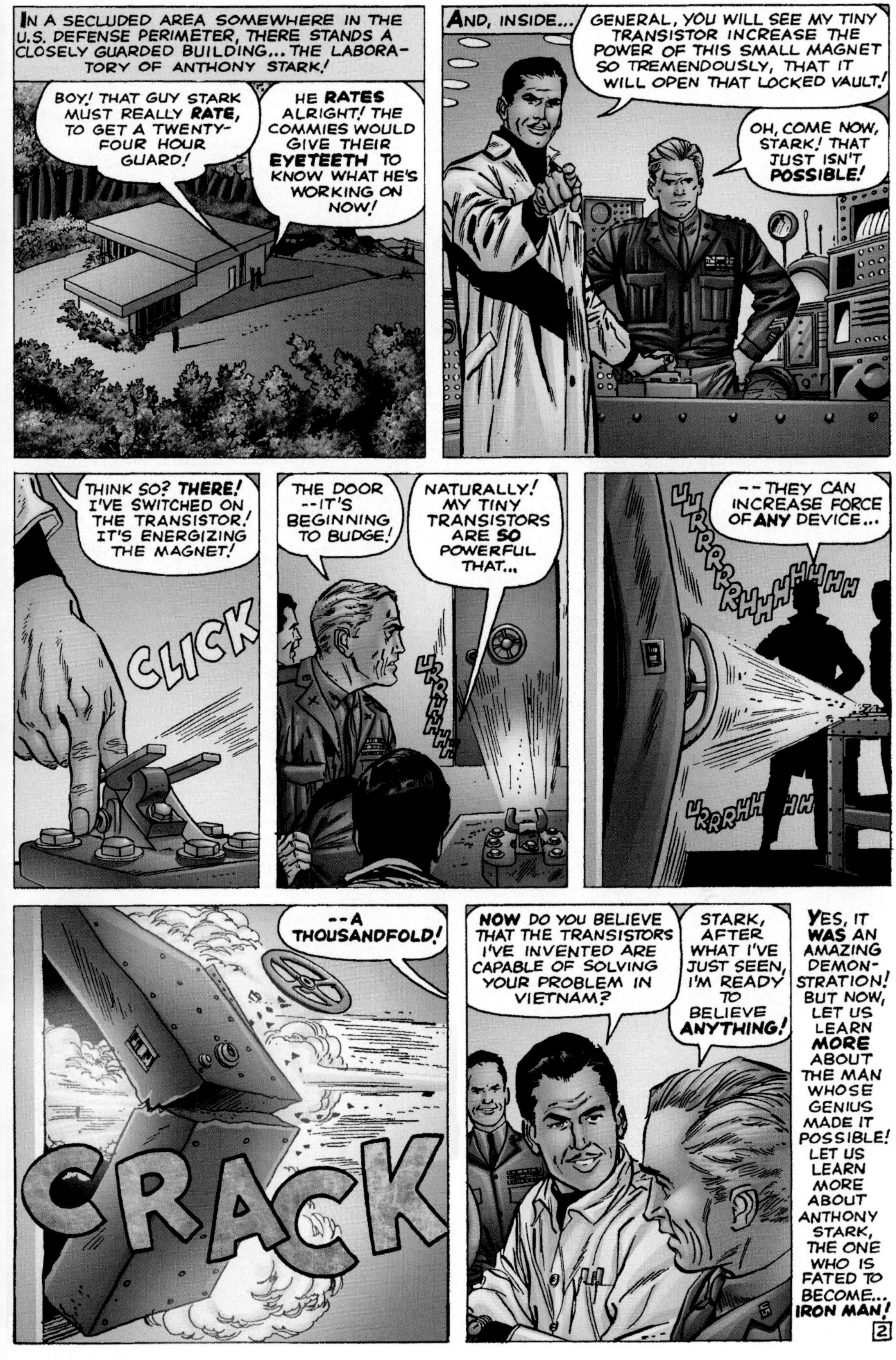

IN A SECLUDED AREA SOMEWHERE IN THE U.S. DEFENSE PERIMETER, THERE STANDS A CLOSELY GUARDED BUILDING... THE LABORATORY OF ANTHONY STARK!
BOY! THAT GUY STARK MUST REALLY **RATE**, TO GET A TWENTY-FOUR HOUR GUARD!
HE **RATES** ALRIGHT! THE COMMIES WOULD GIVE THEIR **EYETEETH** TO KNOW WHAT HE'S WORKING ON NOW!
AND, INSIDE...
GENERAL, YOU WILL SEE MY TINY TRANSISTOR INCREASE THE POWER OF THIS SMALL MAGNET SO TREMENDOUSLY, THAT IT WILL OPEN THAT LOCKED VAULT!
OH, COME NOW, STARK! THAT JUST ISN'T **POSSIBLE!**
THINK SO? **THERE!** I'VE SWITCHED ON THE TRANSISTOR! IT'S ENERGIZING THE MAGNET!
CLICK
THE DOOR --IT'S BEGINNING TO BUDGE!
NATURALLY! MY TINY TRANSISTORS ARE **SO** POWERFUL THAT...
URRHHHH
--THEY CAN INCREASE FORCE OF **ANY** DEVICE...
URRRRRHHHHHHHHH
URRRHHHHH
--A THOUSANDFOLD!
CRACK
NOW DO YOU BELIEVE THAT THE TRANSISTORS I'VE INVENTED ARE CAPABLE OF SOLVING YOUR PROBLEM IN VIETNAM?
STARK, AFTER WHAT I'VE JUST SEEN, I'M READY TO BELIEVE **ANYTHING!**
YES, IT **WAS** AN AMAZING DEMONSTRATION! BUT NOW, LET US LEARN **MORE** ABOUT THE MAN WHOSE GENIUS MADE IT POSSIBLE! LET US LEARN MORE ABOUT ANTHONY STARK, THE ONE WHO IS FATED TO BECOME... **IRON MAN!**

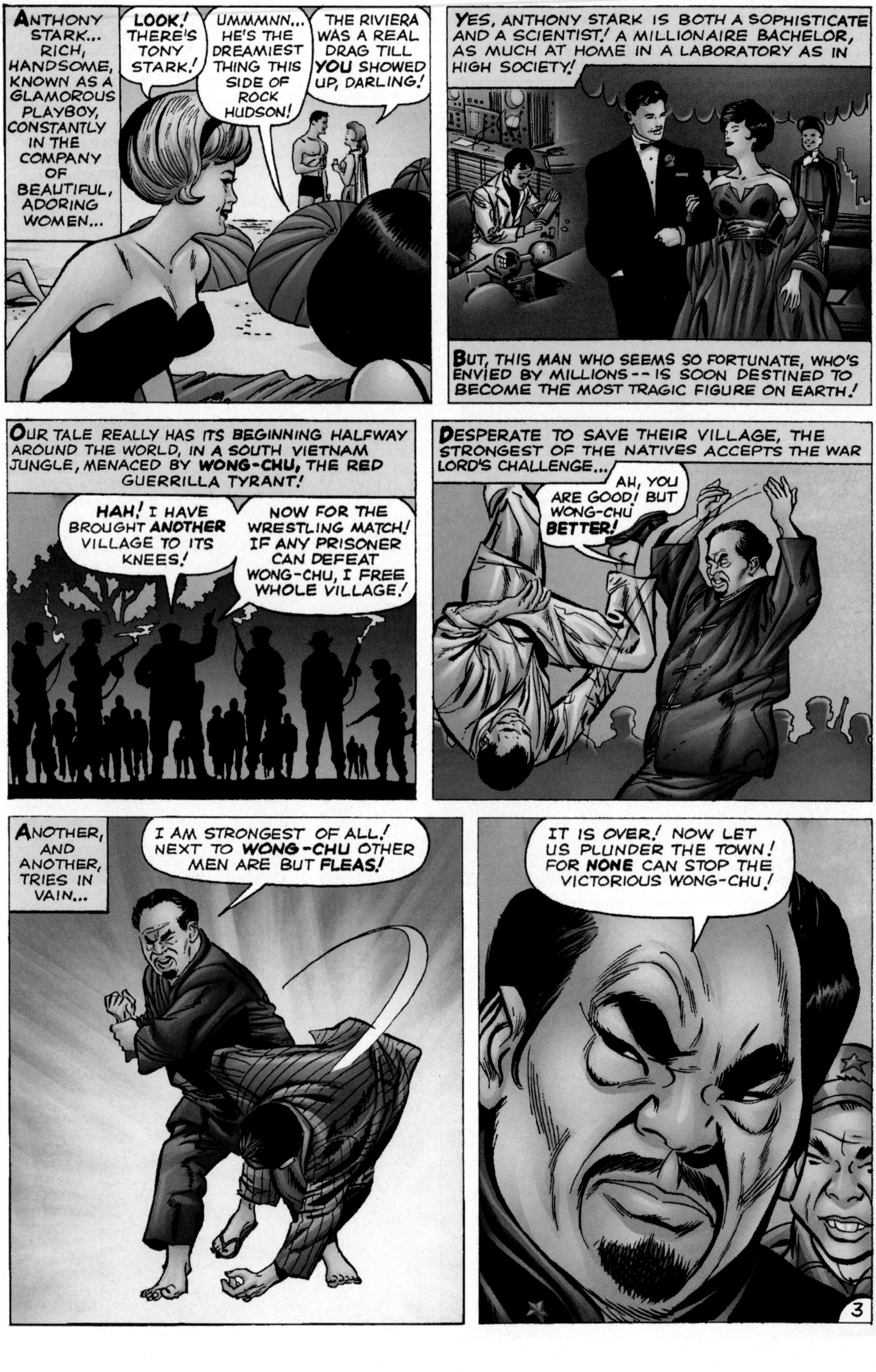
ANTHONY STARK... RICH, HANDSOME, KNOWN AS A GLAMOROUS PLAYBOY, CONSTANTLY IN THE COMPANY OF BEAUTIFUL, ADORING WOMEN...
LOOK! THERE'S TONY STARK!
UMMMNN... HE'S THE DREAMIEST THING THIS SIDE OF ROCK HUDSON!
THE RIVIERA WAS A REAL DRAG TILL YOU SHOWED UP, DARLING!
YES, ANTHONY STARK IS BOTH A SOPHISTICATE AND A SCIENTIST! A MILLIONAIRE BACHELOR, AS MUCH AT HOME IN A LABORATORY AS IN HIGH SOCIETY!
BUT, THIS MAN WHO SEEMS SO FORTUNATE, WHO'S ENVIED BY MILLIONS -- IS SOON DESTINED TO BECOME THE MOST TRAGIC FIGURE ON EARTH!
OUR TALE REALLY HAS ITS BEGINNING HALFWAY AROUND THE WORLD, IN A SOUTH VIETNAM JUNGLE, MENACED BY WONG-CHU, THE RED GUERRILLA TYRANT!
HAH! I HAVE BROUGHT ANOTHER VILLAGE TO ITS KNEES!
NOW FOR THE WRESTLING MATCH! IF ANY PRISONER CAN DEFEAT WONG-CHU, I FREE WHOLE VILLAGE!
DESPERATE TO SAVE THEIR VILLAGE, THE STRONGEST OF THE NATIVES ACCEPTS THE WAR LORD'S CHALLENGE...
AH, YOU ARE GOOD! BUT WONG-CHU BETTER!
ANOTHER, AND ANOTHER, TRIES IN VAIN...
I AM STRONGEST OF ALL! NEXT TO WONG-CHU OTHER MEN ARE BUT FLEAS!
IT IS OVER! NOW LET US PLUNDER THE TOWN! FOR NONE CAN STOP THE VICTORIOUS WONG-CHU!
3

MEANWHILE, ON THE OUTSKIRTS OF THE JUNGLE...

THE RED GUERRILLAS OUTNUMBER US! OUR HEAVY ARTILLERY COULD BEAT THEM, BUT WE CAN'T TRANSPORT SUCH BIG WEAPONS THROUGH THE DENSE JUNGLE!

SO, THAT'S WHERE MY MIDGET TRANSISTORS COME IN, EH?

RIGHT! THANKS TO YOUR INVENTIONS, OUR MORTARS ARE NO LARGER OR HEAVIER THAN FLASHLIGHTS! OUR MEN CAN CARRY THEM ANYWHERE!

TAKE COVER! THERE'S THE ENEMY! YOU'LL SEE YOUR GUNS IN ACTION NOW!

THAT'S WHY I WAS SENT HERE! TO MAKE SURE THEY WORK AS WELL AS PLANNED! IF NOT, I'LL FIX 'EM ON THE SPOT!

JUST LOOK AT THE REDS RETREAT!

STARK, YOUR WEAPONS ARE EVERYTHING WE HOPED FOR!

BATTLE-FILLED MINUTES LATER...

THE REDS NEVER KNEW WHAT HIT THEM!

BUT, THE JUNGLE HOLDS A THOUSAND PERILS! SOME NATURAL, OTHERS MAN MADE...

AND, TRIPPING OVER A SMALL CONCEALED STRING LEADS TO DISASTER...

BAROOM

A BOOBY-TRAP! OHHH...

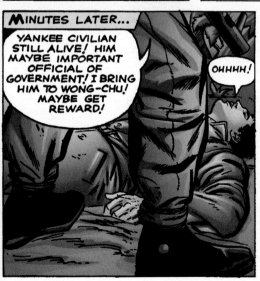

MINUTES LATER...

YANKEE CIVILIAN STILL ALIVE! HIM MAYBE IMPORTANT OFFICIAL OF GOVERNMENT! I BRING HIM TO WONG-CHU! MAYBE GET REWARD!

OHHHH!

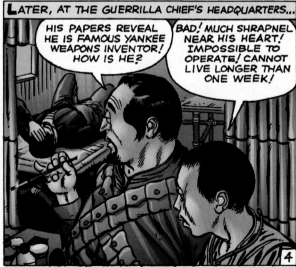

LATER, AT THE GUERRILLA CHIEF'S HEADQUARTERS...

HIS PAPERS REVEAL HE IS FAMOUS YANKEE WEAPONS INVENTOR! HOW IS HE?

BAD! MUCH SHRAPNEL NEAR HIS HEART! IMPOSSIBLE TO OPERATE! CANNOT LIVE LONGER THAN ONE WEEK!

4

IN A FEW DAYS SHRAPNEL WILL REACH HIS HEART-- THEN HE WILL DIE! **NOTHING** CAN SAVE HIM!

BAH! WE CAN **USE** HIS GENIUS! WONG-CHU WILL **TRICK** HIM INTO SPENDING HIS LAST DAYS ON EARTH WORKING FOR **US!** IS HE STRONG ENOUGH NOW?

YES, HE CAN WORK TILL SHRAPNEL REACHES HEART!

WE KNOW YOU ARE AMERICAN WEAPONS INVENTOR! IF YOU DESIGN POWERFUL NEW WEAPON FOR **ME**, AFTERWARDS I HAVE SURGEON SAVE YOUR LIFE!

HE'S LYING... IF THEY **COULD** THEY'D DO IT **NOW**, TO BE SURE I LIVE LONG ENOUGH TO DESIGN WEAPONS FOR THEM!

I KNOW I'VE ONLY DAYS TO LIVE, BUT MY LAST ACT WILL BE TO DEFEAT THIS **GRINNING, SMIRKING, RED TERRORIST!**

ALL RIGHT, WONG-CHU, I'LL **DO** IT!

I KNEW YOU WOULD NOT HESITATE TO BETRAY YOUR COUNTRY TO SAVE YOURSELF!

HERE ROOM WHERE YOU WORK! PLENTY OF SCRAP IRON! PLENTY TOOLS!

THIS I PROMISE YOU... I SHALL BUILD THE MOST FANTASTIC WEAPON OF ALL TIME!

I'LL **BUILD** IT, ALRIGHT, BUT IT WILL BE **MINE**...

--MADE FOR ONLY **ONE** PURPOSE-- **TO KEEP ME ALIVE!**

CLICK!

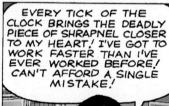

EVERY TICK OF THE CLOCK BRINGS THE DEADLY PIECE OF SHRAPNEL CLOSER TO MY HEART! I'VE GOT TO WORK FASTER THAN I'VE EVER WORKED BEFORE! CAN'T AFFORD A SINGLE MISTAKE!

THEN, ON THE SECOND DAY OF TONY STARK'S RACE AGAINST TIME...

THIS OLD ONE, PROFESSOR YINSEN! ONCE GREAT SCIENTIST! NOW LOWLY MAN-SERVANT OF WONG-CHU.. ...WILL **HELP** YOU BUILD WEAPON!

NO! I WILL **NEVER** HELP THE EVIL RED TYRANTS! **NEVER!!**

5.

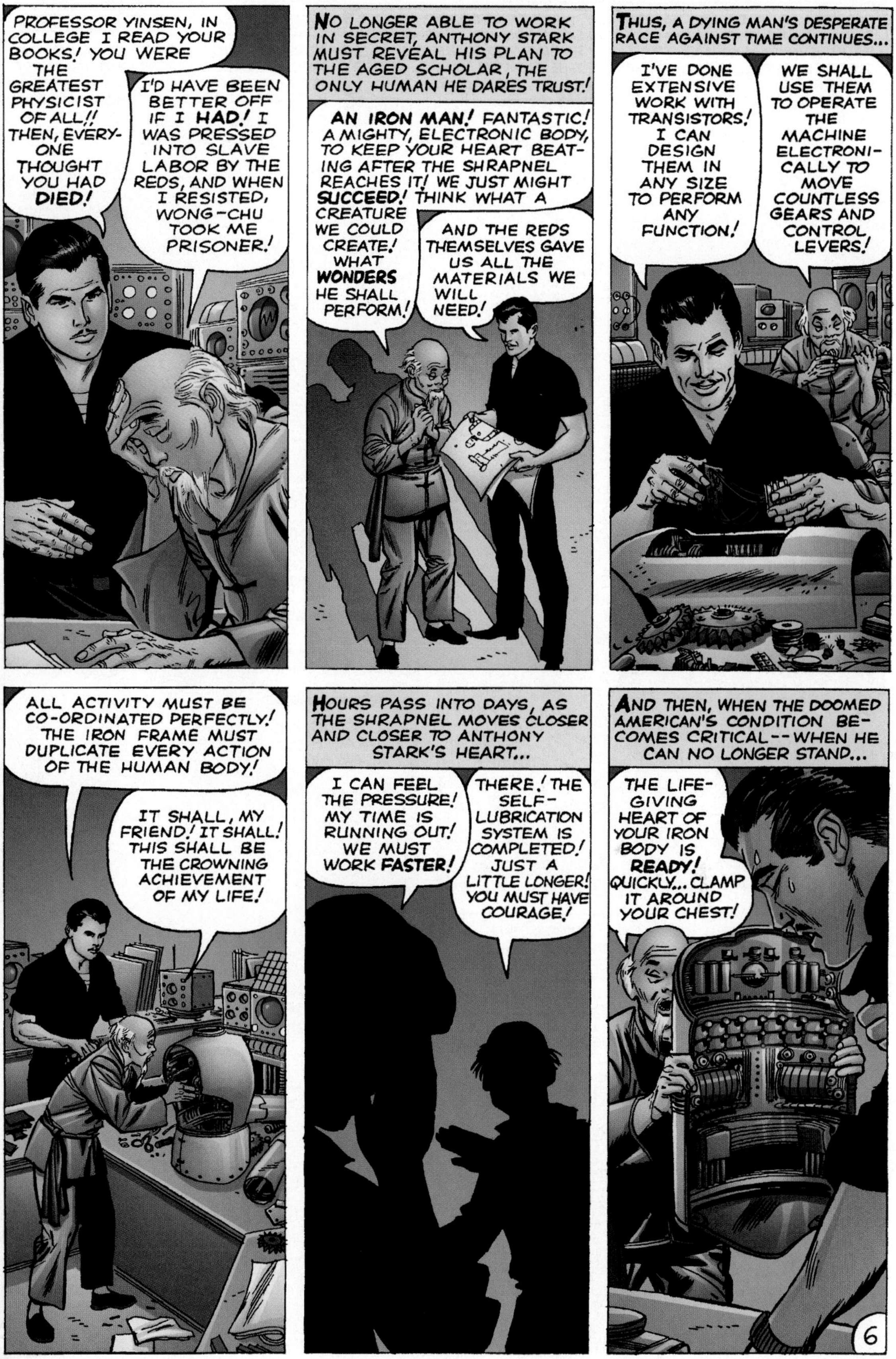
PROFESSOR YINSEN, IN COLLEGE I READ YOUR BOOKS! YOU WERE THE GREATEST PHYSICIST OF ALL!! THEN, EVERYONE THOUGHT YOU HAD DIED!
I'D HAVE BEEN BETTER OFF IF I HAD! I WAS PRESSED INTO SLAVE LABOR BY THE REDS, AND WHEN I RESISTED, WONG-CHU TOOK ME PRISONER!
NO LONGER ABLE TO WORK IN SECRET, ANTHONY STARK MUST REVEAL HIS PLAN TO THE AGED SCHOLAR, THE ONLY HUMAN HE DARES TRUST!
AN IRON MAN! FANTASTIC! A MIGHTY, ELECTRONIC BODY, TO KEEP YOUR HEART BEATING AFTER THE SHRAPNEL REACHES IT! WE JUST MIGHT SUCCEED! THINK WHAT A CREATURE WE COULD CREATE! WHAT WONDERS HE SHALL PERFORM!
AND THE REDS THEMSELVES GAVE US ALL THE MATERIALS WE WILL NEED!
THUS, A DYING MAN'S DESPERATE RACE AGAINST TIME CONTINUES...
I'VE DONE EXTENSIVE WORK WITH TRANSISTORS! I CAN DESIGN THEM IN ANY SIZE TO PERFORM ANY FUNCTION!
WE SHALL USE THEM TO OPERATE THE MACHINE ELECTRONICALLY TO MOVE COUNTLESS GEARS AND CONTROL LEVERS!
ALL ACTIVITY MUST BE CO-ORDINATED PERFECTLY! THE IRON FRAME MUST DUPLICATE EVERY ACTION OF THE HUMAN BODY!
IT SHALL, MY FRIEND! IT SHALL! THIS SHALL BE THE CROWNING ACHIEVEMENT OF MY LIFE!
HOURS PASS INTO DAYS, AS THE SHRAPNEL MOVES CLOSER AND CLOSER TO ANTHONY STARK'S HEART...
I CAN FEEL THE PRESSURE! MY TIME IS RUNNING OUT! WE MUST WORK FASTER!
THERE! THE SELF-LUBRICATION SYSTEM IS COMPLETED! JUST A LITTLE LONGER! YOU MUST HAVE COURAGE!
AND THEN, WHEN THE DOOMED AMERICAN'S CONDITION BECOMES CRITICAL--WHEN HE CAN NO LONGER STAND...
THE LIFE-GIVING HEART OF YOUR IRON BODY IS READY! QUICKLY... CLAMP IT AROUND YOUR CHEST!
6

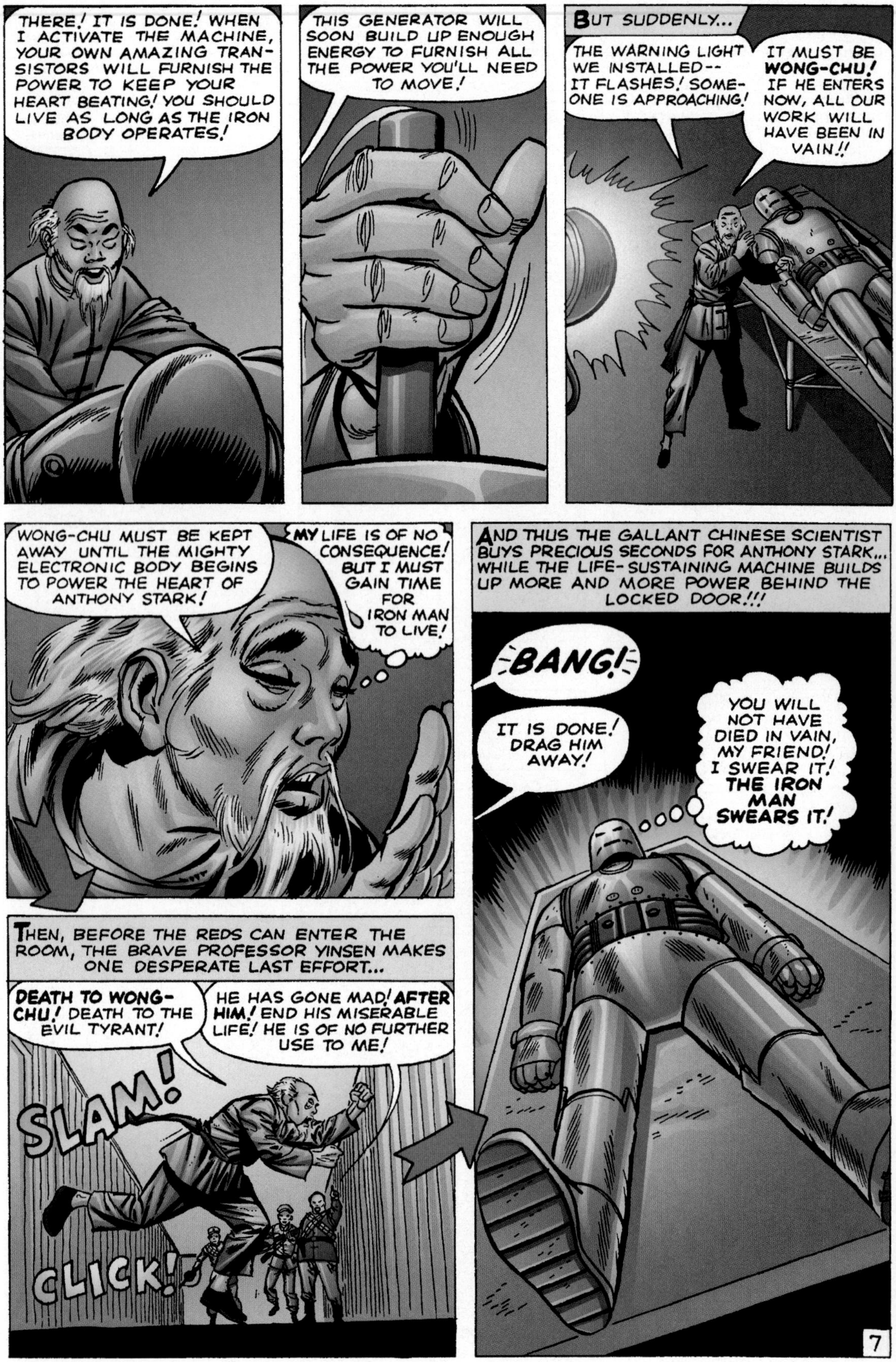
THERE! IT IS DONE! WHEN I ACTIVATE THE MACHINE, YOUR OWN AMAZING TRANSISTORS WILL FURNISH THE POWER TO KEEP YOUR HEART BEATING! YOU SHOULD LIVE AS LONG AS THE IRON BODY OPERATES!
THIS GENERATOR WILL SOON BUILD UP ENOUGH ENERGY TO FURNISH ALL THE POWER YOU'LL NEED TO MOVE!
BUT SUDDENLY...
THE WARNING LIGHT WE INSTALLED-- IT FLASHES! SOMEONE IS APPROACHING!
IT MUST BE **WONG-CHU!** IF HE ENTERS NOW, ALL OUR WORK WILL HAVE BEEN IN VAIN!!
WONG-CHU MUST BE KEPT AWAY UNTIL THE MIGHTY ELECTRONIC BODY BEGINS TO POWER THE HEART OF ANTHONY STARK!
MY LIFE IS OF NO CONSEQUENCE! BUT I MUST GAIN TIME FOR IRON MAN TO LIVE!
THEN, BEFORE THE REDS CAN ENTER THE ROOM, THE BRAVE PROFESSOR YINSEN MAKES ONE DESPERATE LAST EFFORT...
DEATH TO WONG-CHU! DEATH TO THE EVIL TYRANT!
HE HAS GONE MAD! **AFTER HIM!** END HIS MISERABLE LIFE! HE IS OF NO FURTHER USE TO ME!
SLAM!
CLICK!
AND THUS THE GALLANT CHINESE SCIENTIST BUYS PRECIOUS SECONDS FOR ANTHONY STARK... WHILE THE LIFE-SUSTAINING MACHINE BUILDS UP MORE AND MORE POWER BEHIND THE LOCKED DOOR!!!
BANG!
IT IS DONE! DRAG HIM AWAY!
YOU WILL NOT HAVE DIED IN VAIN, MY FRIEND! I SWEAR IT! **THE IRON MAN SWEARS IT!**

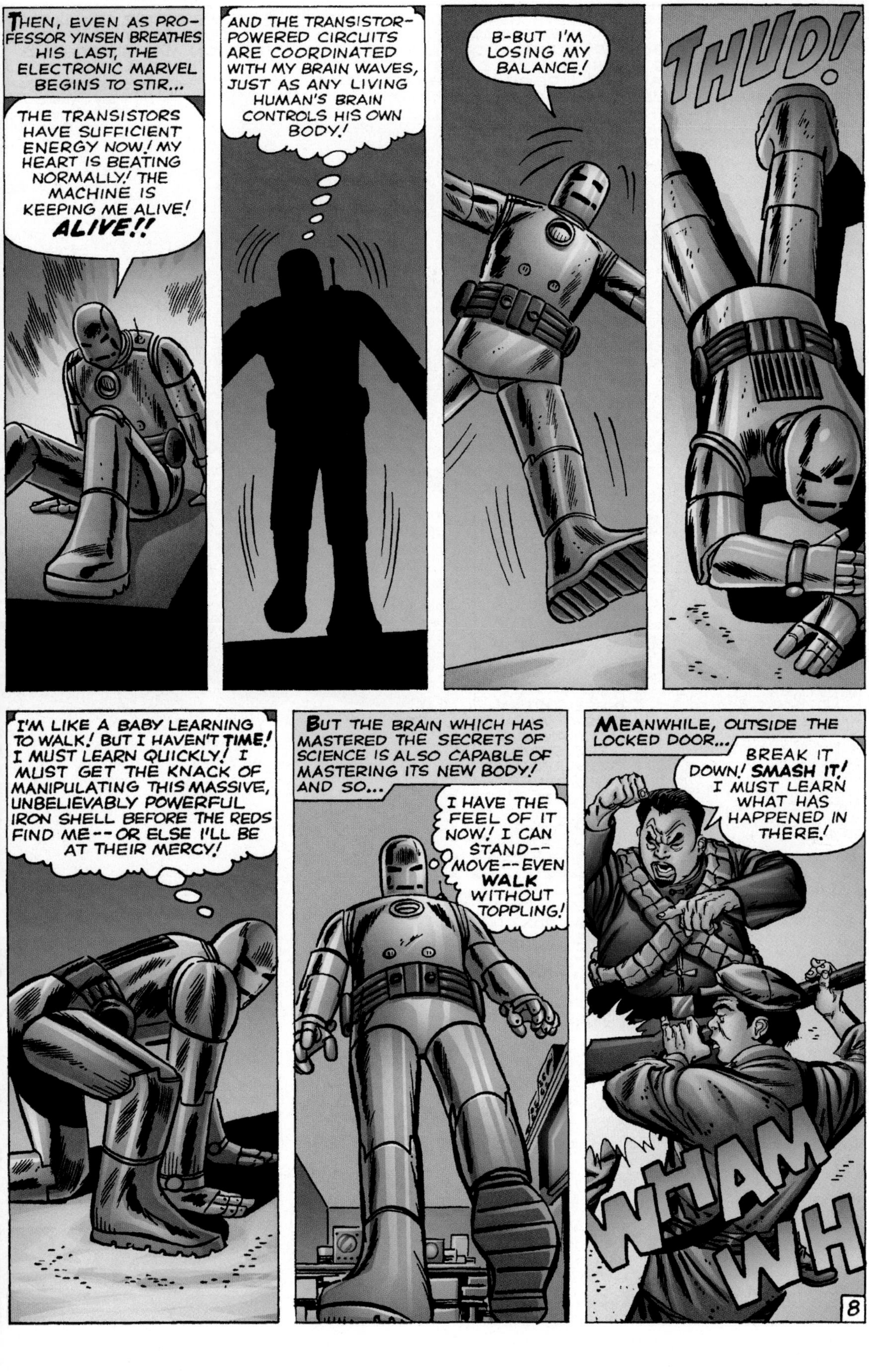
THEN, EVEN AS PROFESSOR YINSEN BREATHES HIS LAST, THE ELECTRONIC MARVEL BEGINS TO STIR...
THE TRANSISTORS HAVE SUFFICIENT ENERGY NOW! MY HEART IS BEATING NORMALLY! THE MACHINE IS KEEPING ME ALIVE! ALIVE!!
AND THE TRANSISTOR-POWERED CIRCUITS ARE COORDINATED WITH MY BRAIN WAVES, JUST AS ANY LIVING HUMAN'S BRAIN CONTROLS HIS OWN BODY!
B-BUT I'M LOSING MY BALANCE!
THUD!
I'M LIKE A BABY LEARNING TO WALK! BUT I HAVEN'T TIME! I MUST LEARN QUICKLY! I MUST GET THE KNACK OF MANIPULATING THIS MASSIVE, UNBELIEVABLY POWERFUL IRON SHELL BEFORE THE REDS FIND ME--OR ELSE I'LL BE AT THEIR MERCY!
BUT THE BRAIN WHICH HAS MASTERED THE SECRETS OF SCIENCE IS ALSO CAPABLE OF MASTERING ITS NEW BODY! AND SO...
I HAVE THE FEEL OF IT NOW! I CAN STAND--MOVE--EVEN WALK WITHOUT TOPPLING!
MEANWHILE, OUTSIDE THE LOCKED DOOR...
BREAK IT DOWN! SMASH IT! I MUST LEARN WHAT HAS HAPPENED IN THERE!
WHAM
WH
8

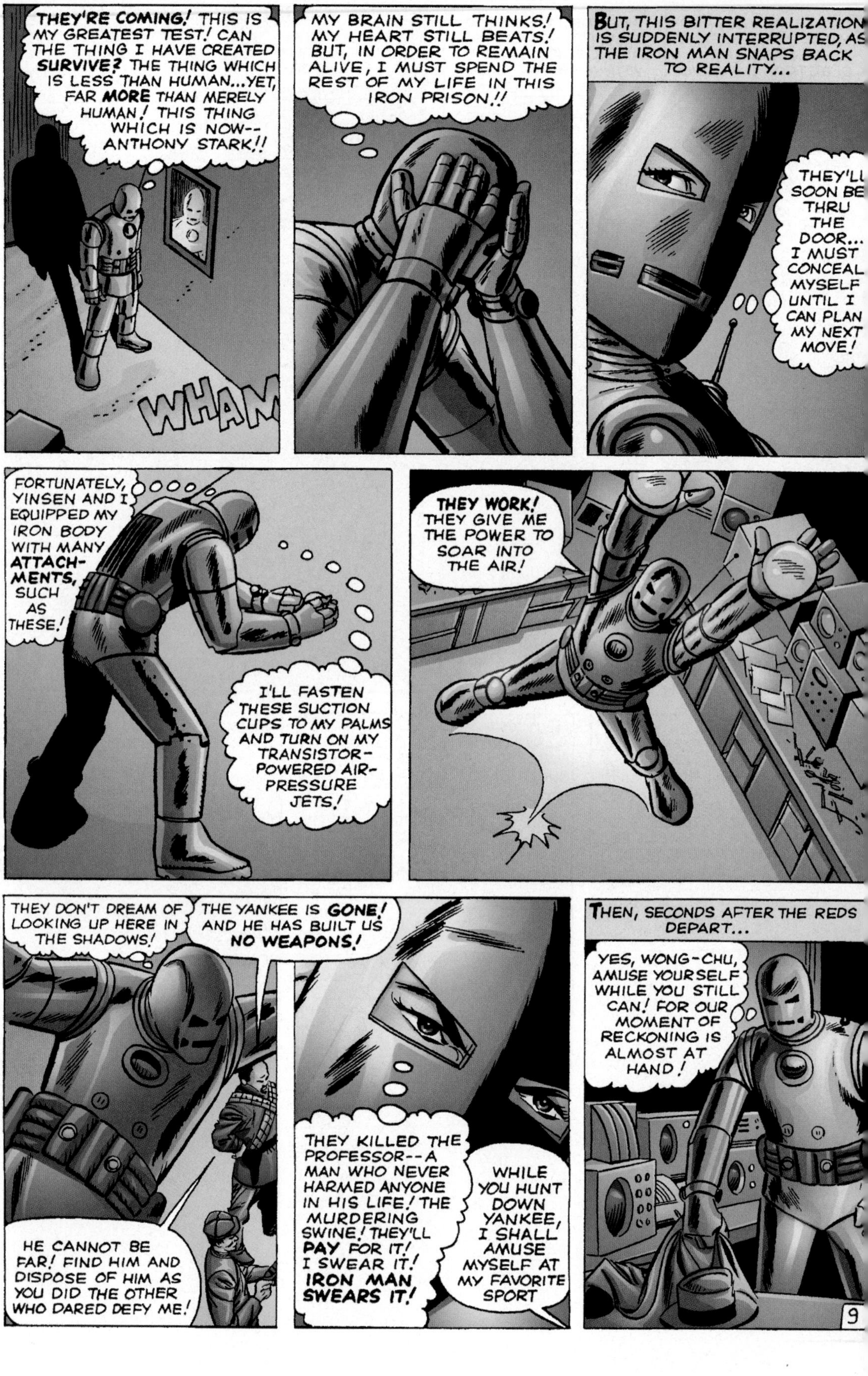
THEY'RE COMING! THIS IS MY GREATEST TEST! CAN THE THING I HAVE CREATED SURVIVE? THE THING WHICH IS LESS THAN HUMAN...YET, FAR MORE THAN MERELY HUMAN! THIS THING WHICH IS NOW--ANTHONY STARK!!
WHAM
MY BRAIN STILL THINKS! MY HEART STILL BEATS! BUT, IN ORDER TO REMAIN ALIVE, I MUST SPEND THE REST OF MY LIFE IN THIS IRON PRISON!!
BUT, THIS BITTER REALIZATION IS SUDDENLY INTERRUPTED, AS THE IRON MAN SNAPS BACK TO REALITY...
THEY'LL SOON BE THRU THE DOOR... I MUST CONCEAL MYSELF UNTIL I CAN PLAN MY NEXT MOVE!
FORTUNATELY, YINSEN AND I EQUIPPED MY IRON BODY WITH MANY ATTACHMENTS, SUCH AS THESE!
I'LL FASTEN THESE SUCTION CUPS TO MY PALMS AND TURN ON MY TRANSISTOR-POWERED AIR-PRESSURE JETS!
THEY WORK! THEY GIVE ME THE POWER TO SOAR INTO THE AIR!
THEY DON'T DREAM OF LOOKING UP HERE IN THE SHADOWS!
THE YANKEE IS GONE! AND HE HAS BUILT US NO WEAPONS!
HE CANNOT BE FAR! FIND HIM AND DISPOSE OF HIM AS YOU DID THE OTHER WHO DARED DEFY ME!
THEY KILLED THE PROFESSOR--A MAN WHO NEVER HARMED ANYONE IN HIS LIFE! THE MURDERING SWINE! THEY'LL PAY FOR IT! I SWEAR IT! IRON MAN SWEARS IT!
WHILE YOU HUNT DOWN YANKEE, I SHALL AMUSE MYSELF AT MY FAVORITE SPORT
THEN, SECONDS AFTER THE REDS DEPART...
YES, WONG-CHU, AMUSE YOURSELF WHILE YOU STILL CAN! FOR OUR MOMENT OF RECKONING IS ALMOST AT HAND!
9

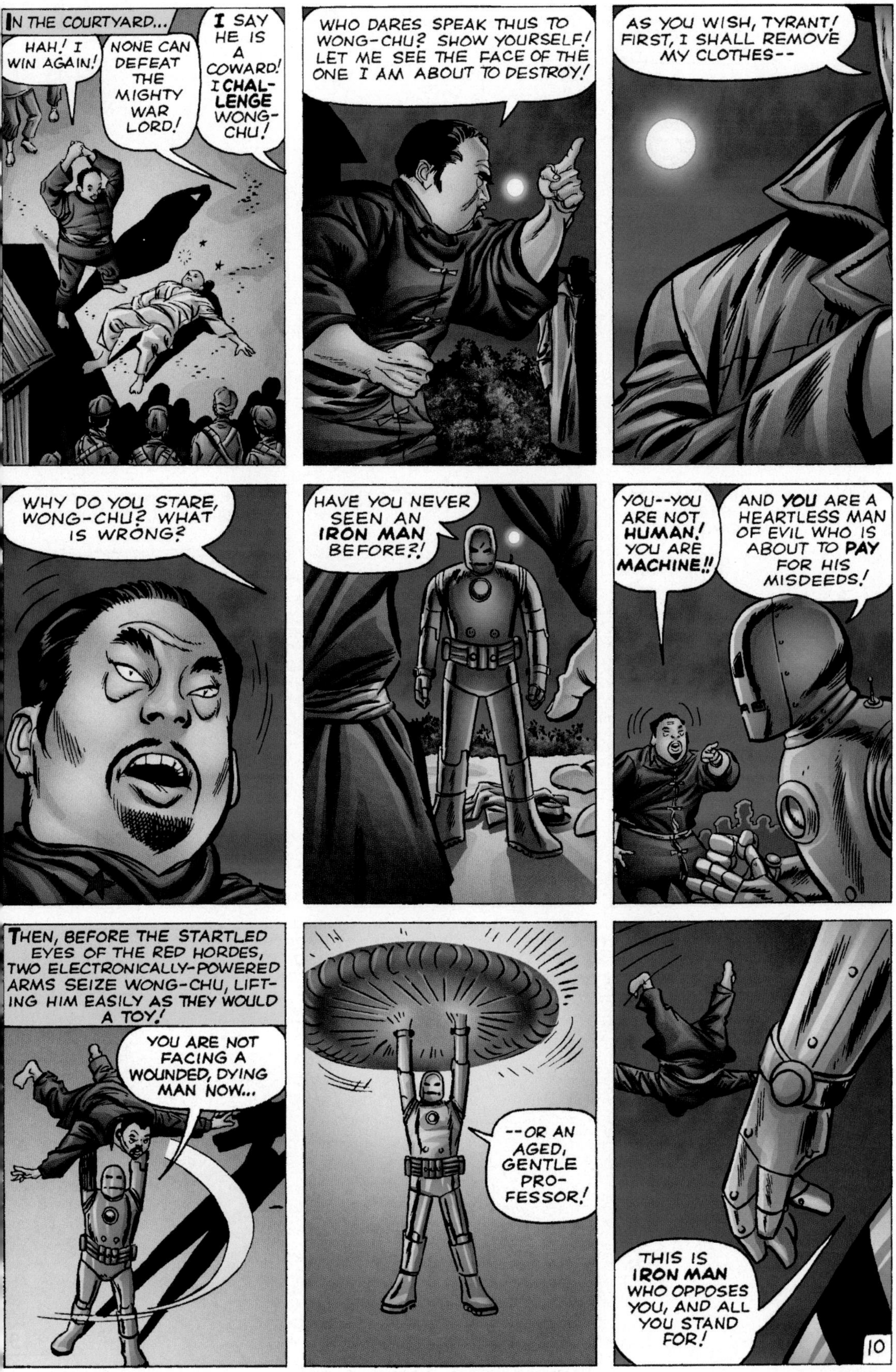
IN THE COURTYARD...
HAH! I WIN AGAIN!
NONE CAN DEFEAT THE MIGHTY WAR LORD!
I SAY HE IS A COWARD! I CHALLENGE WONG-CHU!
WHO DARES SPEAK THUS TO WONG-CHU? SHOW YOURSELF! LET ME SEE THE FACE OF THE ONE I AM ABOUT TO DESTROY!
AS YOU WISH, TYRANT! FIRST, I SHALL REMOVE MY CLOTHES--
WHY DO YOU STARE, WONG-CHU? WHAT IS WRONG?
HAVE YOU NEVER SEEN AN IRON MAN BEFORE?!
YOU--YOU ARE NOT HUMAN! YOU ARE MACHINE!!
AND YOU ARE A HEARTLESS MAN OF EVIL WHO IS ABOUT TO PAY FOR HIS MISDEEDS!
THEN, BEFORE THE STARTLED EYES OF THE RED HORDES, TWO ELECTRONICALLY-POWERED ARMS SEIZE WONG-CHU, LIFTING HIM EASILY AS THEY WOULD A TOY!
YOU ARE NOT FACING A WOUNDED, DYING MAN NOW...
--OR AN AGED, GENTLE PROFESSOR!
THIS IS IRON MAN WHO OPPOSES YOU, AND ALL YOU STAND FOR!
10

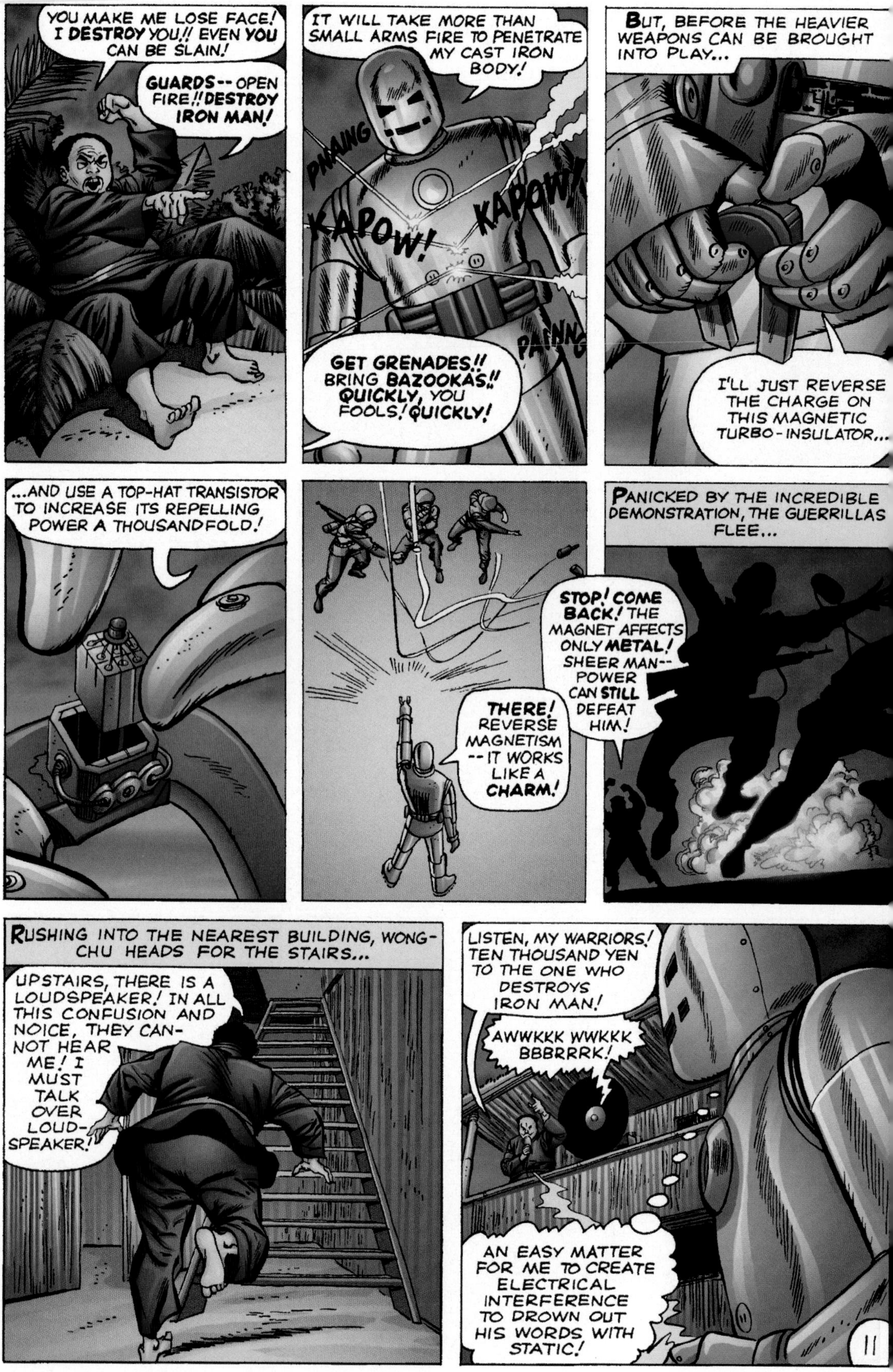
YOU MAKE ME LOSE FACE! I DESTROY YOU!! EVEN YOU CAN BE SLAIN!
GUARDS--OPEN FIRE!! DESTROY IRON MAN!
IT WILL TAKE MORE THAN SMALL ARMS FIRE TO PENETRATE MY CAST IRON BODY!
PWAING
KAPOW!
KAPOW!
PWING
GET GRENADES!! BRING BAZOOKAS!! QUICKLY, YOU FOOLS! QUICKLY!
BUT, BEFORE THE HEAVIER WEAPONS CAN BE BROUGHT INTO PLAY...
I'LL JUST REVERSE THE CHARGE ON THIS MAGNETIC TURBO-INSULATOR...
...AND USE A TOP-HAT TRANSISTOR TO INCREASE ITS REPELLING POWER A THOUSANDFOLD!
THERE! REVERSE MAGNETISM--IT WORKS LIKE A CHARM!
PANICKED BY THE INCREDIBLE DEMONSTRATION, THE GUERRILLAS FLEE...
STOP! COME BACK! THE MAGNET AFFECTS ONLY METAL! SHEER MAN-POWER CAN STILL DEFEAT HIM!
RUSHING INTO THE NEAREST BUILDING, WONG-CHU HEADS FOR THE STAIRS...
UPSTAIRS, THERE IS A LOUDSPEAKER! IN ALL THIS CONFUSION AND NOICE, THEY CAN-NOT HEAR ME! I MUST TALK OVER LOUD-SPEAKER!
LISTEN, MY WARRIORS! TEN THOUSAND YEN TO THE ONE WHO DESTROYS IRON MAN!
AWWKKK WWKKK BBBRRRK!
AN EASY MATTER FOR ME TO CREATE ELECTRICAL INTERFERENCE TO DROWN OUT HIS WORDS WITH STATIC!
11

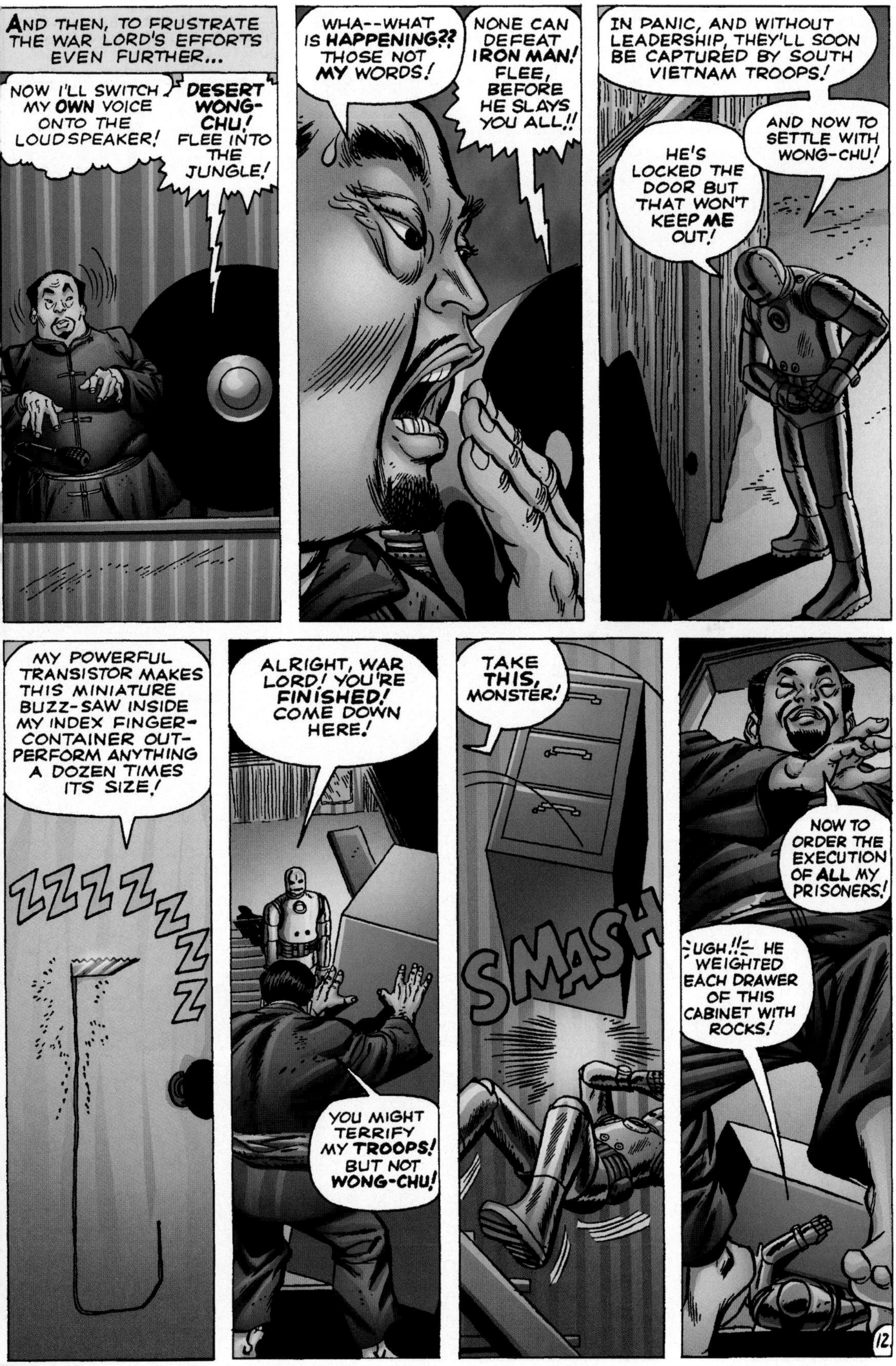
AND THEN, TO FRUSTRATE THE WAR LORD'S EFFORTS EVEN FURTHER...
NOW I'LL SWITCH MY OWN VOICE ONTO THE LOUDSPEAKER!
DESERT WONG-CHU! FLEE INTO THE JUNGLE!
WHA--WHAT IS HAPPENING?? THOSE NOT MY WORDS!
NONE CAN DEFEAT IRON MAN! FLEE, BEFORE HE SLAYS YOU ALL!!
IN PANIC, AND WITHOUT LEADERSHIP, THEY'LL SOON BE CAPTURED BY SOUTH VIETNAM TROOPS!
AND NOW TO SETTLE WITH WONG-CHU!
HE'S LOCKED THE DOOR BUT THAT WON'T KEEP ME OUT!
MY POWERFUL TRANSISTOR MAKES THIS MINIATURE BUZZ-SAW INSIDE MY INDEX FINGER-CONTAINER OUT-PERFORM ANYTHING A DOZEN TIMES ITS SIZE!
ZZZZZZZZ
ALRIGHT, WAR LORD! YOU'RE FINISHED! COME DOWN HERE!
YOU MIGHT TERRIFY MY TROOPS! BUT NOT WONG-CHU!
TAKE THIS, MONSTER!
SMASH
NOW TO ORDER THE EXECUTION OF ALL MY PRISONERS!
UGH!! HE WEIGHTED EACH DRAWER OF THIS CABINET WITH ROCKS!
12

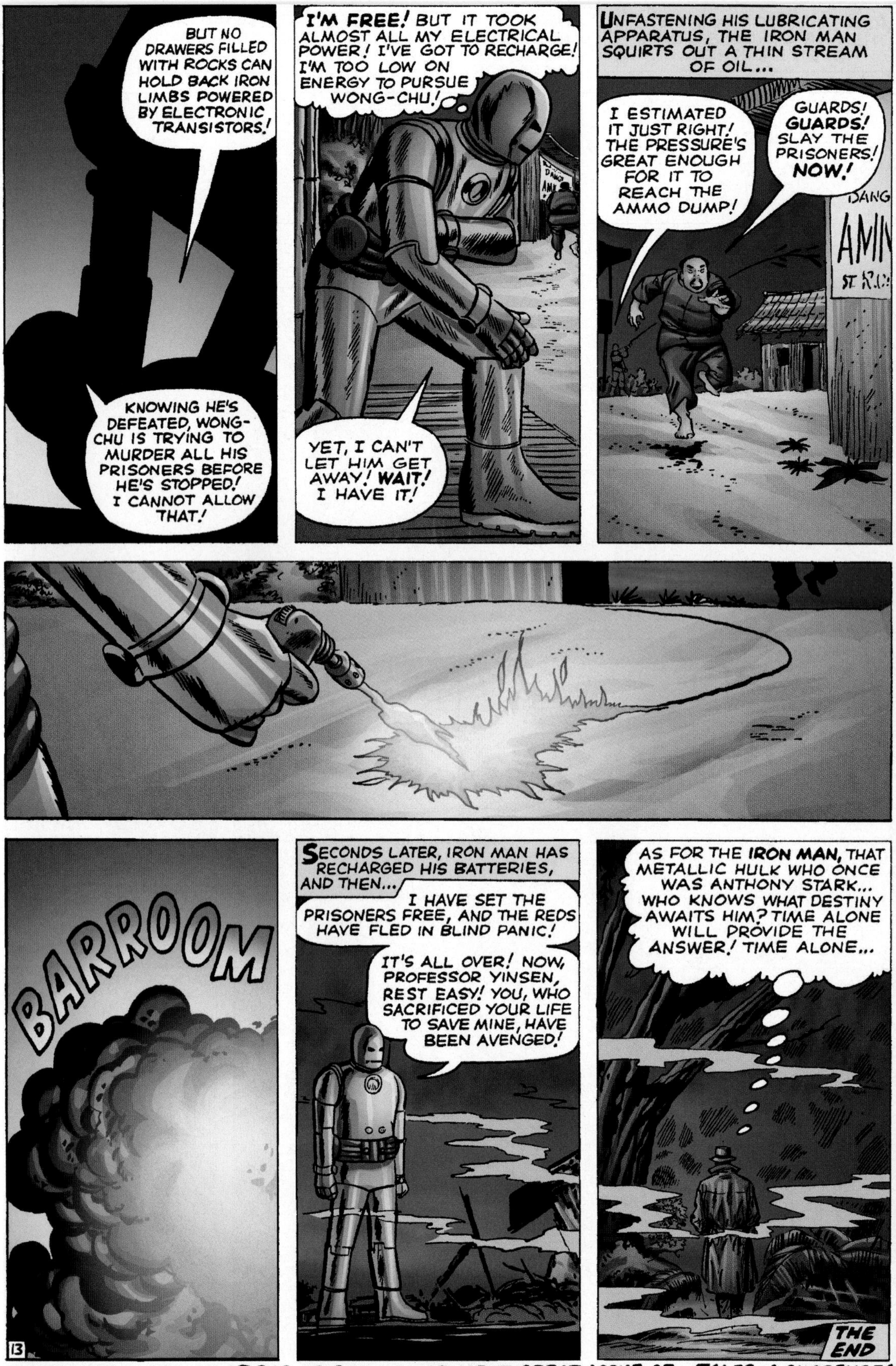
BUT NO DRAWERS FILLED WITH ROCKS CAN HOLD BACK IRON LIMBS POWERED BY ELECTRONIC TRANSISTORS!
KNOWING HE'S DEFEATED, WONG-CHU IS TRYING TO MURDER ALL HIS PRISONERS BEFORE HE'S STOPPED! I CANNOT ALLOW THAT!
I'M FREE! BUT IT TOOK ALMOST ALL MY ELECTRICAL POWER! I'VE GOT TO RECHARGE! I'M TOO LOW ON ENERGY TO PURSUE WONG-CHU!
YET, I CAN'T LET HIM GET AWAY! WAIT! I HAVE IT!
UNFASTENING HIS LUBRICATING APPARATUS, THE IRON MAN SQUIRTS OUT A THIN STREAM OF OIL...
I ESTIMATED IT JUST RIGHT! THE PRESSURE'S GREAT ENOUGH FOR IT TO REACH THE AMMO DUMP!
GUARDS! GUARDS! SLAY THE PRISONERS! NOW!
BARROOM
SECONDS LATER, IRON MAN HAS RECHARGED HIS BATTERIES, AND THEN...
I HAVE SET THE PRISONERS FREE, AND THE REDS HAVE FLED IN BLIND PANIC!
IT'S ALL OVER! NOW, PROFESSOR YINSEN, REST EASY! YOU, WHO SACRIFICED YOUR LIFE TO SAVE MINE, HAVE BEEN AVENGED!
AS FOR THE IRON MAN, THAT METALLIC HULK WHO ONCE WAS ANTHONY STARK... WHO KNOWS WHAT DESTINY AWAITS HIM? TIME ALONE WILL PROVIDE THE ANSWER! TIME ALONE...
THE END

DON'T MISS MORE OF *IRON MAN* IN THE NEXT GREAT ISSUE OF... *TALES of SUSPENSE!*

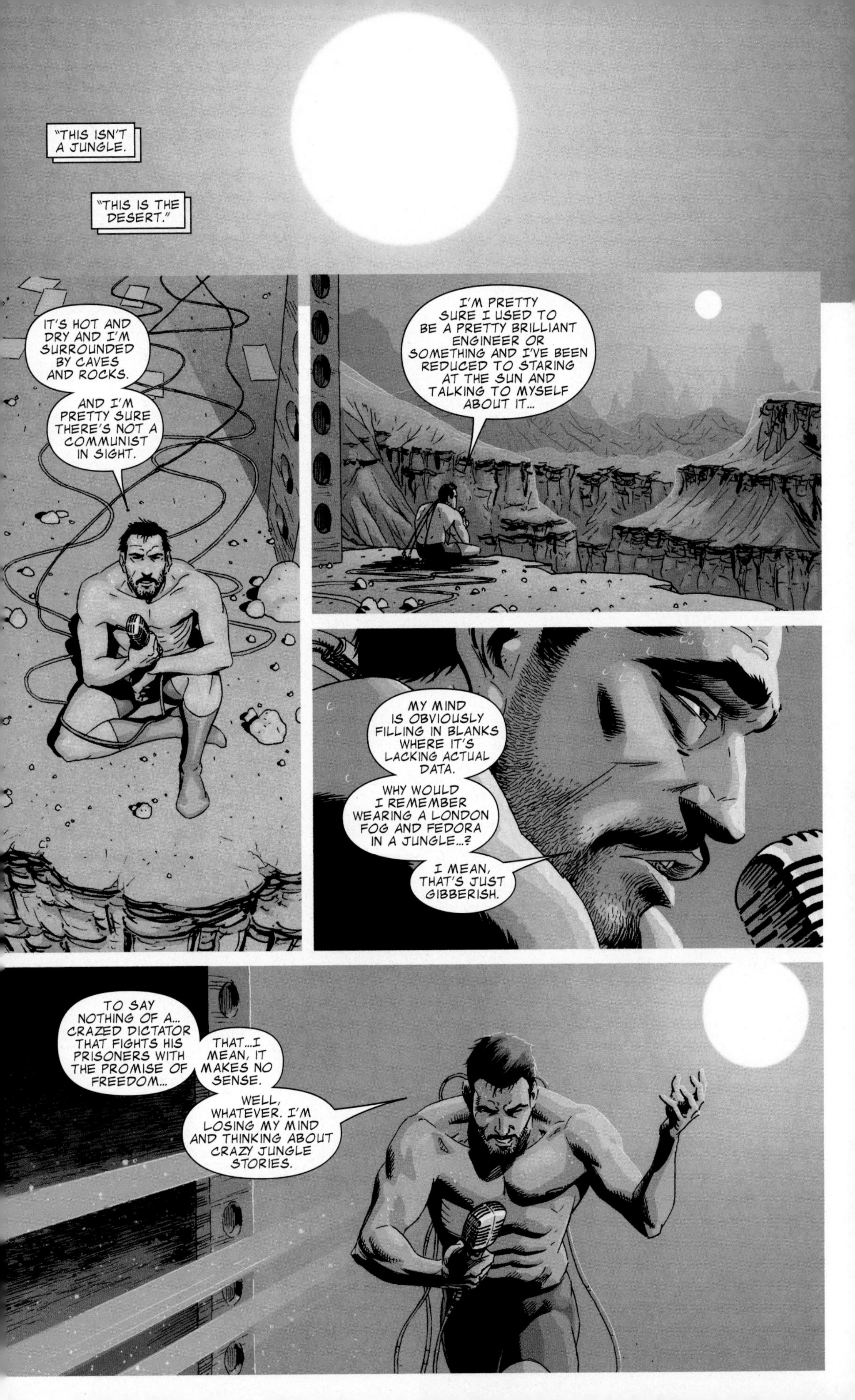
"THIS ISN'T A JUNGLE.
"THIS IS THE DESERT."
IT'S HOT AND DRY AND I'M SURROUNDED BY CAVES AND ROCKS.
AND I'M PRETTY SURE THERE'S NOT A COMMUNIST IN SIGHT.
I'M PRETTY SURE I USED TO BE A PRETTY BRILLIANT ENGINEER OR SOMETHING AND I'VE BEEN REDUCED TO STARING AT THE SUN AND TALKING TO MYSELF ABOUT IT...
MY MIND IS OBVIOUSLY FILLING IN BLANKS WHERE IT'S LACKING ACTUAL DATA.
WHY WOULD I REMEMBER WEARING A LONDON FOG AND FEDORA IN A JUNGLE...?
I MEAN, THAT'S JUST GIBBERISH.
TO SAY NOTHING OF A... CRAZED DICTATOR THAT FIGHTS HIS PRISONERS WITH THE PROMISE OF FREEDOM...
THAT...I MEAN, IT MAKES NO SENSE.
WELL, WHATEVER. I'M LOSING MY MIND AND THINKING ABOUT CRAZY JUNGLE STORIES.

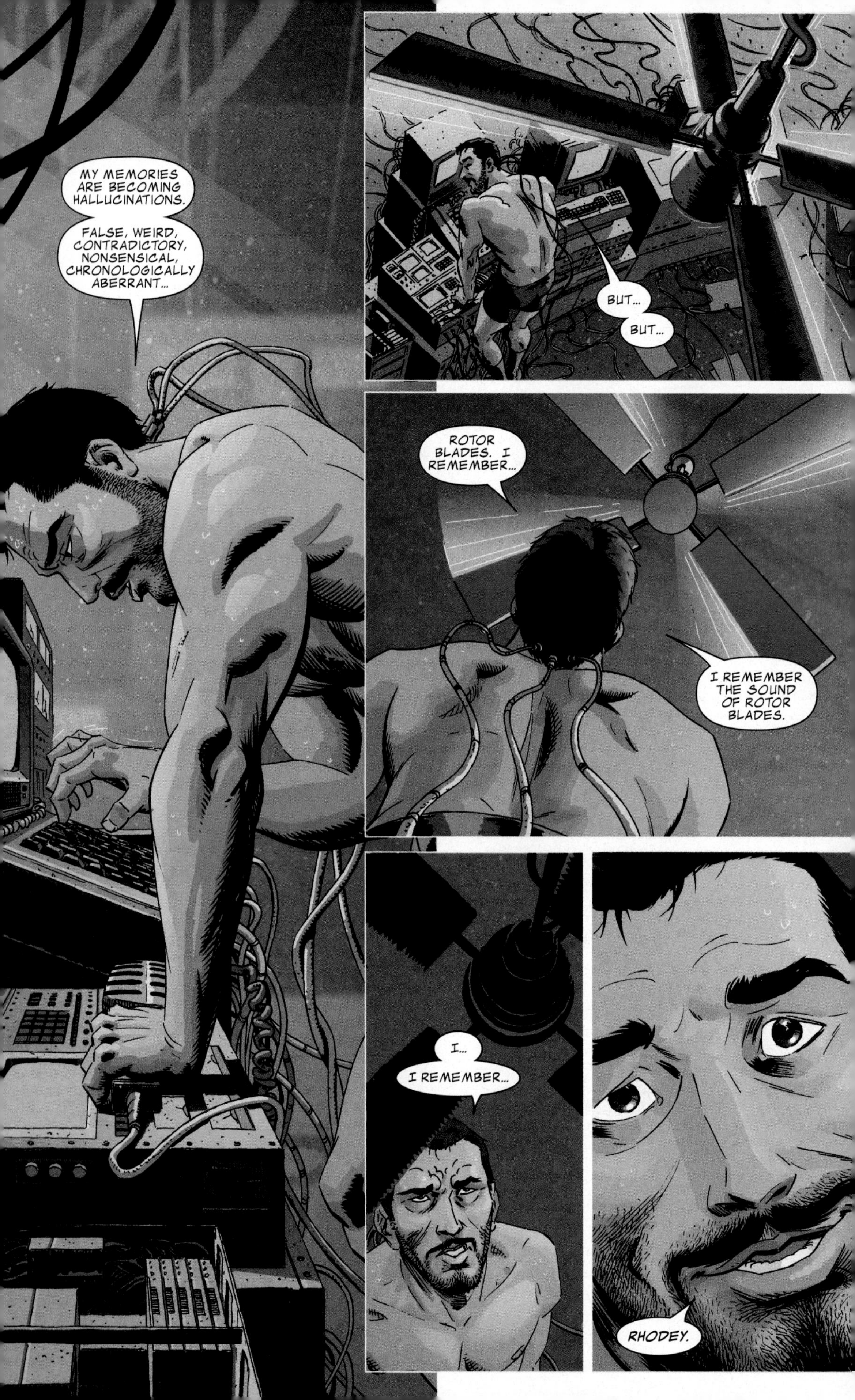
MY MEMORIES ARE BECOMING HALLUCINATIONS.
FALSE, WEIRD, CONTRADICTORY, NONSENSICAL, CHRONOLOGICALLY ABERRANT...
BUT...
BUT...
ROTOR BLADES. I REMEMBER...
I REMEMBER THE SOUND OF ROTOR BLADES.
I...
I REMEMBER...
RHODEY.

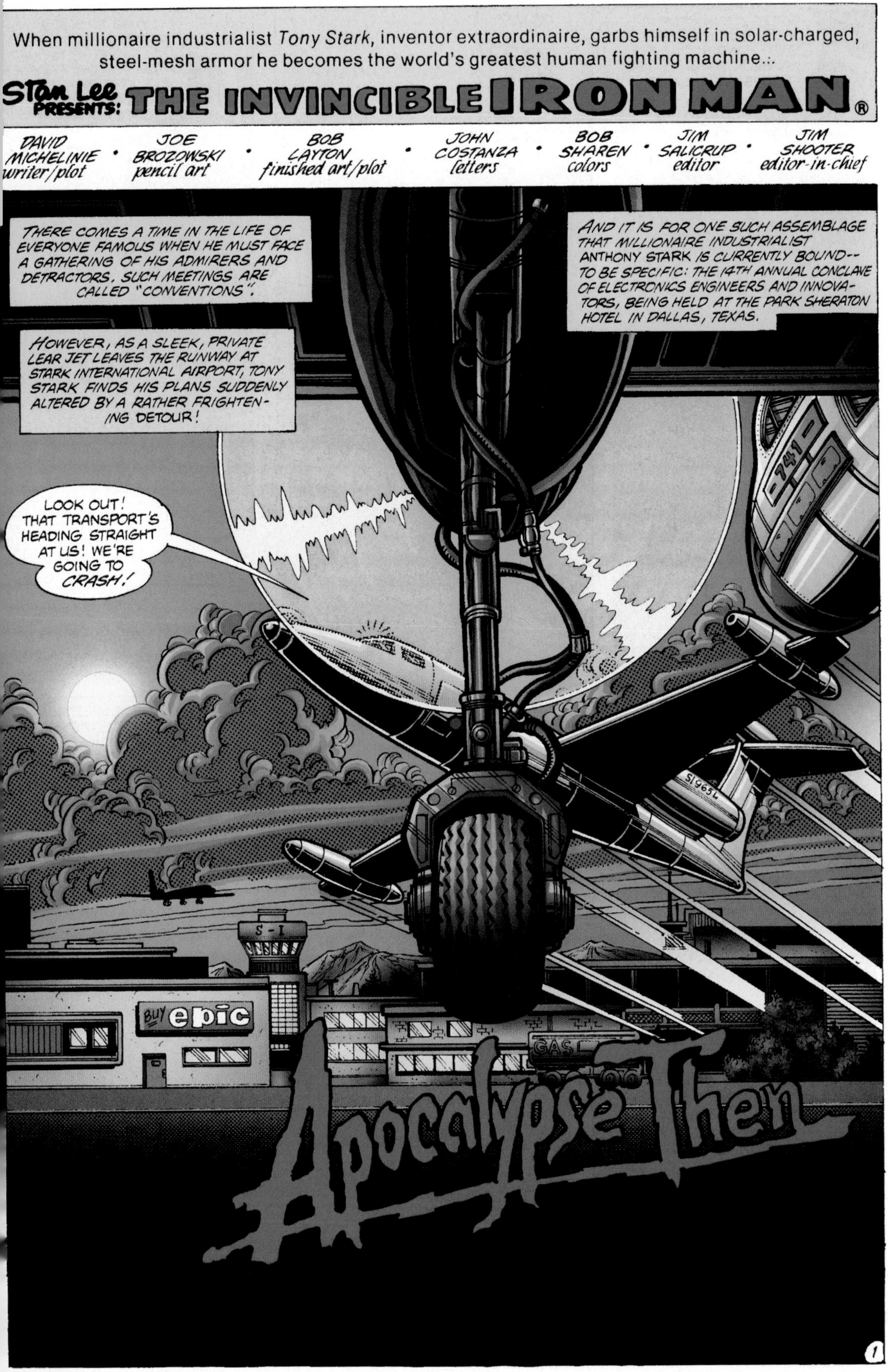
When millionaire industrialist *Tony Stark*, inventor extraordinaire, garbs himself in solar-charged, steel-mesh armor he becomes the world's greatest human fighting machine...
STAN LEE PRESENTS: THE INVINCIBLE IRON MAN®
DAVID MICHELINIE writer/plot • JOE BROZOWSKI pencil art • BOB LAYTON finished art/plot • JOHN COSTANZA letters • BOB SHAREN colors • JIM SALICRUP editor • JIM SHOOTER editor-in-chief
THERE COMES A TIME IN THE LIFE OF EVERYONE FAMOUS WHEN HE MUST FACE A GATHERING OF HIS ADMIRERS AND DETRACTORS. SUCH MEETINGS ARE CALLED "CONVENTIONS".
AND IT IS FOR ONE SUCH ASSEMBLAGE THAT MILLIONAIRE INDUSTRIALIST ANTHONY STARK IS CURRENTLY BOUND-- TO BE SPECIFIC: THE 14TH ANNUAL CONCLAVE OF ELECTRONICS ENGINEERS AND INNOVATORS, BEING HELD AT THE PARK SHERATON HOTEL IN DALLAS, TEXAS.
HOWEVER, AS A SLEEK, PRIVATE LEAR JET LEAVES THE RUNWAY AT STARK INTERNATIONAL AIRPORT, TONY STARK FINDS HIS PLANS SUDDENLY ALTERED BY A RATHER FRIGHTENING DETOUR!
LOOK OUT! THAT TRANSPORT'S HEADING STRAIGHT AT US! WE'RE GOING TO CRASH!
741
SI965L
S-I
BUY epic
GAS
Apocalypse Then
1

NOT IF I CAN HELP IT, CHIEF! BUT YOU'D BETTER START HANDIN' OUT THE AIRSICK BAGS, 'CAUSE THIS IS GONNA BE--

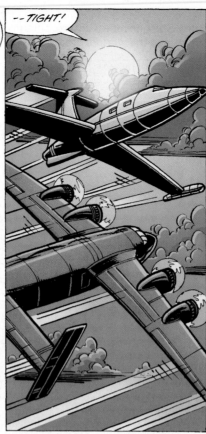

--TIGHT!

;G...G... GULP!;

TOWER TO S.I.-1. SORRY ABOUT THAT LITTLE MIX-UP. WE HAD A TEMPORARY PROBLEM WITH OUR GROUND CONTROL READOUT. GLAD NO ONE WAS HURT.

YOU'LL PROBABLY HAVE TO MAKE A STATEMENT TO AN F.A.A. HEARING WHEN YOU GET BACK, THOUGH.

I GOT A STATEMENT I'D LIKE TO MAKE RIGHT NOW, DUDE, 'CEPT IT'D PRO-BABLY MELT YOUR EARPHONES!

UH, RIGHT. TOWER OUT!

RHODEY, HAVE I EVER TOLD YOU THAT YOUR FLYING SKILLS MAKE WALDO PEPPER LOOK LIKE A KID WITH A KITE?

Y'MEAN THIS WEEK?

SERIOUSLY, JIM, I SOMETIMES THINK YOU COULD FLY THE PANTS OFF OF IRON MAN HIMSELF. AND AS FOR HAVING JUST SAVED MY LIFE--

2

SAY, BOSS, FORGET IT. I WAS JUST DOIN' MY JOB.

BUT, SETTLING BACK INTO THE CRUSHED VELOUR OF THE SEAT CUSHION, TONY STARK KNOWS THAT LIFE-SAVING IS NOT A PART OF HIS PILOT'S SALARIED DUTIES. FOR IF IT HAD BEEN--

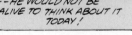

--HE WOULD NOT BE ALIVE TO THINK ABOUT IT TODAY!

THE GLEAMING-NEW LEAR JET SHOOTS SOUTH-WARDS THROUGH THE AFTERNOON SKY, AND THE RELAXING INVENTOR FINDS HIS MIND FILING BACKWARDS, SIFTING THROUGH MEMORIES--

--ARRIVING FINALLY AT SOUTHEAST ASIA DURING THE VIETNAMESE WAR, WHERE HE HAD COME TO TEST HIS THEORIES OF REVERSE MAGNETISM WITH NEW AMERICAN ORDNANCE...

...AND HAD INSTEAD FALLEN VICTIM TO ONE OF THE VIET CONG'S OLDEST WEAPONS, THE BOOBY-TRAPPED MINE...

WHRAAWWWW

...ONE THAT HAD LEFT A PIECE OF SHRAPNEL LODGED DANGEROUSLY CLOSE TO HIS HEART.

3

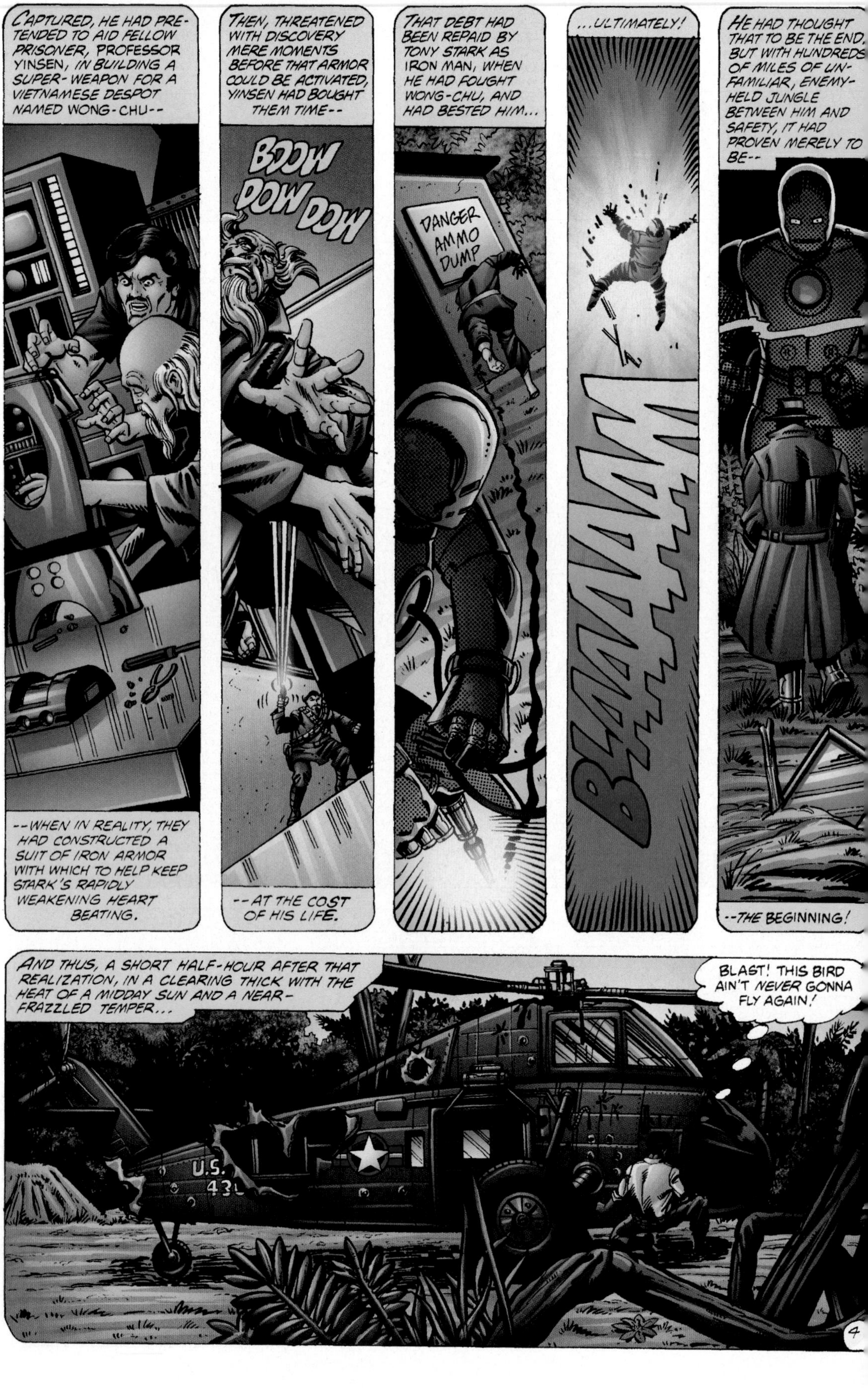
CAPTURED, HE HAD PRETENDED TO AID FELLOW PRISONER, PROFESSOR YINSEN, IN BUILDING A SUPER-WEAPON FOR A VIETNAMESE DESPOT NAMED WONG-CHU--
--WHEN IN REALITY, THEY HAD CONSTRUCTED A SUIT OF IRON ARMOR WITH WHICH TO HELP KEEP STARK'S RAPIDLY WEAKENING HEART BEATING.
THEN, THREATENED WITH DISCOVERY MERE MOMENTS BEFORE THAT ARMOR COULD BE ACTIVATED, YINSEN HAD BOUGHT THEM TIME--
BDOW DOW DOW
--AT THE COST OF HIS LIFE.
THAT DEBT HAD BEEN REPAID BY TONY STARK AS IRON MAN, WHEN HE HAD FOUGHT WONG-CHU, AND HAD BESTED HIM...
DANGER AMMO DUMP
...ULTIMATELY!
BLAAAAM
HE HAD THOUGHT THAT TO BE THE END. BUT WITH HUNDREDS OF MILES OF UNFAMILIAR, ENEMY-HELD JUNGLE BETWEEN HIM AND SAFETY, IT HAD PROVEN MERELY TO BE--
--THE BEGINNING!
AND THUS, A SHORT HALF-HOUR AFTER THAT REALIZATION, IN A CLEARING THICK WITH THE HEAT OF A MIDDAY SUN AND A NEAR-FRAZZLED TEMPER...
BLAST! THIS BIRD AIN'T NEVER GONNA FLY AGAIN!
U.S.
43

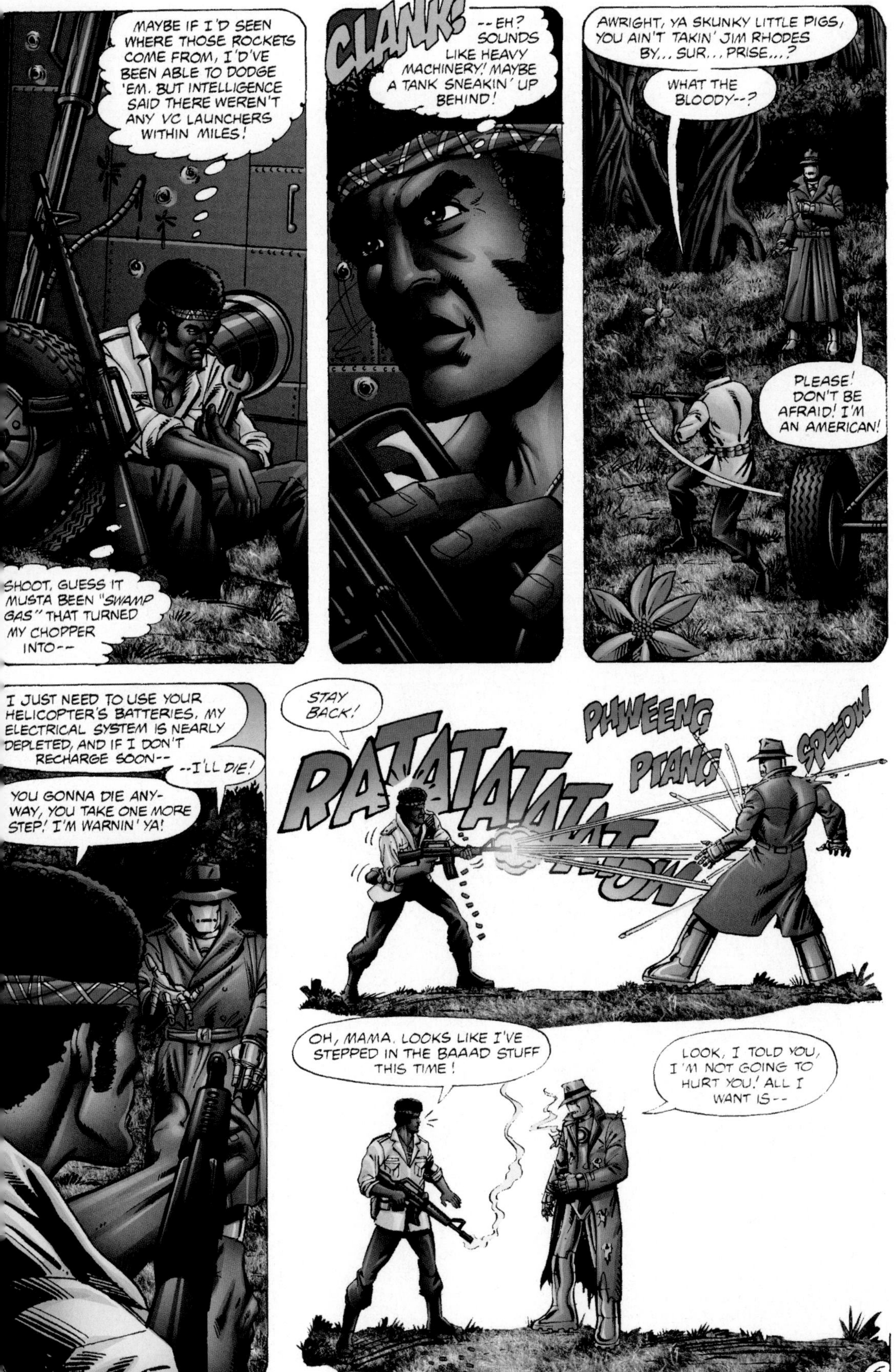

MAYBE IF I'D SEEN WHERE THOSE ROCKETS COME FROM, I'D'VE BEEN ABLE TO DODGE 'EM. BUT INTELLIGENCE SAID THERE WEREN'T ANY VC LAUNCHERS WITHIN MILES!
SHOOT, GUESS IT MUSTA BEEN "SWAMP GAS" THAT TURNED MY CHOPPER INTO--
CLANK!
--EH? SOUNDS LIKE HEAVY MACHINERY! MAYBE A TANK SNEAKIN' UP BEHIND!
AWRIGHT, YA SKUNKY LITTLE PIGS, YOU AIN'T TAKIN' JIM RHODES BY... SUR... PRISE...?
WHAT THE BLOODY--?
PLEASE! DON'T BE AFRAID! I'M AN AMERICAN!
I JUST NEED TO USE YOUR HELICOPTER'S BATTERIES. MY ELECTRICAL SYSTEM IS NEARLY DEPLETED, AND IF I DON'T RECHARGE SOON--
--I'LL DIE!
YOU GONNA DIE ANYWAY, YOU TAKE ONE MORE STEP! I'M WARNIN' YA!
STAY BACK!
RATATATATATATOW
PHWEENG
PTANG
SPEEOW
OH, MAMA. LOOKS LIKE I'VE STEPPED IN THE BAAAD STUFF THIS TIME!
LOOK, I TOLD YOU, I'M NOT GOING TO HURT YOU! ALL I WANT IS--

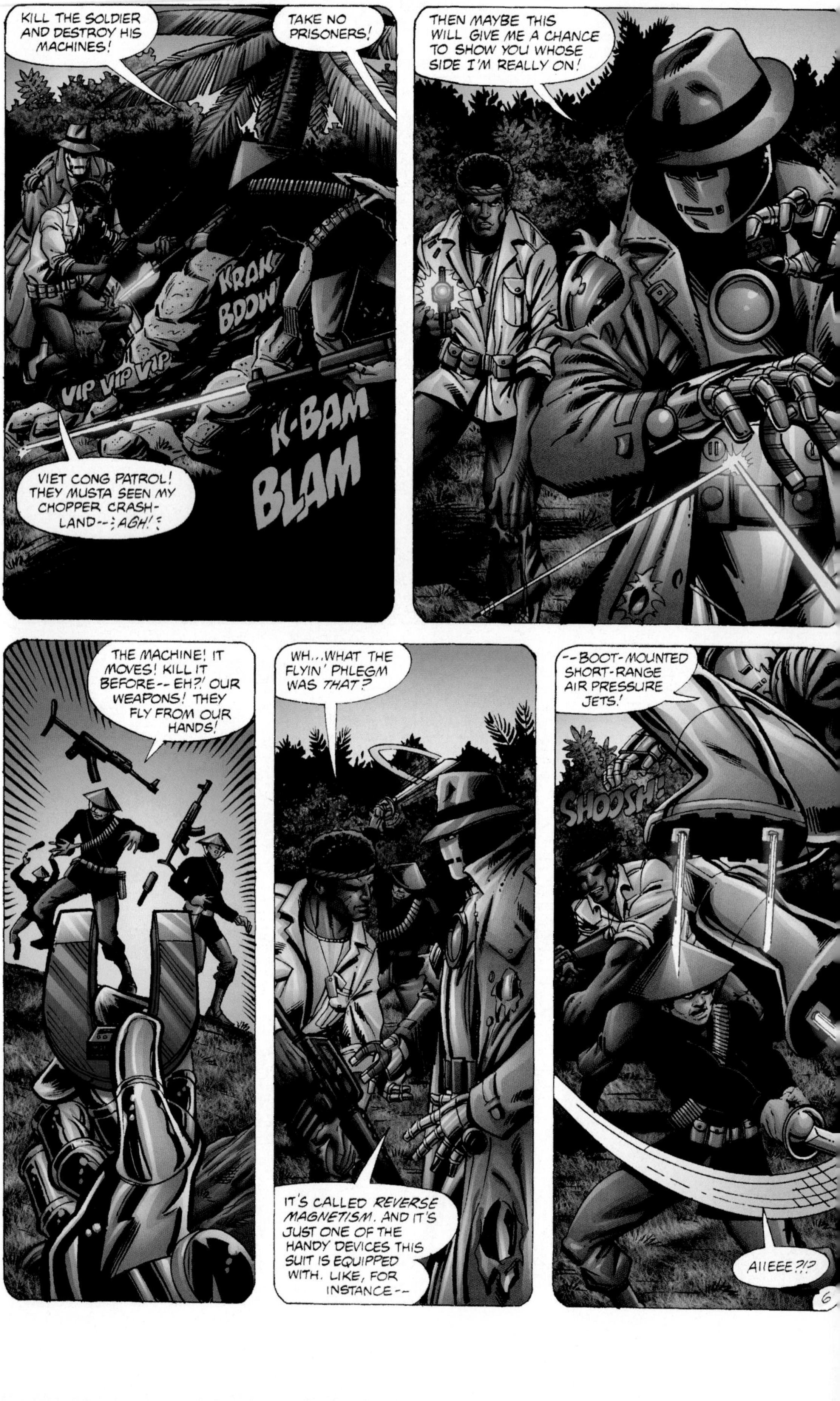

KILL THE SOLDIER AND DESTROY HIS MACHINES!
TAKE NO PRISONERS!
KRAK BOOM
VIP VIP VIP
K-BAM BLAM
VIET CONG PATROL! THEY MUSTA SEEN MY CHOPPER CRASH-LAND-- AGH!
THEN MAYBE THIS WILL GIVE ME A CHANCE TO SHOW YOU WHOSE SIDE I'M REALLY ON!
THE MACHINE! IT MOVES! KILL IT BEFORE-- EH?! OUR WEAPONS! THEY FLY FROM OUR HANDS!
WH...WHAT THE FLYIN' PHLEGM WAS THAT?
IT'S CALLED REVERSE MAGNETISM. AND IT'S JUST ONE OF THE HANDY DEVICES THIS SUIT IS EQUIPPED WITH. LIKE, FOR INSTANCE--
--BOOT-MOUNTED SHORT-RANGE AIR PRESSURE JETS!
SHOOSH!
AIIEEE?!?

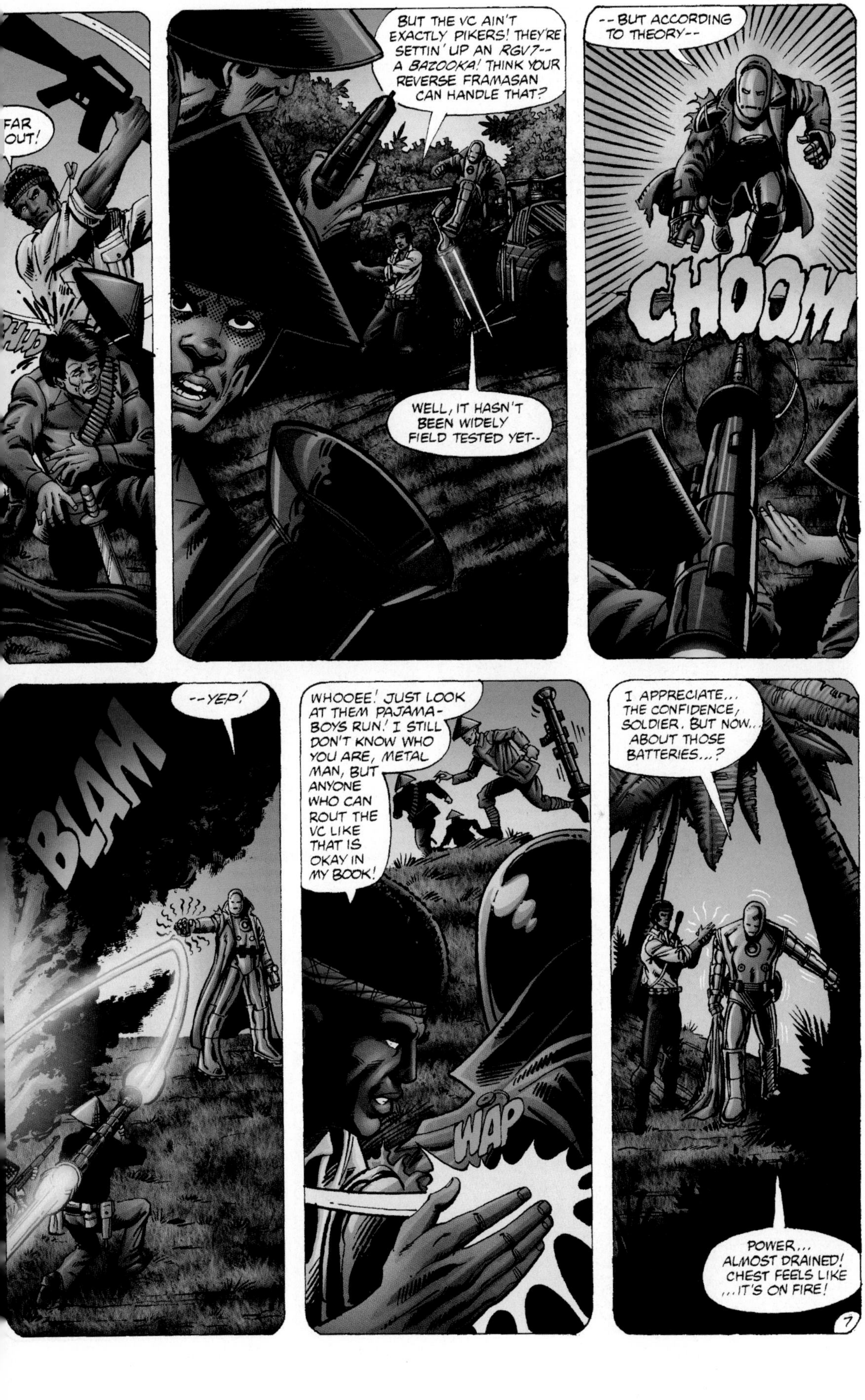
FAR OUT!
BUT THE VC AIN'T EXACTLY PIKERS! THEY'RE SETTIN' UP AN RGV7-- A BAZOOKA! THINK YOUR REVERSE FRAMASAN CAN HANDLE THAT?
WELL, IT HASN'T BEEN WIDELY FIELD TESTED YET--
-- BUT ACCORDING TO THEORY--
CHOOM
BLAM
--YEP!
WHOOEE! JUST LOOK AT THEM PAJAMA-BOYS RUN! I STILL DON'T KNOW WHO YOU ARE, METAL MAN, BUT ANYONE WHO CAN ROUT THE VC LIKE THAT IS OKAY IN MY BOOK!
WAP
I APPRECIATE... THE CONFIDENCE, SOLDIER. BUT NOW... ABOUT THOSE BATTERIES...?
POWER... ALMOST DRAINED! CHEST FEELS LIKE ...IT'S ON FIRE!

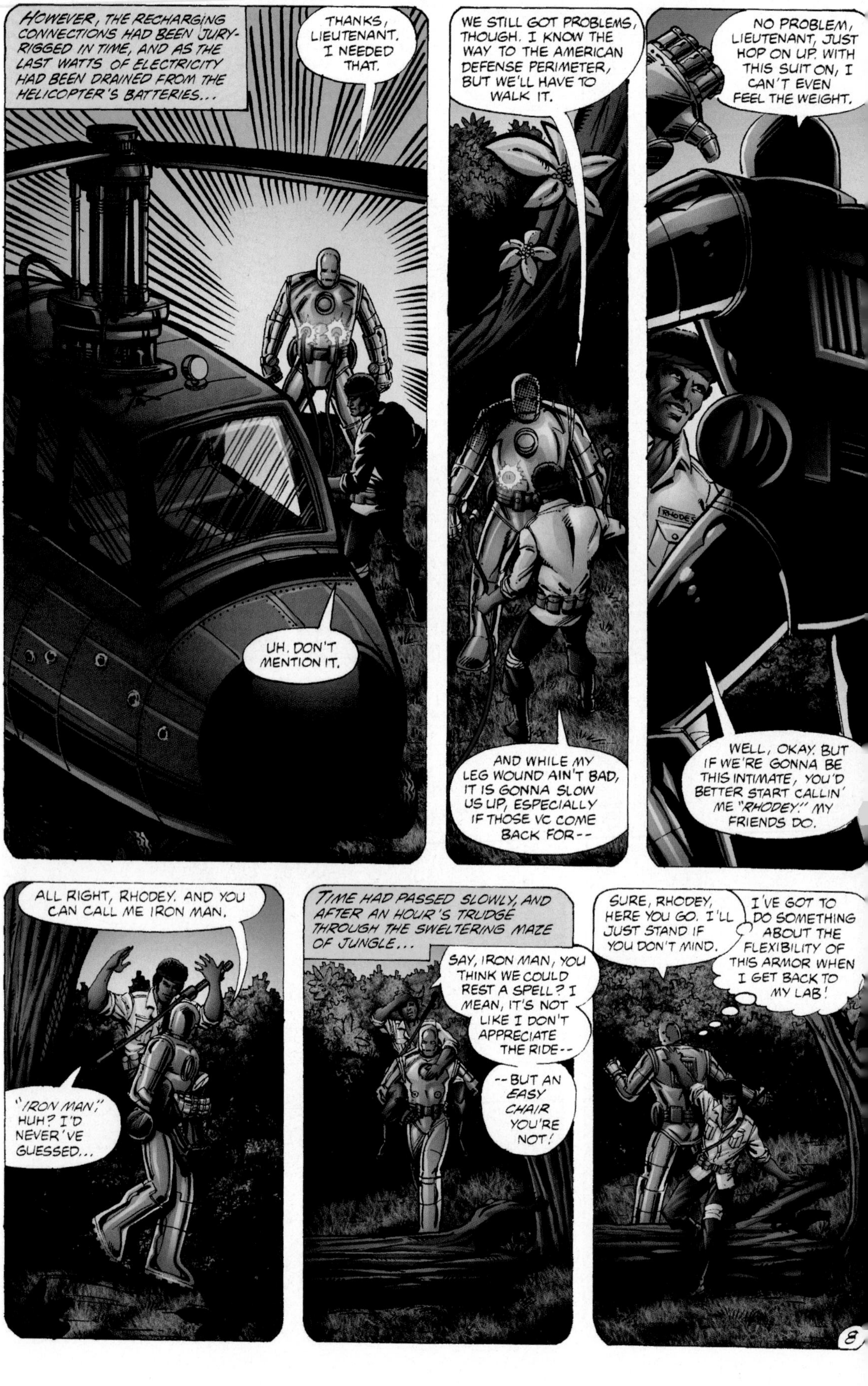
HOWEVER, THE RECHARGING CONNECTIONS HAD BEEN JURY-RIGGED IN TIME, AND AS THE LAST WATTS OF ELECTRICITY HAD BEEN DRAINED FROM THE HELICOPTER'S BATTERIES...
THANKS, LIEUTENANT. I NEEDED THAT.
UH. DON'T MENTION IT.
WE STILL GOT PROBLEMS, THOUGH. I KNOW THE WAY TO THE AMERICAN DEFENSE PERIMETER, BUT WE'LL HAVE TO WALK IT.
AND WHILE MY LEG WOUND AIN'T BAD, IT IS GONNA SLOW US UP, ESPECIALLY IF THOSE VC COME BACK FOR--
NO PROBLEM, LIEUTENANT, JUST HOP ON UP. WITH THIS SUIT ON, I CAN'T EVEN FEEL THE WEIGHT.
RHODES
WELL, OKAY. BUT IF WE'RE GONNA BE THIS INTIMATE, YOU'D BETTER START CALLIN' ME "RHODEY." MY FRIENDS DO.
ALL RIGHT, RHODEY. AND YOU CAN CALL ME IRON MAN.
"IRON MAN," HUH? I'D NEVER'VE GUESSED...
TIME HAD PASSED SLOWLY, AND AFTER AN HOUR'S TRUDGE THROUGH THE SWELTERING MAZE OF JUNGLE...
SAY, IRON MAN, YOU THINK WE COULD REST A SPELL? I MEAN, IT'S NOT LIKE I DON'T APPRECIATE THE RIDE--
--BUT AN EASY CHAIR YOU'RE NOT!
SURE, RHODEY, HERE YOU GO. I'LL JUST STAND IF YOU DON'T MIND.
I'VE GOT TO DO SOMETHING ABOUT THE FLEXIBILITY OF THIS ARMOR WHEN I GET BACK TO MY LAB!
8

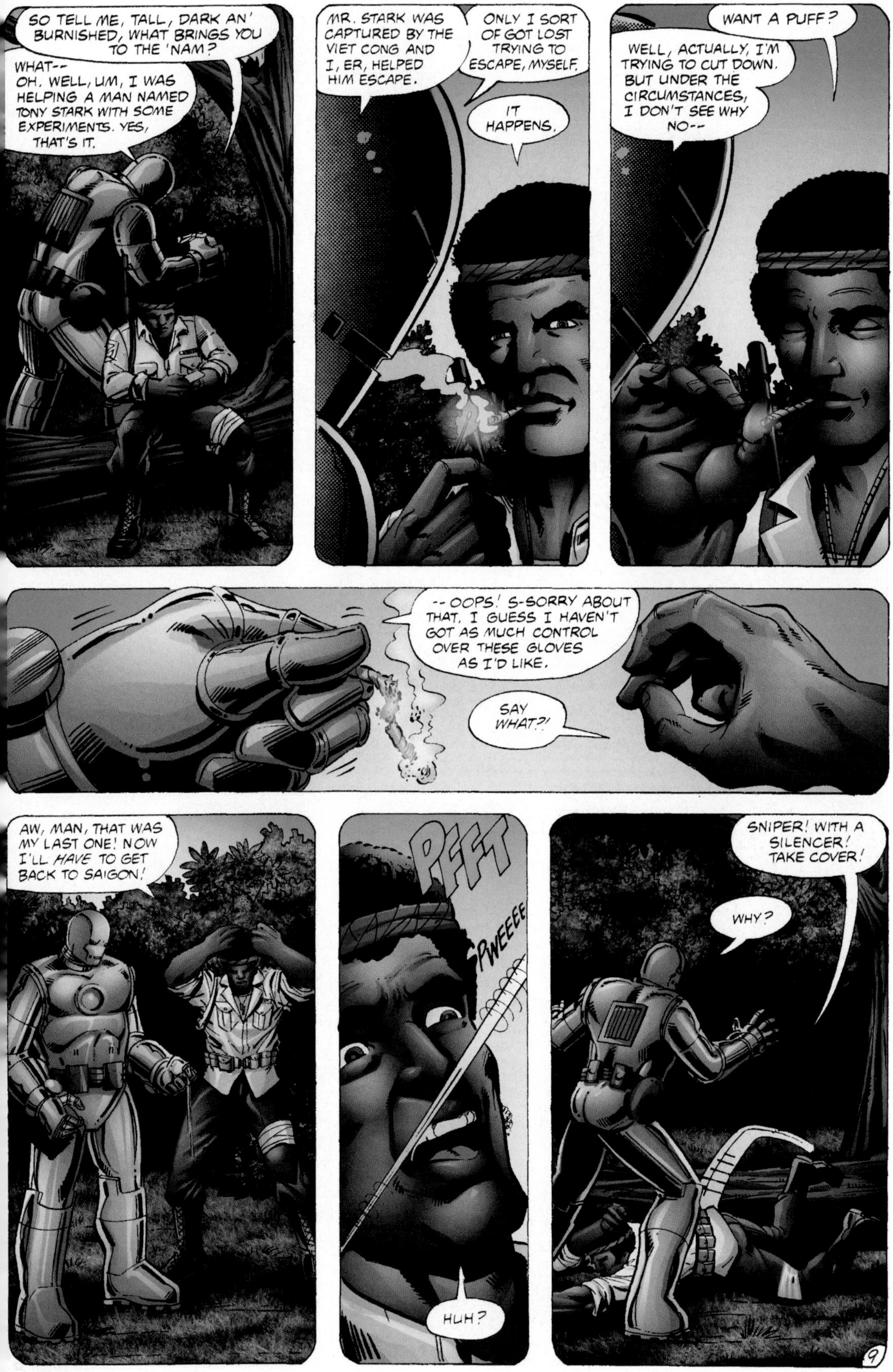
SO TELL ME, TALL, DARK AN' BURNISHED, WHAT BRINGS YOU TO THE 'NAM?
WHAT-- OH. WELL, UM, I WAS HELPING A MAN NAMED TONY STARK WITH SOME EXPERIMENTS. YES, THAT'S IT.
MR. STARK WAS CAPTURED BY THE VIET CONG AND I, ER, HELPED HIM ESCAPE.
ONLY I SORT OF GOT LOST TRYING TO ESCAPE, MYSELF.
IT HAPPENS.
WANT A PUFF?
WELL, ACTUALLY, I'M TRYING TO CUT DOWN. BUT UNDER THE CIRCUMSTANCES, I DON'T SEE WHY NO--
-- OOPS! S-SORRY ABOUT THAT. I GUESS I HAVEN'T GOT AS MUCH CONTROL OVER THESE GLOVES AS I'D LIKE.
SAY WHAT?!
AW, MAN, THAT WAS MY LAST ONE! NOW I'LL HAVE TO GET BACK TO SAIGON!
PFFT
PWEEEE
HUH?
SNIPER! WITH A SILENCER! TAKE COVER!
WHY?

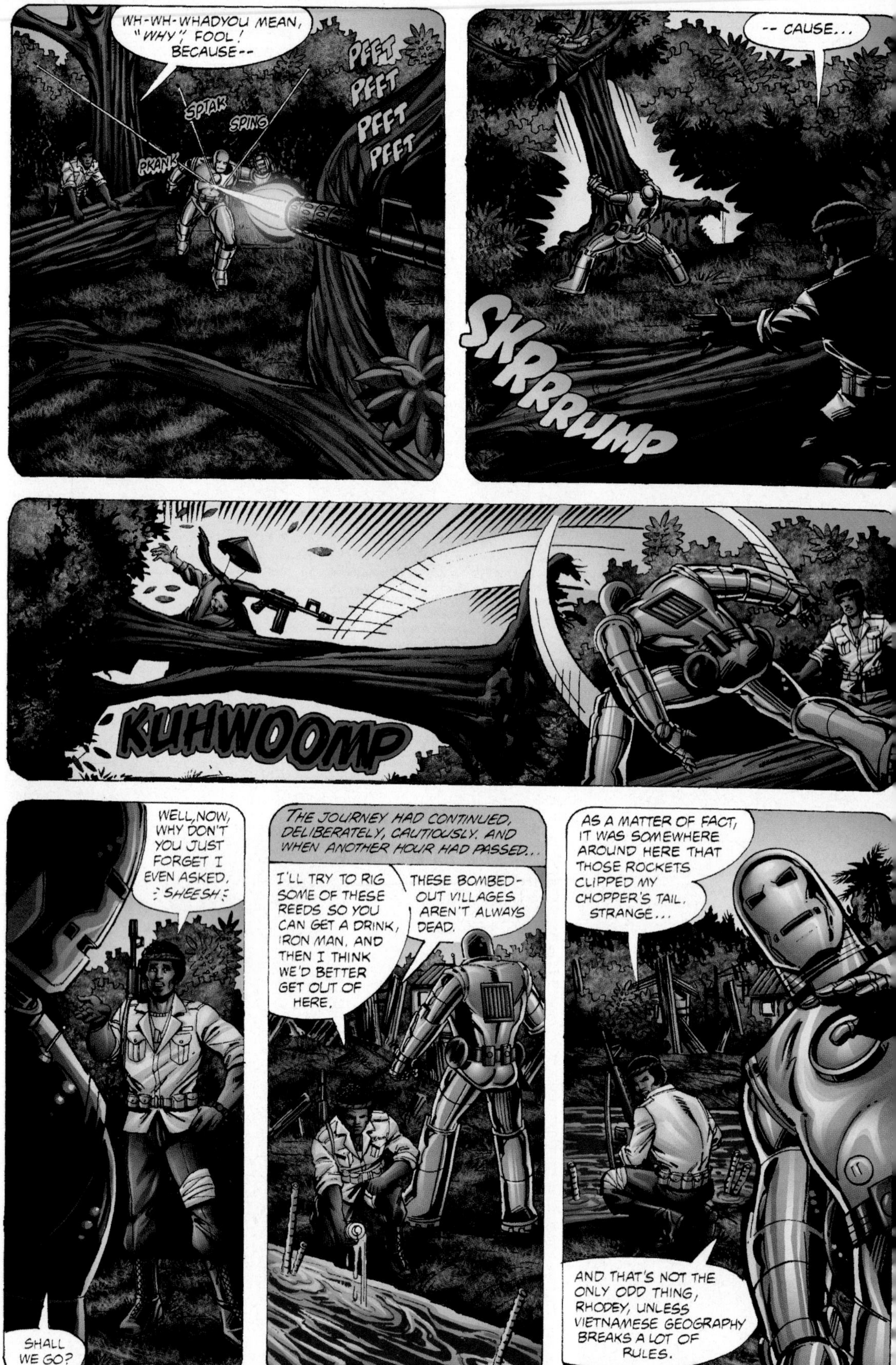
WH-WH-WHADYOU MEAN, "WHY," FOOL! BECAUSE--
SPTAK
SPING
PKANK
PFFT
PFFT
PFFT
PFFT
-- CAUSE...
SKRRRUMP
KUHWOOMP
WELL, NOW, WHY DON'T YOU JUST FORGET I EVEN ASKED. SHEESH
SHALL WE GO?
THE JOURNEY HAD CONTINUED, DELIBERATELY, CAUTIOUSLY. AND WHEN ANOTHER HOUR HAD PASSED...
I'LL TRY TO RIG SOME OF THESE REEDS SO YOU CAN GET A DRINK, IRON MAN, AND THEN I THINK WE'D BETTER GET OUT OF HERE.
THESE BOMBED-OUT VILLAGES AREN'T ALWAYS DEAD.
AS A MATTER OF FACT, IT WAS SOMEWHERE AROUND HERE THAT THOSE ROCKETS CLIPPED MY CHOPPER'S TAIL. STRANGE...
AND THAT'S NOT THE ONLY ODD THING, RHODEY, UNLESS VIETNAMESE GEOGRAPHY BREAKS A LOT OF RULES.
10

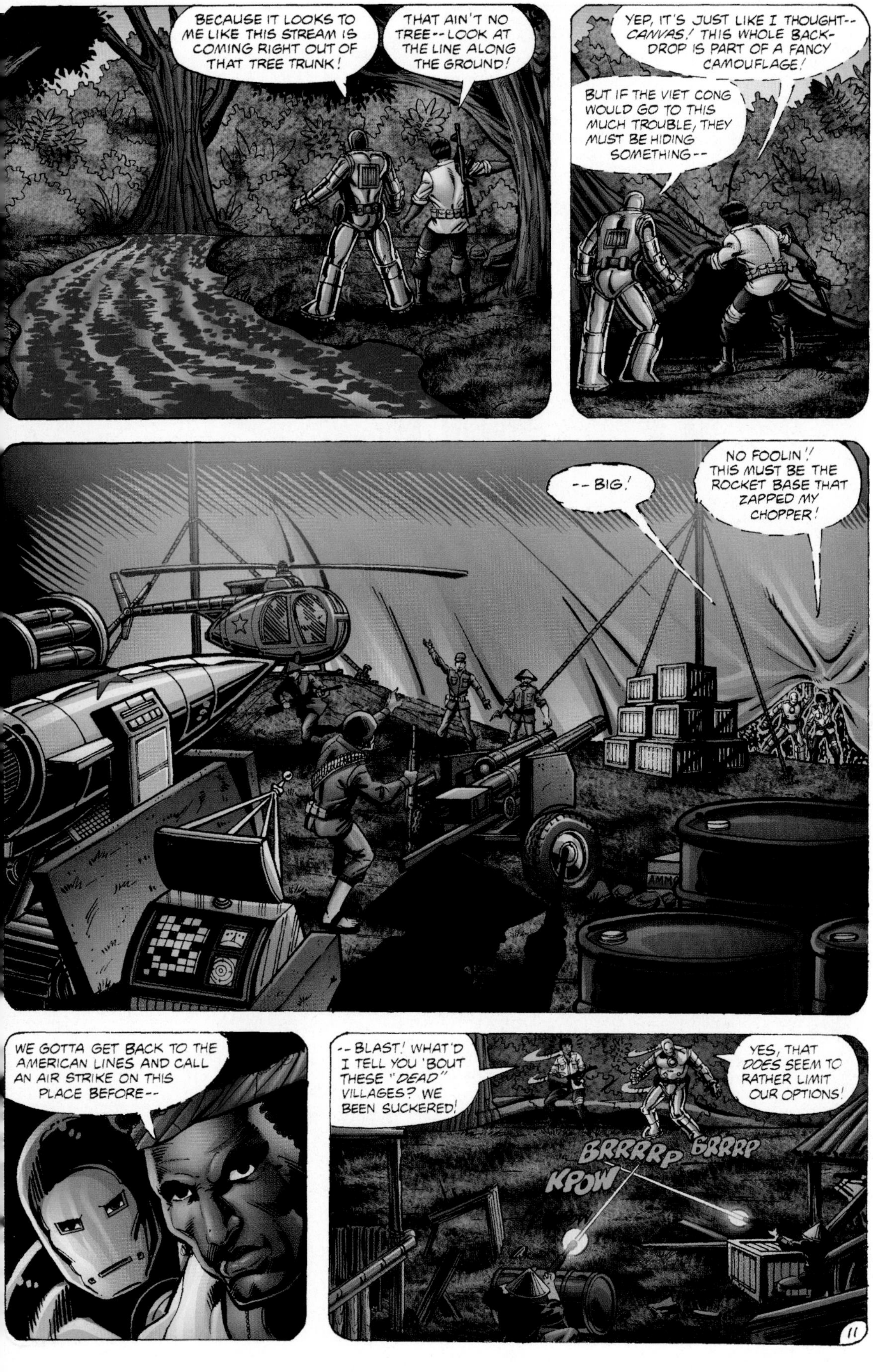

BECAUSE IT LOOKS TO ME LIKE THIS STREAM IS COMING RIGHT OUT OF THAT TREE TRUNK!
THAT AIN'T NO TREE--LOOK AT THE LINE ALONG THE GROUND!
YEP, IT'S JUST LIKE I THOUGHT--CANVAS! THIS WHOLE BACKDROP IS PART OF A FANCY CAMOUFLAGE!
BUT IF THE VIET CONG WOULD GO TO THIS MUCH TROUBLE, THEY MUST BE HIDING SOMETHING--
--BIG!
NO FOOLIN'! THIS MUST BE THE ROCKET BASE THAT ZAPPED MY CHOPPER!
AMMO
WE GOTTA GET BACK TO THE AMERICAN LINES AND CALL AN AIR STRIKE ON THIS PLACE BEFORE--
--BLAST! WHAT'D I TELL YOU 'BOUT THESE "DEAD" VILLAGES? WE BEEN SUCKERED!
YES, THAT DOES SEEM TO RATHER LIMIT OUR OPTIONS!
BRRRRP
BRRRP
KPOW

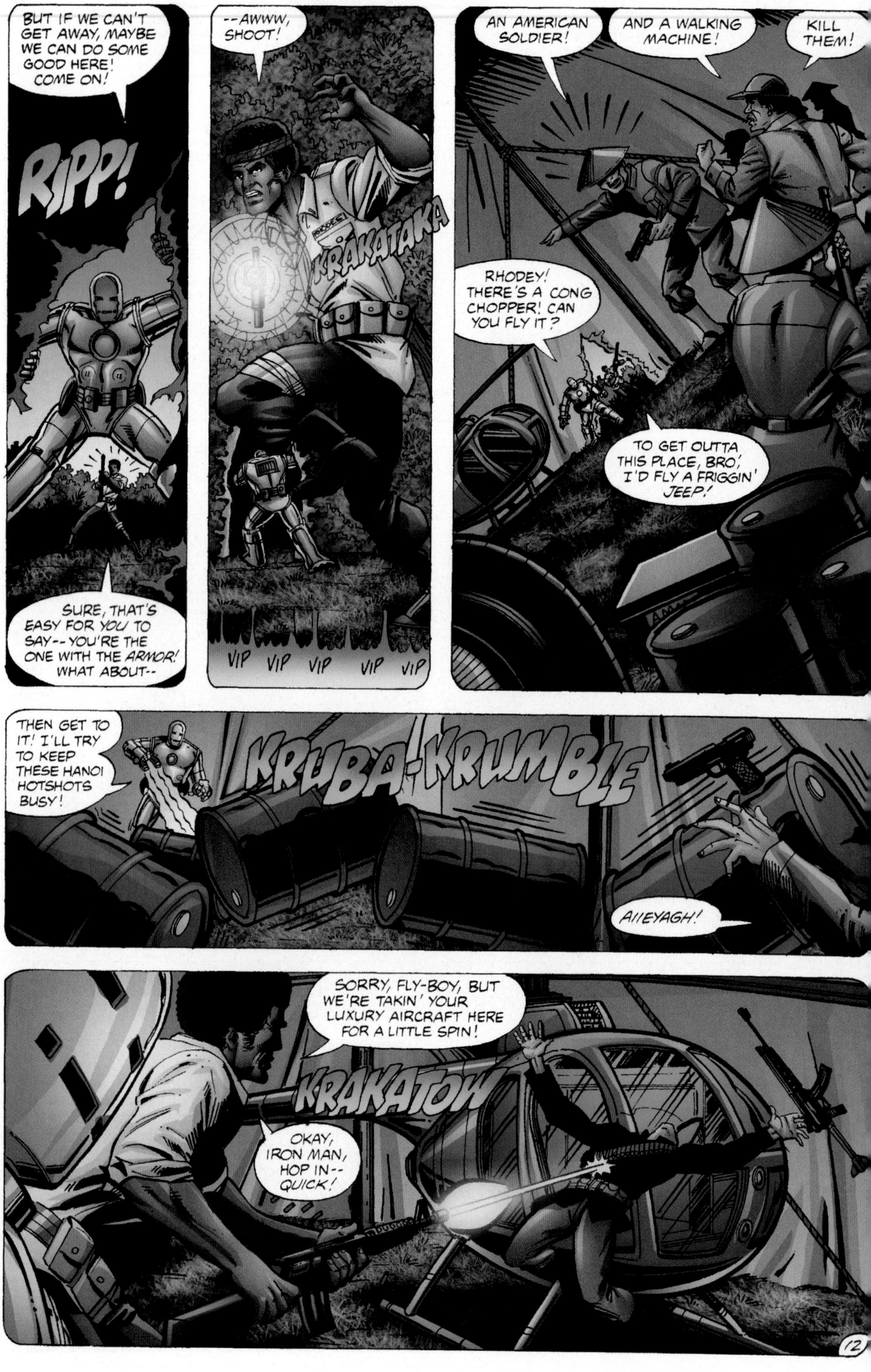

BUT IF WE CAN'T GET AWAY, MAYBE WE CAN DO SOME GOOD HERE! COME ON!
RIPP!
SURE, THAT'S EASY FOR YOU TO SAY-- YOU'RE THE ONE WITH THE ARMOR! WHAT ABOUT--
--AWWW, SHOOT!
KRAKATAKA
VIP VIP VIP VIP VIP
AN AMERICAN SOLDIER!
AND A WALKING MACHINE!
KILL THEM!
RHODEY! THERE'S A CONG CHOPPER! CAN YOU FLY IT?
TO GET OUTTA THIS PLACE, BRO, I'D FLY A FRIGGIN' JEEP!
THEN GET TO IT! I'LL TRY TO KEEP THESE HANOI HOTSHOTS BUSY!
KRUBA-KRUMBLE
AIIEYAGH!
SORRY, FLY-BOY, BUT WE'RE TAKIN' YOUR LUXURY AIRCRAFT HERE FOR A LITTLE SPIN!
KRAKATOW
OKAY, IRON MAN, HOP IN-- QUICK!

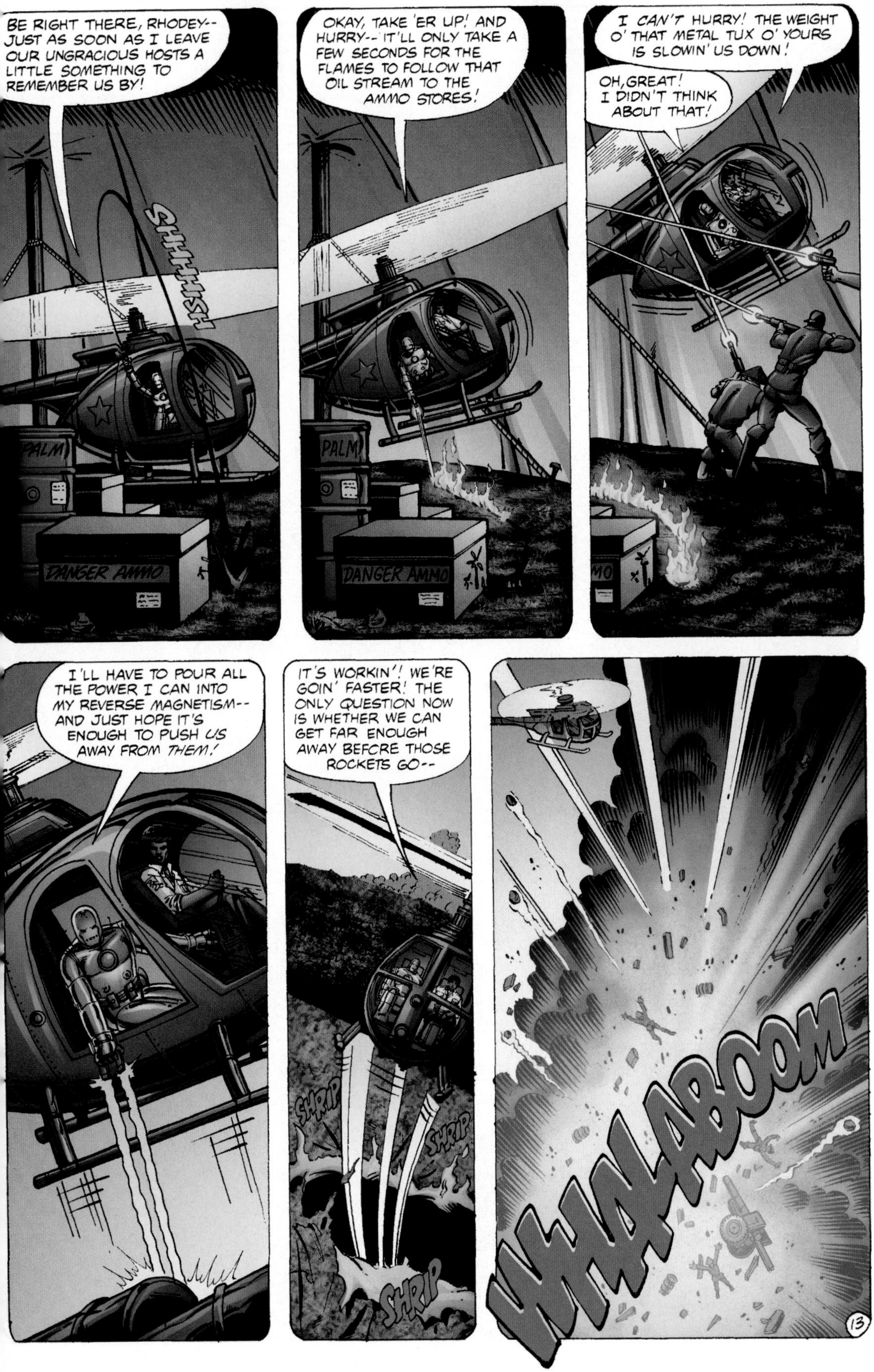
BE RIGHT THERE, RHODEY-- JUST AS SOON AS I LEAVE OUR UNGRACIOUS HOSTS A LITTLE SOMETHING TO REMEMBER US BY!
SHHHHSH!
OKAY, TAKE 'ER UP! AND HURRY-- IT'LL ONLY TAKE A FEW SECONDS FOR THE FLAMES TO FOLLOW THAT OIL STREAM TO THE AMMO STORES!
PALM
DANGER AMMO
I CAN'T HURRY! THE WEIGHT O' THAT METAL TUX O' YOURS IS SLOWIN' US DOWN!
OH, GREAT! I DIDN'T THINK ABOUT THAT!
I'LL HAVE TO POUR ALL THE POWER I CAN INTO MY REVERSE MAGNETISM-- AND JUST HOPE IT'S ENOUGH TO PUSH US AWAY FROM THEM!
IT'S WORKIN'! WE'RE GOIN' FASTER! THE ONLY QUESTION NOW IS WHETHER WE CAN GET FAR ENOUGH AWAY BEFORE THOSE ROCKETS GO--
SHRIP
SHRIP
SHRIP
WHHAABOOM

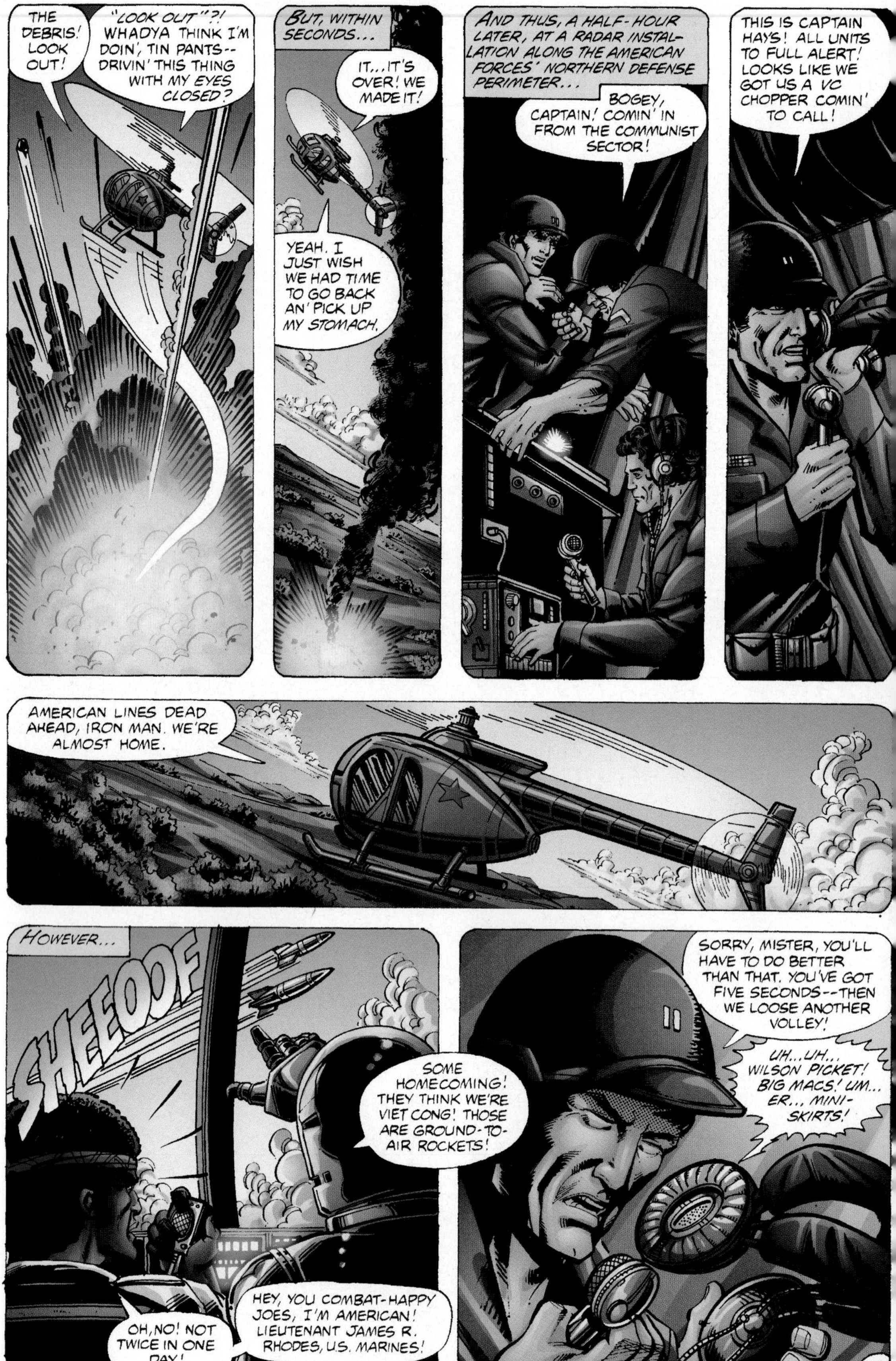
THE DEBRIS! LOOK OUT!
"LOOK OUT"?! WHADYA THINK I'M DOIN', TIN PANTS-- DRIVIN' THIS THING WITH MY EYES CLOSED?
BUT, WITHIN SECONDS...
IT...IT'S OVER! WE MADE IT!
YEAH. I JUST WISH WE HAD TIME TO GO BACK AN' PICK UP MY STOMACH.
AND THUS, A HALF-HOUR LATER, AT A RADAR INSTALLATION ALONG THE AMERICAN FORCES' NORTHERN DEFENSE PERIMETER...
BOGEY, CAPTAIN! COMIN' IN FROM THE COMMUNIST SECTOR!
THIS IS CAPTAIN HAYS! ALL UNITS TO FULL ALERT! LOOKS LIKE WE GOT US A VC CHOPPER COMIN' TO CALL!
AMERICAN LINES DEAD AHEAD, IRON MAN. WE'RE ALMOST HOME.
HOWEVER...
SHEEOOF
SOME HOMECOMING! THEY THINK WE'RE VIET CONG! THOSE ARE GROUND-TO-AIR ROCKETS!
OH, NO! NOT TWICE IN ONE DAY!
HEY, YOU COMBAT-HAPPY JOES, I'M AMERICAN! LIEUTENANT JAMES R. RHODES, U.S. MARINES!
SORRY, MISTER, YOU'LL HAVE TO DO BETTER THAN THAT. YOU'VE GOT FIVE SECONDS--THEN WE LOOSE ANOTHER VOLLEY!
UH...UH... WILSON PICKET! BIG MACS! UM... ER..., MINI-SKIRTS!
14

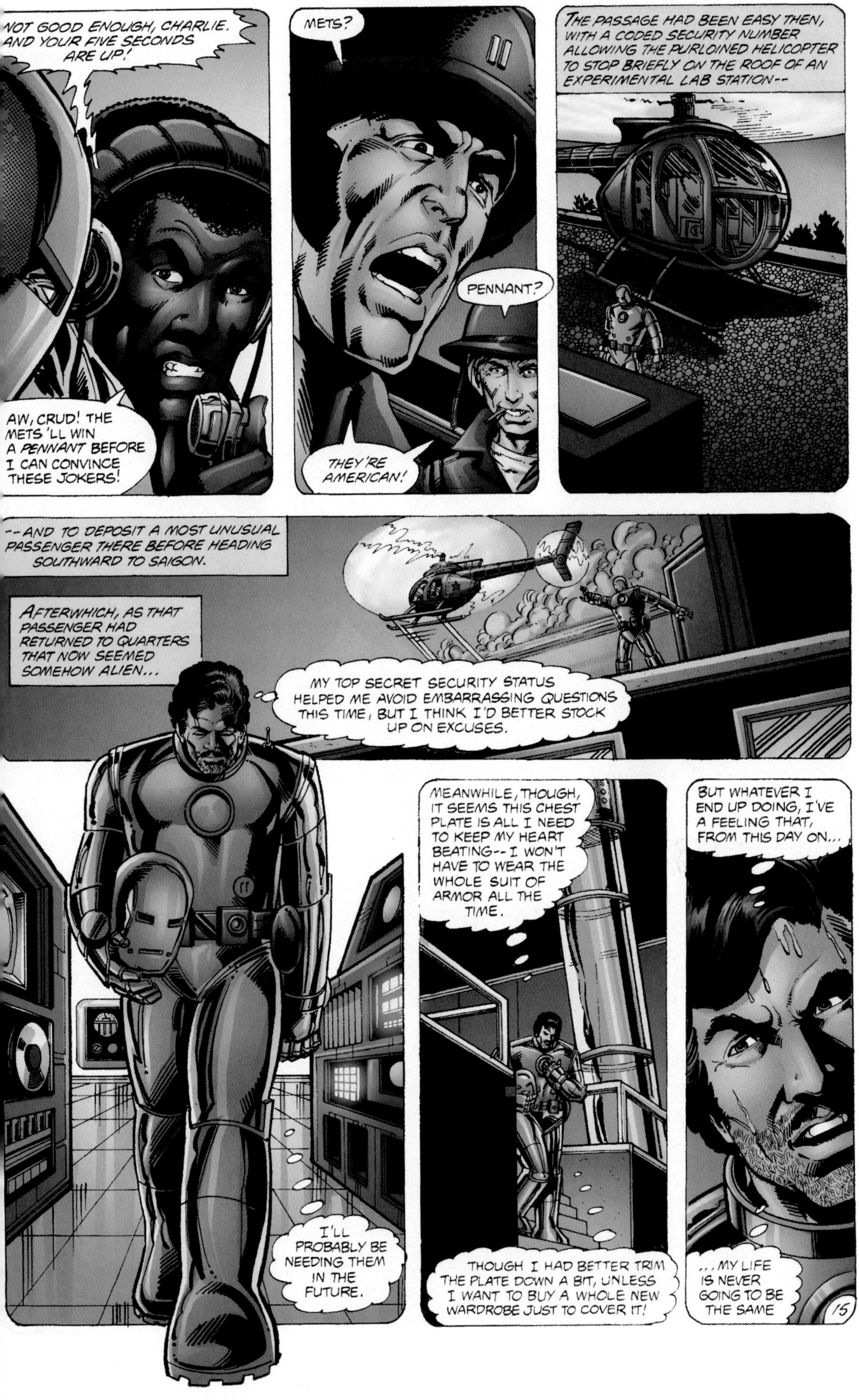
NOT GOOD ENOUGH, CHARLIE. AND YOUR FIVE SECONDS ARE UP!
AW, CRUD! THE METS'LL WIN A PENNANT BEFORE I CAN CONVINCE THESE JOKERS!
METS?
PENNANT?
THEY'RE AMERICAN!
THE PASSAGE HAD BEEN EASY THEN, WITH A CODED SECURITY NUMBER ALLOWING THE PURLOINED HELICOPTER TO STOP BRIEFLY ON THE ROOF OF AN EXPERIMENTAL LAB STATION--
--AND TO DEPOSIT A MOST UNUSUAL PASSENGER THERE BEFORE HEADING SOUTHWARD TO SAIGON.
AFTERWHICH, AS THAT PASSENGER HAD RETURNED TO QUARTERS THAT NOW SEEMED SOMEHOW ALIEN...
MY TOP SECRET SECURITY STATUS HELPED ME AVOID EMBARRASSING QUESTIONS THIS TIME, BUT I THINK I'D BETTER STOCK UP ON EXCUSES.
I'LL PROBABLY BE NEEDING THEM IN THE FUTURE.
MEANWHILE, THOUGH, IT SEEMS THIS CHEST PLATE IS ALL I NEED TO KEEP MY HEART BEATING-- I WON'T HAVE TO WEAR THE WHOLE SUIT OF ARMOR ALL THE TIME.
THOUGH I HAD BETTER TRIM THE PLATE DOWN A BIT, UNLESS I WANT TO BUY A WHOLE NEW WARDROBE JUST TO COVER IT!
BUT WHATEVER I END UP DOING, I'VE A FEELING THAT, FROM THIS DAY ON...
...MY LIFE IS NEVER GOING TO BE THE SAME
15

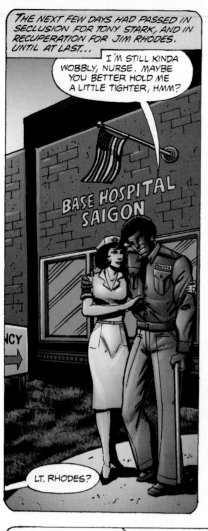

THE NEXT FEW DAYS HAD PASSED IN SECLUSION FOR TONY STARK, AND IN RECUPERATION FOR JIM RHODES. UNTIL AT LAST...

I'M STILL KINDA WOBBLY, NURSE. MAYBE YOU BETTER HOLD ME A LITTLE TIGHTER, HMM?

BASE HOSPITAL SAIGON

LT. RHODES?

HOW DO YOU DO? I'M TONY STARK.

"STARK"? YOU THE GUY THAT IRON DUDE WAS TALKIN' ABOUT?

THAT'S RIGHT. HE TOLD ME ALL ABOUT HOW YOU HELPED HIM GET TO SAFETY, AND I WANTED TO THANK YOU.

I WOULD HAVE LOST A VERY CLOSE FRIEND IF IRON MAN HADN'T MADE IT.

MR. STARK, I THINK WE BOTH DID OUR SHARE O' SAVIN'.

NEVERTHELESS, YOU'RE A GOOD MAN. IF I EVER REQUIRE THE SERVICES OF A PILOT WHILE I'M HERE, I HOPE YOU'LL BE AVAILABLE.

AND IF YOU NEED A JOB WHEN THESE HOSTILITIES ARE OVER, PLEASE DON'T HESITATE TO GIVE ME A CALL.

THANKS FOR THE OFFER, MR. STARK. ONCE I FINISH CLEANIN' UP THESE JUNGLES FOR UNCLE SAM, I'LL SURE KEEP THAT IN MIND.

16

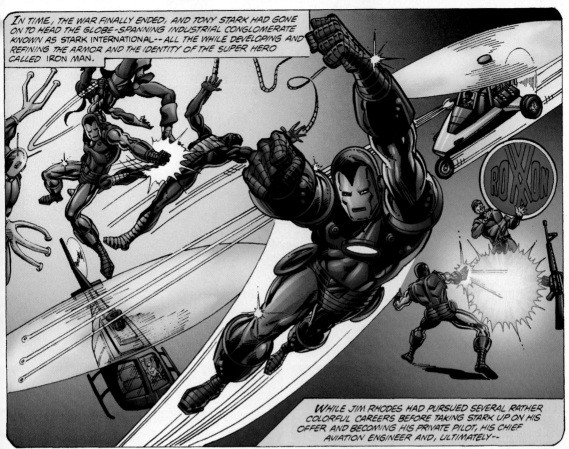

IN TIME, THE WAR FINALLY ENDED, AND TONY STARK HAD GONE ON TO HEAD THE GLOBE-SPANNING INDUSTRIAL CONGLOMERATE KNOWN AS STARK INTERNATIONAL--ALL THE WHILE DEVELOPING AND REFINING THE ARMOR AND THE IDENTITY OF THE SUPER HERO CALLED IRON MAN.

WHILE JIM RHODES HAD PURSUED SEVERAL RATHER COLORFUL CAREERS BEFORE TAKING STARK UP ON HIS OFFER AND BECOMING HIS PRIVATE PILOT, HIS CHIEF AVIATION ENGINEER AND, ULTIMATELY--

--HIS FRIEND...

HEY, TONY. BOSS!

WHA--OH. SORRY. GUESS I WAS DAYDREAMING.

WE'RE ALMOST TO DALLAS. YOU WANT TO TAKE US IN?

NO, THANKS. I'M A GOOD PILOT--BUT I PREFER BEING FLOWN BY THE BEST.

AW, SHUCKS, CHIEF, YOU KEEP THAT UP YOU'RE GONNA TURN MY HEAD. AND UNTIL WE GET BACK ON THE GROUND--

--THAT COULD BE DOWNRIGHT DANGEROUS!

CUTE, RHODEY, REAL CUTE...

17

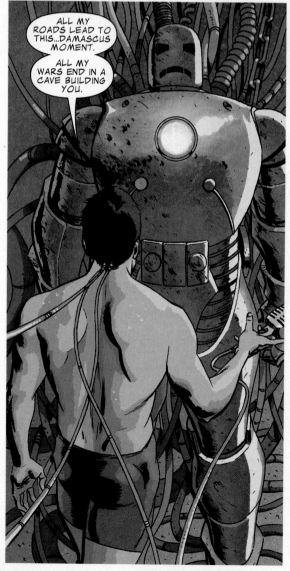

MAYBE IT DOESN'T MATTER, WHETHER IT'S HERE OR IN VIETNAM OR CAMBODIA OR RWANDA OR BOSNIA OR IRAQ.

DOES THE WAR MATTER?

ALL MY ROADS LEAD TO THIS...DAMASCUS MOMENT.

ALL MY WARS END IN A CAVE BUILDING YOU.

I'VE GOT MYSELF INTO TROUBLE THAT HIDING OUT INSIDE OF YOU WON'T FIX.

AND I'M AFRAID.

"I'M AFRAID AND I'M FORGETTING EVERYTHING I EVER KNEW INCLUDING WHY I EVER MADE YOU IN THE FIRST PLACE.

"SO JUST TRY NOT TO FORGET THIS PART, TONY--"

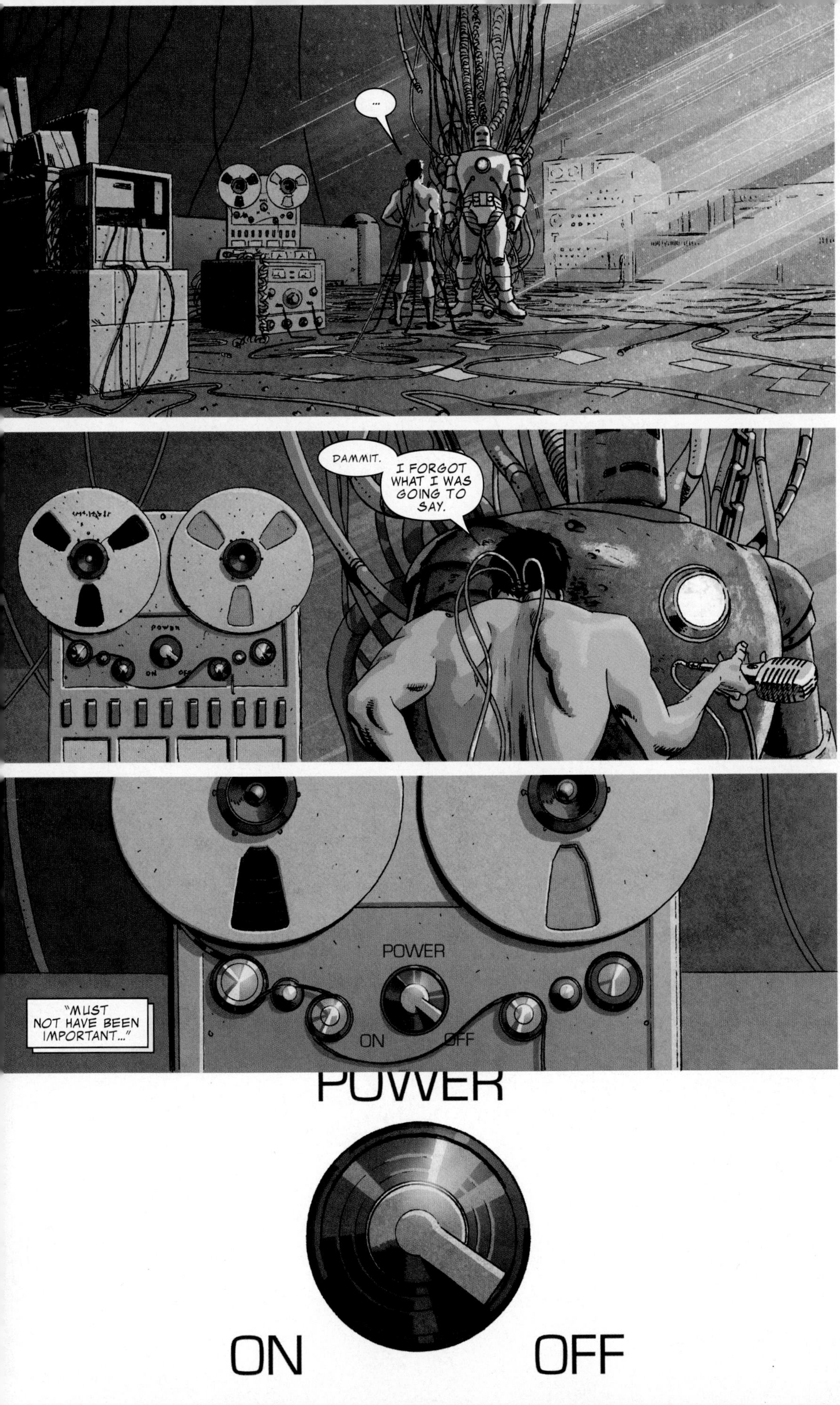
...
DAMMIT.
I FORGOT WHAT I WAS GOING TO SAY.
POWER
ON
"MUST NOT HAVE BEEN IMPORTANT..."
POWER
ON
OFF

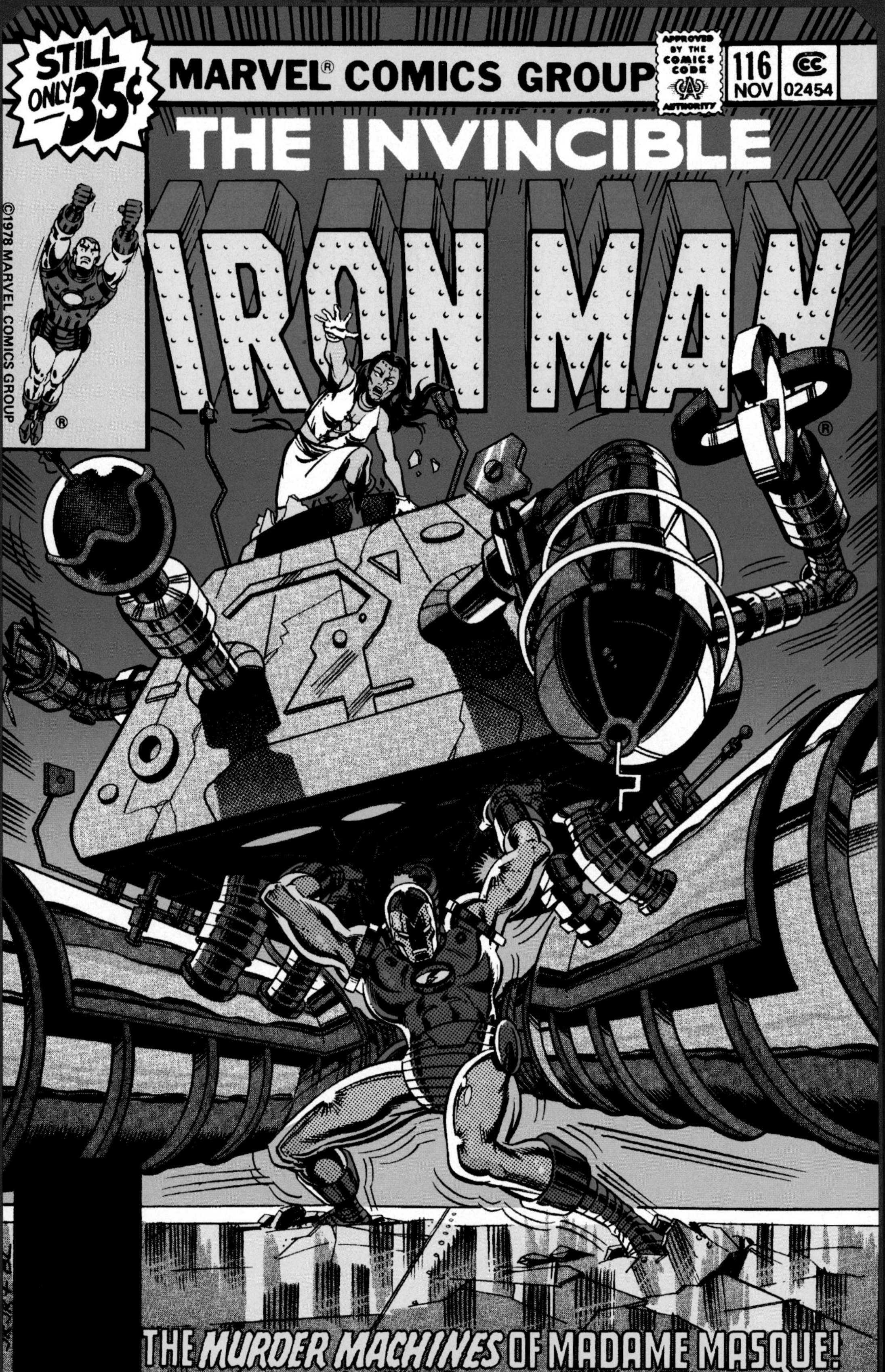
STILL ONLY 35¢
MARVEL® COMICS GROUP
APPROVED BY THE COMICS CODE AUTHORITY
116 NOV
CC 02454
THE INVINCIBLE
IRON MAN®
©1978 MARVEL COMICS GROUP
THE MURDER MACHINES OF MADAME MASQUE!

When millionaire industrialist *Tony Stark*, inventor extraordinaire, garbs himself in solar-charged, steel-mesh *armor* he becomes the world's greatest human fighting machine...

Stan Lee PRESENTS: THE INVINCIBLE IRON MAN®

DAVID MICHELINIE PLOT / WORDS / JOHN ROMITA Jr. PENCILS / BOB LAYTON PLOT / INKS / A. KAWECKI LETTERS / G. ROUSSOS COLORS / ROGER STERN EDITOR / JIM SHOOTER EDITOR-IN-CHIEF

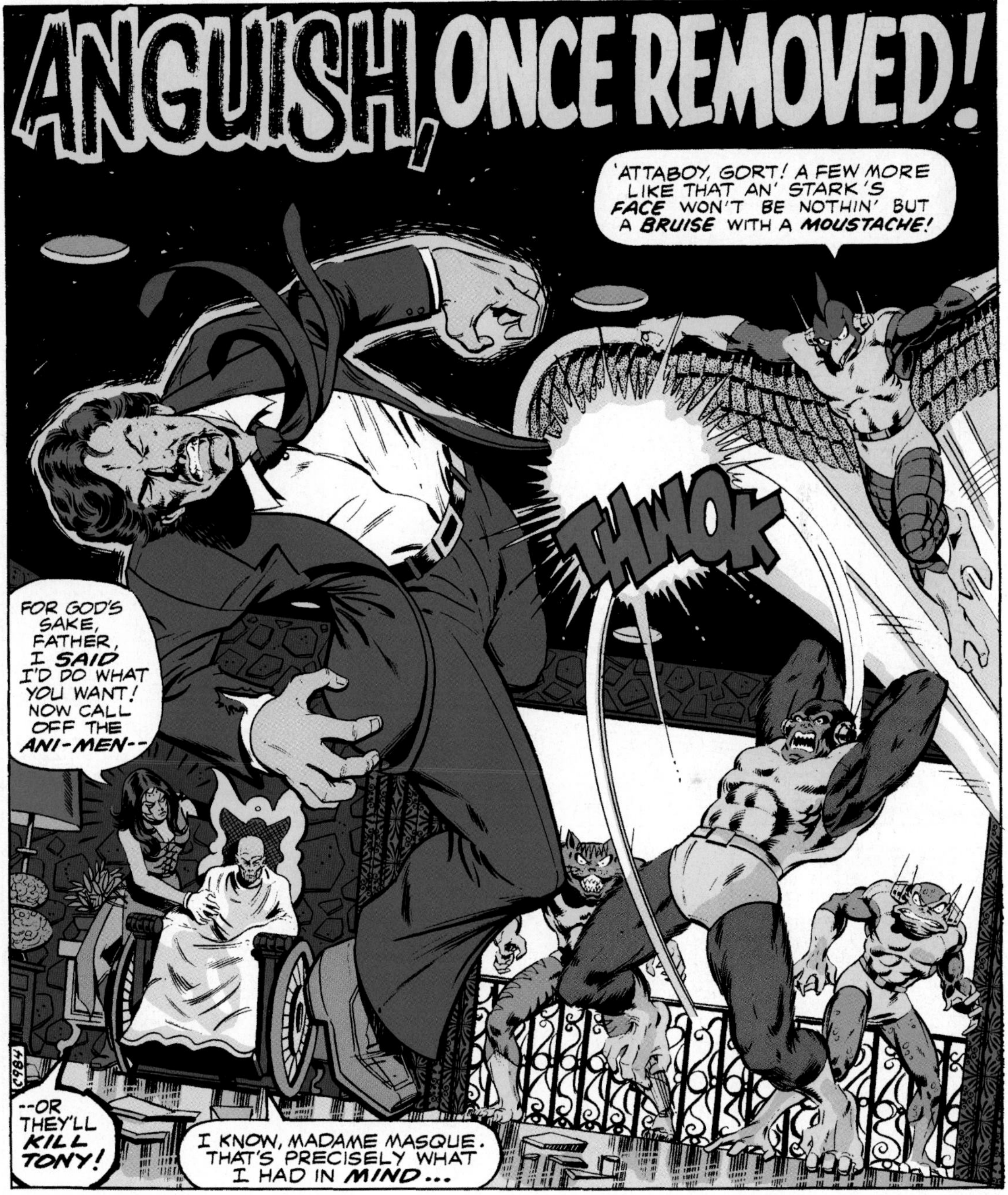

ANGUISH, ONCE REMOVED!
'ATTABOY, GORT! A FEW MORE LIKE THAT AN' STARK'S FACE WON'T BE NOTHIN' BUT A BRUISE WITH A MOUSTACHE!
THWOK
FOR GOD'S SAKE, FATHER, I SAID I'D DO WHAT YOU WANT! NOW CALL OFF THE ANI-MEN--
--OR THEY'LL KILL TONY!
I KNOW, MADAME MASQUE. THAT'S PRECISELY WHAT I HAD IN MIND...
©1984

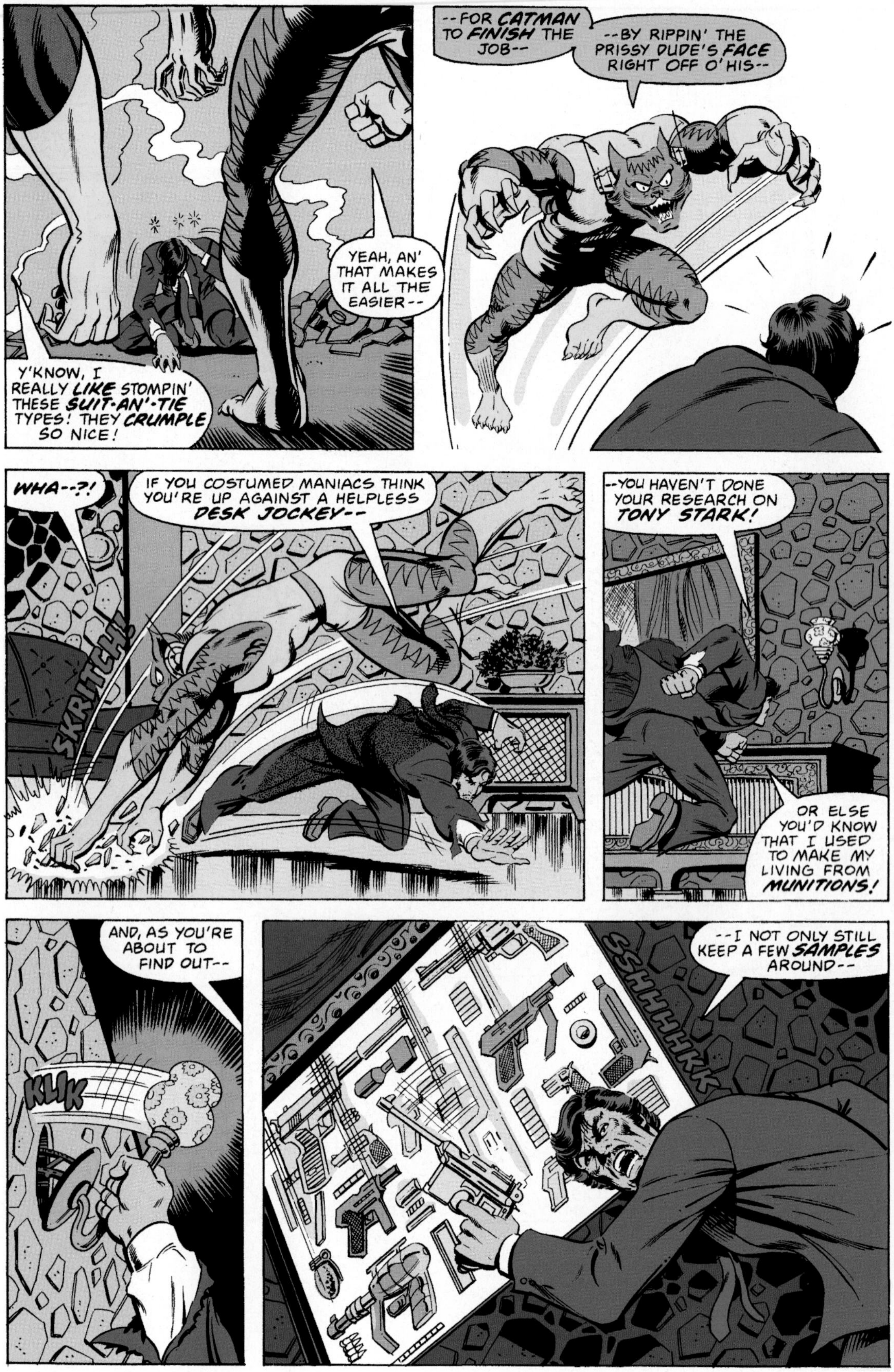

Y'KNOW, I REALLY LIKE STOMPIN' THESE SUIT-AN'-TIE TYPES! THEY CRUMPLE SO NICE!
YEAH, AN' THAT MAKES IT ALL THE EASIER--
--FOR CATMAN TO FINISH THE JOB--
--BY RIPPIN' THE PRISSY DUDE'S FACE RIGHT OFF O'HIS--
WHA--?!
IF YOU COSTUMED MANIACS THINK YOU'RE UP AGAINST A HELPLESS DESK JOCKEY--
SKRITCH!
--YOU HAVEN'T DONE YOUR RESEARCH ON TONY STARK!
OR ELSE YOU'D KNOW THAT I USED TO MAKE MY LIVING FROM MUNITIONS!
AND, AS YOU'RE ABOUT TO FIND OUT--
KLIK
SSHHHHKK
--I NOT ONLY STILL KEEP A FEW SAMPLES AROUND--

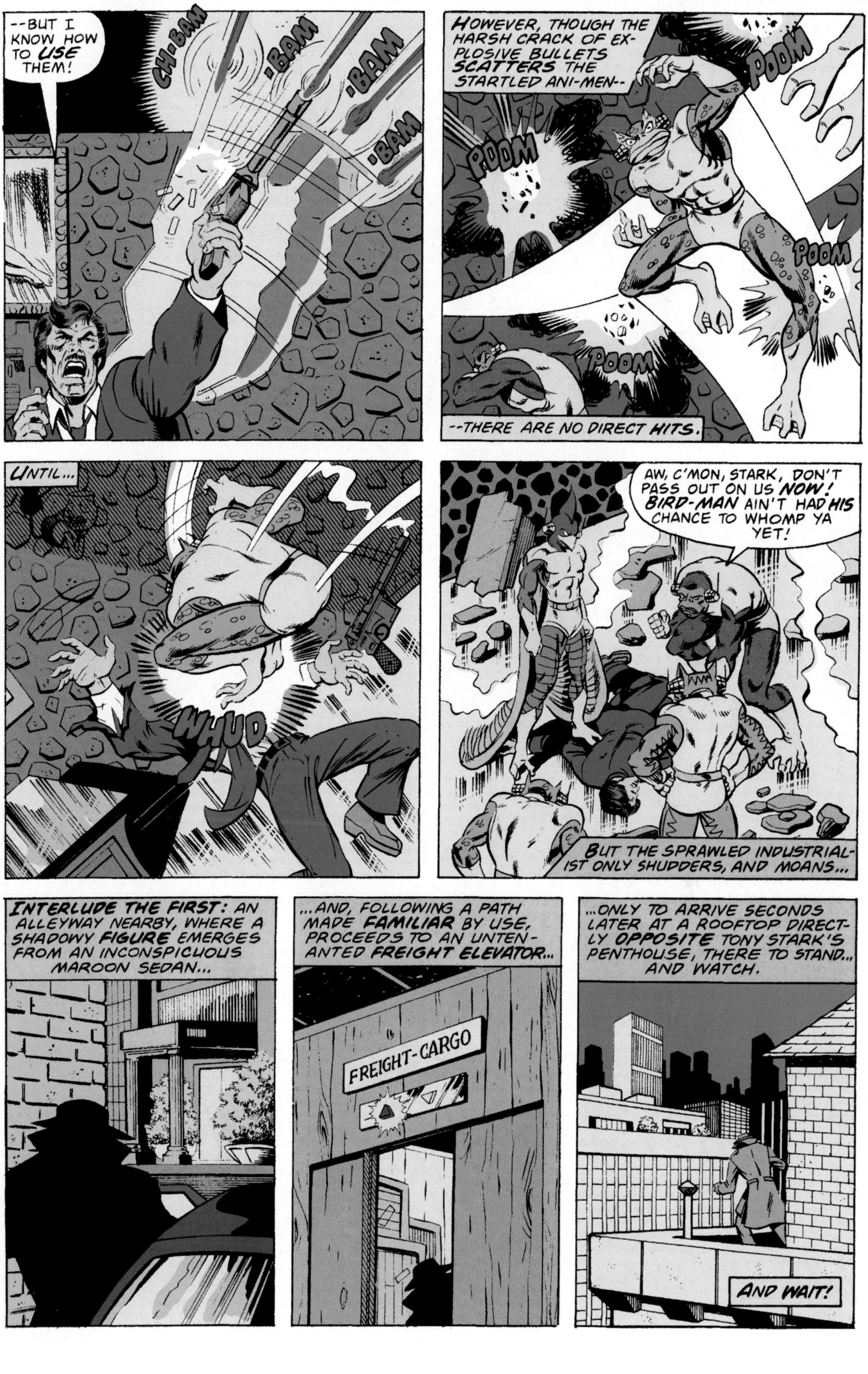
--BUT I KNOW HOW TO USE THEM!
CH-BAM
'BAM
'BAM
'BAM
HOWEVER, THOUGH THE HARSH CRACK OF EXPLOSIVE BULLETS SCATTERS THE STARTLED ANI-MEN--
POOM
POOM
POOM
POOM
--THERE ARE NO DIRECT HITS.
UNTIL...
WHUD
AW, C'MON, STARK, DON'T PASS OUT ON US NOW! BIRD-MAN AIN'T HAD HIS CHANCE TO WHOMP YA YET!
BUT THE SPRAWLED INDUSTRIALIST ONLY SHUDDERS, AND MOANS...
INTERLUDE THE FIRST: AN ALLEYWAY NEARBY, WHERE A SHADOWY FIGURE EMERGES FROM AN INCONSPICUOUS MAROON SEDAN...
...AND, FOLLOWING A PATH MADE FAMILIAR BY USE, PROCEEDS TO AN UNTENANTED FREIGHT ELEVATOR...
FREIGHT-CARGO
...ONLY TO ARRIVE SECONDS LATER AT A ROOFTOP DIRECTLY OPPOSITE TONY STARK'S PENTHOUSE, THERE TO STAND... AND WATCH.
AND WAIT!

ENOUGH, FATHER! YOU MADE ME *CHOOSE* BETWEEN YOU AND TONY-- AND I *DID!*

BUT THAT WAS WITH THE PROMISE THAT TONY WOULDN'T BE *HURT!*

I KNOW, WHITNEY. BUT YOU'LL HAVE TO... FORGIVE ME MY LITTLE ...*FABRICATION.*.

YOU SEE, I'VE BEEN THROUGH *TOO MUCH* ...TO LET STARK RE-MAIN...A *THREAT!*

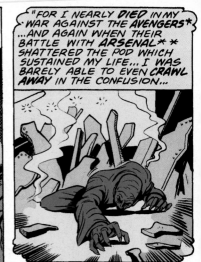

"FOR I NEARLY *DIED* IN MY WAR AGAINST THE *AVENGERS* * ...AND AGAIN WHEN THEIR BATTLE WITH *ARSENAL* * * SHATTERED THE POD WHICH SUSTAINED MY LIFE... I WAS BARELY ABLE TO EVEN *CRAWL AWAY* IN THE CONFUSION...

* AVENGERS #166
* * IRON MAN #114   --ROG.

"BUT ONCE FREE, I KNEW THAT UNLESS I REGAINED MY *STOLEN YOUTH,* * MY SURVIVAL COULD BE COUNTED IN *DAYS!* AND SO I RE-CRUITED THE *ANI-MEN*--

"--KNOWING THAT THEIR ANIMAL INSTINCTS AND CRIMINAL CUNNING WOULD SOON LEAD ME TO--

* AGAIN, IN AVENGERS #166--R.

"--*YOU!* AND ONCE YOUR UNFORTUNATE *LOVER* IS DISPOSED OF...THERE WILL BE NO BARRIERS TO KEEP YOU FROM HELPING ME...*REVERSE* THE AGING PROCESS...

"...WILL THERE...

"...*DAUGHTER?*"

INTERLUDE THE SECOND: THE ROOFTOP...

I'VE BEEN DOGGING STARK'S TRAIL FOR WEEKS--EVEN TO HIS PRIVATE *OFFICE* AT STARK INTERNA-TIONAL *--AND HE NEVER ONCE *SUSPECTED!*

BUT THEN, THAT'S JUST *CHILD'S PLAY* FOR--

*IM #113--R.

--THE *SPYMASTER!*

AND NOW, IT'S TIME FOR THE FRIENDLY FOLKS WHO *HIRED* ME--

--TO GET THEIR *MONEY'S WORTH!*

THLIK

AND THUS, WITH THE SINGLE THRUST OF A YELLOW-GLOVED THUMB--

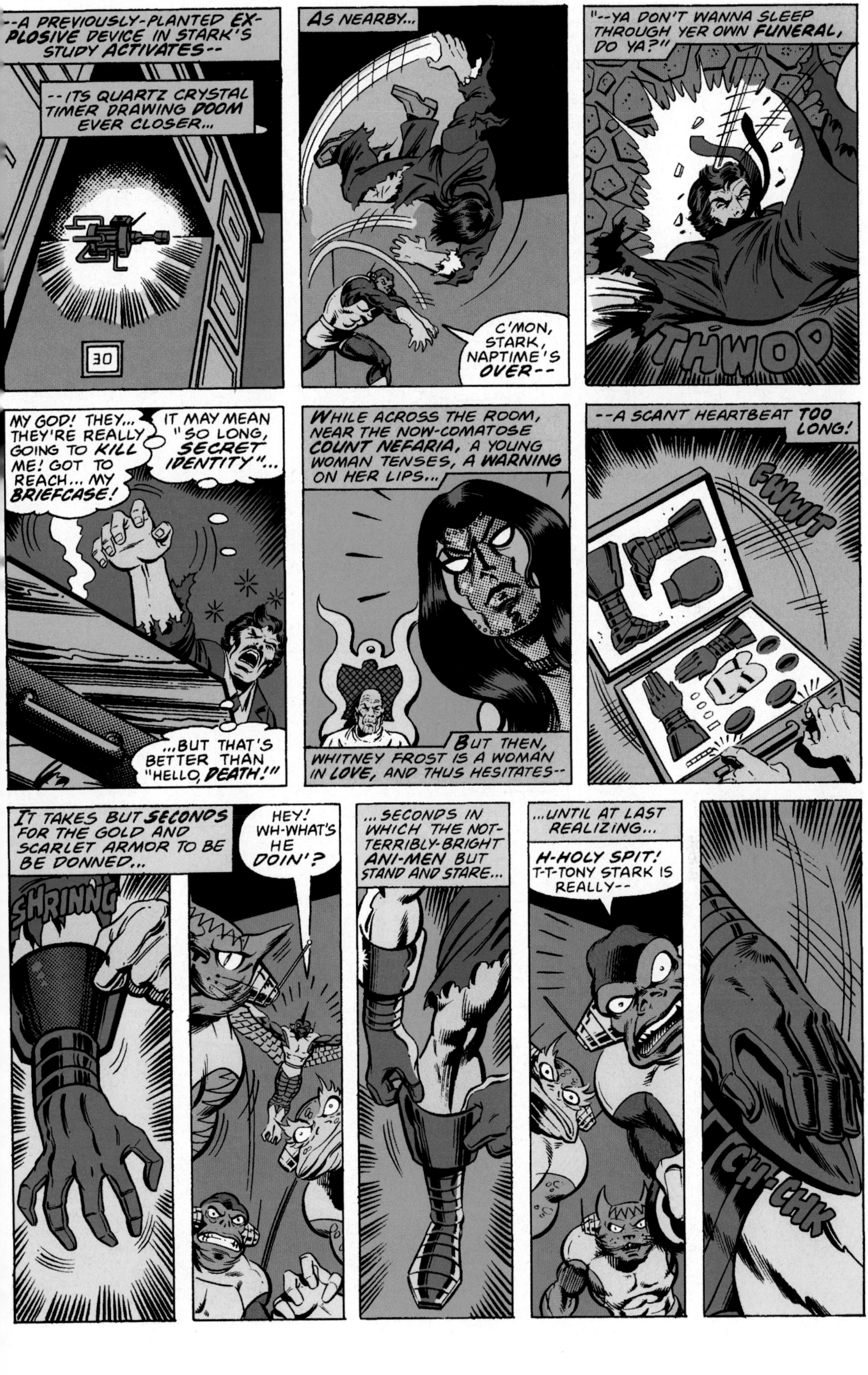
--A PREVIOUSLY-PLANTED EXPLOSIVE DEVICE IN STARK'S STUDY ACTIVATES--
--ITS QUARTZ CRYSTAL TIMER DRAWING DOOM EVER CLOSER...
30
AS NEARBY...
C'MON, STARK, NAPTIME'S OVER--
"--YA DON'T WANNA SLEEP THROUGH YER OWN FUNERAL, DO YA?"
THWOD
MY GOD! THEY... THEY'RE REALLY GOING TO KILL ME! GOT TO REACH... MY BRIEFCASE!
IT MAY MEAN "SO LONG, SECRET IDENTITY"...
...BUT THAT'S BETTER THAN "HELLO, DEATH!"
WHILE ACROSS THE ROOM, NEAR THE NOW-COMATOSE COUNT NEFARIA, A YOUNG WOMAN TENSES, A WARNING ON HER LIPS...
BUT THEN, WHITNEY FROST IS A WOMAN IN LOVE, AND THUS HESITATES--
--A SCANT HEARTBEAT TOO LONG!
FWWIT
IT TAKES BUT SECONDS FOR THE GOLD AND SCARLET ARMOR TO BE BE DONNED...
SHRINNG
HEY! WH-WHAT'S HE DOIN'?
...SECONDS IN WHICH THE NOT-TERRIBLY-BRIGHT ANI-MEN BUT STAND AND STARE...
...UNTIL AT LAST REALIZING...
H-HOLY SPIT! T-T-TONY STARK IS REALLY--
CH-CHK

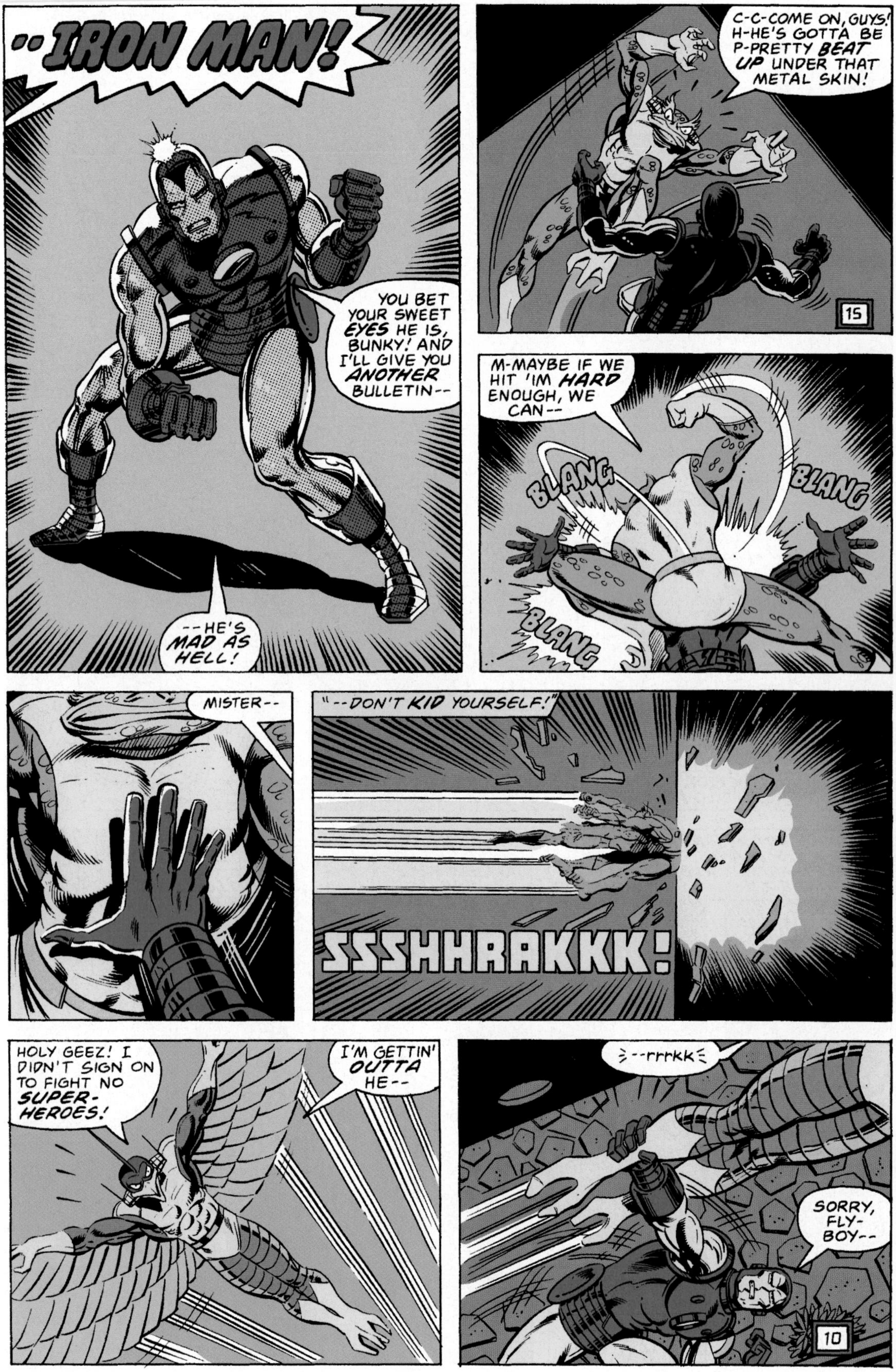
--IRON MAN!
YOU BET YOUR SWEET EYES HE IS, BUNKY! AND I'LL GIVE YOU ANOTHER BULLETIN--
--HE'S MAD AS HELL!
C-C-COME ON, GUYS! H-HE'S GOTTA BE P-PRETTY BEAT UP UNDER THAT METAL SKIN!
15
M-MAYBE IF WE HIT 'IM HARD ENOUGH, WE CAN--
BLANG
BLANG
BLANG
MISTER--
"--DON'T KID YOURSELF!"
SSSHHRAKKK!
HOLY GEEZ! I DIDN'T SIGN ON TO FIGHT NO SUPER-HEROES!
I'M GETTIN' OUTTA HE--
--rrrkk
SORRY, FLY-BOY--
10

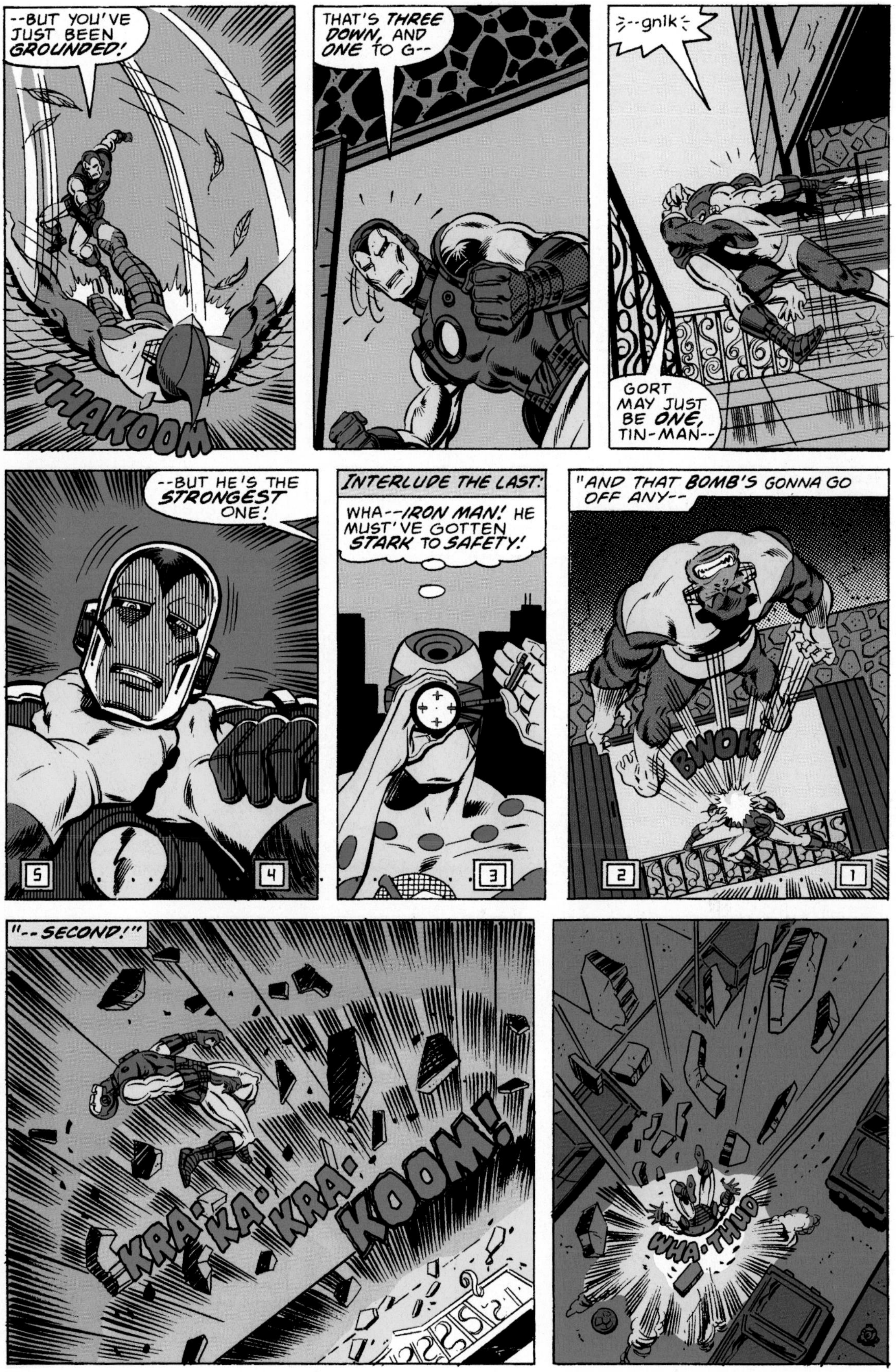
--BUT YOU'VE JUST BEEN GROUNDED!
THAKOOM
THAT'S THREE DOWN, AND ONE TO G--
--gnlk
GORT MAY JUST BE ONE, TIN-MAN--
--BUT HE'S THE STRONGEST ONE!
5
4
INTERLUDE THE LAST:
WHA--IRON MAN! HE MUST'VE GOTTEN STARK TO SAFETY!
3
"AND THAT BOMB'S GONNA GO OFF ANY--
BWOK
2
1
"--SECOND!"
KRA-KA-KRA-KOOM!
WHA-THUD

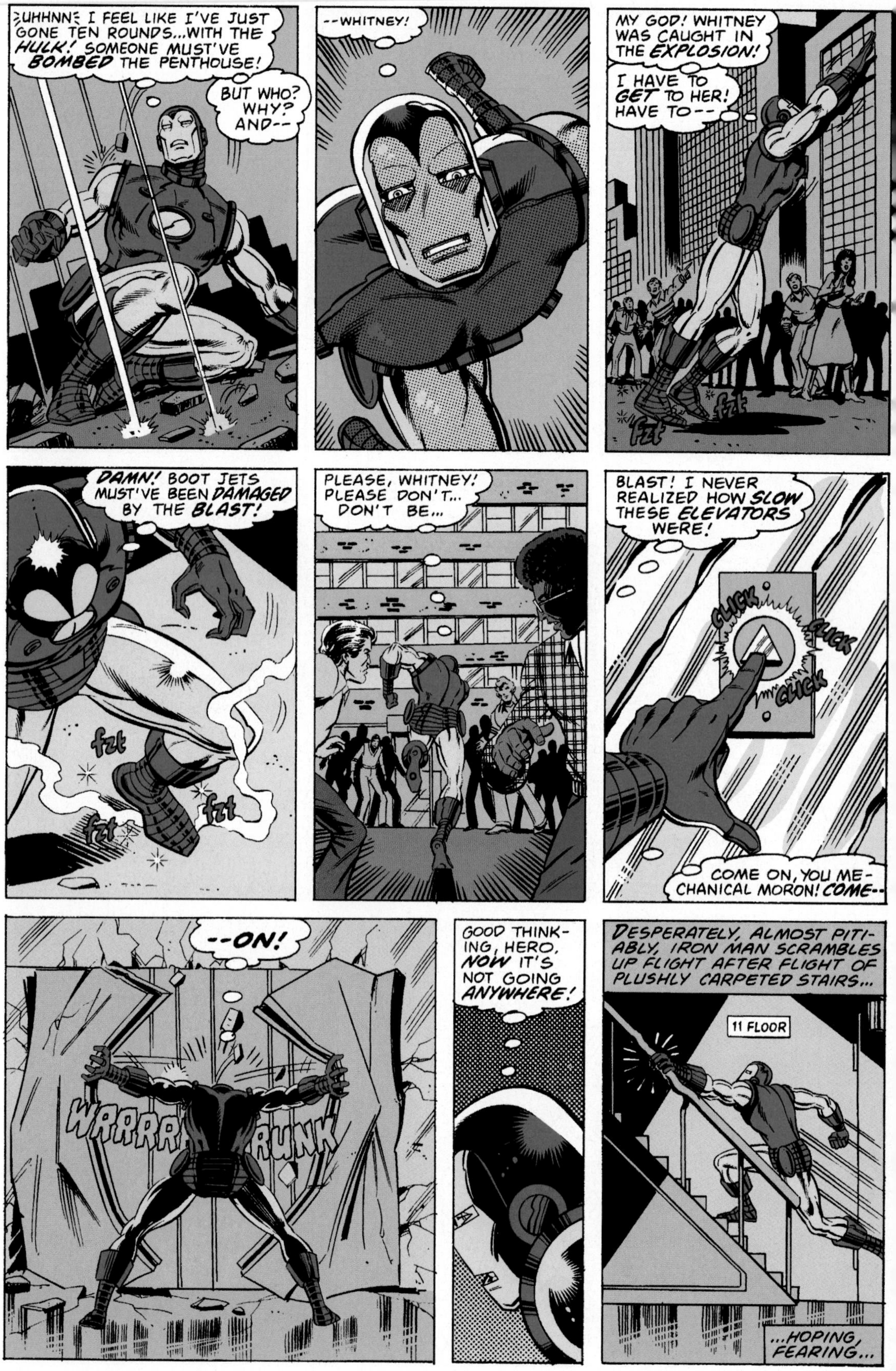
UHHHNN! I FEEL LIKE I'VE JUST GONE TEN ROUNDS...WITH THE HULK! SOMEONE MUST'VE BOMBED THE PENTHOUSE!
BUT WHO? WHY? AND--
--WHITNEY!
MY GOD! WHITNEY WAS CAUGHT IN THE EXPLOSION!
I HAVE TO GET TO HER! HAVE TO--
fzt
fzt
DAMN! BOOT JETS MUST'VE BEEN DAMAGED BY THE BLAST!
fzt
fzt
fzt
PLEASE, WHITNEY! PLEASE DON'T... DON'T BE...
BLAST! I NEVER REALIZED HOW SLOW THESE ELEVATORS WERE!
CLICK
CLICK
CLICK
COME ON, YOU ME-CHANICAL MORON! COME--
--ON!
WRRRR
RUNK
GOOD THINK-ING, HERO. NOW IT'S NOT GOING ANYWHERE!
DESPERATELY, ALMOST PITI-ABLY, IRON MAN SCRAMBLES UP FLIGHT AFTER FLIGHT OF PLUSHLY CARPETED STAIRS...
11 FLOOR
...HOPING, FEARING...

...YET ALL THE WHILE *KNOWING* WHAT HE WILL FIND...

OH... GOD.

FOR A MOMENT, HE STANDS SILENT...AND THEN, BENDING GENTLY, HE LIFTS A PIECE OF TATTERED CLOTH FROM THE RUBBLE, HOLDING IT AS IF THE REMNANT OF A DREAM--

--THE SOUND OF BREATHS TOO SHALLOWLY TAKEN COMING FROM BEHIND THE METAL OF HIS MASK.

UNTIL...

≶PUFF PUFF≷ IRON MAN! BOY, AM I GLAD *YOU* SHOWED UP! I WOULDA BEEN HERE *SOONER* MYSELF ≶PANT≷ ONLY--

--I WAS *DECKED* BY YOUR *GIRLFRIEND* PUSHIN' SOME OL' GEEZER IN A *WHEELCHAIR* OUT THE SERVICE ENTRANCE! I--

WHAT?! SHE'S *ALIVE?*

WHICH WAY DID THEY *GO,* MAN! *WHICH WAY?*

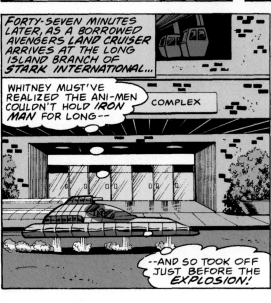

FORTY-SEVEN MINUTES LATER, AS A BORROWED *AVENGERS* LAND CRUISER ARRIVES AT THE LONG ISLAND BRANCH OF STARK *INTERNATIONAL...*

WHITNEY MUST'VE REALIZED THE ANI-MEN COULDN'T HOLD *IRON MAN* FOR LONG--

COMPLEX

--AND SO TOOK OFF JUST BEFORE THE *EXPLOSION!*

AND SINCE THIS IS ONE OF THE FEW RESEARCH FACILITIES *SOPHISTICATED* ENOUGH TO KEEP HER FATHER ALIVE, I'M BETTING THAT THIS IS WHERE SHE *HEADED!*

ONLY...WHY IS THE PLACE *DESERTED?*

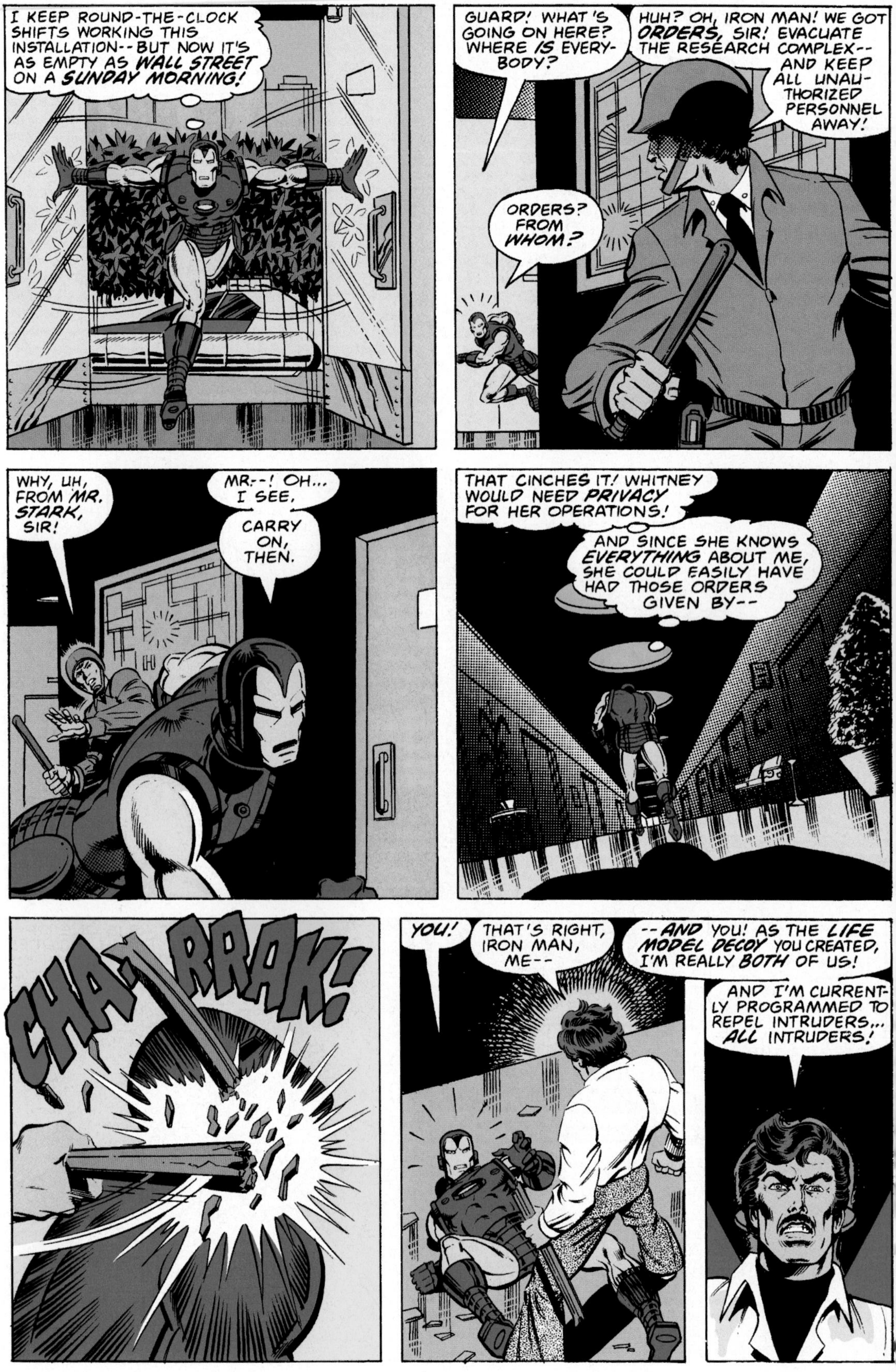
I KEEP ROUND-THE-CLOCK SHIFTS WORKING THIS INSTALLATION--BUT NOW IT'S AS EMPTY AS WALL STREET ON A SUNDAY MORNING!
GUARD! WHAT'S GOING ON HERE? WHERE IS EVERYBODY?
HUH? OH, IRON MAN! WE GOT ORDERS, SIR! EVACUATE THE RESEARCH COMPLEX--AND KEEP ALL UNAUTHORIZED PERSONNEL AWAY!
ORDERS? FROM WHOM?
WHY, UH, FROM MR. STARK, SIR!
MR.--! OH... I SEE.
CARRY ON, THEN.
THAT CINCHES IT! WHITNEY WOULD NEED PRIVACY FOR HER OPERATIONS!
AND SINCE SHE KNOWS EVERYTHING ABOUT ME, SHE COULD EASILY HAVE HAD THOSE ORDERS GIVEN BY--
CHA-RRRAK!
YOU!
THAT'S RIGHT, IRON MAN, ME--
--AND YOU! AS THE LIFE MODEL DECOY YOU CREATED, I'M REALLY BOTH OF US!
AND I'M CURRENTLY PROGRAMMED TO REPEL INTRUDERS... ALL INTRUDERS!

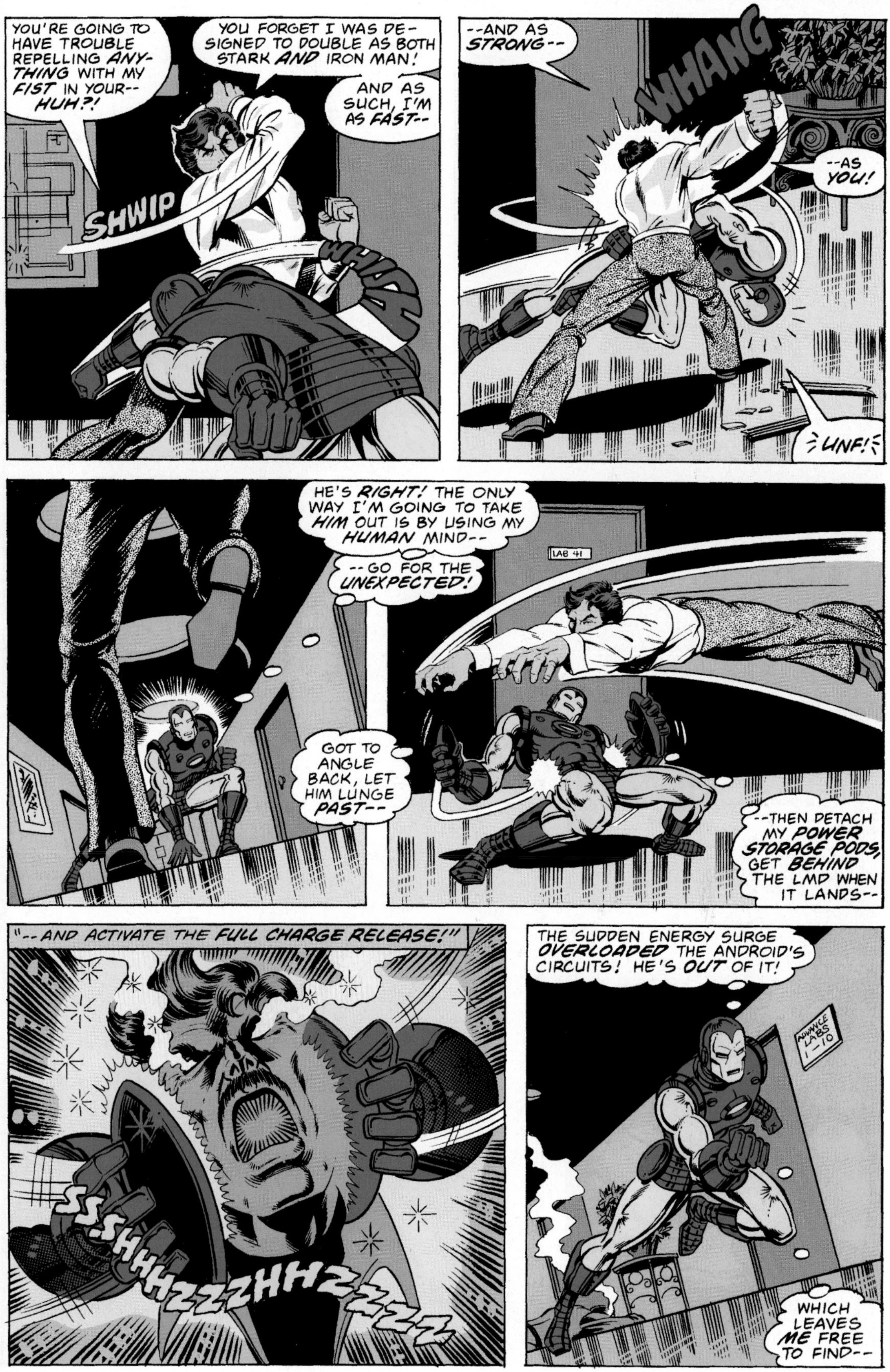
YOU'RE GOING TO HAVE TROUBLE REPELLING ANY-THING WITH MY FIST IN YOUR-- HUH?!
YOU FORGET I WAS DE-SIGNED TO DOUBLE AS BOTH STARK AND IRON MAN!
AND AS SUCH, I'M AS FAST--
SHWIP
WHIP
--AND AS STRONG--
WHANG
--AS YOU!
UNF!
HE'S RIGHT! THE ONLY WAY I'M GOING TO TAKE HIM OUT IS BY USING MY HUMAN MIND--
--GO FOR THE UNEXPECTED!
LAB 41
GOT TO ANGLE BACK, LET HIM LUNGE PAST--
--THEN DETACH MY POWER STORAGE PODS, GET BEHIND THE LMD WHEN IT LANDS--
"--AND ACTIVATE THE FULL CHARGE RELEASE!"
SSSHHHZZZZHHHZZZZZZ
THE SUDDEN ENERGY SURGE OVERLOADED THE ANDROID'S CIRCUITS! HE'S OUT OF IT!
ADVANCE LABS 1-10
WHICH LEAVES ME FREE TO FIND--

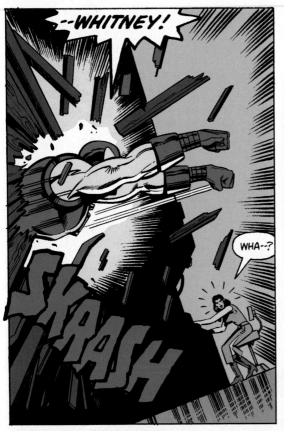

--WHITNEY!

WHA--?

I HOPE YOU REALIZE, YOUNG LADY, THAT YOU SUCCEEDED IN SCARING THE LIVING *BEJEEZUS* OUT OF ME! AND AS SOON AS I GET *NEFARIA* BACK, I INTEND TO--

NO, TONY, PLEASE! I HAVE TO KEEP HIM *ALIVE!*

WHICH IS EXACTLY WHAT *I* INTEND TO DO--BUT AT *AVENGERS' MAN-SION,* WHERE THE REJUVENATION PROCESS CAN BE *MONITORED!*

NEFARIA MAY BE YOUR *FATHER,* WHITNEY--

--BUT HE'S ALSO ONE OF THE MOST *DANGEROUS* MEN IN THE WORLD! AND NO MATTER WHAT I *FEEL*--

--I'M STILL AN *AVENGER!*

I'M SORRY.

PLIP

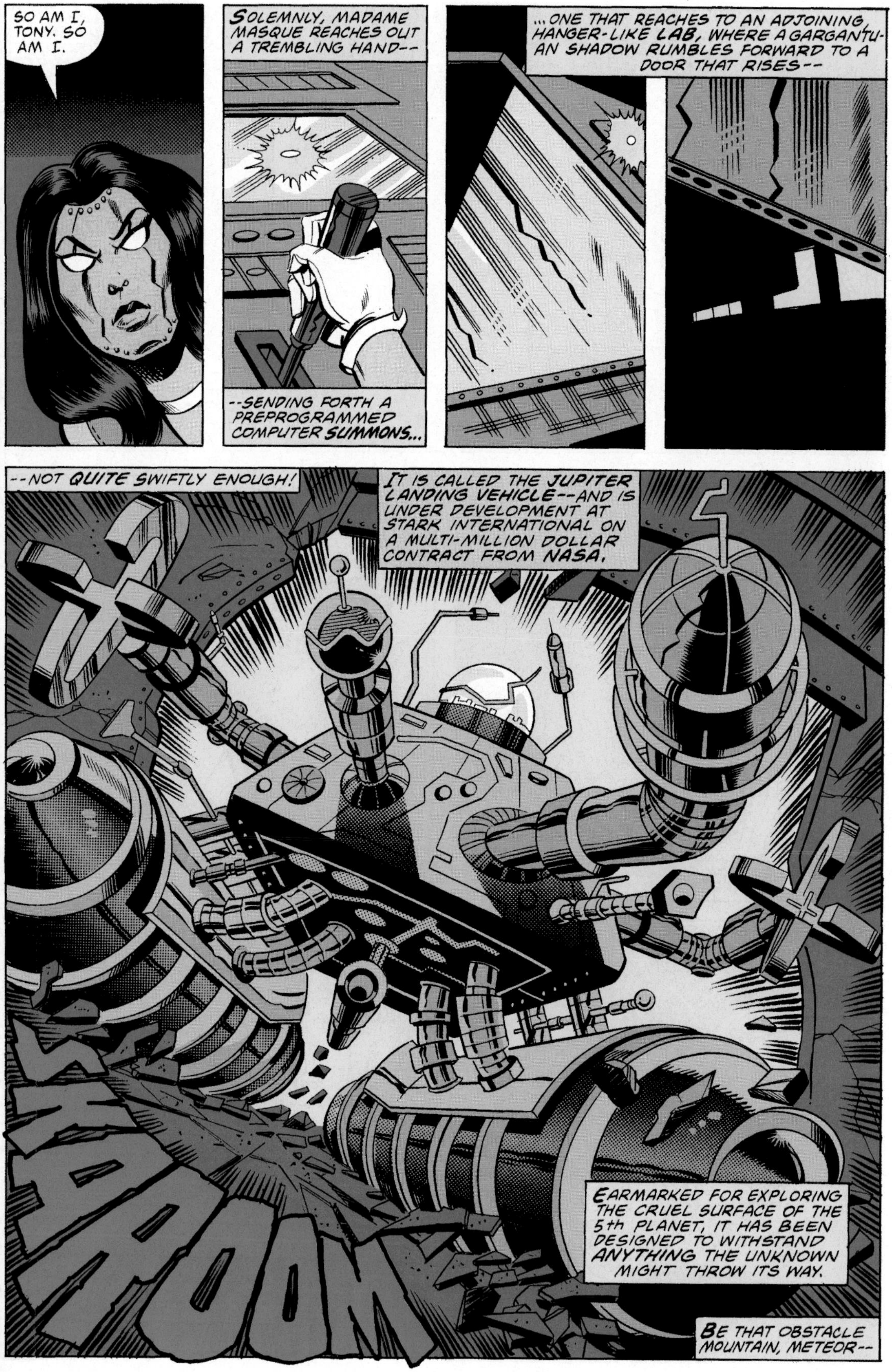
SO AM I, TONY. SO AM I.
SOLEMNLY, MADAME MASQUE REACHES OUT A TREMBLING HAND--
--SENDING FORTH A PREPROGRAMMED COMPUTER SUMMONS...
...ONE THAT REACHES TO AN ADJOINING, HANGER-LIKE LAB, WHERE A GARGANTU-AN SHADOW RUMBLES FORWARD TO A DOOR THAT RISES--
--NOT QUITE SWIFTLY ENOUGH!
IT IS CALLED THE JUPITER LANDING VEHICLE--AND IS UNDER DEVELOPMENT AT STARK INTERNATIONAL ON A MULTI-MILLION DOLLAR CONTRACT FROM NASA.
SKRADOOM
EARMARKED FOR EXPLORING THE CRUEL SURFACE OF THE 5th PLANET, IT HAS BEEN DESIGNED TO WITHSTAND ANYTHING THE UNKNOWN MIGHT THROW ITS WAY.
BE THAT OBSTACLE MOUNTAIN, METEOR--

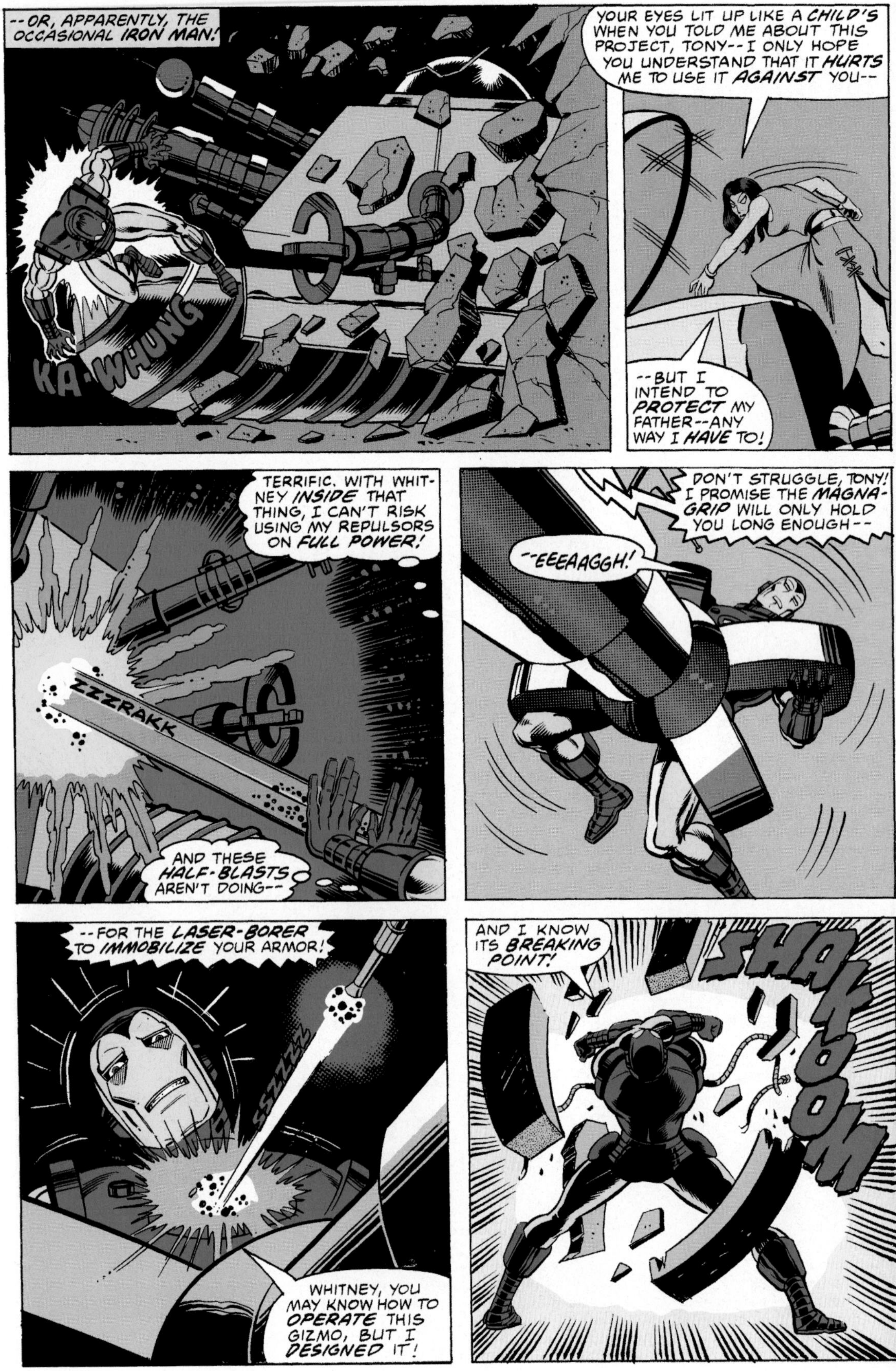
--OR, APPARENTLY, THE OCCASIONAL IRON MAN!
KA-WHUNG
YOUR EYES LIT UP LIKE A CHILD'S WHEN YOU TOLD ME ABOUT THIS PROJECT, TONY--I ONLY HOPE YOU UNDERSTAND THAT IT HURTS ME TO USE IT AGAINST YOU--
--BUT I INTEND TO PROTECT MY FATHER--ANY WAY I HAVE TO!
TERRIFIC. WITH WHITNEY INSIDE THAT THING, I CAN'T RISK USING MY REPULSORS ON FULL POWER!
ZZZRAKK
AND THESE HALF-BLASTS AREN'T DOING--
DON'T STRUGGLE, TONY! I PROMISE THE MAGNA-GRIP WILL ONLY HOLD YOU LONG ENOUGH--
--EEEAAGGH!
--FOR THE LASER-BORER TO IMMOBILIZE YOUR ARMOR!
WHITNEY, YOU MAY KNOW HOW TO OPERATE THIS GIZMO, BUT I DESIGNED IT!
AND I KNOW ITS BREAKING POINT!
SHAKOOM

JUST LIKE I KNOW MY *OWN!*

RRRRATCH

AND, LADY, BELIEVE ME WHEN I TELL YOU--

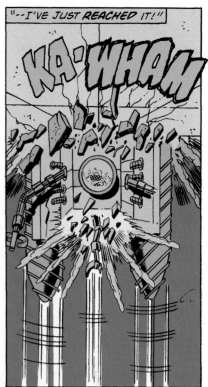

"--I'VE JUST *REACHED* IT!"

KA-WHAM

I SHARED MY *LIFE* WITH YOU, WHITNEY-- MY LOVE, MY *DREAMS!*

AND I DON'T *AP-PRECIATE* HAVING THE WORLD I TRUST-ED YOU WITH TURNED *AGAINST* ME!

KRAK

KRINKLASH

CAPISH?

AND NOW, MS. FROST, WE'RE GOING TO *SETTLE* THIS ONCE AND FOR--

K BLAM BLAM

WHA-- OH, NO!

"THE SECURITY GUARDS MUST HAVE HEARD THE NOISE--

KRAK

KPOW

"--AND THE JLV'S STILL *OPERATING!*"

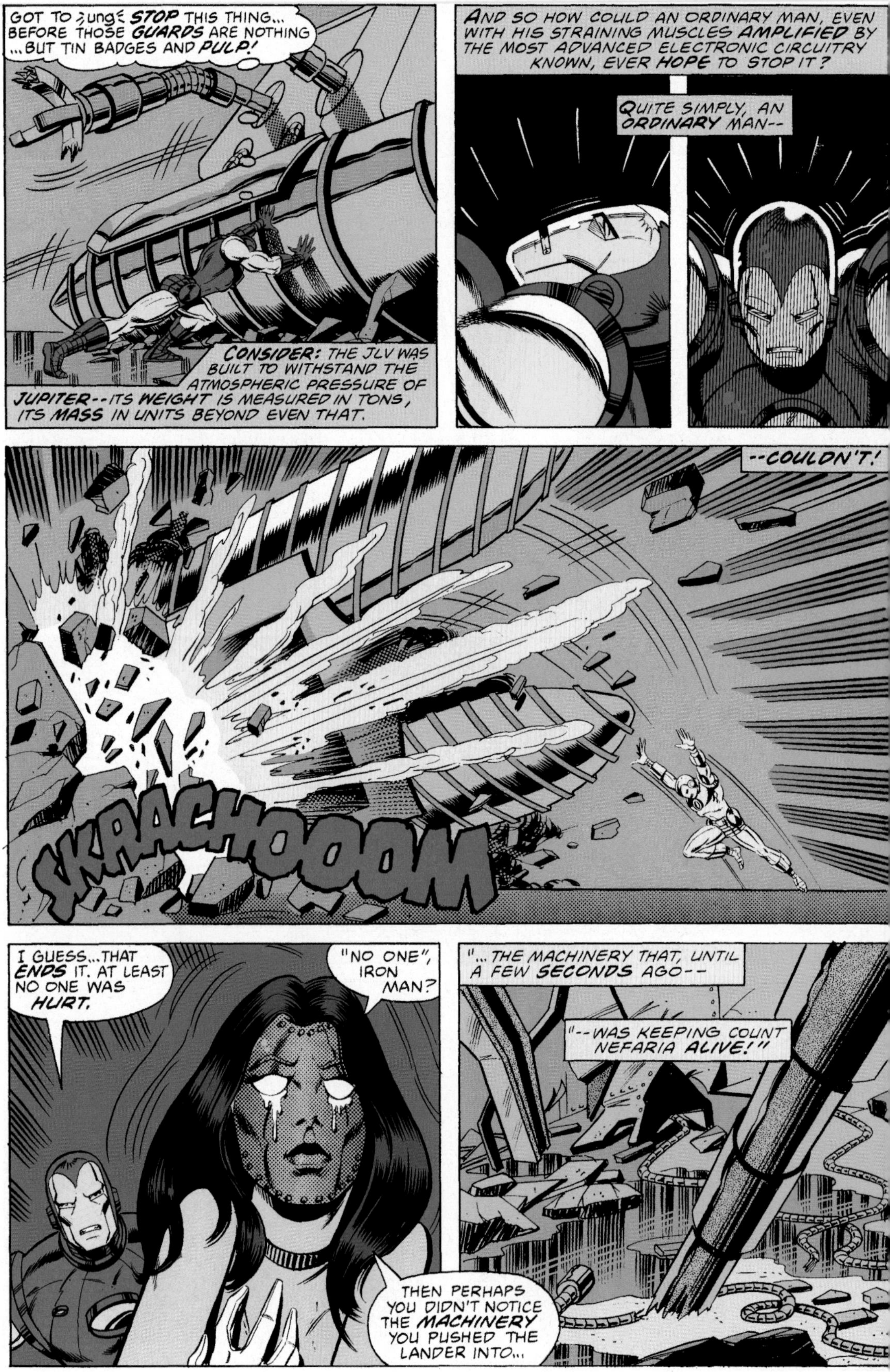

GOT TO ~ung~ STOP THIS THING... BEFORE THOSE GUARDS ARE NOTHING ...BUT TIN BADGES AND PULP!
CONSIDER: THE JLV WAS BUILT TO WITHSTAND THE ATMOSPHERIC PRESSURE OF JUPITER--ITS WEIGHT IS MEASURED IN TONS, ITS MASS IN UNITS BEYOND EVEN THAT.
AND SO HOW COULD AN ORDINARY MAN, EVEN WITH HIS STRAINING MUSCLES AMPLIFIED BY THE MOST ADVANCED ELECTRONIC CIRCUITRY KNOWN, EVER HOPE TO STOP IT?
QUITE SIMPLY, AN ORDINARY MAN--
--COULDN'T!
KKRACHOOOOM
I GUESS...THAT ENDS IT. AT LEAST NO ONE WAS HURT.
"NO ONE", IRON MAN?
THEN PERHAPS YOU DIDN'T NOTICE THE MACHINERY YOU PUSHED THE LANDER INTO...
"...THE MACHINERY THAT, UNTIL A FEW SECONDS AGO--
"--WAS KEEPING COUNT NEFARIA ALIVE!"

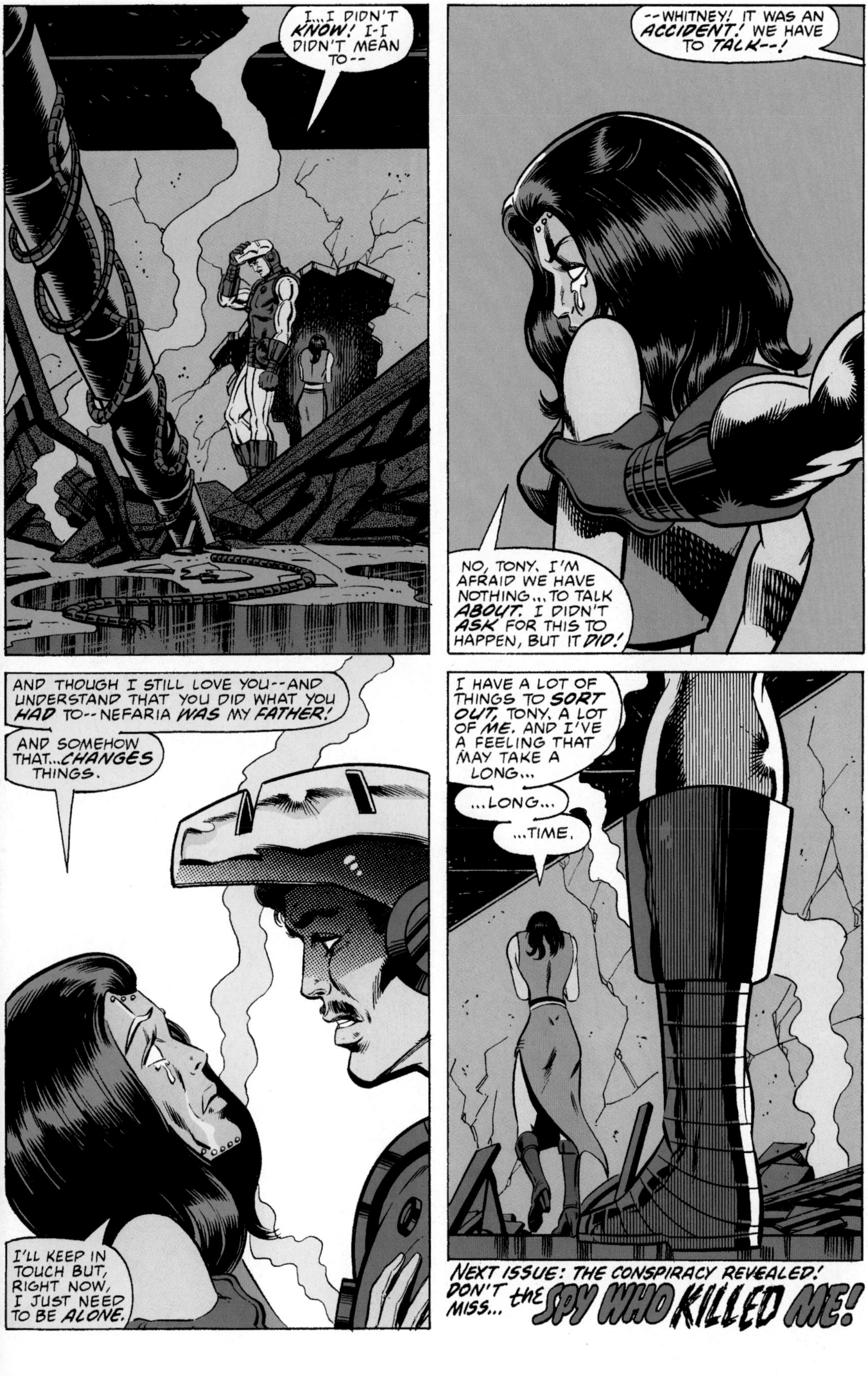
I...I DIDN'T KNOW! I-I DIDN'T MEAN TO--
--WHITNEY! IT WAS AN ACCIDENT! WE HAVE TO TALK--!
NO, TONY. I'M AFRAID WE HAVE NOTHING... TO TALK ABOUT. I DIDN'T ASK FOR THIS TO HAPPEN, BUT IT DID!
AND THOUGH I STILL LOVE YOU--AND UNDERSTAND THAT YOU DID WHAT YOU HAD TO--NEFARIA WAS MY FATHER!
AND SOMEHOW THAT...CHANGES THINGS.
I'LL KEEP IN TOUCH BUT, RIGHT NOW, I JUST NEED TO BE ALONE.
I HAVE A LOT OF THINGS TO SORT OUT, TONY. A LOT OF ME. AND I'VE A FEELING THAT MAY TAKE A LONG...
...LONG...
...TIME.

NEXT ISSUE: THE CONSPIRACY REVEALED! DON'T MISS... the SPY WHO KILLED ME!

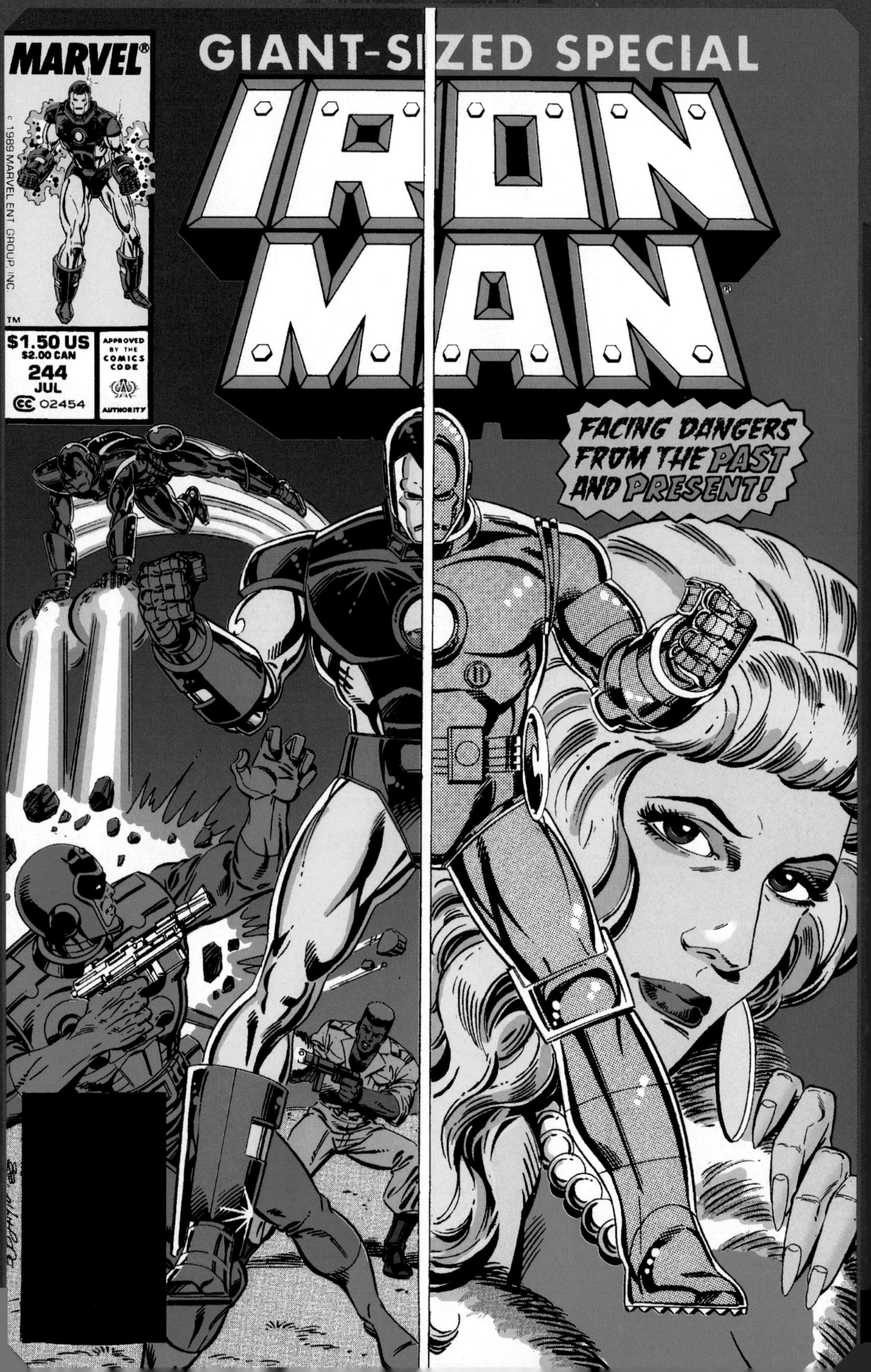
MARVEL®
GIANT-SIZED SPECIAL
IRON MAN®
© 1989 MARVEL ENT GROUP, INC
TM
$1.50 US
$2.00 CAN
244
JUL
02454
APPROVED BY THE COMICS CODE AUTHORITY
FACING DANGERS FROM THE PAST AND PRESENT!

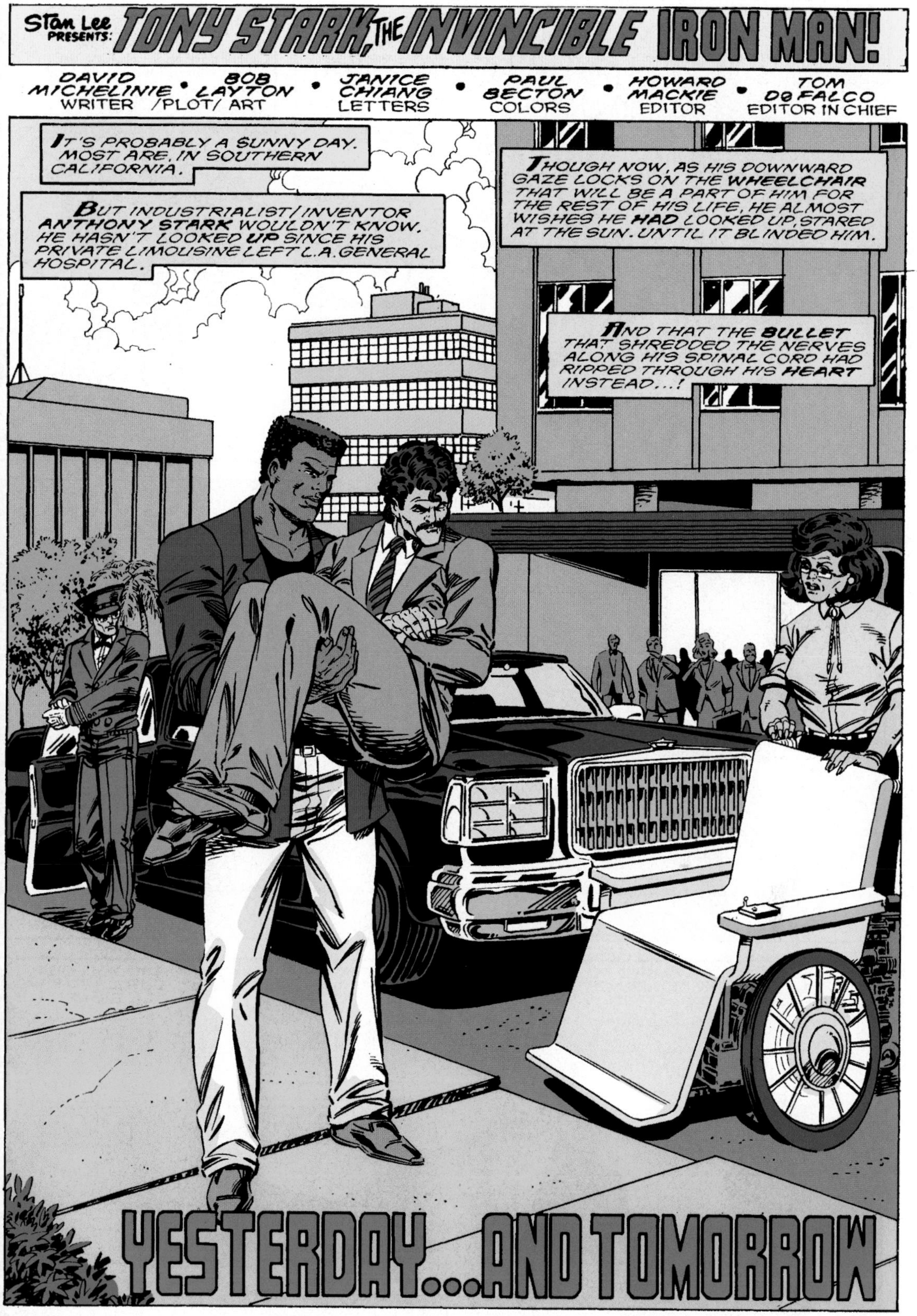

STAN LEE PRESENTS: TONY STARK, THE INVINCIBLE IRON MAN!
DAVID MICHELINIE WRITER • BOB LAYTON /PLOT/ ART • JANICE CHIANG LETTERS • PAUL BECTON COLORS • HOWARD MACKIE EDITOR • TOM DeFALCO EDITOR IN CHIEF
IT'S PROBABLY A SUNNY DAY. MOST ARE, IN SOUTHERN CALIFORNIA.
BUT INDUSTRIALIST/INVENTOR ANTHONY STARK WOULDN'T KNOW. HE HASN'T LOOKED UP SINCE HIS PRIVATE LIMOUSINE LEFT L.A. GENERAL HOSPITAL.
THOUGH NOW, AS HIS DOWNWARD GAZE LOCKS ON THE WHEELCHAIR THAT WILL BE A PART OF HIM FOR THE REST OF HIS LIFE, HE ALMOST WISHES HE HAD LOOKED UP. STARED AT THE SUN. UNTIL IT BLINDED HIM.
AND THAT THE BULLET THAT SHREDDED THE NERVES ALONG HIS SPINAL CORD HAD RIPPED THROUGH HIS HEART INSTEAD...!
YESTERDAY...AND TOMORROW

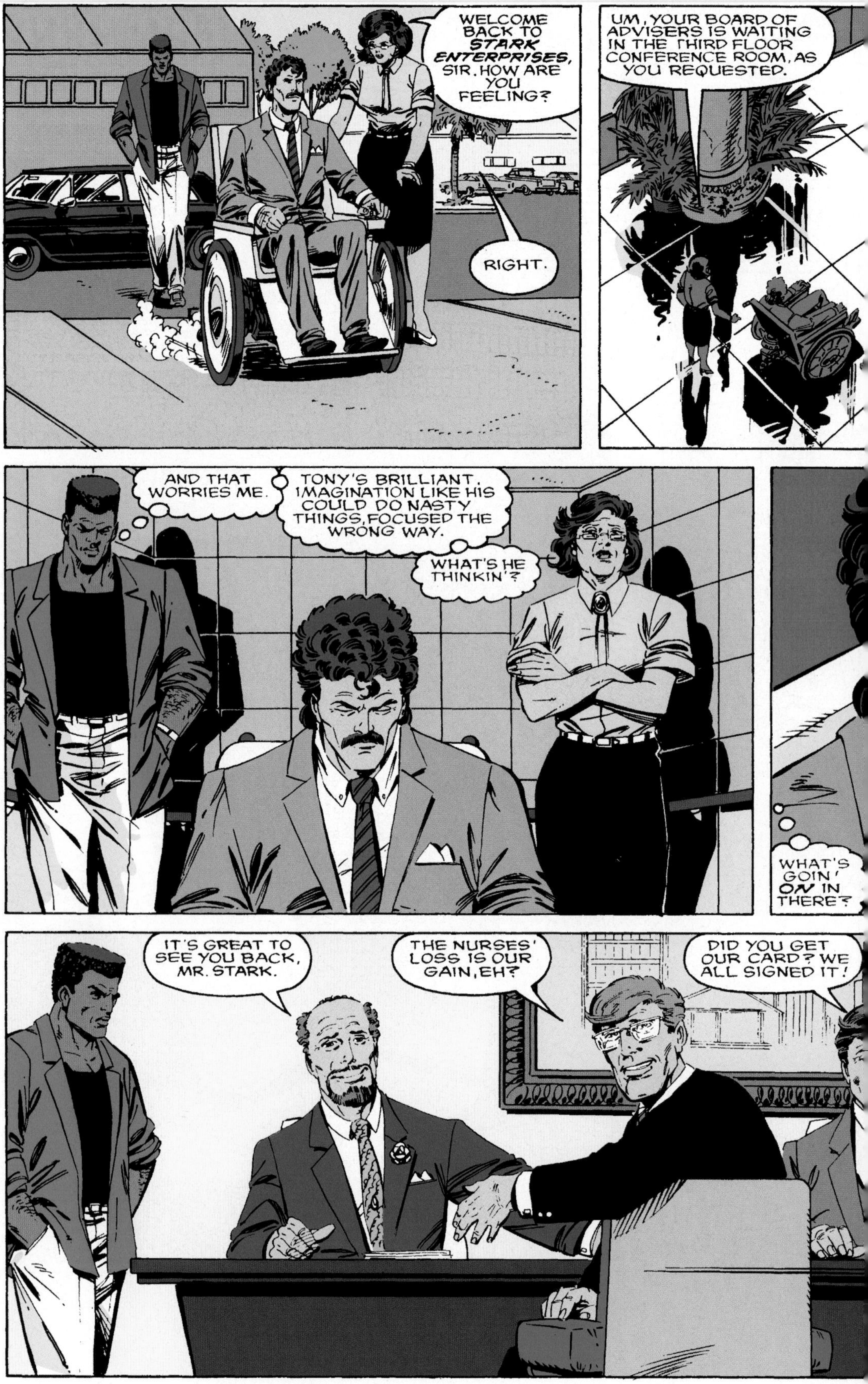
WELCOME BACK TO STARK ENTERPRISES, SIR. HOW ARE YOU FEELING?
RIGHT.
UM, YOUR BOARD OF ADVISERS IS WAITING IN THE THIRD FLOOR CONFERENCE ROOM, AS YOU REQUESTED.
AND THAT WORRIES ME.
TONY'S BRILLIANT. IMAGINATION LIKE HIS COULD DO NASTY THINGS, FOCUSED THE WRONG WAY.
WHAT'S HE THINKIN'?
WHAT'S GOIN' ON IN THERE?
IT'S GREAT TO SEE YOU BACK, MR. STARK.
THE NURSES' LOSS IS OUR GAIN, EH?
DID YOU GET OUR CARD? WE ALL SIGNED IT!

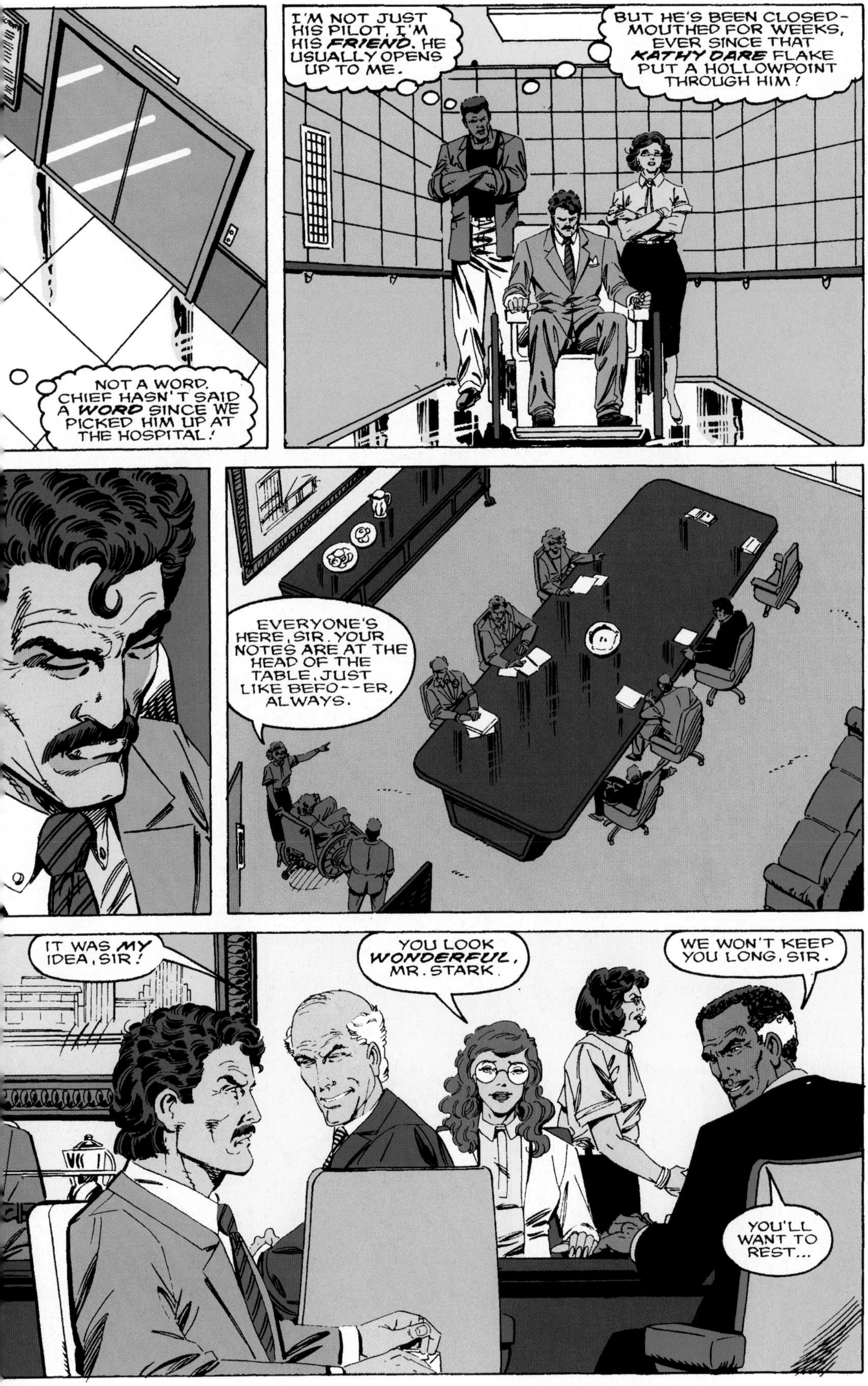

NOT A WORD. CHIEF HASN'T SAID A WORD SINCE WE PICKED HIM UP AT THE HOSPITAL!
I'M NOT JUST HIS PILOT, I'M HIS FRIEND. HE USUALLY OPENS UP TO ME.
BUT HE'S BEEN CLOSED-MOUTHED FOR WEEKS, EVER SINCE THAT KATHY DARE FLAKE PUT A HOLLOWPOINT THROUGH HIM!
EVERYONE'S HERE, SIR. YOUR NOTES ARE AT THE HEAD OF THE TABLE, JUST LIKE BEFO--ER, ALWAYS.
IT WAS MY IDEA, SIR!
YOU LOOK WONDERFUL, MR. STARK.
WE WON'T KEEP YOU LONG, SIR.
YOU'LL WANT TO REST...

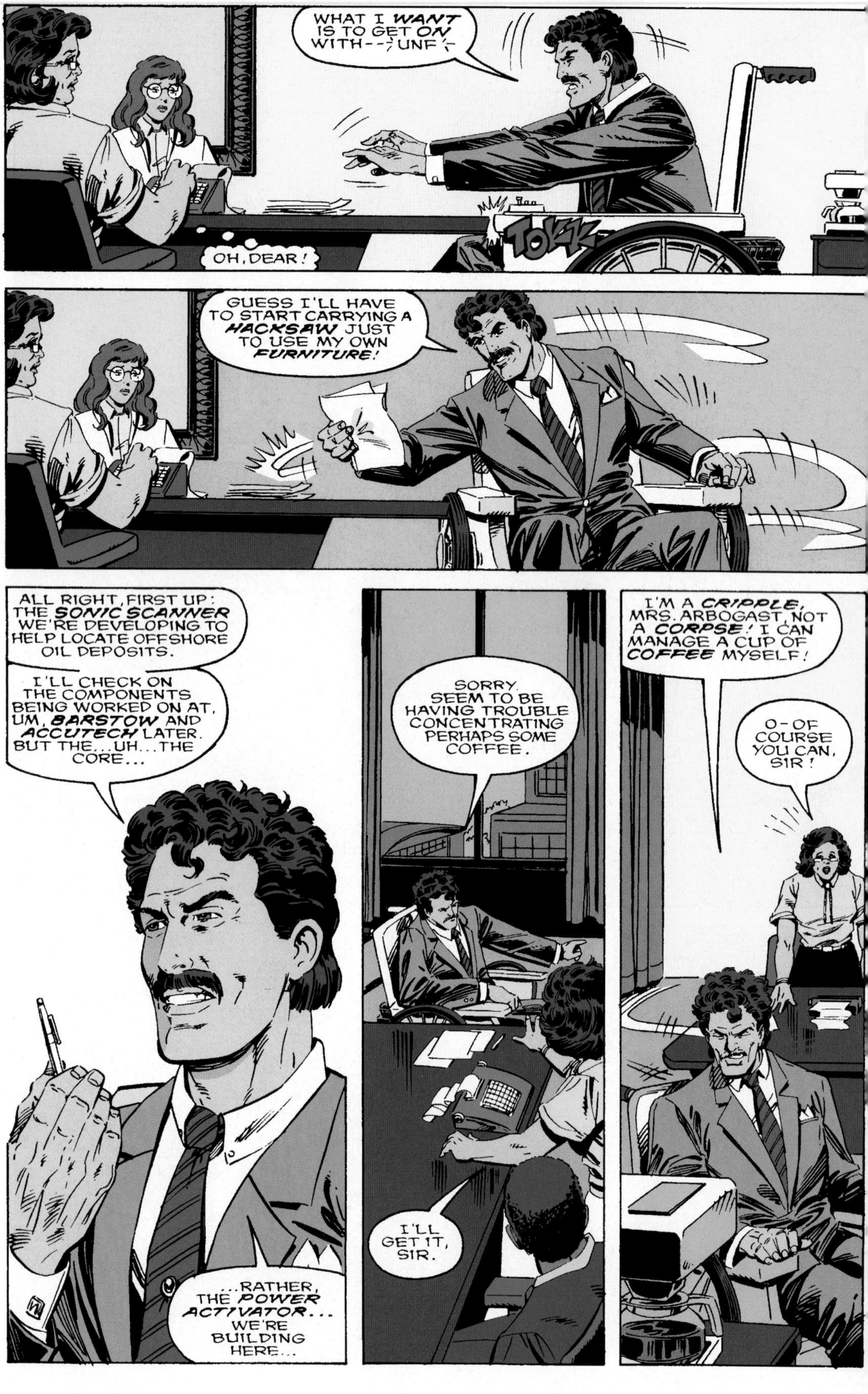
WHAT I WANT IS TO GET ON WITH--UNF
TOKK
OH, DEAR!
GUESS I'LL HAVE TO START CARRYING A HACKSAW JUST TO USE MY OWN FURNITURE!
ALL RIGHT, FIRST UP: THE SONIC SCANNER WE'RE DEVELOPING TO HELP LOCATE OFFSHORE OIL DEPOSITS.
I'LL CHECK ON THE COMPONENTS BEING WORKED ON AT, UM, BARSTOW AND ACCUTECH LATER. BUT THE...UH...THE CORE...
...RATHER, THE POWER ACTIVATOR... WE'RE BUILDING HERE...
SORRY. SEEM TO BE HAVING TROUBLE CONCENTRATING. PERHAPS SOME COFFEE.
I'LL GET IT, SIR.
I'M A CRIPPLE, MRS. ARBOGAST, NOT A CORPSE! I CAN MANAGE A CUP OF COFFEE MYSELF!
O-OF COURSE YOU CAN, SIR!

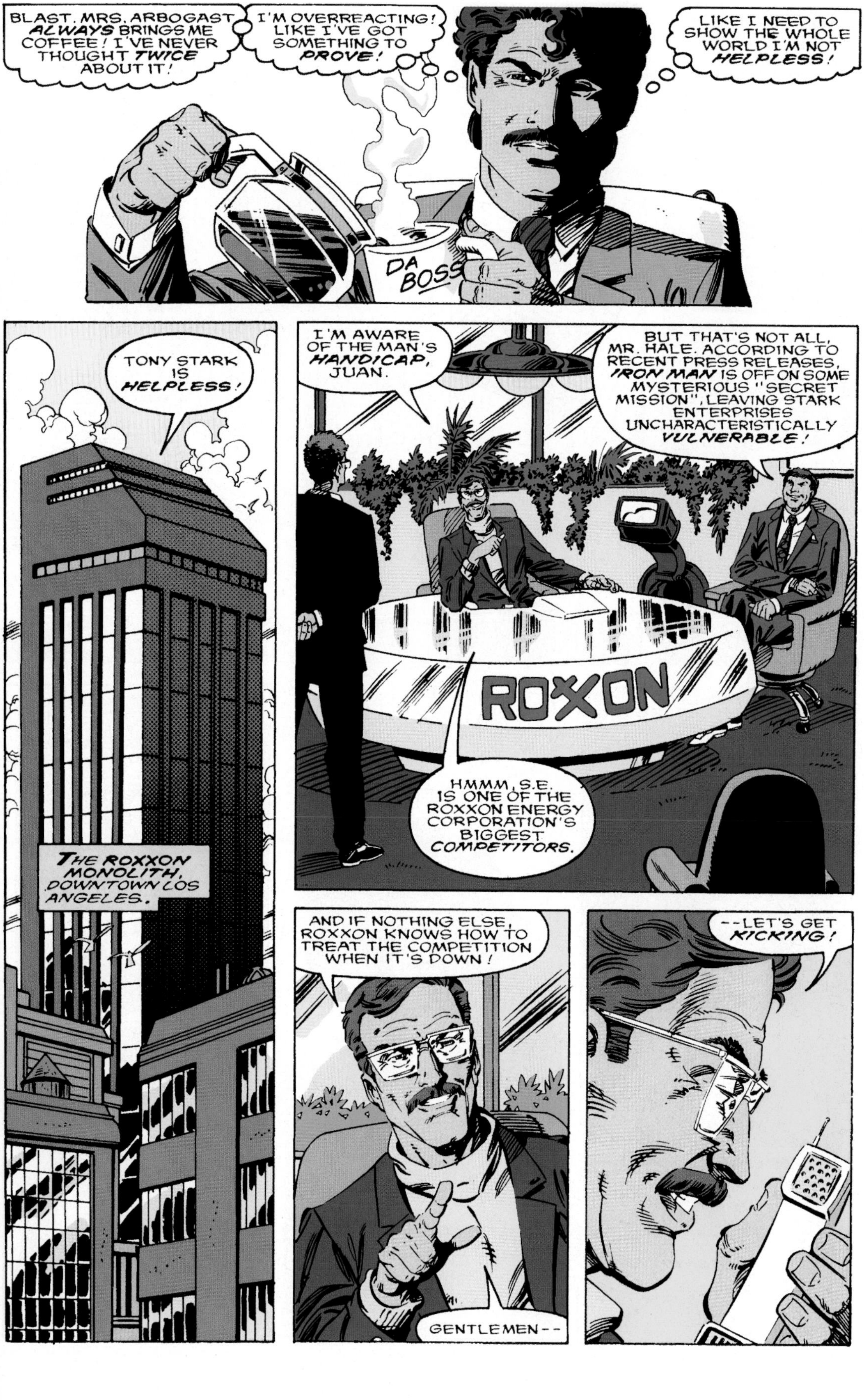
BLAST. MRS. ARBOGAST *ALWAYS* BRINGS ME COFFEE! I'VE NEVER THOUGHT *TWICE* ABOUT IT!
I'M OVERREACTING! LIKE I'VE GOT SOMETHING TO *PROVE*!
LIKE I NEED TO SHOW THE WHOLE WORLD I'M NOT *HELPLESS*!
DA BOSS
TONY STARK IS *HELPLESS*!
THE ROXXON MONOLITH, DOWNTOWN LOS ANGELES.
I'M AWARE OF THE MAN'S *HANDICAP*, JUAN.
BUT THAT'S NOT ALL, MR. HALE. ACCORDING TO RECENT PRESS RELEASES, *IRON MAN* IS OFF ON SOME MYSTERIOUS "SECRET MISSION", LEAVING STARK ENTERPRISES UNCHARACTERISTICALLY *VULNERABLE*!
ROXXON
HMMM, S.E. IS ONE OF THE ROXXON ENERGY CORPORATION'S BIGGEST *COMPETITORS*.
AND IF NOTHING ELSE, ROXXON KNOWS HOW TO TREAT THE COMPETITION WHEN IT'S DOWN!
GENTLEMEN--
--LET'S GET *KICKING*!

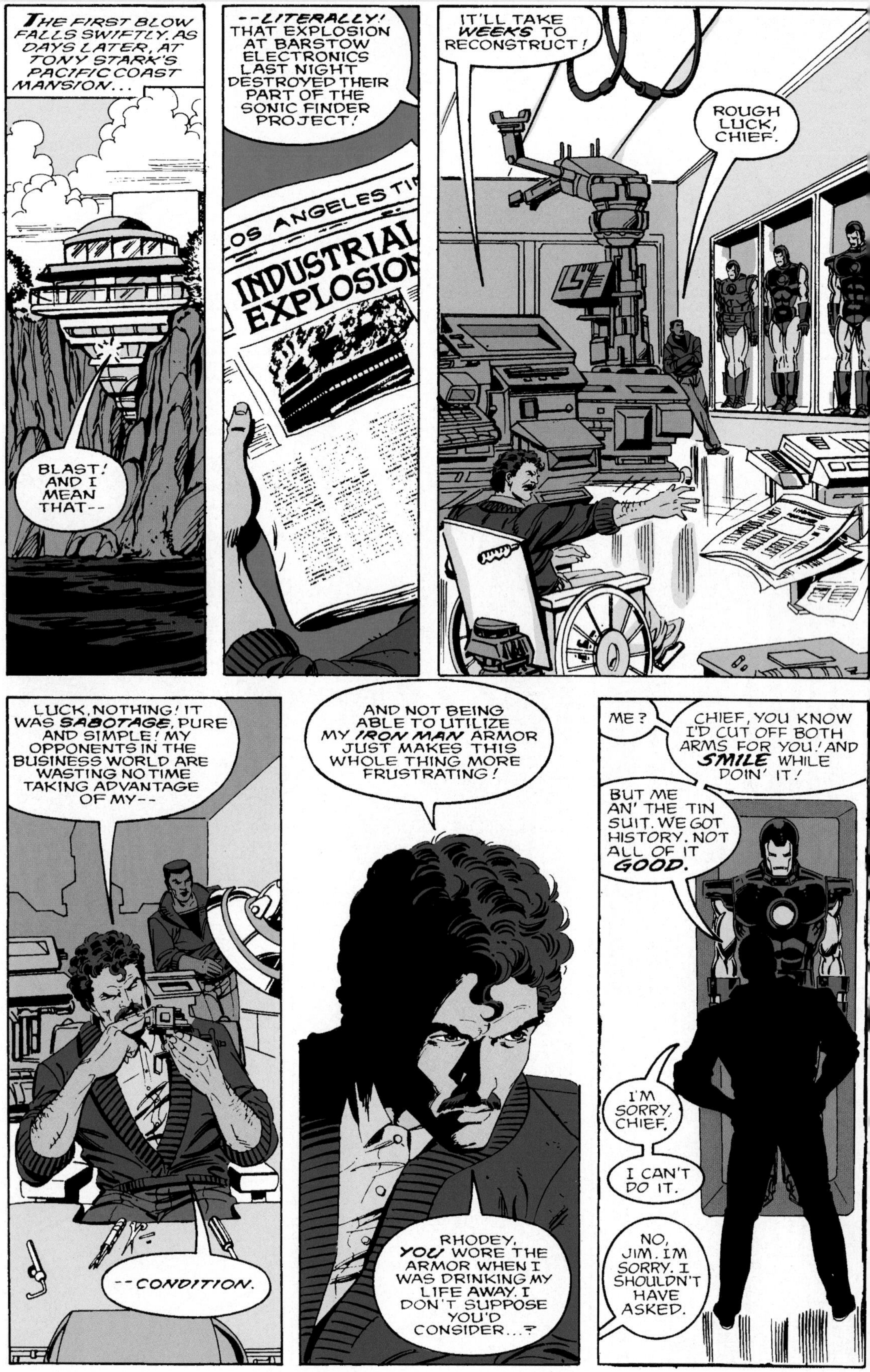
THE FIRST BLOW FALLS SWIFTLY. AS DAYS LATER, AT TONY STARK'S PACIFIC COAST MANSION...
BLAST! AND I MEAN THAT--
--LITERALLY! THAT EXPLOSION AT BARSTOW ELECTRONICS LAST NIGHT DESTROYED THEIR PART OF THE SONIC FINDER PROJECT!
LOS ANGELES TI
INDUSTRIAL EXPLOSION
IT'LL TAKE WEEKS TO RECONSTRUCT!
ROUGH LUCK, CHIEF.
LUCK, NOTHING! IT WAS SABOTAGE, PURE AND SIMPLE! MY OPPONENTS IN THE BUSINESS WORLD ARE WASTING NO TIME TAKING ADVANTAGE OF MY--
--CONDITION.
AND NOT BEING ABLE TO UTILIZE MY IRON MAN ARMOR JUST MAKES THIS WHOLE THING MORE FRUSTRATING!
RHODEY, YOU WORE THE ARMOR WHEN I WAS DRINKING MY LIFE AWAY. I DON'T SUPPOSE YOU'D CONSIDER...?
ME?
CHIEF, YOU KNOW I'D CUT OFF BOTH ARMS FOR YOU! AND SMILE WHILE DOIN' IT!
BUT ME AN' THE TIN SUIT. WE GOT HISTORY. NOT ALL OF IT GOOD.
I'M SORRY, CHIEF.
I CAN'T DO IT.
NO, JIM. I'M SORRY. I SHOULDN'T HAVE ASKED.

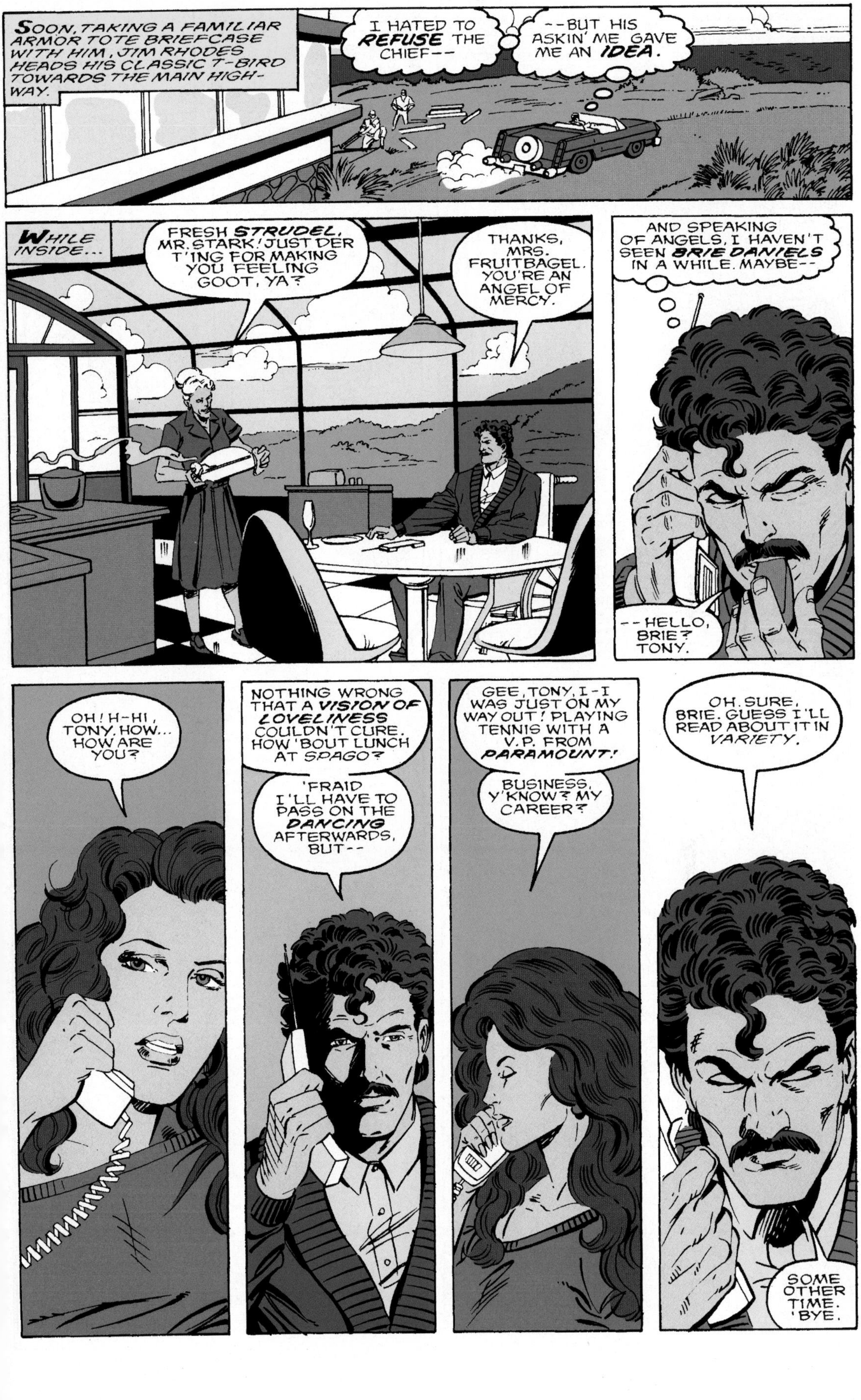
SOON, TAKING A FAMILIAR ARMOR TOTE BRIEFCASE WITH HIM, JIM RHODES HEADS HIS CLASSIC T-BIRD TOWARDS THE MAIN HIGHWAY.
I HATED TO REFUSE THE CHIEF--
--BUT HIS ASKIN' ME GAVE ME AN IDEA.
WHILE INSIDE...
FRESH STRUDEL, MR. STARK! JUST DER T'ING FOR MAKING YOU FEELING GOOT, YA?
THANKS, MRS. FRUITBAGEL. YOU'RE AN ANGEL OF MERCY.
AND SPEAKING OF ANGELS, I HAVEN'T SEEN BRIE DANIELS IN A WHILE. MAYBE--
--HELLO, BRIE? TONY.
OH! H-HI, TONY. HOW... HOW ARE YOU?
NOTHING WRONG THAT A VISION OF LOVELINESS COULDN'T CURE. HOW 'BOUT LUNCH AT SPAGO?
'FRAID I'LL HAVE TO PASS ON THE DANCING AFTERWARDS, BUT--
GEE, TONY, I-I WAS JUST ON MY WAY OUT! PLAYING TENNIS WITH A V.P. FROM PARAMOUNT!
BUSINESS, Y'KNOW? MY CAREER?
OH. SURE, BRIE. GUESS I'LL READ ABOUT IT IN VARIETY.
SOME OTHER TIME. 'BYE.

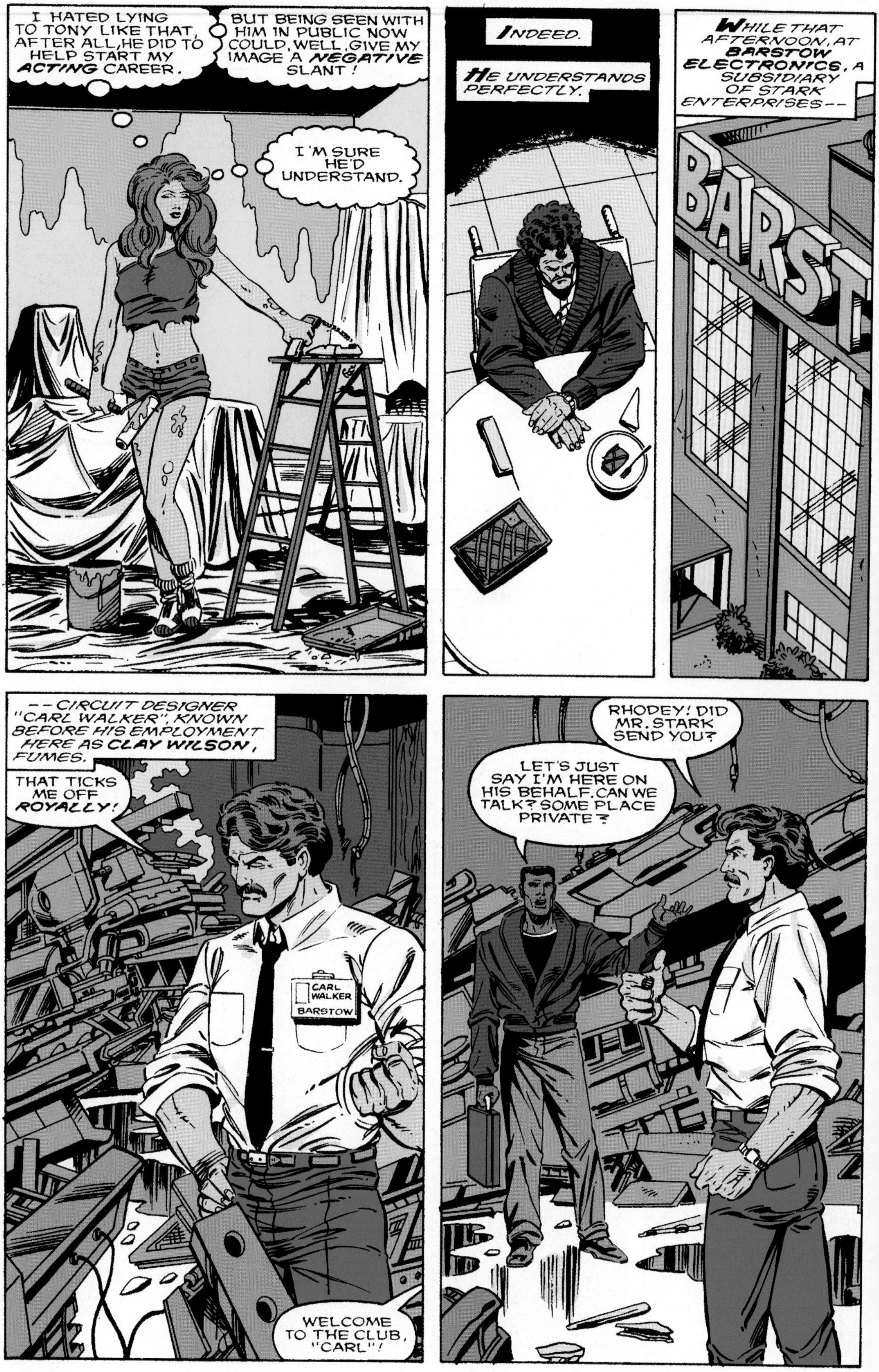
I HATED LYING TO TONY LIKE THAT, AFTER ALL, HE DID TO HELP START MY ACTING CAREER.
BUT BEING SEEN WITH HIM IN PUBLIC NOW COULD, WELL, GIVE MY IMAGE A NEGATIVE SLANT!
I'M SURE HE'D UNDERSTAND.
INDEED.
HE UNDERSTANDS PERFECTLY.
WHILE THAT AFTERNOON, AT BARSTOW ELECTRONICS, A SUBSIDIARY OF STARK ENTERPRISES--
BARST
--CIRCUIT DESIGNER "CARL WALKER", KNOWN BEFORE HIS EMPLOYMENT HERE AS CLAY WILSON, FUMES.
THAT TICKS ME OFF ROYALLY!
CARL WALKER
BARSTOW
WELCOME TO THE CLUB, "CARL"!
RHODEY! DID MR. STARK SEND YOU?
LET'S JUST SAY I'M HERE ON HIS BEHALF. CAN WE TALK? SOME PLACE PRIVATE?

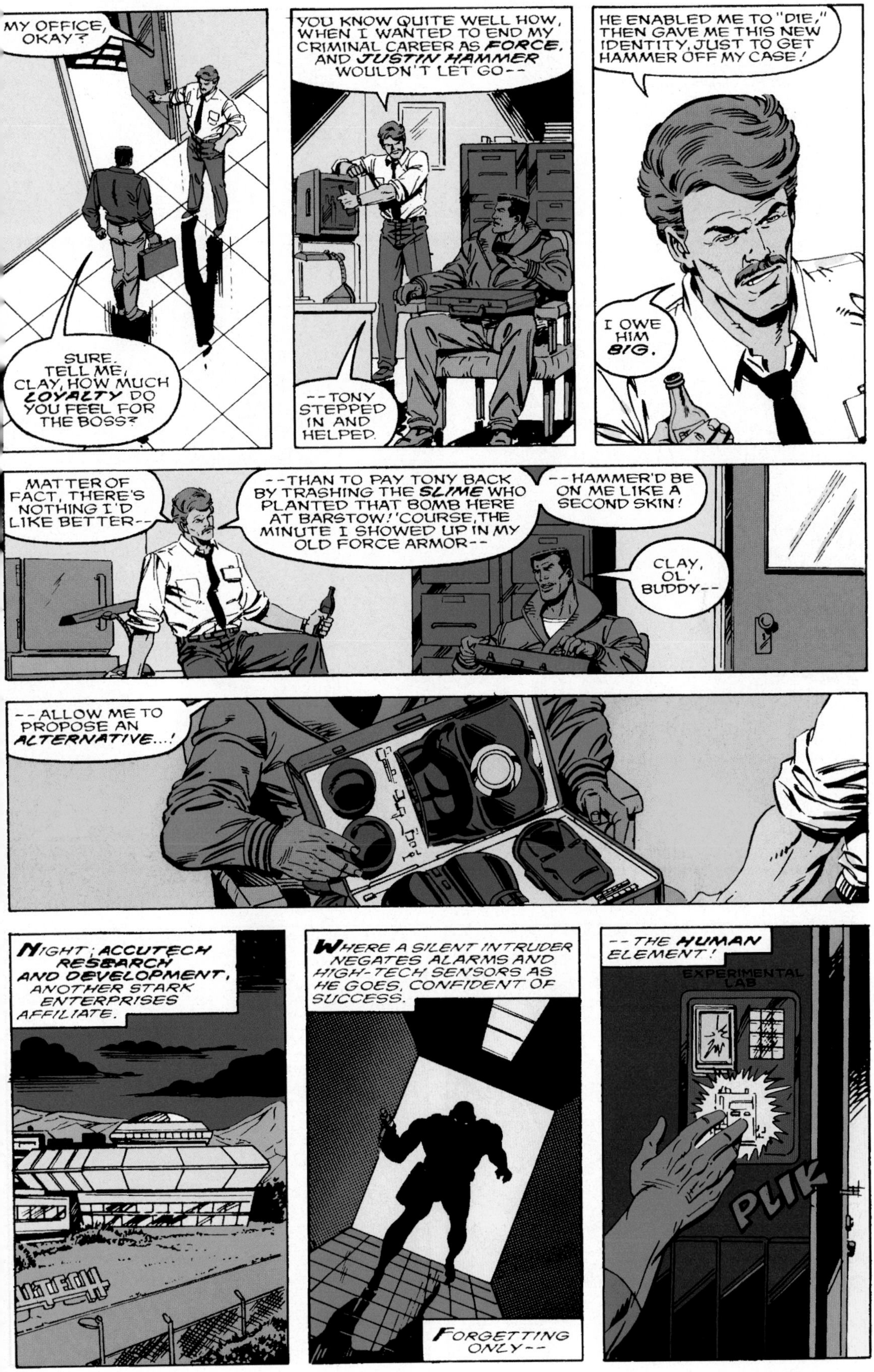
MY OFFICE, OKAY?
SURE. TELL ME, CLAY, HOW MUCH LOYALTY DO YOU FEEL FOR THE BOSS?
YOU KNOW QUITE WELL HOW, WHEN I WANTED TO END MY CRIMINAL CAREER AS FORCE, AND JUSTIN HAMMER WOULDN'T LET GO--
--TONY STEPPED IN AND HELPED.
HE ENABLED ME TO "DIE," THEN GAVE ME THIS NEW IDENTITY, JUST TO GET HAMMER OFF MY CASE!
I OWE HIM BIG.
MATTER OF FACT, THERE'S NOTHING I'D LIKE BETTER--
--THAN TO PAY TONY BACK BY TRASHING THE SLIME WHO PLANTED THAT BOMB HERE AT BARSTOW! 'COURSE, THE MINUTE I SHOWED UP IN MY OLD FORCE ARMOR--
--HAMMER'D BE ON ME LIKE A SECOND SKIN!
CLAY, OL' BUDDY--
--ALLOW ME TO PROPOSE AN ALTERNATIVE...!
NIGHT: ACCUTECH RESEARCH AND DEVELOPMENT, ANOTHER STARK ENTERPRISES AFFILIATE.
WHERE A SILENT INTRUDER NEGATES ALARMS AND HIGH-TECH SENSORS AS HE GOES, CONFIDENT OF SUCCESS.
FORGETTING ONLY--
--THE HUMAN ELEMENT!
EXPERIMENTAL LAB
PLIK

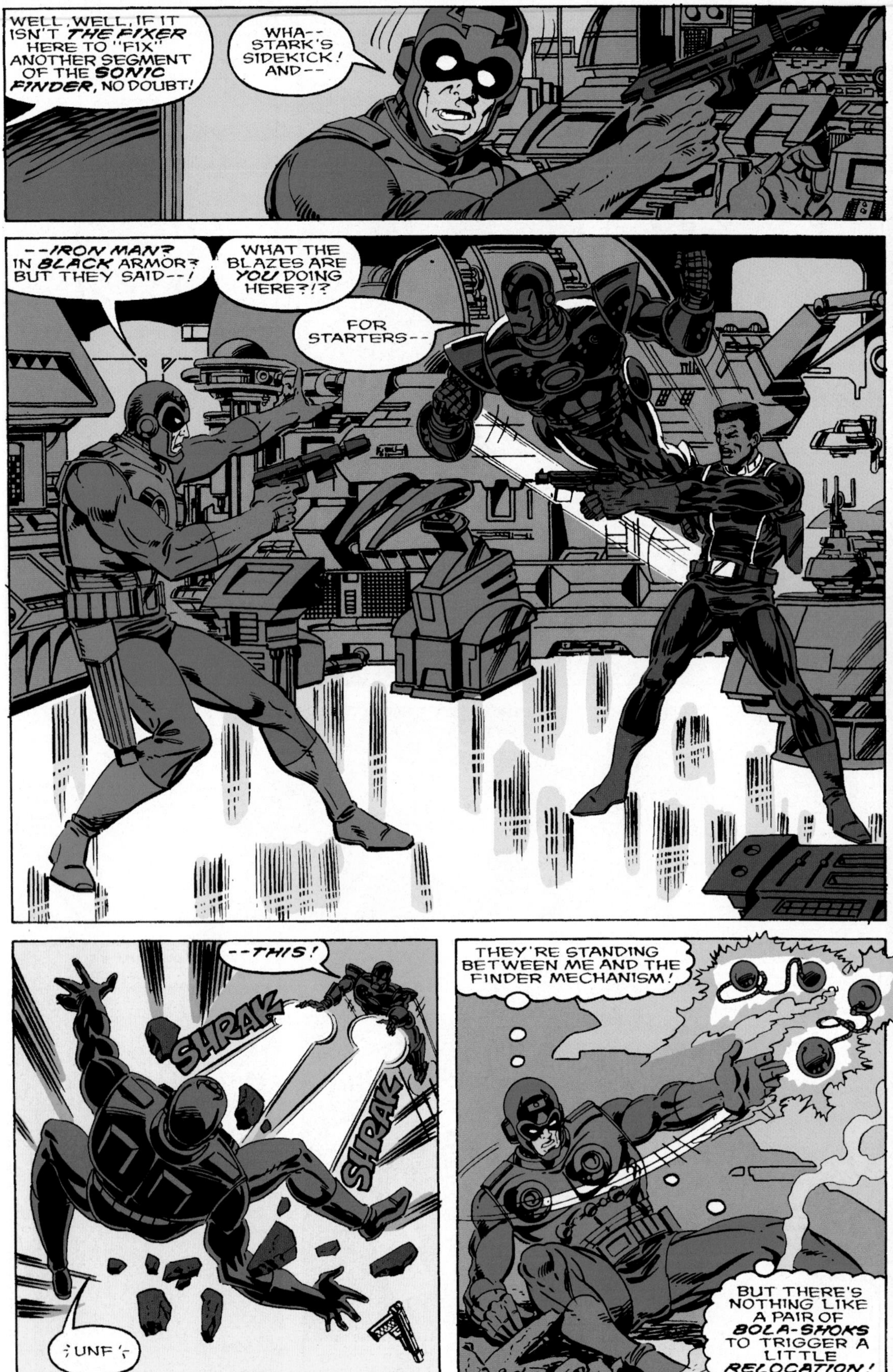

WELL, WELL, IF IT ISN'T THE FIXER HERE TO "FIX" ANOTHER SEGMENT OF THE SONIC FINDER, NO DOUBT!
WHA-- STARK'S SIDEKICK! AND--
--IRON MAN? IN BLACK ARMOR? BUT THEY SAID--!
WHAT THE BLAZES ARE YOU DOING HERE?!?
FOR STARTERS--
--THIS!
SHRAK
SHRAK
UNF
THEY'RE STANDING BETWEEN ME AND THE FINDER MECHANISM!
BUT THERE'S NOTHING LIKE A PAIR OF BOLA-SHOKS TO TRIGGER A LITTLE RELOCATION!

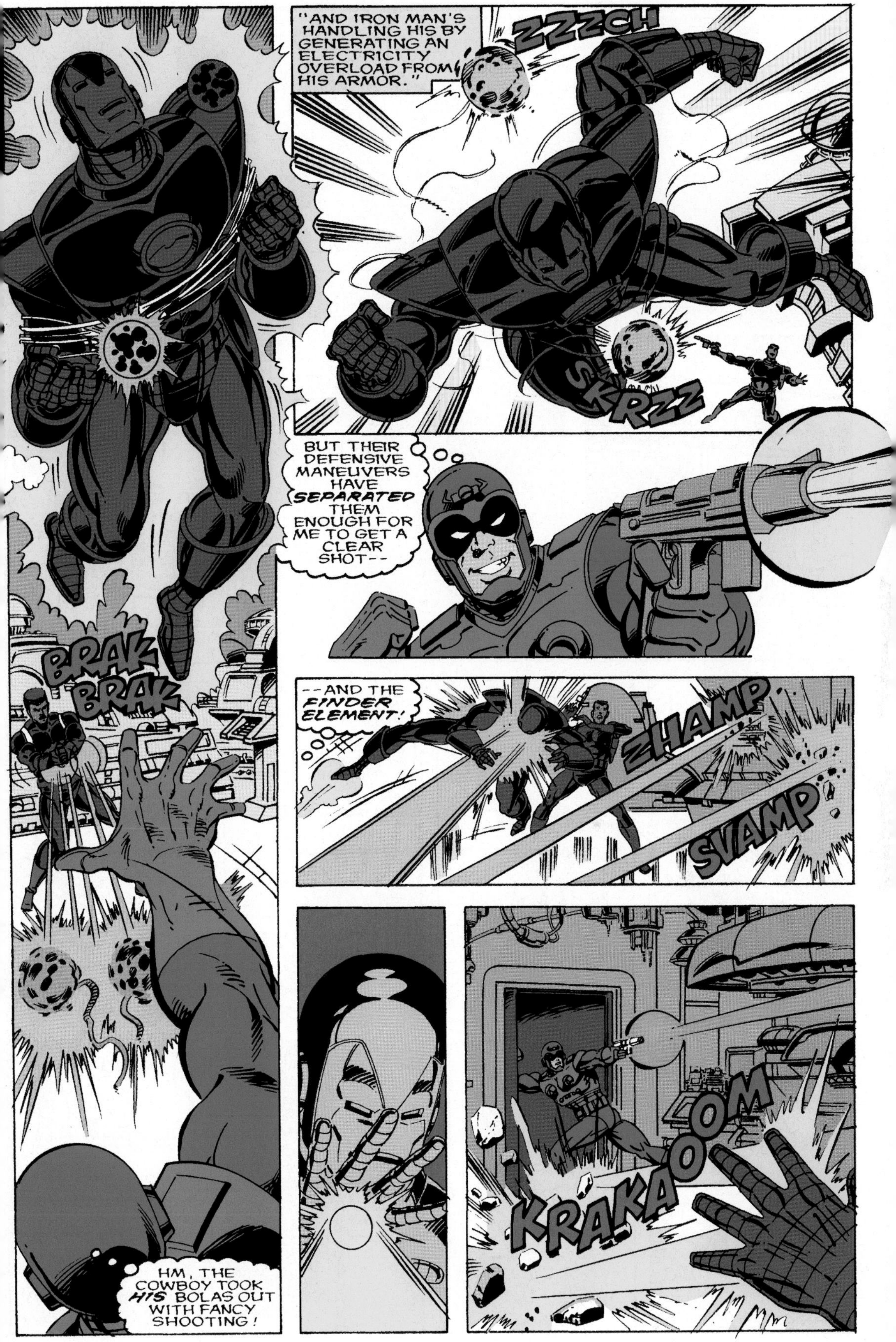

"AND IRON MAN'S HANDLING HIS BY GENERATING AN ELECTRICITY OVERLOAD FROM HIS ARMOR."
ZZZCH
SKRZZ
BUT THEIR DEFENSIVE MANEUVERS HAVE SEPARATED THEM ENOUGH FOR ME TO GET A CLEAR SHOT--
BRAK BRAK
--AND THE FINDER ELEMENT!
ZHAMP
SVAMP
HM, THE COWBOY TOOK HIS BOLAS OUT WITH FANCY SHOOTING!
KRAKAOOM

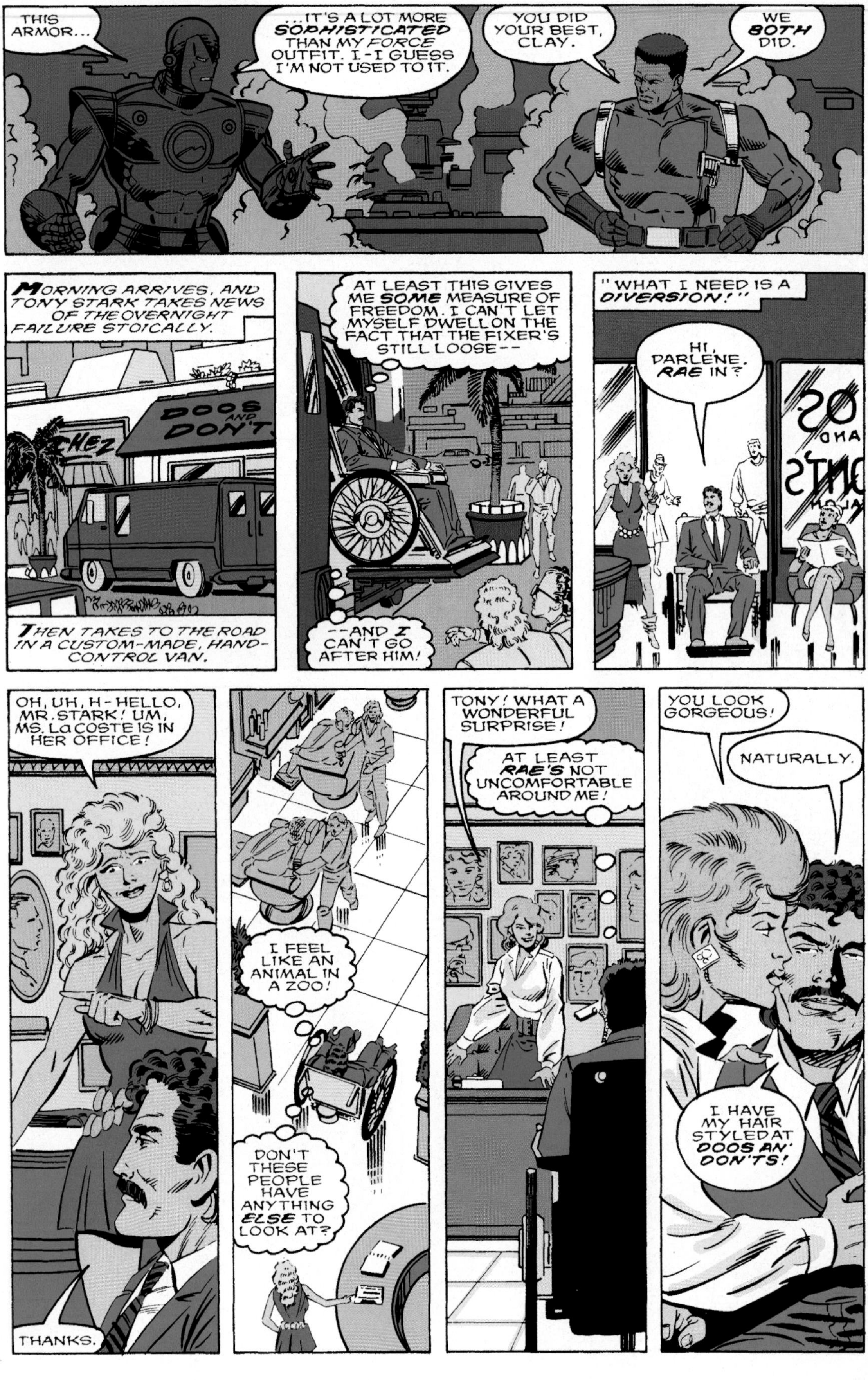
THIS ARMOR...
...IT'S A LOT MORE SOPHISTICATED THAN MY FORCE OUTFIT. I-I GUESS I'M NOT USED TO IT.
YOU DID YOUR BEST, CLAY.
WE BOTH DID.
MORNING ARRIVES, AND TONY STARK TAKES NEWS OF THE OVERNIGHT FAILURE STOICALLY.
CHEZ
DOOS AND DON'TS
THEN TAKES TO THE ROAD IN A CUSTOM-MADE, HAND-CONTROL VAN.
AT LEAST THIS GIVES ME SOME MEASURE OF FREEDOM. I CAN'T LET MYSELF DWELL ON THE FACT THAT THE FIXER'S STILL LOOSE--
--AND I CAN'T GO AFTER HIM!
"WHAT I NEED IS A DIVERSION!"
HI, DARLENE. RAE IN?
OH, UH, H-HELLO, MR. STARK! UM, MS. La COSTE IS IN HER OFFICE!
THANKS.
I FEEL LIKE AN ANIMAL IN A ZOO!
DON'T THESE PEOPLE HAVE ANYTHING ELSE TO LOOK AT?
TONY! WHAT A WONDERFUL SURPRISE!
AT LEAST RAE'S NOT UNCOMFORTABLE AROUND ME!
YOU LOOK GORGEOUS!
NATURALLY.
I HAVE MY HAIR STYLED AT DOOS AN' DON'TS!

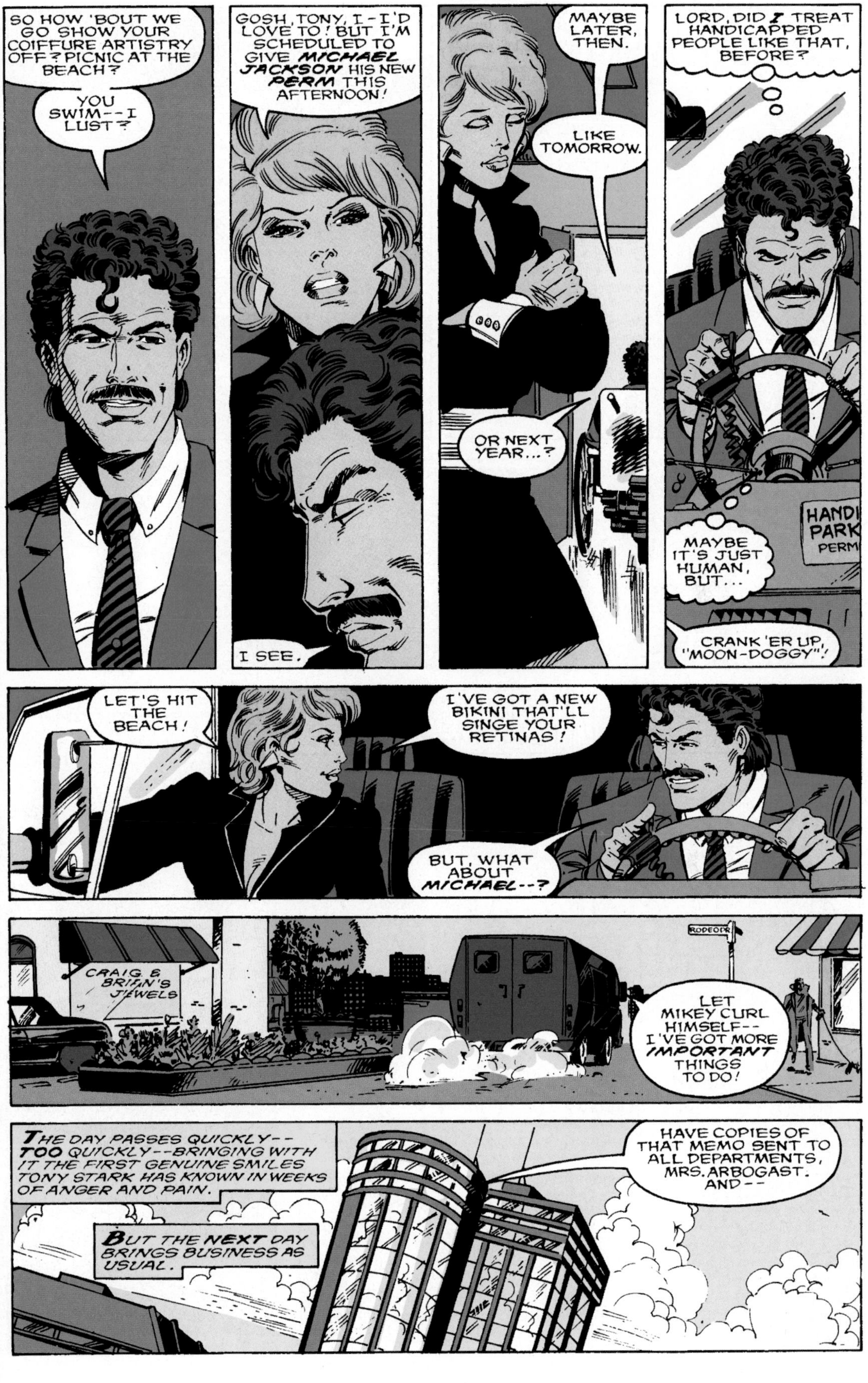

SO HOW 'BOUT WE GO SHOW YOUR COIFFURE ARTISTRY OFF? PICNIC AT THE BEACH?
YOU SWIM--I LUST?
GOSH, TONY, I-I'D LOVE TO! BUT I'M SCHEDULED TO GIVE MICHAEL JACKSON HIS NEW PERM THIS AFTERNOON!
I SEE.
MAYBE LATER, THEN.
LIKE TOMORROW.
OR NEXT YEAR...?
LORD, DID I TREAT HANDICAPPED PEOPLE LIKE THAT, BEFORE?
MAYBE IT'S JUST HUMAN, BUT...
HANDI
PARK
PERM
CRANK 'ER UP, "MOON-DOGGY"!
LET'S HIT THE BEACH!
I'VE GOT A NEW BIKINI THAT'LL SINGE YOUR RETINAS!
BUT, WHAT ABOUT MICHAEL--?
CRAIG & BRIAN'S JEWELS
RODEO DR
LET MIKEY CURL HIMSELF--I'VE GOT MORE IMPORTANT THINGS TO DO!
THE DAY PASSES QUICKLY--TOO QUICKLY--BRINGING WITH IT THE FIRST GENUINE SMILES TONY STARK HAS KNOWN IN WEEKS OF ANGER AND PAIN.
BUT THE NEXT DAY BRINGS BUSINESS AS USUAL.
HAVE COPIES OF THAT MEMO SENT TO ALL DEPARTMENTS, MRS. ARBOGAST. AND--

REEOOEEE

INTRUDER ALARM!

OH, MY WORD! LOOK AT *THAT!*

WHAT? *WHAT?*

WHRRRRR

I KNEW IT!

I *KNEW* THIS WOULD HAPPEN!

"THE FIXER USING SOME KIND OF *JET PACK* TO INCREASE HIS MANEUVERABILITY.

"PERIMETER BLISTER CANNONS CAN'T LOCK ON!"

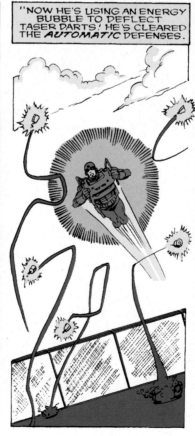
"NOW HE'S USING AN ENERGY BUBBLE TO DEFLECT TASER DARTS! HE'S CLEARED THE *AUTOMATIC* DEFENSES.

"IT'S UP TO RHODEY, CLAY, AND THE *EMERGENCY TEAM* TO STOP HIM!"

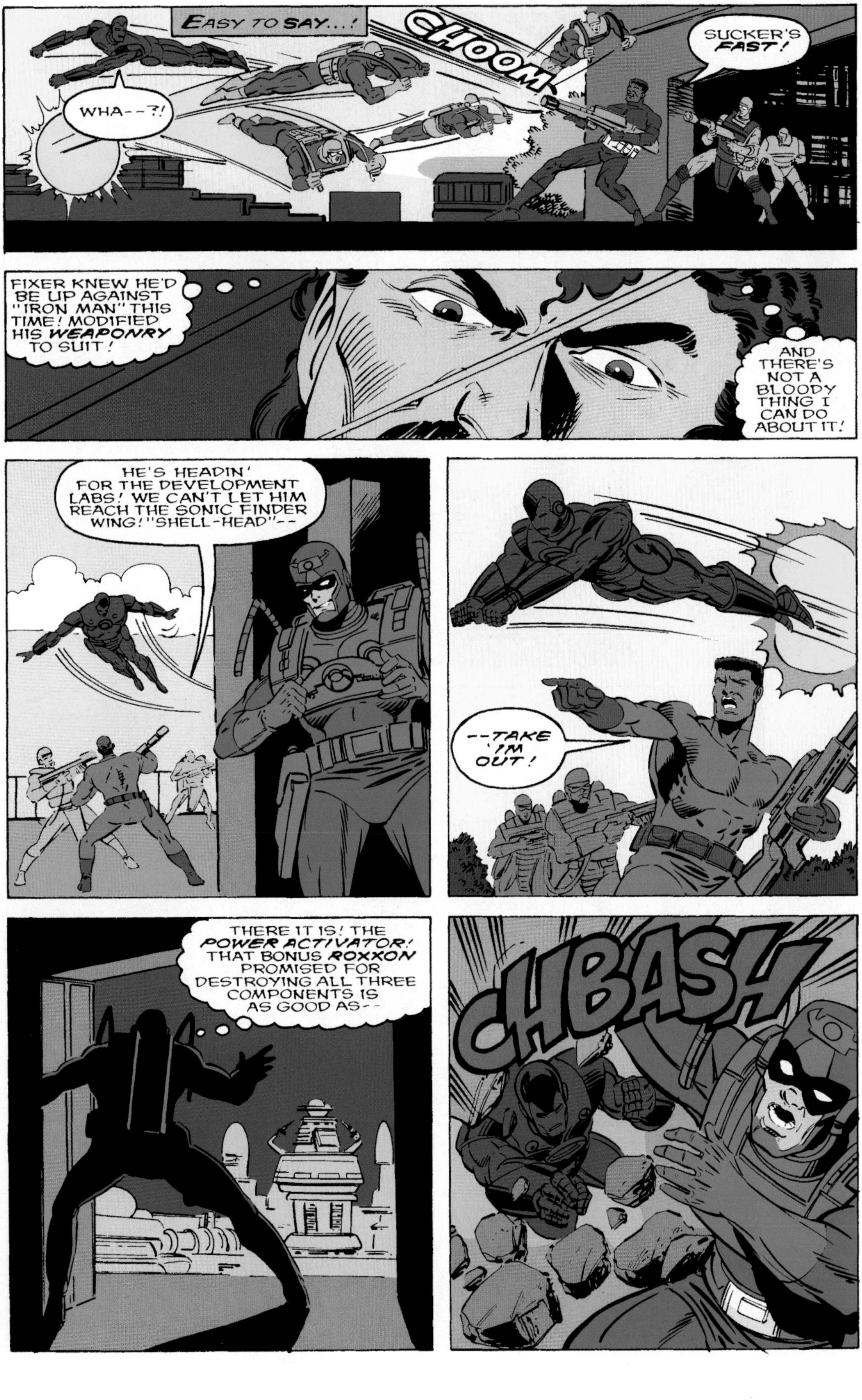
EASY TO SAY...!
CHOOOM
WHA--?!
SUCKER'S FAST!
FIXER KNEW HE'D BE UP AGAINST "IRON MAN" THIS TIME! MODIFIED HIS WEAPONRY TO SUIT!
AND THERE'S NOT A BLOODY THING I CAN DO ABOUT IT!
HE'S HEADIN' FOR THE DEVELOPMENT LABS! WE CAN'T LET HIM REACH THE SONIC FINDER WING! "SHELL-HEAD"--
--TAKE 'IM OUT!
THERE IT IS! THE POWER ACTIVATOR! THAT BONUS ROXXON PROMISED FOR DESTROYING ALL THREE COMPONENTS IS AS GOOD AS--
CHBASH

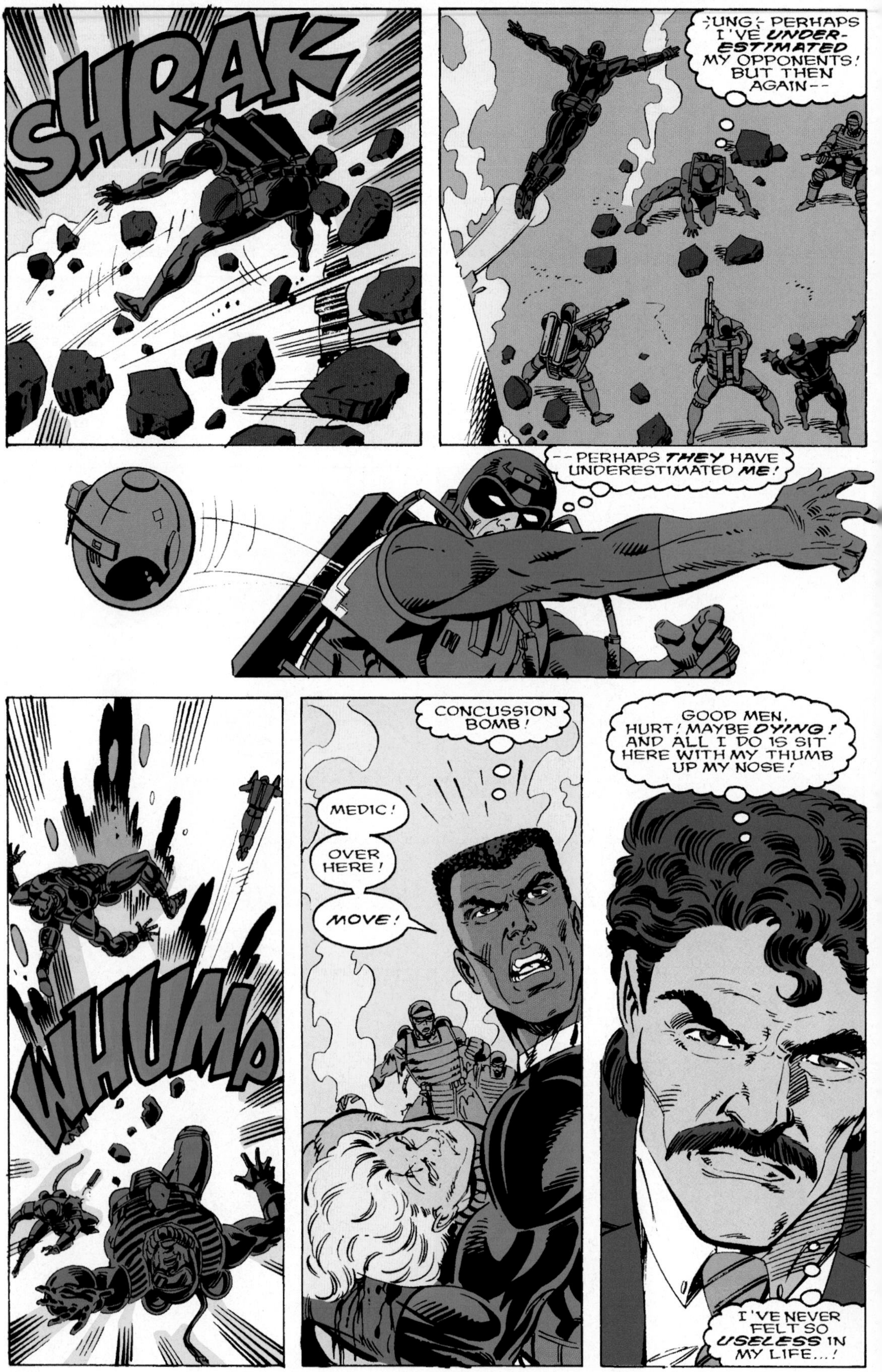
SHRAK
-UNG!- PERHAPS I'VE UNDER-ESTIMATED MY OPPONENTS! BUT THEN AGAIN--
--PERHAPS THEY HAVE UNDERESTIMATED ME!
WHUMP
CONCUSSION BOMB!
MEDIC!
OVER HERE!
MOVE!
GOOD MEN, HURT! MAYBE DYING! AND ALL I DO IS SIT HERE WITH MY THUMB UP MY NOSE!
I'VE NEVER FELT SO USELESS IN MY LIFE...!

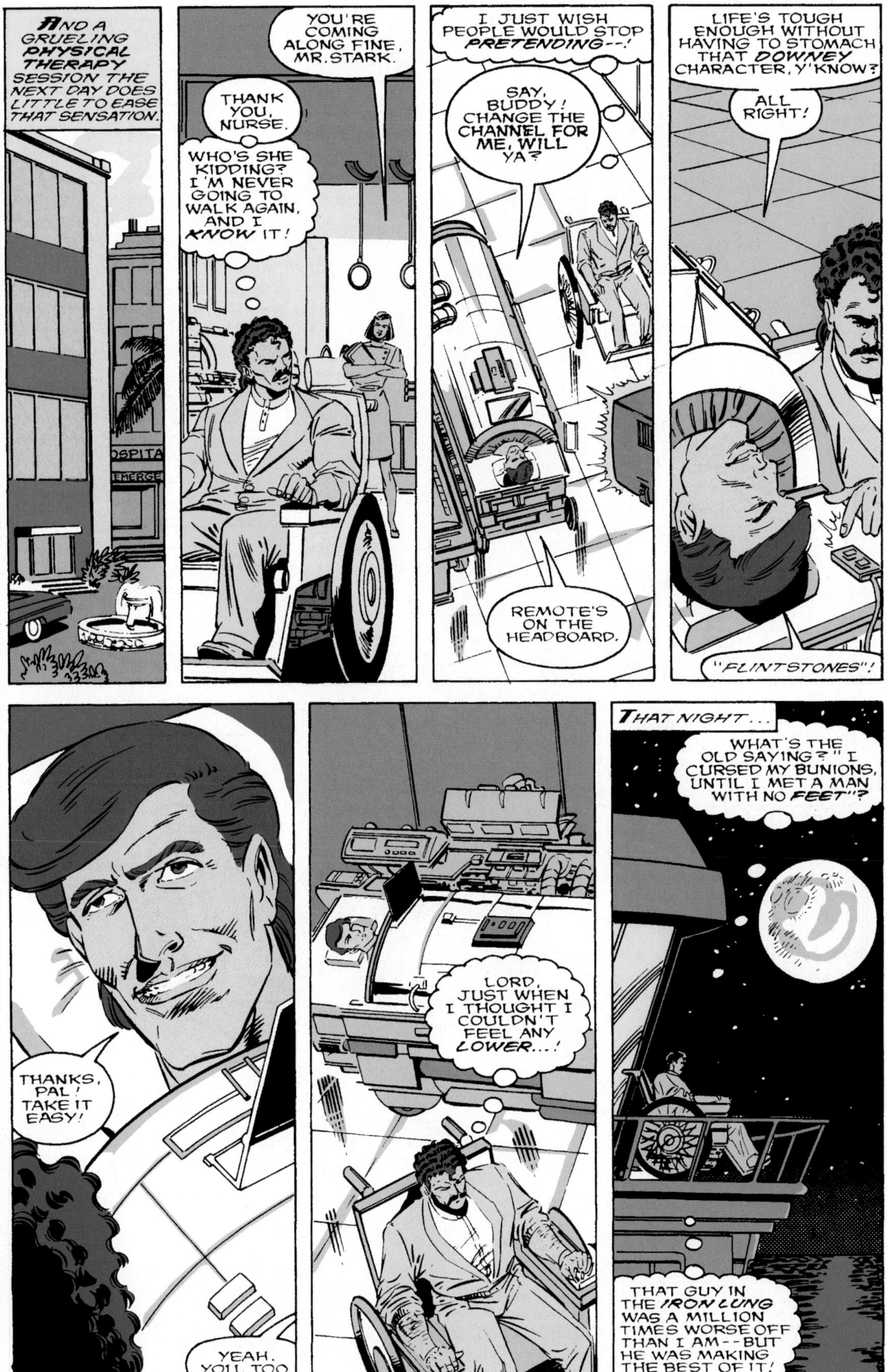
AND A GRUELING PHYSICAL THERAPY SESSION THE NEXT DAY DOES LITTLE TO EASE THAT SENSATION.
YOU'RE COMING ALONG FINE, MR. STARK.
THANK YOU, NURSE.
WHO'S SHE KIDDING? I'M NEVER GOING TO WALK AGAIN, AND I KNOW IT!
I JUST WISH PEOPLE WOULD STOP PRETENDING--!
SAY, BUDDY! CHANGE THE CHANNEL FOR ME, WILL YA?
REMOTE'S ON THE HEADBOARD.
LIFE'S TOUGH ENOUGH WITHOUT HAVING TO STOMACH THAT DOWNEY CHARACTER, Y'KNOW?
ALL RIGHT!
"FLINTSTONES"!
THANKS, PAL! TAKE IT EASY!
YEAH. YOU, TOO.
LORD, JUST WHEN I THOUGHT I COULDN'T FEEL ANY LOWER...!
THAT NIGHT...
WHAT'S THE OLD SAYING? "I CURSED MY BUNIONS, UNTIL I MET A MAN WITH NO FEET"?
THAT GUY IN THE IRON LUNG WAS A MILLION TIMES WORSE OFF THAN I AM--BUT HE WAS MAKING THE BEST OF IT!

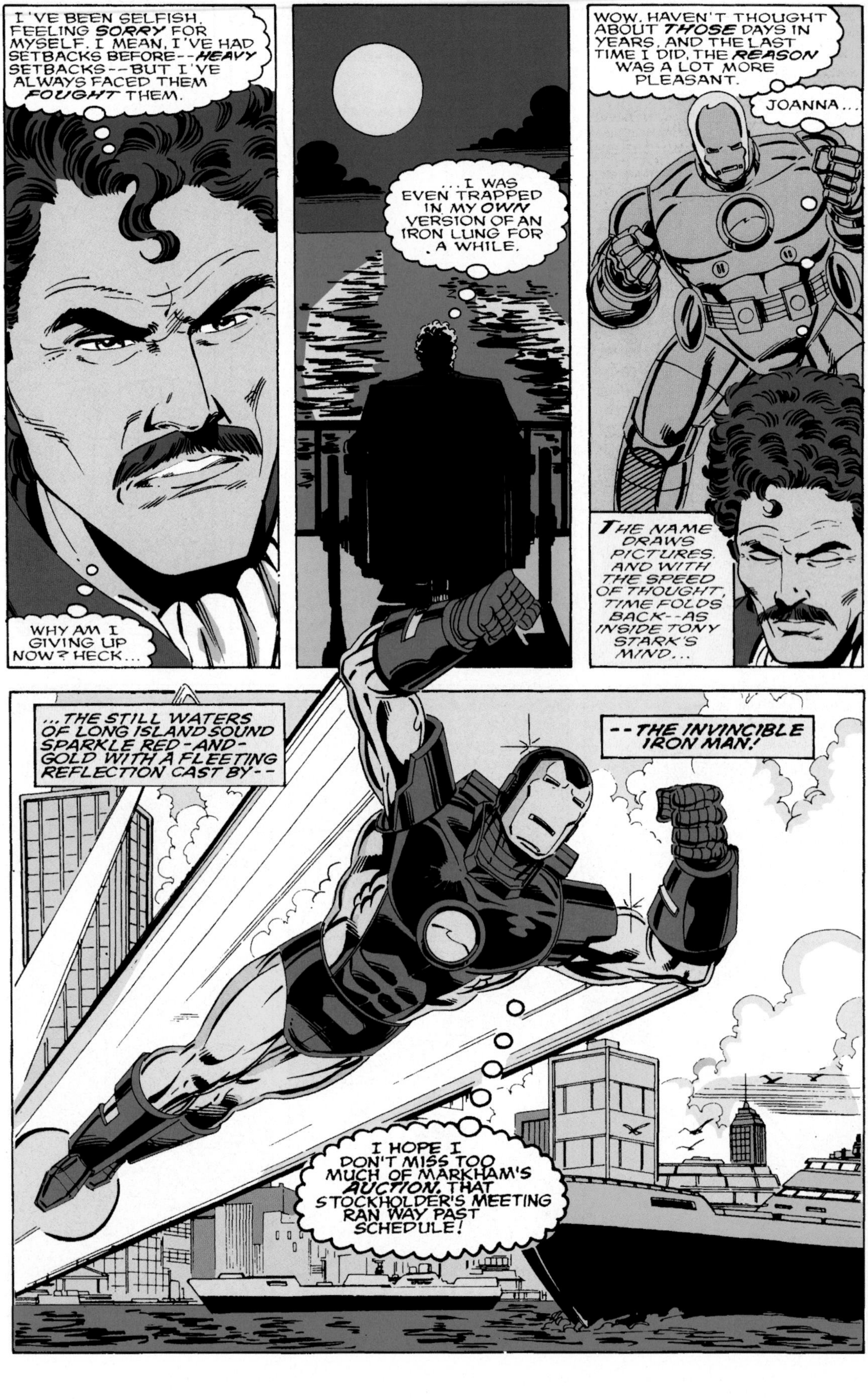
I'VE BEEN SELFISH, FEELING SORRY FOR MYSELF. I MEAN, I'VE HAD SETBACKS BEFORE--HEAVY SETBACKS--BUT I'VE ALWAYS FACED THEM FOUGHT THEM.
WHY AM I GIVING UP NOW? HECK...
...I WAS EVEN TRAPPED IN MY OWN VERSION OF AN IRON LUNG FOR A WHILE.
WOW. HAVEN'T THOUGHT ABOUT THOSE DAYS IN YEARS, AND THE LAST TIME I DID, THE REASON WAS A LOT MORE PLEASANT.
JOANNA...
THE NAME DRAWS PICTURES, AND WITH THE SPEED OF THOUGHT, TIME FOLDS BACK--AS INSIDE TONY STARK'S MIND...
...THE STILL WATERS OF LONG ISLAND SOUND SPARKLE RED-AND-GOLD WITH A FLEETING REFLECTION CAST BY--
--THE INVINCIBLE IRON MAN!
I HOPE I DON'T MISS TOO MUCH OF MARKHAM'S AUCTION. THAT STOCKHOLDER'S MEETING RAN WAY PAST SCHEDULE!

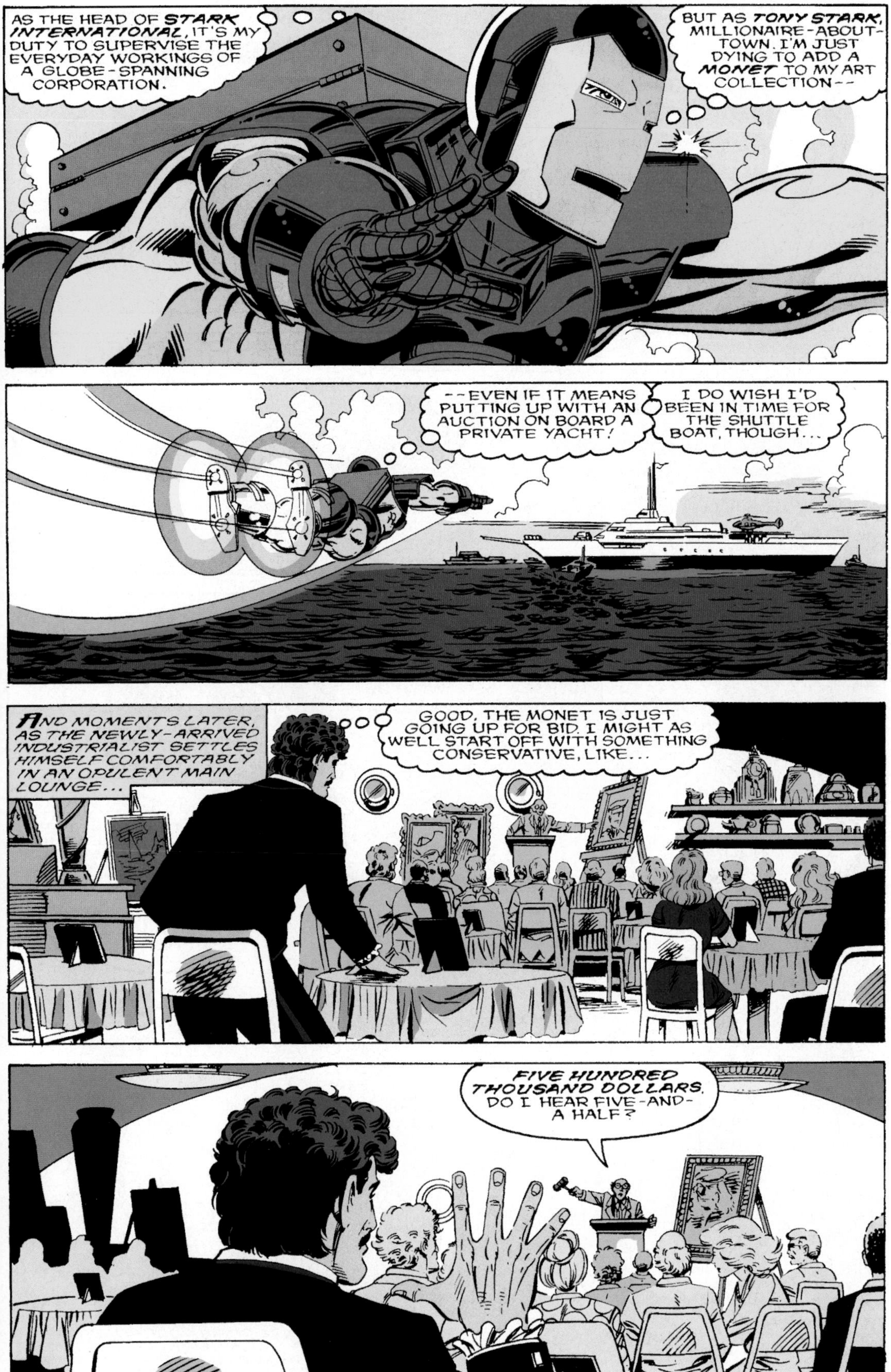
AS THE HEAD OF STARK INTERNATIONAL, IT'S MY DUTY TO SUPERVISE THE EVERYDAY WORKINGS OF A GLOBE-SPANNING CORPORATION.
BUT AS TONY STARK, MILLIONAIRE-ABOUT-TOWN, I'M JUST DYING TO ADD A MONET TO MY ART COLLECTION--
--EVEN IF IT MEANS PUTTING UP WITH AN AUCTION ON BOARD A PRIVATE YACHT!
I DO WISH I'D BEEN IN TIME FOR THE SHUTTLE BOAT, THOUGH...
AND MOMENTS LATER, AS THE NEWLY-ARRIVED INDUSTRIALIST SETTLES HIMSELF COMFORTABLY IN AN OPULENT MAIN LOUNGE...
GOOD, THE MONET IS JUST GOING UP FOR BID. I MIGHT AS WELL START OFF WITH SOMETHING CONSERVATIVE, LIKE...
FIVE HUNDRED THOUSAND DOLLARS. DO I HEAR FIVE-AND-A HALF?

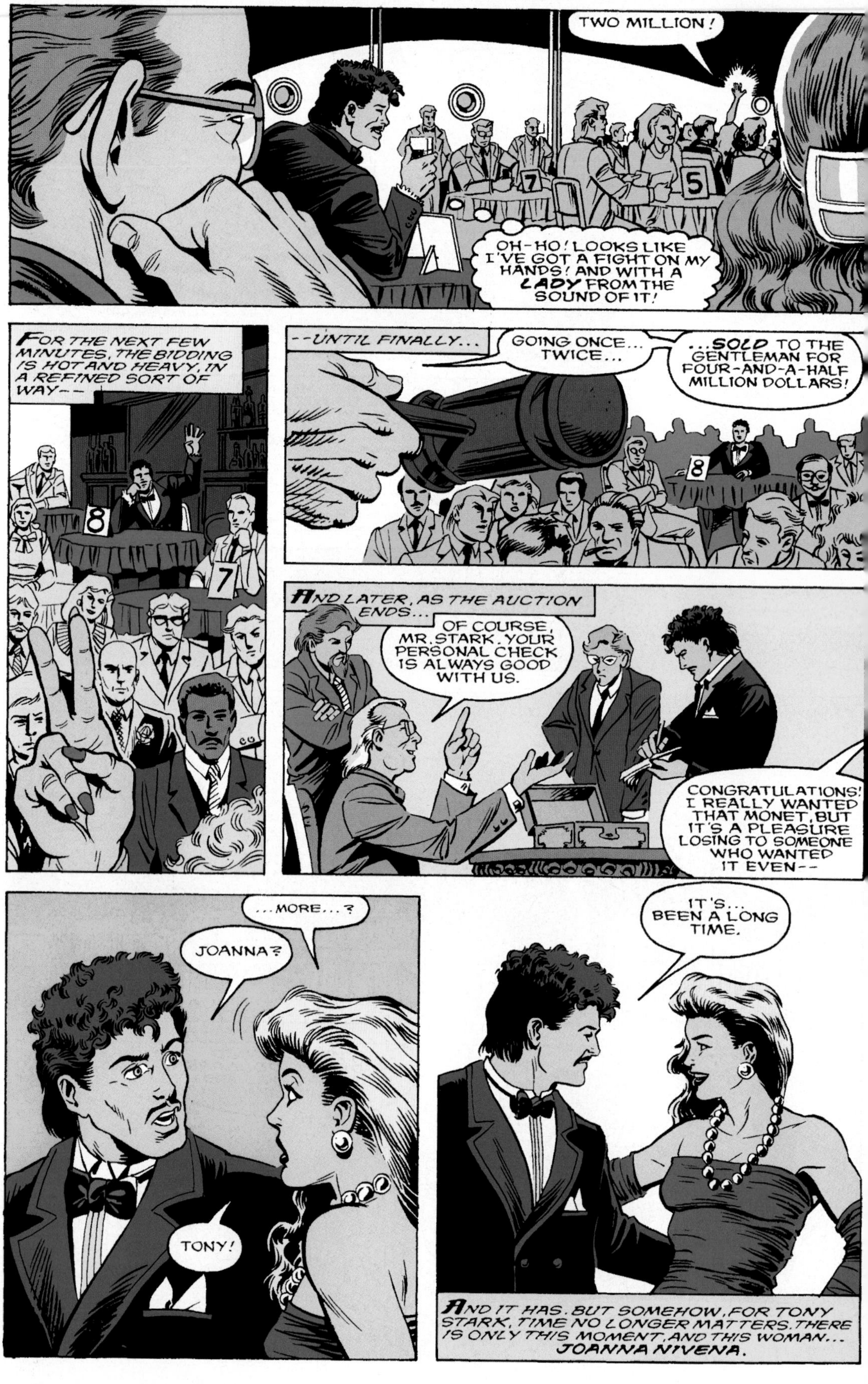
TWO MILLION!
SOLD
OH-HO! LOOKS LIKE I'VE GOT A FIGHT ON MY HANDS! AND WITH A LADY FROM THE SOUND OF IT!
FOR THE NEXT FEW MINUTES, THE BIDDING IS HOT AND HEAVY, IN A REFINED SORT OF WAY--
--UNTIL FINALLY...
GOING ONCE... TWICE...
...SOLD TO THE GENTLEMAN FOR FOUR-AND-A-HALF MILLION DOLLARS!
AND LATER, AS THE AUCTION ENDS...
OF COURSE, MR. STARK. YOUR PERSONAL CHECK IS ALWAYS GOOD WITH US.
CONGRATULATIONS! I REALLY WANTED THAT MONET, BUT IT'S A PLEASURE LOSING TO SOMEONE WHO WANTED IT EVEN--
...MORE...?
JOANNA?
TONY!
IT'S... BEEN A LONG TIME.
AND IT HAS. BUT SOMEHOW, FOR TONY STARK, TIME NO LONGER MATTERS. THERE IS ONLY THIS MOMENT, AND THIS WOMAN... JOANNA NIVENA.

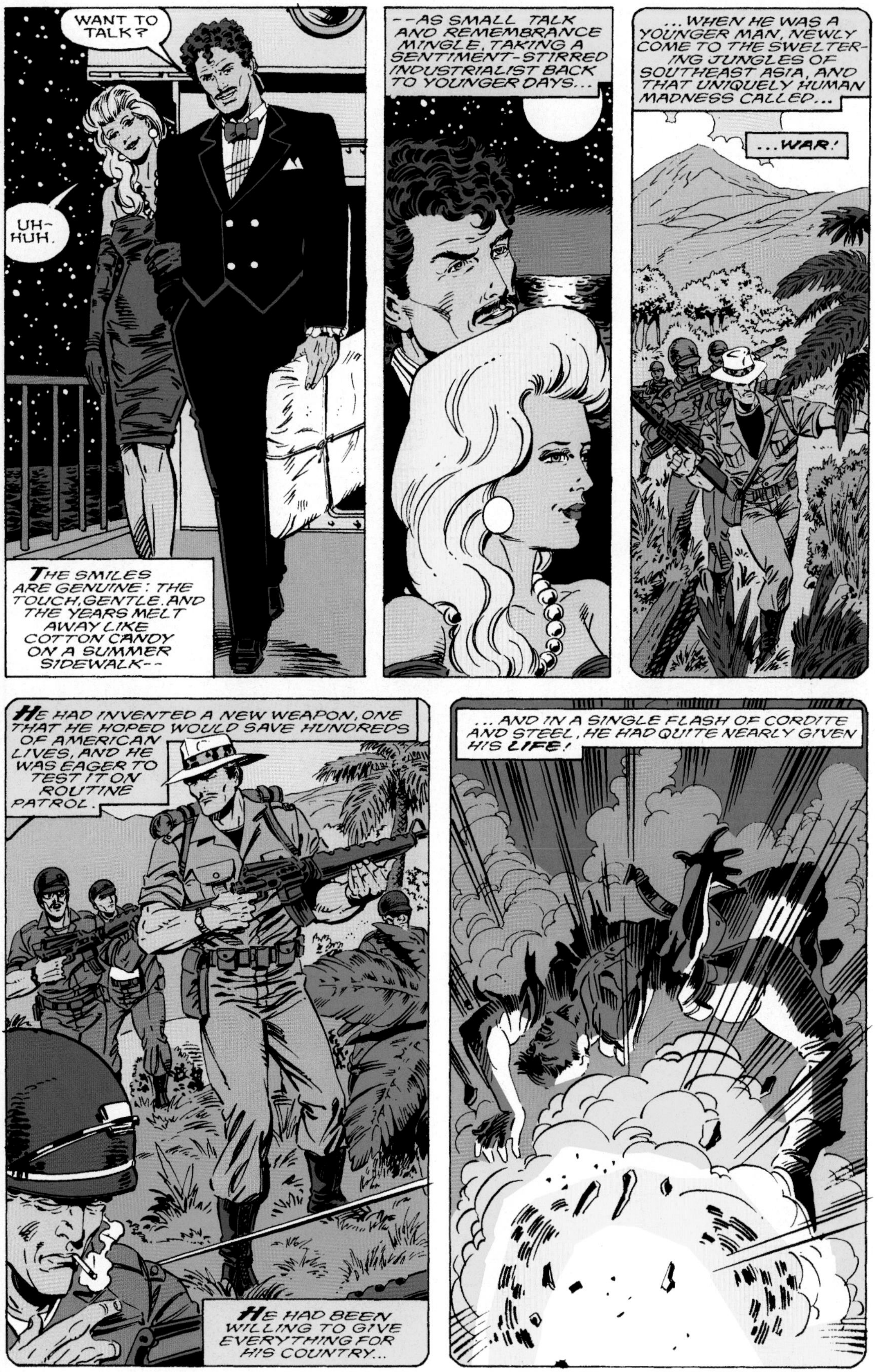
WANT TO TALK?
UH-HUH.
THE SMILES ARE GENUINE: THE TOUCH, GENTLE. AND THE YEARS MELT AWAY LIKE COTTON CANDY ON A SUMMER SIDEWALK--
--AS SMALL TALK AND REMEMBRANCE MINGLE, TAKING A SENTIMENT-STIRRED INDUSTRIALIST BACK TO YOUNGER DAYS...
...WHEN HE WAS A YOUNGER MAN, NEWLY COME TO THE SWELTERING JUNGLES OF SOUTHEAST ASIA, AND THAT UNIQUELY HUMAN MADNESS CALLED...
...WAR!
HE HAD INVENTED A NEW WEAPON, ONE THAT HE HOPED WOULD SAVE HUNDREDS OF AMERICAN LIVES, AND HE WAS EAGER TO TEST IT ON ROUTINE PATROL.
HE HAD BEEN WILLING TO GIVE EVERYTHING FOR HIS COUNTRY...
...AND IN A SINGLE FLASH OF CORDITE AND STEEL, HE HAD QUITE NEARLY GIVEN HIS LIFE!

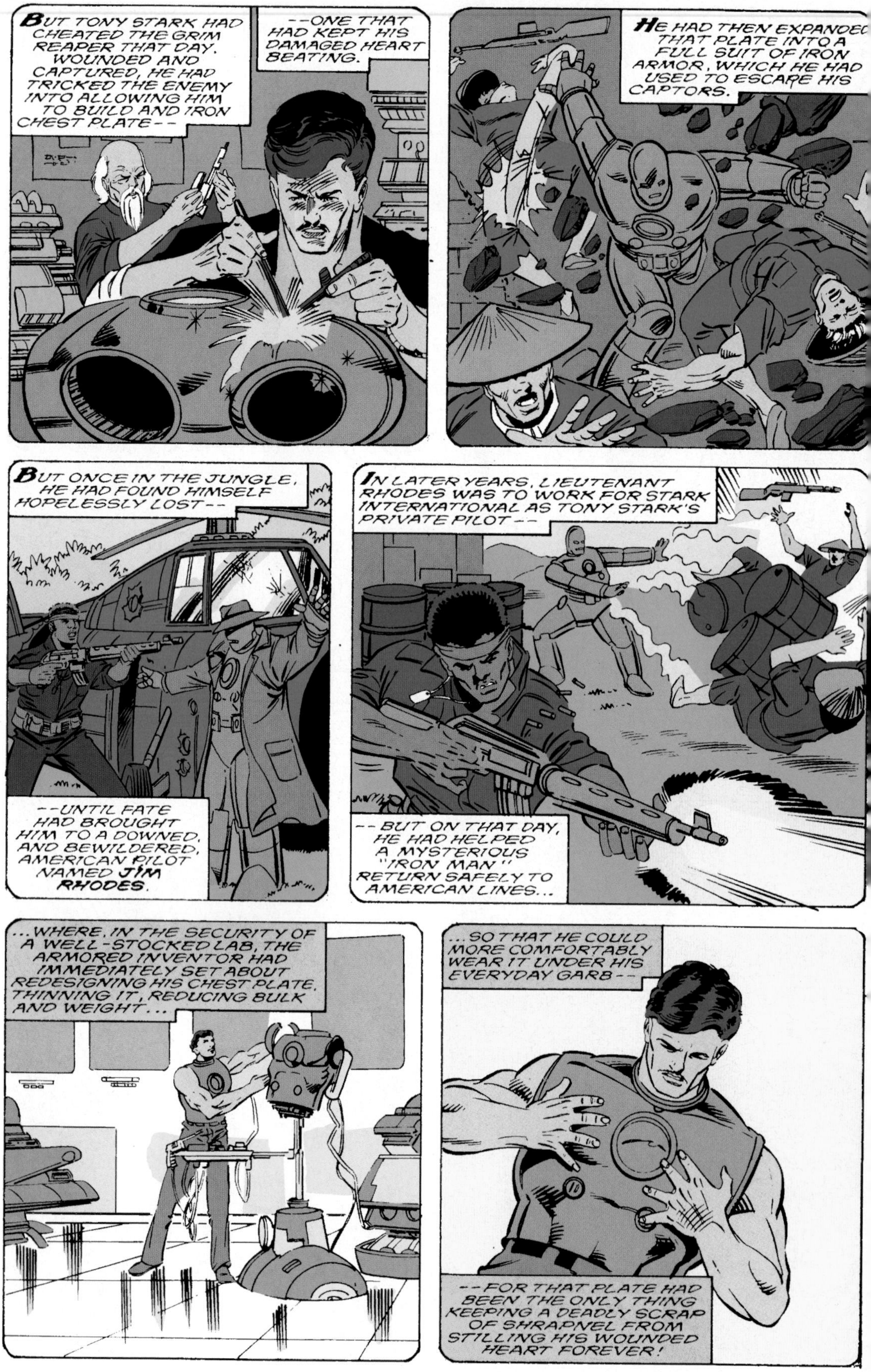
BUT TONY STARK HAD CHEATED THE GRIM REAPER THAT DAY. WOUNDED AND CAPTURED, HE HAD TRICKED THE ENEMY INTO ALLOWING HIM TO BUILD AND IRON CHEST PLATE--
--ONE THAT HAD KEPT HIS DAMAGED HEART BEATING.
HE HAD THEN EXPANDED THAT PLATE INTO A FULL SUIT OF IRON ARMOR, WHICH HE HAD USED TO ESCAPE HIS CAPTORS.
BUT ONCE IN THE JUNGLE, HE HAD FOUND HIMSELF HOPELESSLY LOST--
--UNTIL FATE HAD BROUGHT HIM TO A DOWNED, AND BEWILDERED, AMERICAN PILOT NAMED JIM RHODES.
IN LATER YEARS, LIEUTENANT RHODES WAS TO WORK FOR STARK INTERNATIONAL AS TONY STARK'S PRIVATE PILOT--
--BUT ON THAT DAY, HE HAD HELPED A MYSTERIOUS "IRON MAN" RETURN SAFELY TO AMERICAN LINES...
...WHERE, IN THE SECURITY OF A WELL-STOCKED LAB, THE ARMORED INVENTOR HAD IMMEDIATELY SET ABOUT REDESIGNING HIS CHEST PLATE, THINNING IT, REDUCING BULK AND WEIGHT...
...SO THAT HE COULD MORE COMFORTABLY WEAR IT UNDER HIS EVERYDAY GARB--
--FOR THAT PLATE HAD BEEN THE ONLY THING KEEPING A DEADLY SCRAP OF SHRAPNEL FROM STILLING HIS WOUNDED HEART FOREVER!

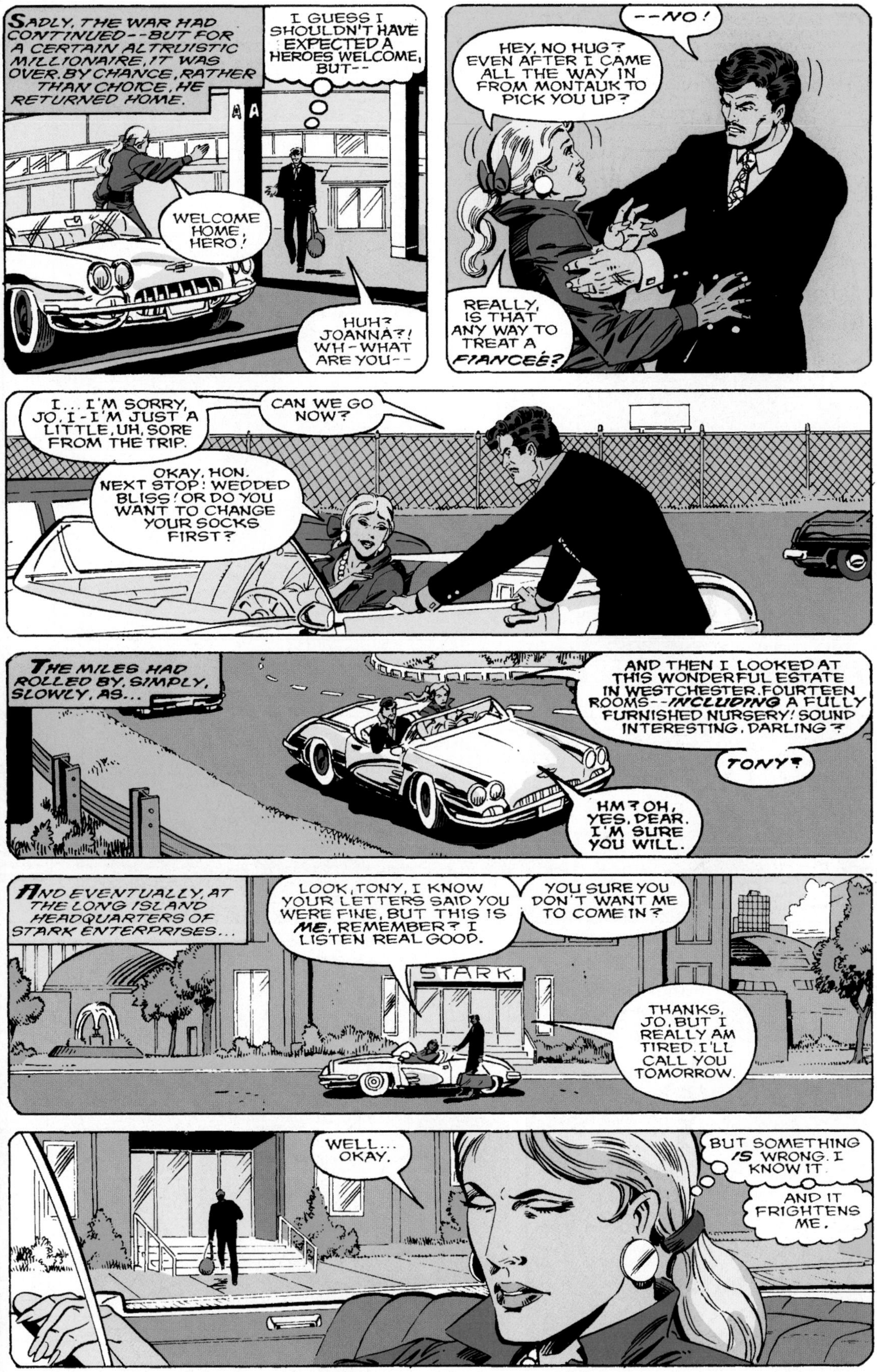
SADLY, THE WAR HAD CONTINUED--BUT FOR A CERTAIN ALTRUISTIC MILLIONAIRE, IT WAS OVER. BY CHANCE, RATHER THAN CHOICE, HE RETURNED HOME.
I GUESS I SHOULDN'T HAVE EXPECTED A HEROES WELCOME, BUT--
WELCOME HOME, HERO!
HUH? JOANNA?! WH-WHAT ARE YOU--
--NO!
HEY, NO HUG? EVEN AFTER I CAME ALL THE WAY IN FROM MONTAUK TO PICK YOU UP?
REALLY, IS THAT ANY WAY TO TREAT A FIANCEÉ?
I... I'M SORRY, JO. I-I'M JUST A LITTLE, UH, SORE FROM THE TRIP.
CAN WE GO NOW?
OKAY, HON. NEXT STOP: WEDDED BLISS! OR DO YOU WANT TO CHANGE YOUR SOCKS FIRST?
THE MILES HAD ROLLED BY, SIMPLY, SLOWLY, AS...
AND THEN I LOOKED AT THIS WONDERFUL ESTATE IN WESTCHESTER. FOURTEEN ROOMS--INCLUDING A FULLY FURNISHED NURSERY! SOUND INTERESTING, DARLING?
TONY?
HM? OH, YES, DEAR. I'M SURE YOU WILL.
AND EVENTUALLY, AT THE LONG ISLAND HEADQUARTERS OF STARK ENTERPRISES...
LOOK, TONY, I KNOW YOUR LETTERS SAID YOU WERE FINE, BUT THIS IS ME, REMEMBER? I LISTEN REAL GOOD.
YOU SURE YOU DON'T WANT ME TO COME IN?
STARK
THANKS, JO, BUT I REALLY AM TIRED. I'LL CALL YOU TOMORROW.
WELL... OKAY.
BUT SOMETHING IS WRONG. I KNOW IT.
AND IT FRIGHTENS ME.

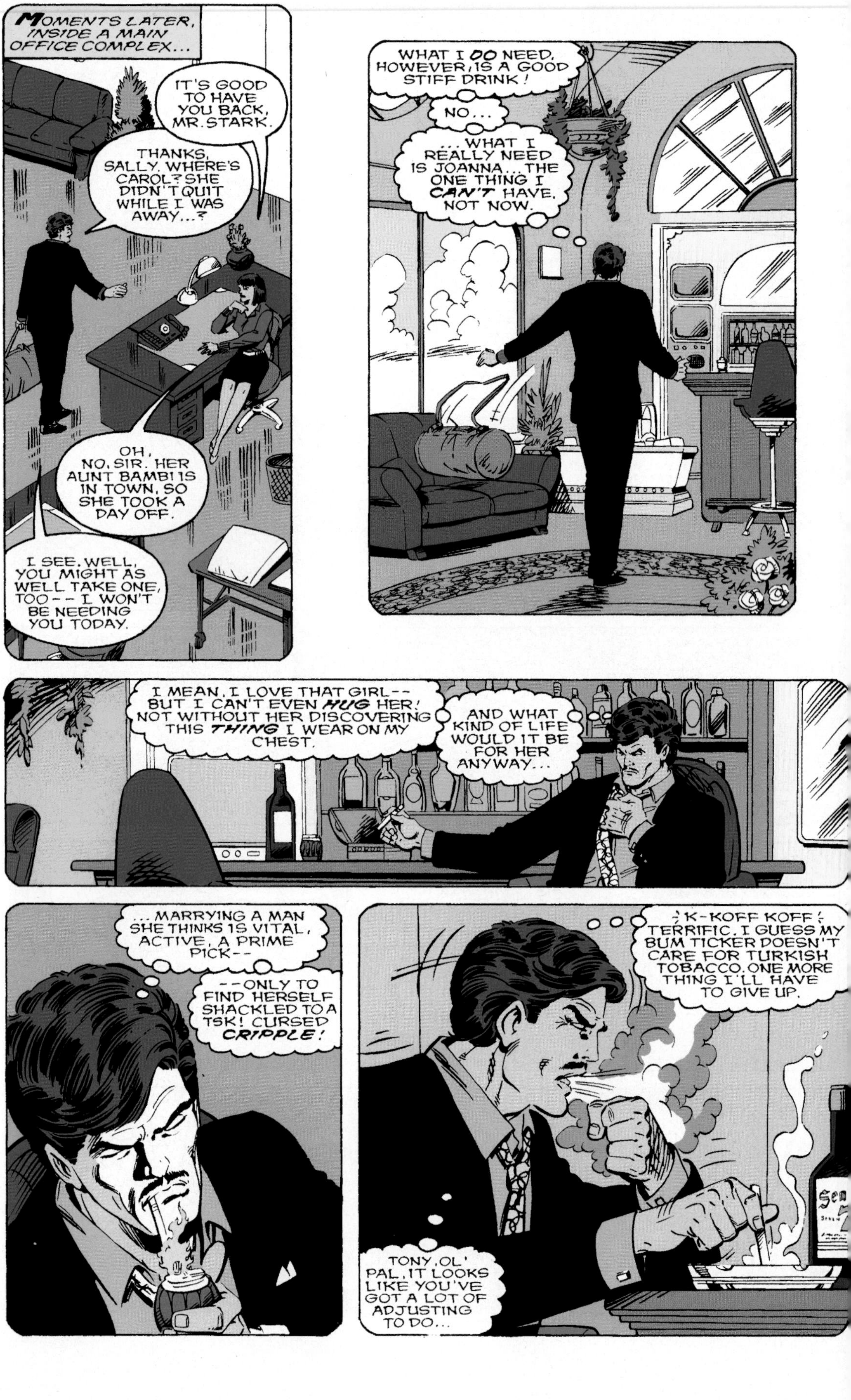
MOMENTS LATER, INSIDE A MAIN OFFICE COMPLEX...
IT'S GOOD TO HAVE YOU BACK, MR. STARK.
THANKS, SALLY. WHERE'S CAROL? SHE DIDN'T QUIT WHILE I WAS AWAY...?
OH, NO, SIR. HER AUNT BAMBI IS IN TOWN, SO SHE TOOK A DAY OFF.
I SEE. WELL, YOU MIGHT AS WELL TAKE ONE, TOO-- I WON'T BE NEEDING YOU TODAY.
WHAT I DO NEED, HOWEVER, IS A GOOD STIFF DRINK!
NO...
...WHAT I REALLY NEED IS JOANNA... THE ONE THING I CAN'T HAVE. NOT NOW.
I MEAN, I LOVE THAT GIRL-- BUT I CAN'T EVEN HUG HER! NOT WITHOUT HER DISCOVERING THIS THING I WEAR ON MY CHEST.
AND WHAT KIND OF LIFE WOULD IT BE FOR HER ANYWAY...
...MARRYING A MAN SHE THINKS IS VITAL, ACTIVE, A PRIME PICK--
--ONLY TO FIND HERSELF SHACKLED TO A TSK! CURSED CRIPPLE!
K-KOFF KOFF! TERRIFIC. I GUESS MY BUM TICKER DOESN'T CARE FOR TURKISH TOBACCO. ONE MORE THING I'LL HAVE TO GIVE UP.
TONY, OL' PAL, IT LOOKS LIKE YOU'VE GOT A LOT OF ADJUSTING TO DO...

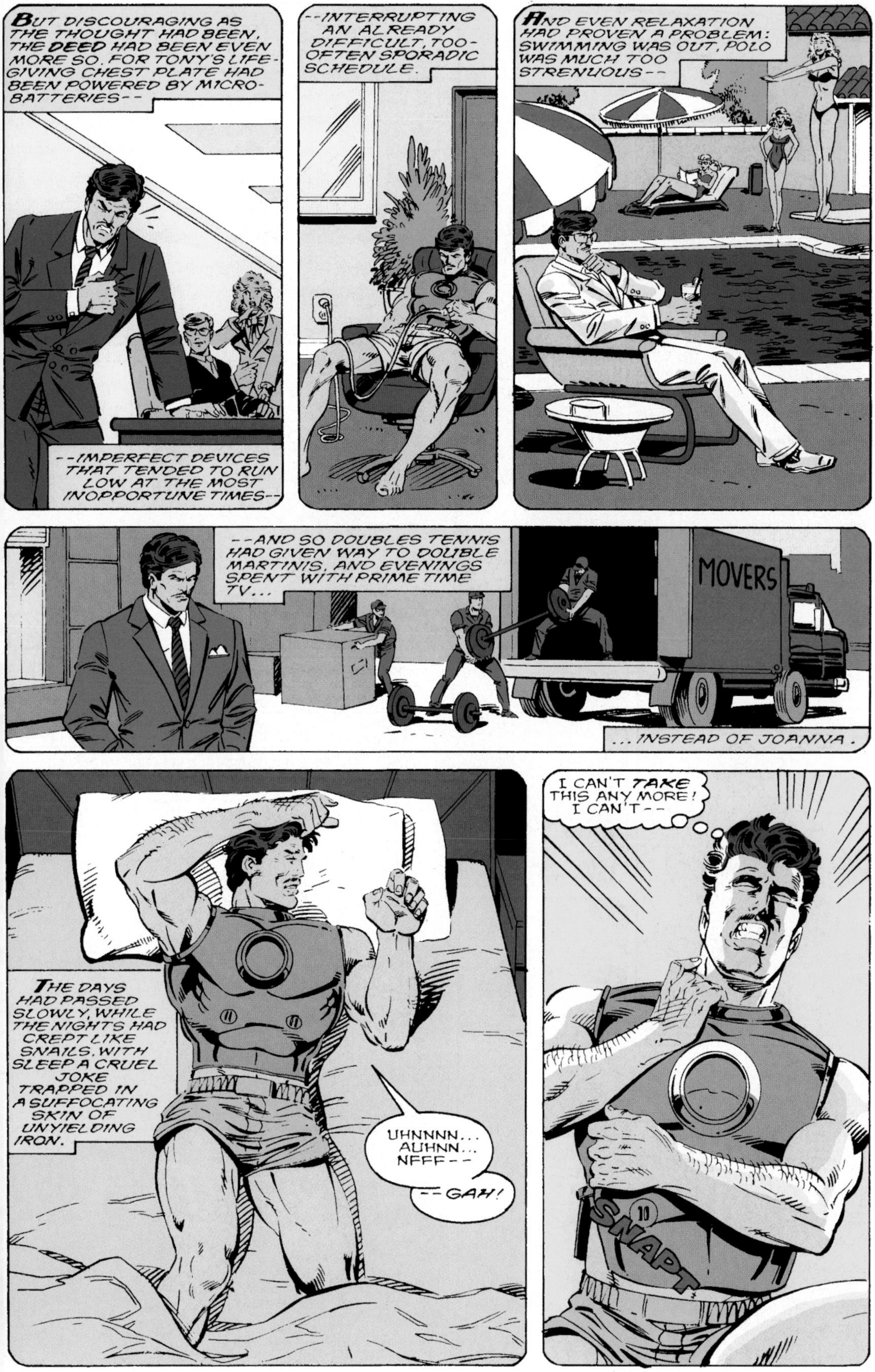
BUT DISCOURAGING AS THE THOUGHT HAD BEEN, THE DEED HAD BEEN EVEN MORE SO. FOR TONY'S LIFE-GIVING CHEST PLATE HAD BEEN POWERED BY MICRO-BATTERIES--
--IMPERFECT DEVICES THAT TENDED TO RUN LOW AT THE MOST INOPPORTUNE TIMES--
--INTERRUPTING AN ALREADY DIFFICULT, TOO-OFTEN SPORADIC SCHEDULE.
AND EVEN RELAXATION HAD PROVEN A PROBLEM: SWIMMING WAS OUT, POLO WAS MUCH TOO STRENUOUS--
--AND SO DOUBLES TENNIS HAD GIVEN WAY TO DOUBLE MARTINIS, AND EVENINGS SPENT WITH PRIME TIME TV...
MOVERS
...INSTEAD OF JOANNA.
THE DAYS HAD PASSED SLOWLY, WHILE THE NIGHTS HAD CREPT LIKE SNAILS, WITH SLEEP A CRUEL JOKE TRAPPED IN A SUFFOCATING SKIN OF UNYIELDING IRON.
UHNNNN... AUHNN... NFFF--
--GAH!
I CAN'T TAKE THIS ANY MORE! I CAN'T--
SNAP!

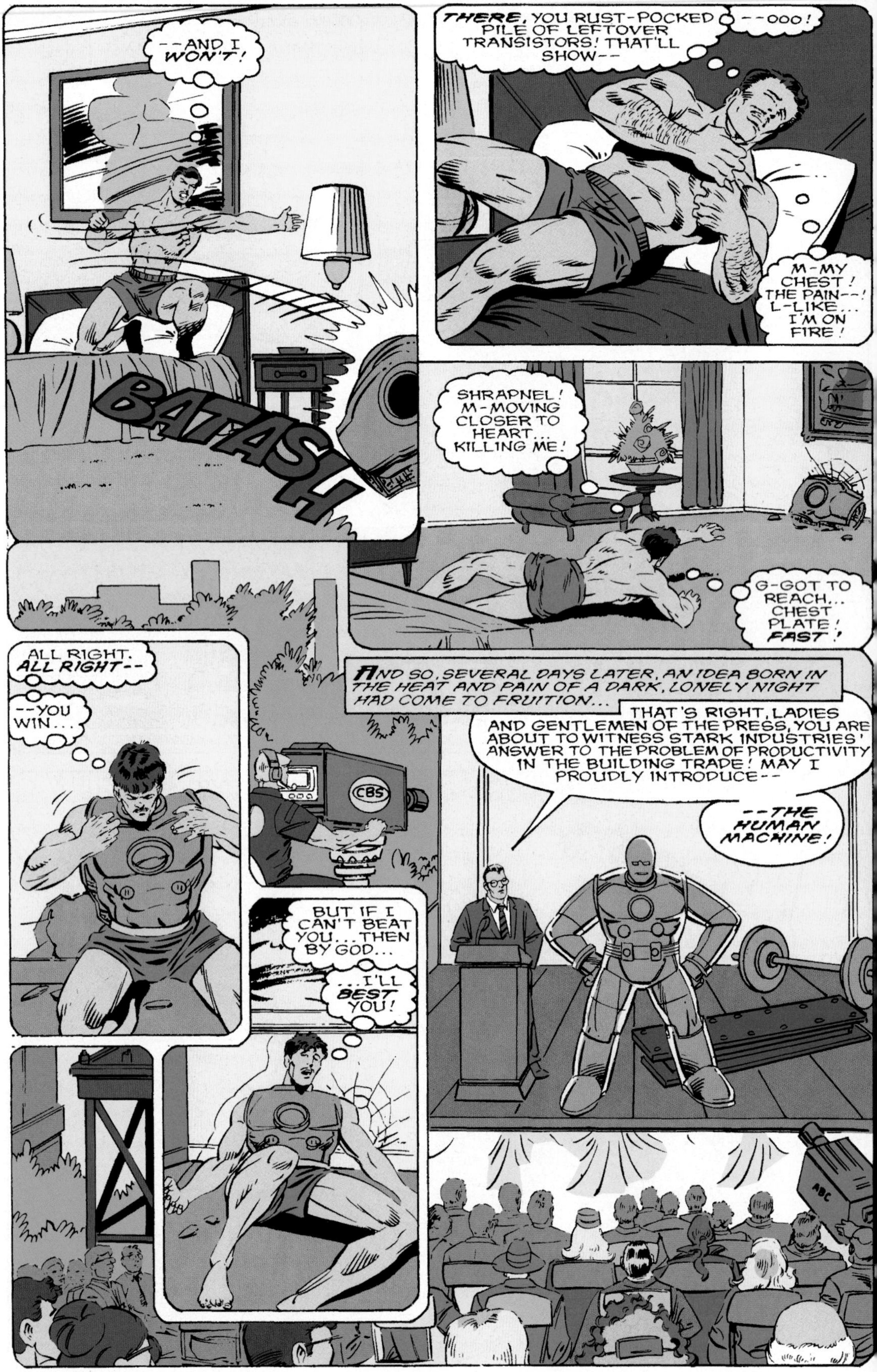
--AND I WON'T!
BATASH
THERE, YOU RUST-POCKED PILE OF LEFTOVER TRANSISTORS! THAT'LL SHOW--
--OOO!
M-MY CHEST! THE PAIN--! L-LIKE... I'M ON FIRE!
SHRAPNEL! M-MOVING CLOSER TO HEART... KILLING ME!
G-GOT TO REACH... CHEST PLATE! FAST!
ALL RIGHT. ALL RIGHT--
--YOU WIN...
BUT IF I CAN'T BEAT YOU... THEN BY GOD...
...I'LL BEST YOU!
AND SO, SEVERAL DAYS LATER, AN IDEA BORN IN THE HEAT AND PAIN OF A DARK, LONELY NIGHT HAD COME TO FRUITION...
THAT'S RIGHT, LADIES AND GENTLEMEN OF THE PRESS, YOU ARE ABOUT TO WITNESS STARK INDUSTRIES' ANSWER TO THE PROBLEM OF PRODUCTIVITY IN THE BUILDING TRADE! MAY I PROUDLY INTRODUCE--
--THE HUMAN MACHINE!
CBS
ABC

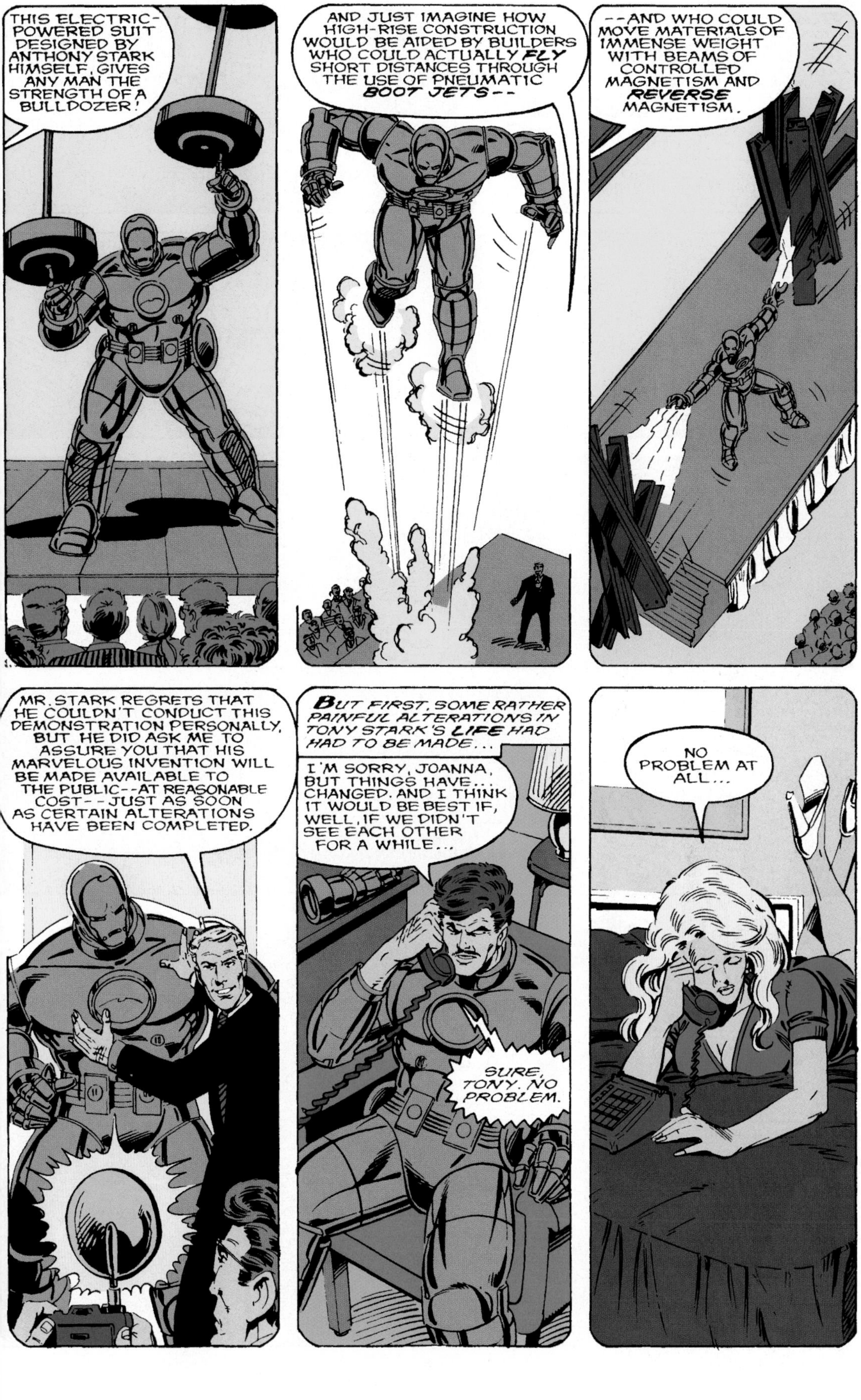
THIS ELECTRIC-POWERED SUIT DESIGNED BY ANTHONY STARK HIMSELF, GIVES ANY MAN THE STRENGTH OF A BULLDOZER!
AND JUST IMAGINE HOW HIGH-RISE CONSTRUCTION WOULD BE AIDED BY BUILDERS WHO COULD ACTUALLY FLY SHORT DISTANCES THROUGH THE USE OF PNEUMATIC BOOT JETS--
--AND WHO COULD MOVE MATERIALS OF IMMENSE WEIGHT WITH BEAMS OF CONTROLLED MAGNETISM AND REVERSE MAGNETISM.
MR. STARK REGRETS THAT HE COULDN'T CONDUCT THIS DEMONSTRATION PERSONALLY, BUT HE DID ASK ME TO ASSURE YOU THAT HIS MARVELOUS INVENTION WILL BE MADE AVAILABLE TO THE PUBLIC--AT REASONABLE COST--JUST AS SOON AS CERTAIN ALTERATIONS HAVE BEEN COMPLETED.
BUT FIRST, SOME RATHER PAINFUL ALTERATIONS IN TONY STARK'S LIFE HAD HAD TO BE MADE...
I'M SORRY, JOANNA, BUT THINGS HAVE... CHANGED. AND I THINK IT WOULD BE BEST IF, WELL, IF WE DIDN'T SEE EACH OTHER FOR A WHILE...
SURE, TONY. NO PROBLEM.
NO PROBLEM AT ALL...

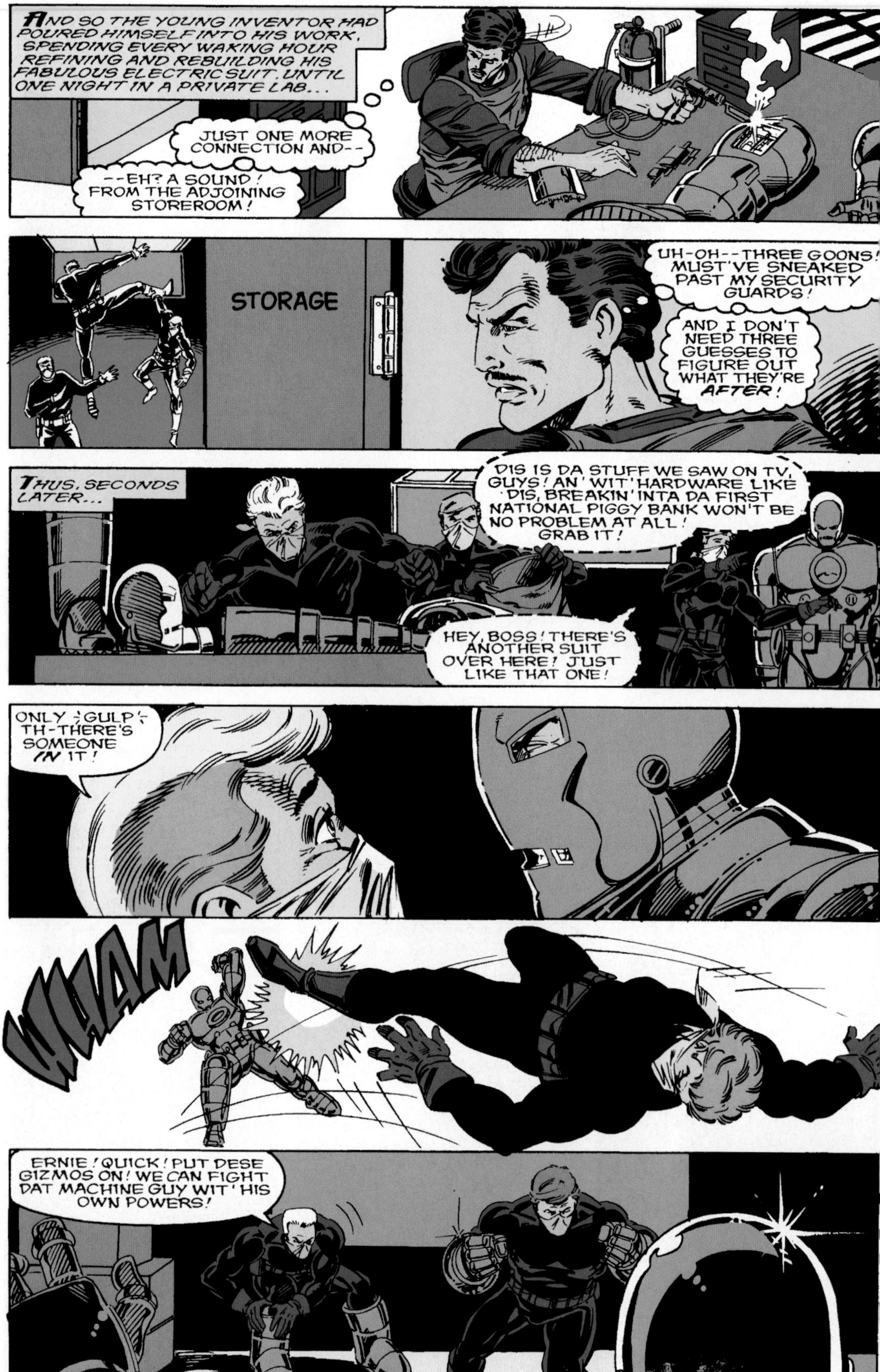
AND SO THE YOUNG INVENTOR HAD POURED HIMSELF INTO HIS WORK, SPENDING EVERY WAKING HOUR REFINING AND REBUILDING HIS FABULOUS ELECTRIC SUIT. UNTIL ONE NIGHT IN A PRIVATE LAB...
JUST ONE MORE CONNECTION AND--
--EH? A SOUND! FROM THE ADJOINING STOREROOM!
STORAGE
UH-OH--THREE GOONS! MUST'VE SNEAKED PAST MY SECURITY GUARDS!
AND I DON'T NEED THREE GUESSES TO FIGURE OUT WHAT THEY'RE AFTER!
THUS, SECONDS LATER...
DIS IS DA STUFF WE SAW ON TV, GUYS! AN' WIT' HARDWARE LIKE DIS, BREAKIN' INTA DA FIRST NATIONAL PIGGY BANK WON'T BE NO PROBLEM AT ALL! GRAB IT!
HEY, BOSS! THERE'S ANOTHER SUIT OVER HERE! JUST LIKE THAT ONE!
ONLY -GULP- TH-THERE'S SOMEONE IN IT!
WHAM
ERNIE! QUICK! PUT DESE GIZMOS ON! WE CAN FIGHT DAT MACHINE GUY WIT' HIS OWN POWERS!

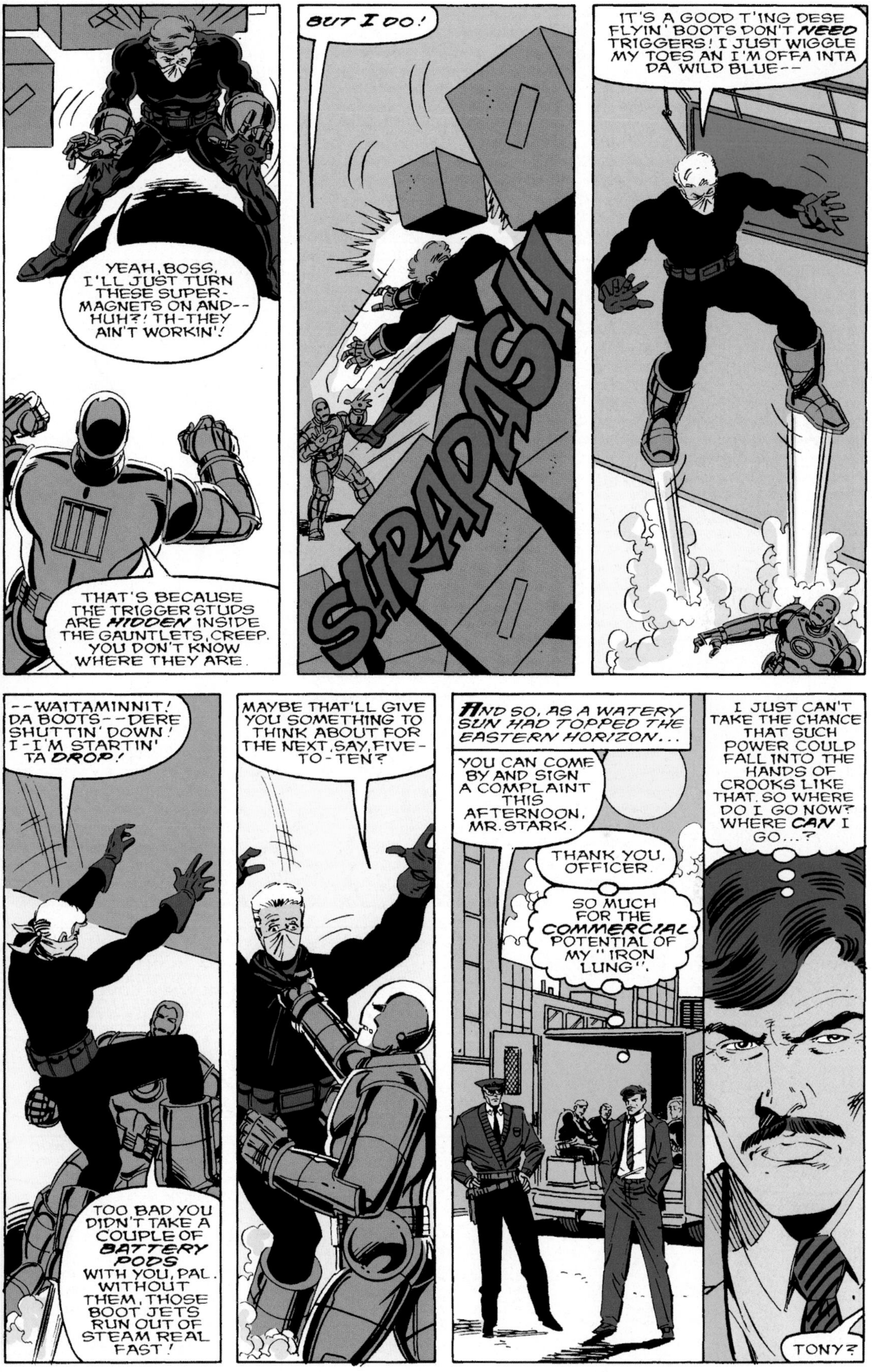
YEAH, BOSS. I'LL JUST TURN THESE SUPER-MAGNETS ON AND-- HUH?! TH-THEY AIN'T WORKIN'!
THAT'S BECAUSE THE TRIGGER STUDS ARE HIDDEN INSIDE THE GAUNTLETS, CREEP. YOU DON'T KNOW WHERE THEY ARE.
BUT I DO!
SHRAPASH!
IT'S A GOOD T'ING DESE FLYIN' BOOTS DON'T NEED TRIGGERS! I JUST WIGGLE MY TOES AN I'M OFFA INTA DA WILD BLUE--
--WAITAMINNIT! DA BOOTS--DERE SHUTTIN' DOWN! I-I'M STARTIN' TA DROP!
TOO BAD YOU DIDN'T TAKE A COUPLE OF BATTERY PODS WITH YOU, PAL. WITHOUT THEM, THOSE BOOT JETS RUN OUT OF STEAM REAL FAST!
MAYBE THAT'LL GIVE YOU SOMETHING TO THINK ABOUT FOR THE NEXT, SAY, FIVE-TO-TEN?
AND SO, AS A WATERY SUN HAD TOPPED THE EASTERN HORIZON...
YOU CAN COME BY AND SIGN A COMPLAINT THIS AFTERNOON, MR. STARK.
THANK YOU, OFFICER.
SO MUCH FOR THE COMMERCIAL POTENTIAL OF MY "IRON LUNG".
I JUST CAN'T TAKE THE CHANCE THAT SUCH POWER COULD FALL INTO THE HANDS OF CROOKS LIKE THAT. SO WHERE DO I GO NOW? WHERE CAN I GO...?
TONY?

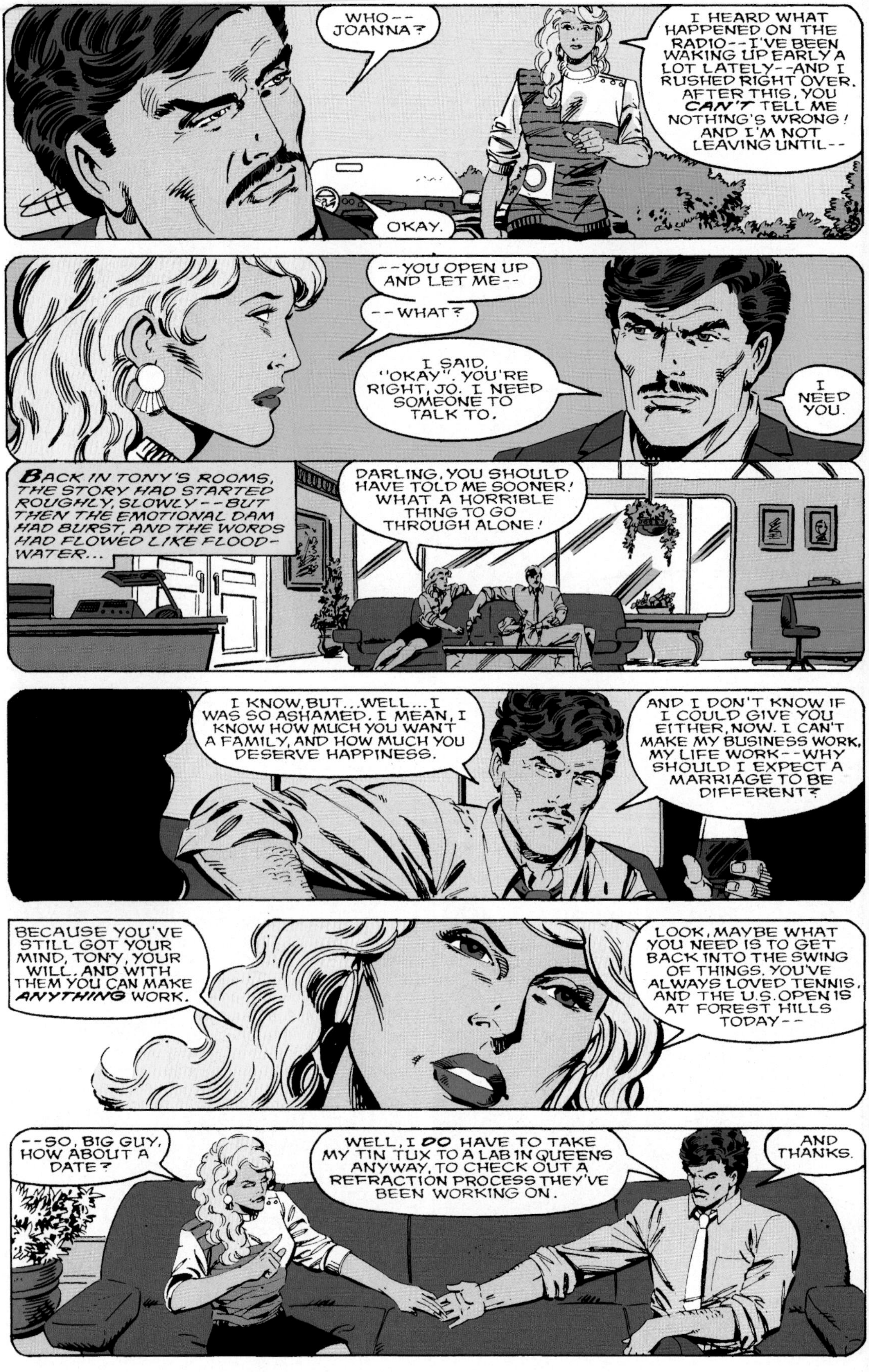
WHO-- JOANNA?
I HEARD WHAT HAPPENED ON THE RADIO--I'VE BEEN WAKING UP EARLY A LOT LATELY--AND I RUSHED RIGHT OVER. AFTER THIS, YOU CAN'T TELL ME NOTHING'S WRONG! AND I'M NOT LEAVING UNTIL--
OKAY.
--YOU OPEN UP AND LET ME--
--WHAT?
I SAID, "OKAY". YOU'RE RIGHT, JO. I NEED SOMEONE TO TALK TO.
I NEED YOU.
BACK IN TONY'S ROOMS, THE STORY HAD STARTED ROUGHLY, SLOWLY--BUT THEN THE EMOTIONAL DAM HAD BURST, AND THE WORDS HAD FLOWED LIKE FLOOD-WATER...
DARLING, YOU SHOULD HAVE TOLD ME SOONER! WHAT A HORRIBLE THING TO GO THROUGH ALONE!
I KNOW, BUT...WELL...I WAS SO ASHAMED. I MEAN, I KNOW HOW MUCH YOU WANT A FAMILY, AND HOW MUCH YOU DESERVE HAPPINESS.
AND I DON'T KNOW IF I COULD GIVE YOU EITHER, NOW. I CAN'T MAKE MY BUSINESS WORK, MY LIFE WORK--WHY SHOULD I EXPECT A MARRIAGE TO BE DIFFERENT?
BECAUSE YOU'VE STILL GOT YOUR MIND, TONY, YOUR WILL. AND WITH THEM YOU CAN MAKE ANYTHING WORK.
LOOK, MAYBE WHAT YOU NEED IS TO GET BACK INTO THE SWING OF THINGS. YOU'VE ALWAYS LOVED TENNIS, AND THE U.S. OPEN IS AT FOREST HILLS TODAY--
--SO, BIG GUY, HOW ABOUT A DATE?
WELL, I DO HAVE TO TAKE MY TIN TUX TO A LAB IN QUEENS ANYWAY, TO CHECK OUT A REFRACTION PROCESS THEY'VE BEEN WORKING ON.
AND THANKS.

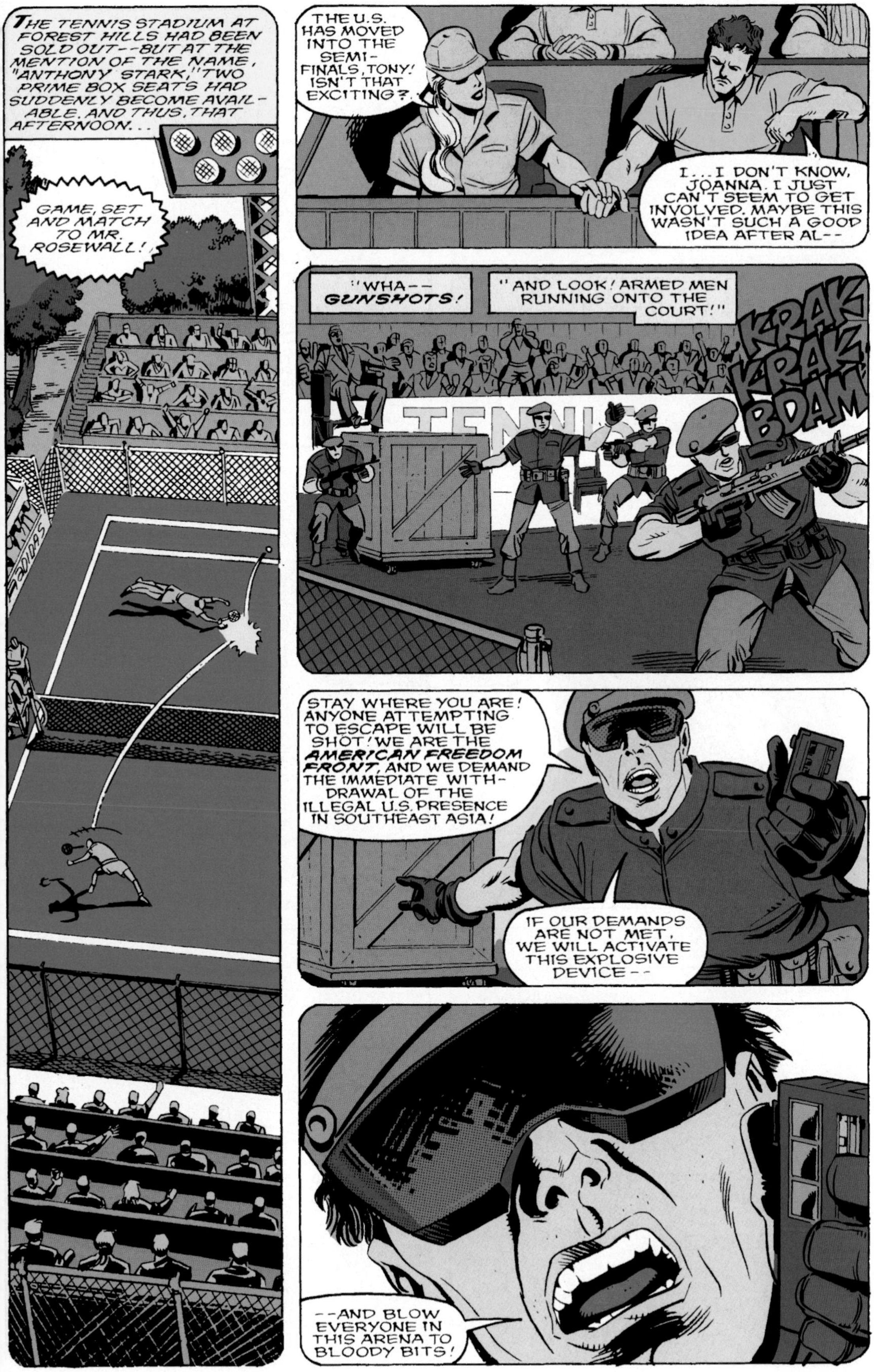
THE TENNIS STADIUM AT FOREST HILLS HAD BEEN SOLD OUT--BUT AT THE MENTION OF THE NAME, "ANTHONY STARK," TWO PRIME BOX SEATS HAD SUDDENLY BECOME AVAIL-ABLE. AND THUS, THAT AFTERNOON...
GAME, SET AND MATCH TO MR. ROSEWALL!
THE U.S. HAS MOVED INTO THE SEMI-FINALS, TONY! ISN'T THAT EXCITING?
I...I DON'T KNOW, JOANNA. I JUST CAN'T SEEM TO GET INVOLVED. MAYBE THIS WASN'T SUCH A GOOD IDEA AFTER AL--
"WHA-- GUNSHOTS!
"AND LOOK! ARMED MEN RUNNING ONTO THE COURT!"
KRAK KRAK BDAM
STAY WHERE YOU ARE! ANYONE ATTEMPTING TO ESCAPE WILL BE SHOT! WE ARE THE AMERICAN FREEDOM FRONT, AND WE DEMAND THE IMMEDIATE WITH-DRAWAL OF THE ILLEGAL U.S. PRESENCE IN SOUTHEAST ASIA!
IF OUR DEMANDS ARE NOT MET, WE WILL ACTIVATE THIS EXPLOSIVE DEVICE--
--AND BLOW EVERYONE IN THIS ARENA TO BLOODY BITS!

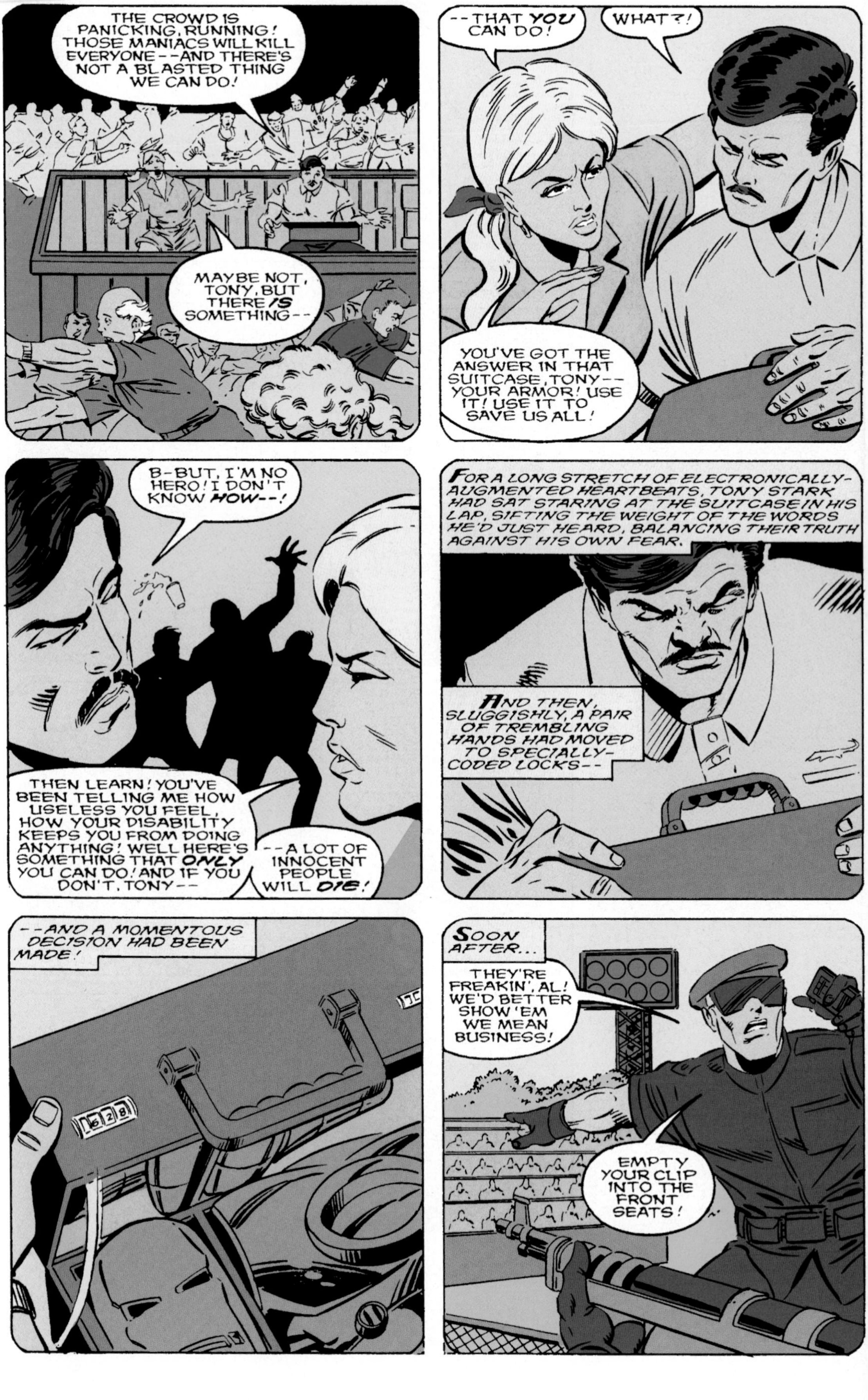
THE CROWD IS PANICKING, RUNNING! THOSE MANIACS WILL KILL EVERYONE--AND THERE'S NOT A BLASTED THING WE CAN DO!
MAYBE NOT, TONY, BUT THERE IS SOMETHING--
--THAT YOU CAN DO!
WHAT?!
YOU'VE GOT THE ANSWER IN THAT SUITCASE, TONY--YOUR ARMOR! USE IT! USE IT TO SAVE US ALL!
B-BUT, I'M NO HERO! I DON'T KNOW HOW--!
THEN LEARN! YOU'VE BEEN TELLING ME HOW USELESS YOU FEEL, HOW YOUR DISABILITY KEEPS YOU FROM DOING ANYTHING! WELL HERE'S SOMETHING THAT ONLY YOU CAN DO! AND IF YOU DON'T, TONY--
--A LOT OF INNOCENT PEOPLE WILL DIE!
FOR A LONG STRETCH OF ELECTRONICALLY-AUGMENTED HEARTBEATS, TONY STARK HAD SAT STARING AT THE SUITCASE IN HIS LAP, SIFTING THE WEIGHT OF THE WORDS HE'D JUST HEARD, BALANCING THEIR TRUTH AGAINST HIS OWN FEAR.
AND THEN, SLUGGISHLY, A PAIR OF TREMBLING HANDS HAD MOVED TO SPECIALLY-CODED LOCKS--
--AND A MOMENTOUS DECISION HAD BEEN MADE!
SOON AFTER...
THEY'RE FREAKIN', AL! WE'D BETTER SHOW 'EM WE MEAN BUSINESS!
EMPTY YOUR CLIP INTO THE FRONT SEATS!

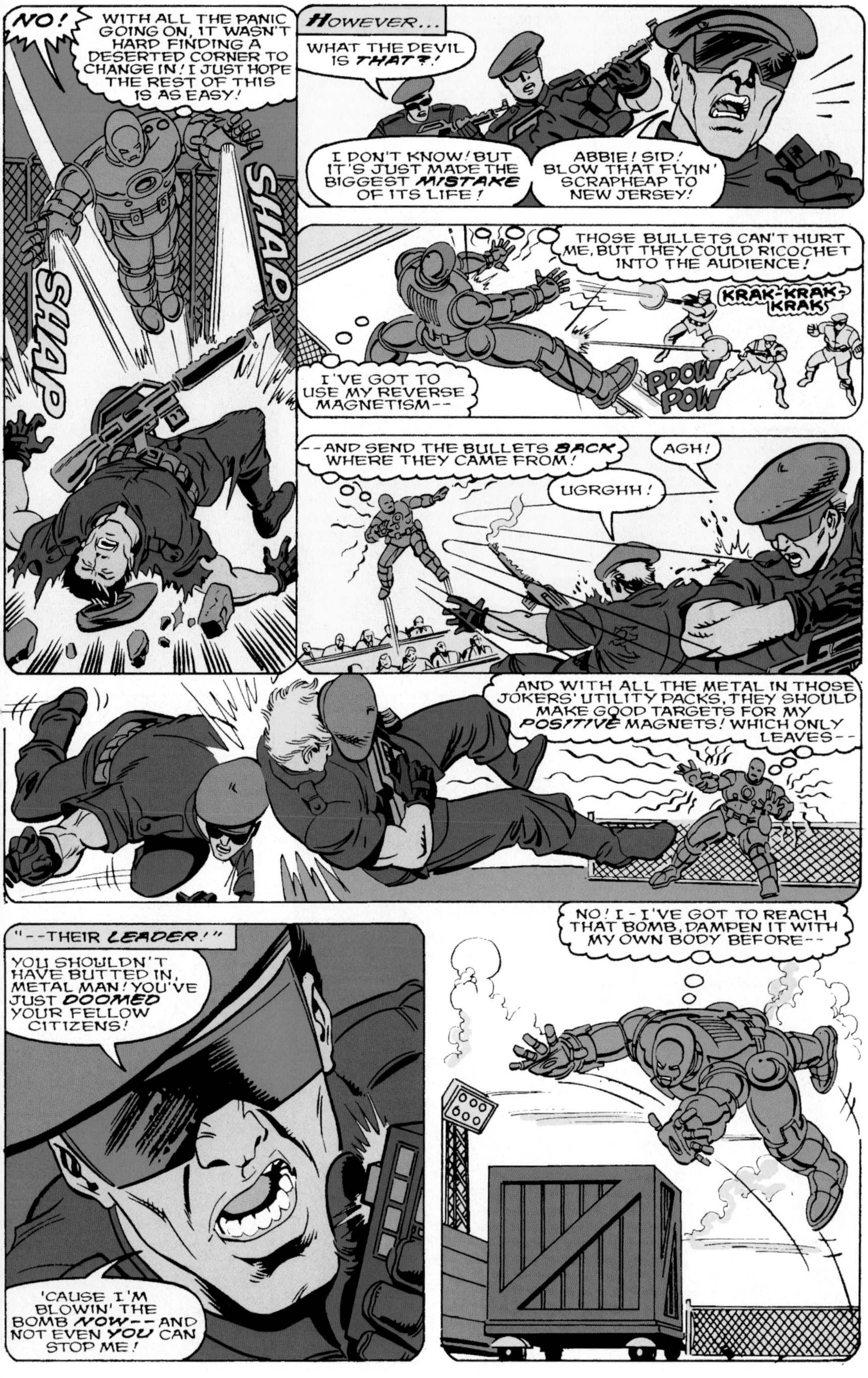
NO!
WITH ALL THE PANIC GOING ON, IT WASN'T HARD FINDING A DESERTED CORNER TO CHANGE IN! I JUST HOPE THE REST OF THIS IS AS EASY!
SHAP
SHAP
SHAP
HOWEVER...
WHAT THE DEVIL IS THAT?!
I DON'T KNOW! BUT IT'S JUST MADE THE BIGGEST MISTAKE OF ITS LIFE!
ABBIE! SID! BLOW THAT FLYIN' SCRAPHEAP TO NEW JERSEY!
THOSE BULLETS CAN'T HURT ME, BUT THEY COULD RICOCHET INTO THE AUDIENCE!
KRAK-KRAK-KRAK
I'VE GOT TO USE MY REVERSE MAGNETISM--
PDOW POW
--AND SEND THE BULLETS BACK WHERE THEY CAME FROM!
AGH!
UGRGHH!
AND WITH ALL THE METAL IN THOSE JOKERS' UTILITY PACKS, THEY SHOULD MAKE GOOD TARGETS FOR MY POSITIVE MAGNETS! WHICH ONLY LEAVES--
"--THEIR LEADER!"
YOU SHOULDN'T HAVE BUTTED IN, METAL MAN! YOU'VE JUST DOOMED YOUR FELLOW CITIZENS!
'CAUSE I'M BLOWIN' THE BOMB NOW--AND NOT EVEN YOU CAN STOP ME!
NO! I-I'VE GOT TO REACH THAT BOMB, DAMPEN IT WITH MY OWN BODY BEFORE--

IN SOUTHEAST ASIA, TONY STARK HAD HAD NO WARNING OF THE EXPLOSION THAT WAS TO CHANGE HIS LIFE; IN FOREST HILLS, HE HAD HAD EVERY WARNING.

BUT NO CHOICE.

FAHBOOOM

TH-THAT METAL GUY-- HE'S STILL ALIVE! FLOATING BACK TO THE GROUND!

I'VE GOTTA GET OUT--

SORRY, PUNK, YOU'RE NOT GOING ANYWHERE!

NOT WHILE I CAN CREATE AN OIL SLICK OUT OF MY ARMOR'S INTERNAL LUBRICATION!

--WHNG?!

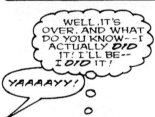

WELL, IT'S OVER. AND WHAT DO YOU KNOW--I ACTUALLY DID IT! I'LL BE-- I DID IT!

YAAAAYY!

THAT "IRON MAN" SAVED OUR LIVES!

HE'S A HERO!

GOLLY! YA THINK HE'LL GIMME HIS AUTOGRAPH?

HURRAY!

INSIDE A SUIT OF SOON-TO-BE FAMILIAR ARMOR, A SMILE HAD BLOSSOMED ON A MUSTACHIOED FACE--

--WHILE THE FATIGUE IN AN OVERTAXED HEART HAD CHANGED A GLOWING SWELL OF HONEST PRIDE.

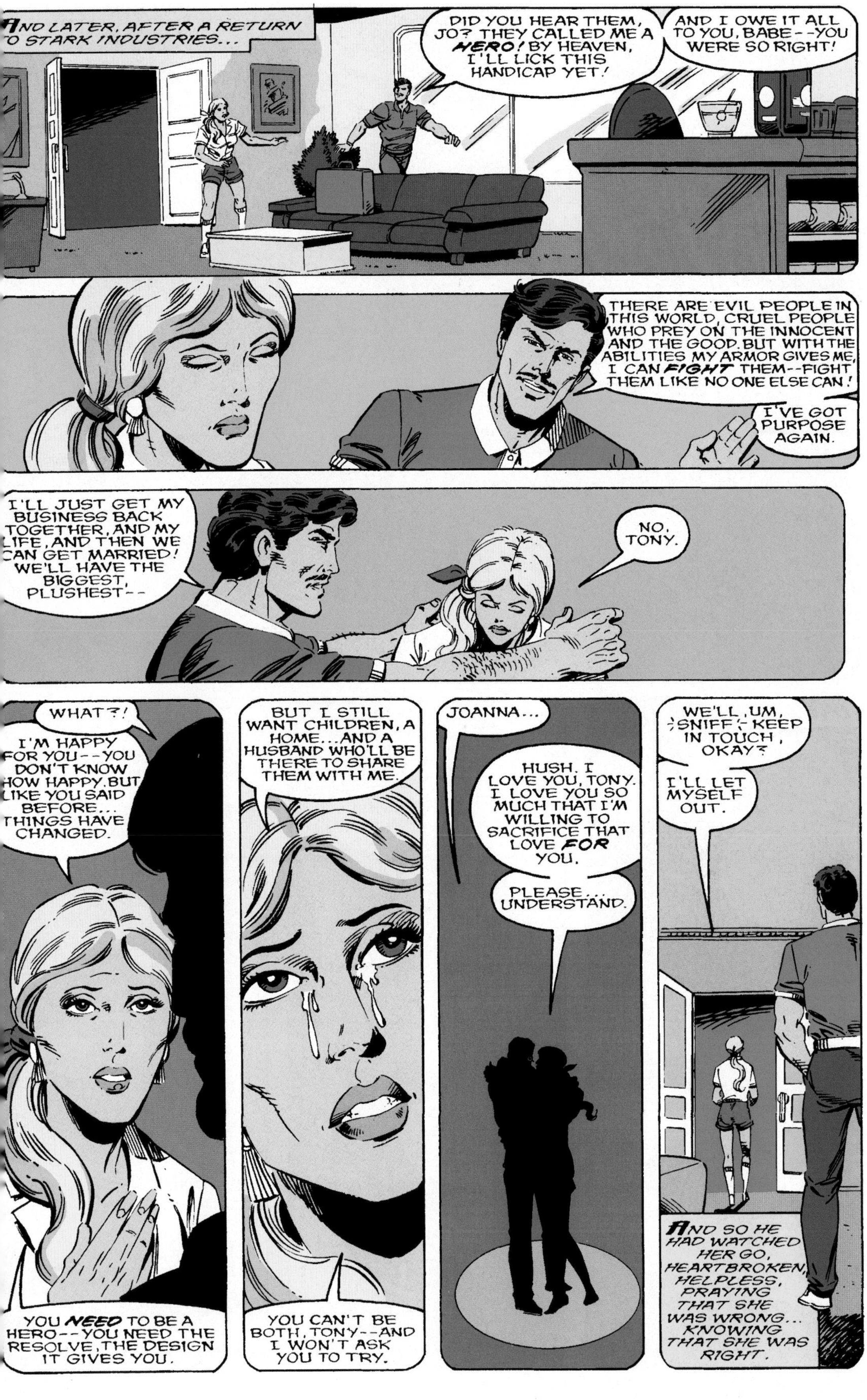
AND LATER, AFTER A RETURN TO STARK INDUSTRIES...
DID YOU HEAR THEM, JO? THEY CALLED ME A HERO! BY HEAVEN, I'LL LICK THIS HANDICAP YET!
AND I OWE IT ALL TO YOU, BABE--YOU WERE SO RIGHT!
THERE ARE EVIL PEOPLE IN THIS WORLD, CRUEL PEOPLE WHO PREY ON THE INNOCENT AND THE GOOD. BUT WITH THE ABILITIES MY ARMOR GIVES ME, I CAN FIGHT THEM--FIGHT THEM LIKE NO ONE ELSE CAN!
I'VE GOT PURPOSE AGAIN.
I'LL JUST GET MY BUSINESS BACK TOGETHER, AND MY LIFE, AND THEN WE CAN GET MARRIED! WE'LL HAVE THE BIGGEST, PLUSHEST--
NO, TONY.
WHAT?!
I'M HAPPY FOR YOU--YOU DON'T KNOW HOW HAPPY. BUT LIKE YOU SAID BEFORE... THINGS HAVE CHANGED.
YOU NEED TO BE A HERO--YOU NEED THE RESOLVE, THE DESIGN IT GIVES YOU.
BUT I STILL WANT CHILDREN, A HOME... AND A HUSBAND WHO'LL BE THERE TO SHARE THEM WITH ME.
YOU CAN'T BE BOTH, TONY--AND I WON'T ASK YOU TO TRY.
JOANNA...
HUSH. I LOVE YOU, TONY. I LOVE YOU SO MUCH THAT I'M WILLING TO SACRIFICE THAT LOVE FOR YOU.
PLEASE... UNDERSTAND.
WE'LL, UM, -SNIFF- KEEP IN TOUCH, OKAY?
I'LL LET MYSELF OUT.
AND SO HE HAD WATCHED HER GO, HEARTBROKEN, HELPLESS, PRAYING THAT SHE WAS WRONG... KNOWING THAT SHE WAS RIGHT.

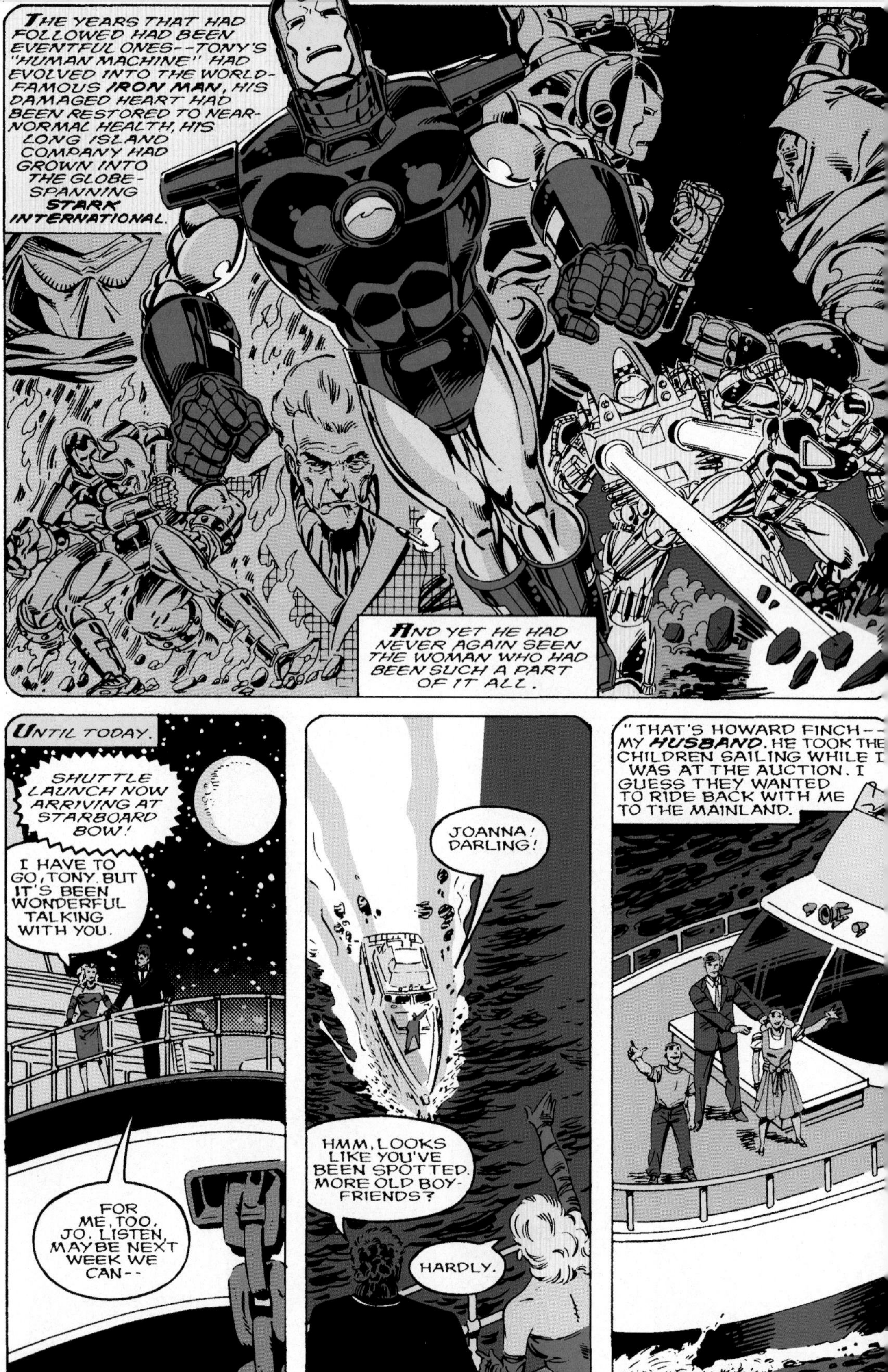
THE YEARS THAT HAD FOLLOWED HAD BEEN EVENTFUL ONES--TONY'S "HUMAN MACHINE" HAD EVOLVED INTO THE WORLD-FAMOUS IRON MAN, HIS DAMAGED HEART HAD BEEN RESTORED TO NEAR-NORMAL HEALTH, HIS LONG ISLAND COMPANY HAD GROWN INTO THE GLOBE-SPANNING STARK INTERNATIONAL.
AND YET HE HAD NEVER AGAIN SEEN THE WOMAN WHO HAD BEEN SUCH A PART OF IT ALL.
UNTIL TODAY.
SHUTTLE LAUNCH NOW ARRIVING AT STARBOARD BOW!
I HAVE TO GO, TONY. BUT IT'S BEEN WONDERFUL TALKING WITH YOU.
FOR ME, TOO, JO. LISTEN, MAYBE NEXT WEEK WE CAN--
JOANNA! DARLING!
HMM, LOOKS LIKE YOU'VE BEEN SPOTTED. MORE OLD BOY-FRIENDS?
HARDLY.
"THAT'S HOWARD FINCH--MY HUSBAND. HE TOOK THE CHILDREN SAILING WHILE I WAS AT THE AUCTION. I GUESS THEY WANTED TO RIDE BACK WITH ME TO THE MAINLAND.

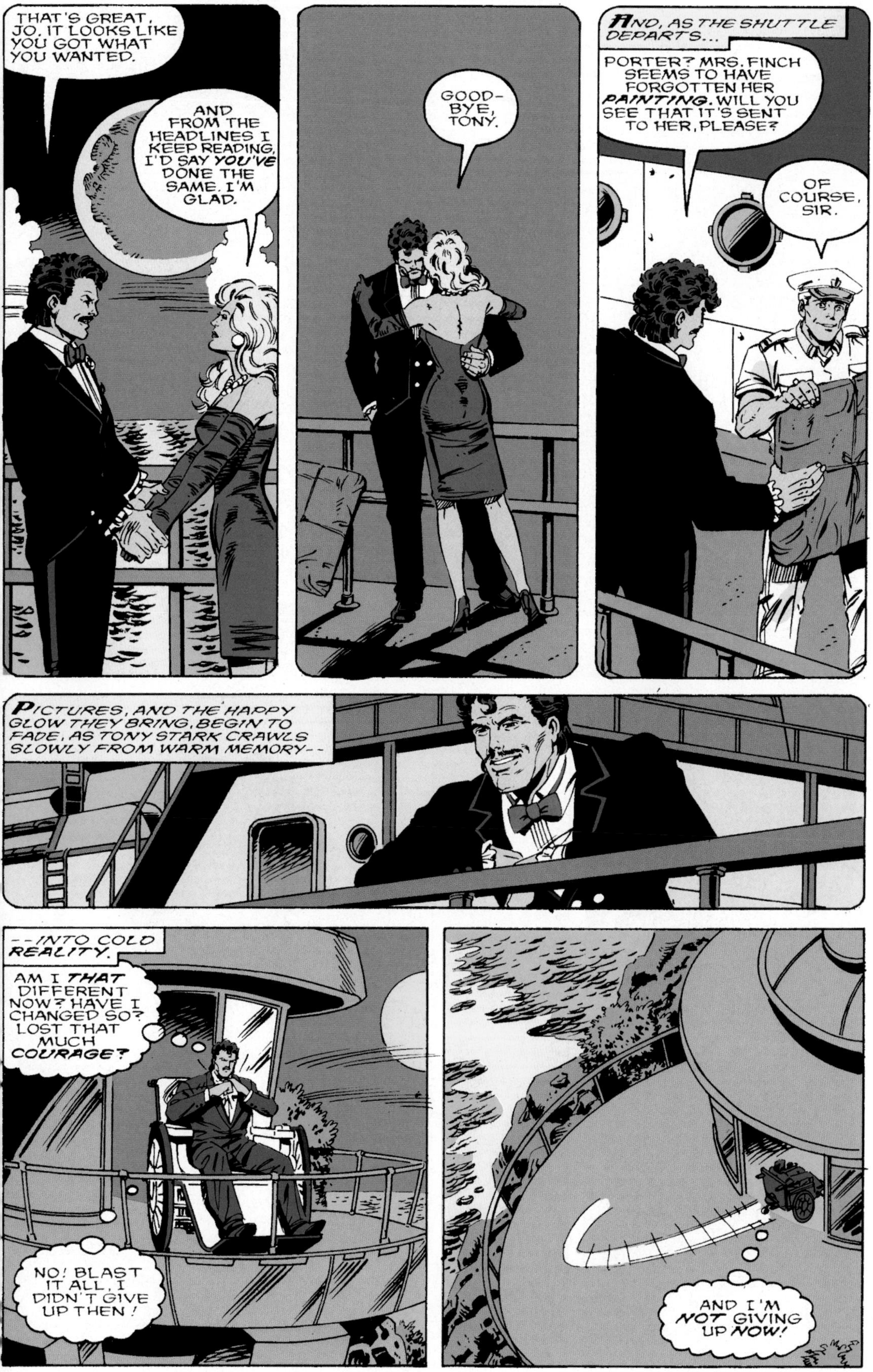

THAT'S GREAT, JO. IT LOOKS LIKE YOU GOT WHAT YOU WANTED.
AND FROM THE HEADLINES I KEEP READING, I'D SAY YOU'VE DONE THE SAME. I'M GLAD.
GOOD-BYE, TONY.
AND, AS THE SHUTTLE DEPARTS...
PORTER? MRS. FINCH SEEMS TO HAVE FORGOTTEN HER PAINTING. WILL YOU SEE THAT IT'S SENT TO HER, PLEASE?
OF COURSE, SIR.
PICTURES, AND THE HAPPY GLOW THEY BRING, BEGIN TO FADE, AS TONY STARK CRAWLS SLOWLY FROM WARM MEMORY--
--INTO COLD REALITY.
AM I THAT DIFFERENT NOW? HAVE I CHANGED SO? LOST THAT MUCH COURAGE?
NO! BLAST IT ALL, I DIDN'T GIVE UP THEN!
AND I'M NOT GIVING UP NOW!

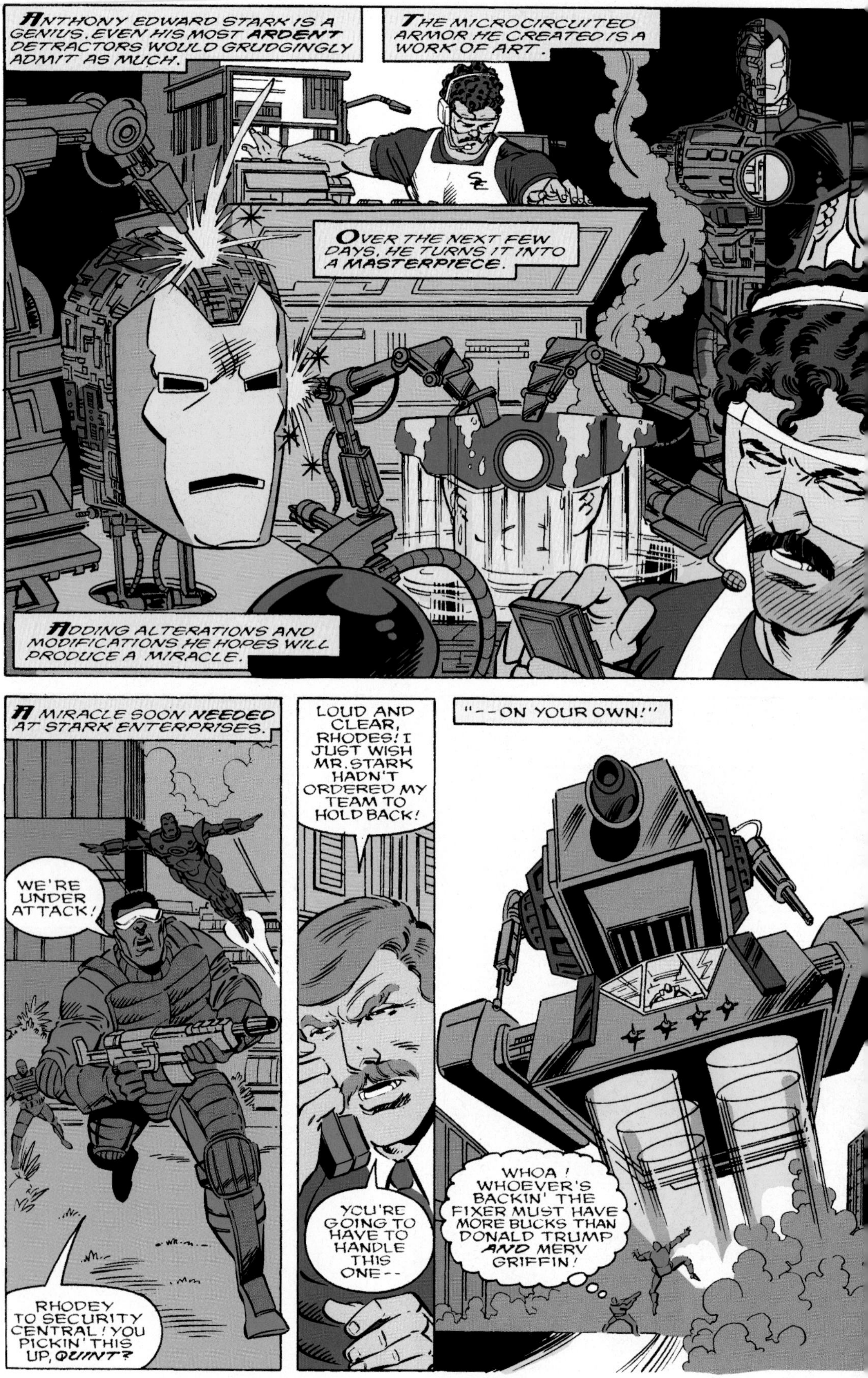
ANTHONY EDWARD STARK IS A GENIUS. EVEN HIS MOST ARDENT DETRACTORS WOULD GRUDGINGLY ADMIT AS MUCH.
THE MICROCIRCUITED ARMOR HE CREATED IS A WORK OF ART.
OVER THE NEXT FEW DAYS, HE TURNS IT INTO A MASTERPIECE.
ADDING ALTERATIONS AND MODIFICATIONS HE HOPES WILL PRODUCE A MIRACLE.
A MIRACLE SOON NEEDED AT STARK ENTERPRISES.
WE'RE UNDER ATTACK!
RHODEY TO SECURITY CENTRAL! YOU PICKIN' THIS UP, QUINT?
LOUD AND CLEAR, RHODES! I JUST WISH MR. STARK HADN'T ORDERED MY TEAM TO HOLD BACK!
YOU'RE GOING TO HAVE TO HANDLE THIS ONE--
"--ON YOUR OWN!"
WHOA! WHOEVER'S BACKIN' THE FIXER MUST HAVE MORE BUCKS THAN DONALD TRUMP AND MERV GRIFFIN!

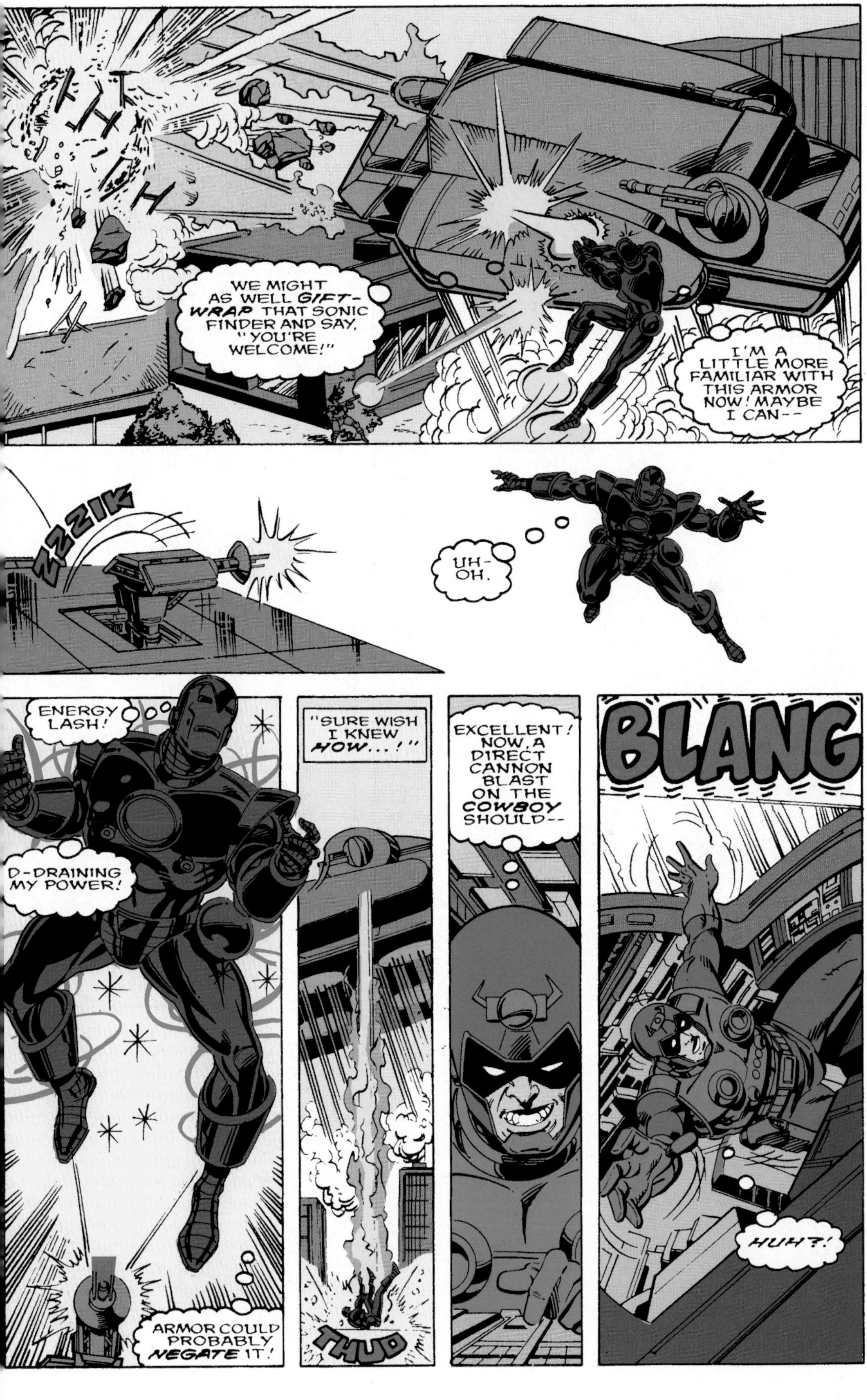

WE MIGHT AS WELL GIFT-WRAP THAT SONIC FINDER AND SAY, "YOU'RE WELCOME!"
I'M A LITTLE MORE FAMILIAR WITH THIS ARMOR NOW! MAYBE I CAN--
ZZZIK
UH-OH.
ENERGY LASH!
D-DRAINING MY POWER!
ARMOR COULD PROBABLY NEGATE IT!
"SURE WISH I KNEW HOW...!"
THUD
EXCELLENT! NOW, A DIRECT CANNON BLAST ON THE COWBOY SHOULD--
BLANG
HUH?!

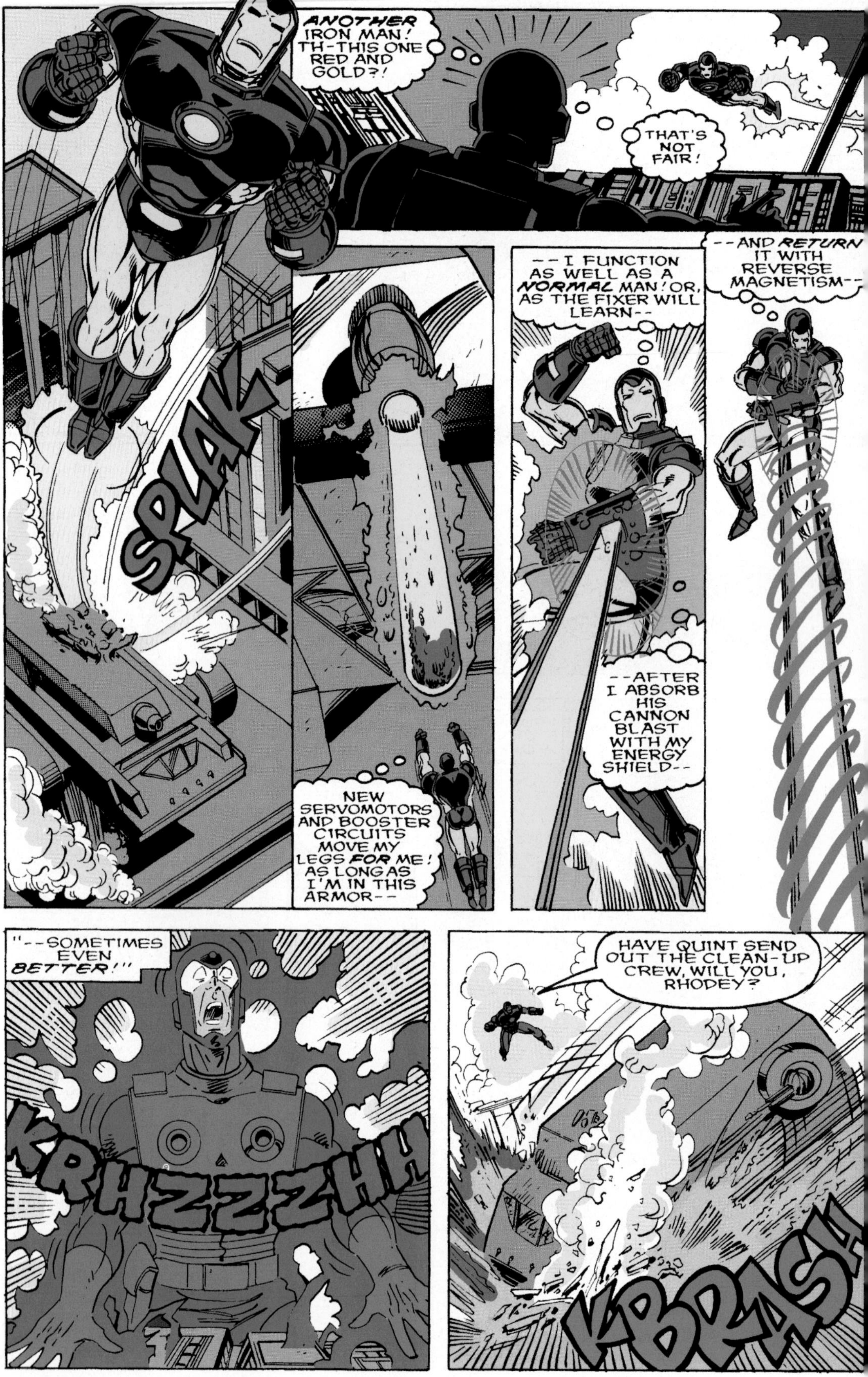
ANOTHER IRON MAN! TH-THIS ONE RED AND GOLD?!
THAT'S NOT FAIR!
SPLAK
NEW SERVOMOTORS AND BOOSTER CIRCUITS MOVE MY LEGS FOR ME! AS LONG AS I'M IN THIS ARMOR--
--I FUNCTION AS WELL AS A NORMAL MAN! OR, AS THE FIXER WILL LEARN--
--AFTER I ABSORB HIS CANNON BLAST WITH MY ENERGY SHIELD--
--AND RETURN IT WITH REVERSE MAGNETISM--
"--SOMETIMES EVEN BETTER!"
KRHZZZHH
HAVE QUINT SEND OUT THE CLEAN-UP CREW, WILL YOU, RHODEY?
KBRASH

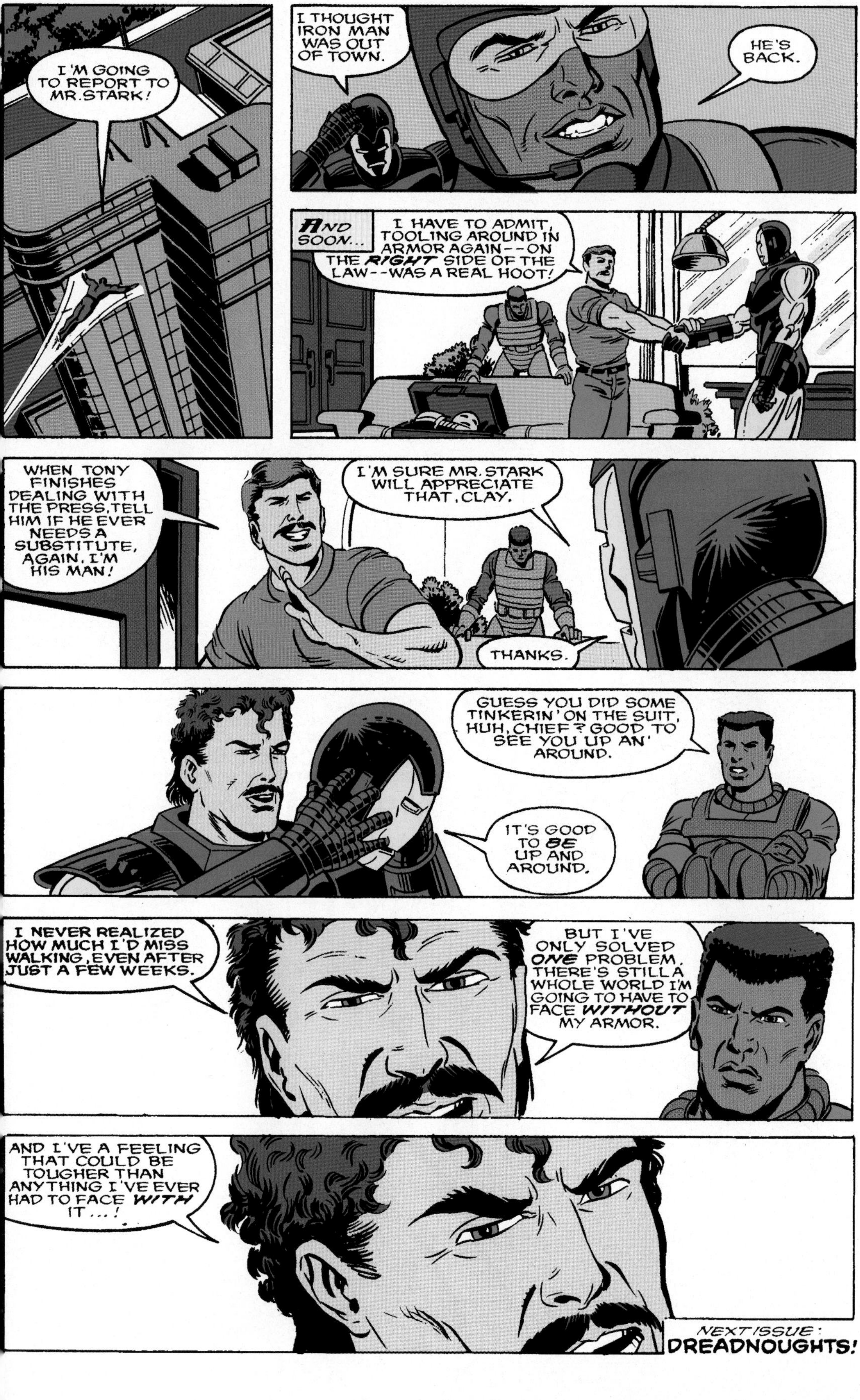
I'M GOING TO REPORT TO MR. STARK!
I THOUGHT IRON MAN WAS OUT OF TOWN.
HE'S BACK.
AND SOON...
I HAVE TO ADMIT, TOOLING AROUND IN ARMOR AGAIN--ON THE RIGHT SIDE OF THE LAW--WAS A REAL HOOT!
WHEN TONY FINISHES DEALING WITH THE PRESS, TELL HIM IF HE EVER NEEDS A SUBSTITUTE, AGAIN, I'M HIS MAN!
I'M SURE MR. STARK WILL APPRECIATE THAT, CLAY.
THANKS.
GUESS YOU DID SOME TINKERIN' ON THE SUIT, HUH, CHIEF? GOOD TO SEE YOU UP AN' AROUND.
IT'S GOOD TO BE UP AND AROUND.
I NEVER REALIZED HOW MUCH I'D MISS WALKING, EVEN AFTER JUST A FEW WEEKS.
BUT I'VE ONLY SOLVED ONE PROBLEM. THERE'S STILL A WHOLE WORLD I'M GOING TO HAVE TO FACE WITHOUT MY ARMOR.
AND I'VE A FEELING THAT COULD BE TOUGHER THAN ANYTHING I'VE EVER HAD TO FACE WITH IT...!
NEXT ISSUE: DREADNOUGHTS!

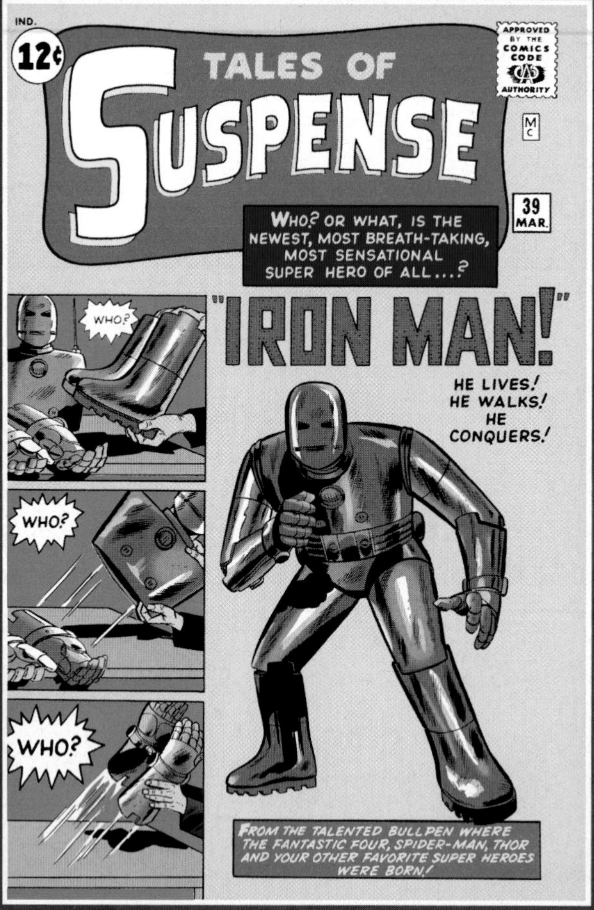
12¢
APPROVED BY THE COMICS CODE AUTHORITY
TALES OF SUSPENSE
39 MAR.
WHO? OR WHAT, IS THE NEWEST, MOST BREATH-TAKING, MOST SENSATIONAL SUPER HERO OF ALL...?
"IRON MAN!"
HE LIVES! HE WALKS! HE CONQUERS!
WHO?
WHO?
WHO?
FROM THE TALENTED BULLPEN WHERE THE FANTASTIC FOUR, SPIDER-MAN, THOR AND YOUR OTHER FAVORITE SUPER HEROES WERE BORN!

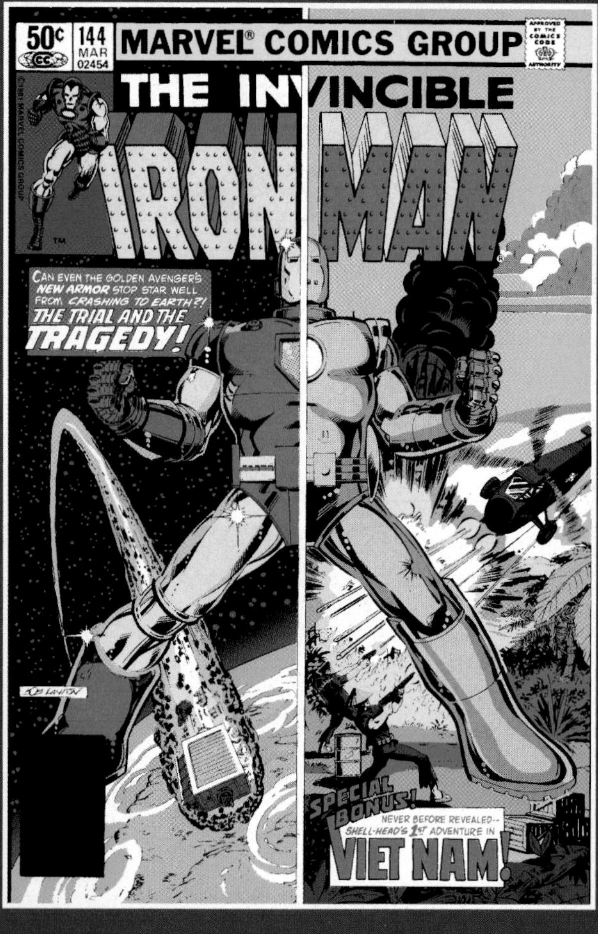
50¢
144 MAR 02454
MARVEL COMICS GROUP
APPROVED BY THE COMICS CODE AUTHORITY
©1981 MARVEL COMICS GROUP
THE INVINCIBLE
IRON MAN
CAN EVEN THE GOLDEN AVENGER'S NEW ARMOR STOP STAR WELL FROM CRASHING TO EARTH?!
THE TRIAL AND THE TRAGEDY!
SPECIAL BONUS!
NEVER BEFORE REVEALED-- SHELL-HEAD'S 1ST ADVENTURE IN
VIET NAM!